THE
FEDERAL RESERVE

THE
FEDERAL RESERVE

An Intentional Mystery

by
Thibaut de Saint Phalle

Foreword by Dr. Fritz Leutwiler
Preface by Charles E. Lord

PRAEGER

New York
Westport, Connecticut
London

Library of Congress Cataloging in Publication Data

De Saint Phalle, Thibaut.
  The Federal Reserve.

  Includes index.
  1. Board of Governors of the Federal Reserve
System (U.S.)   2. Banking law – United States.
I. Title.
HG2563.D39   1984   332.1'1'0973   84-15879
ISBN 0-275-90083-5 (alk. paper)
ISBN 0-275-91803-3 (pbk.: alk. paper)

Library of Congress Catalog Card Number: 84-15879
ISBN: 0-275-90083-5

First published in 1985

Praeger Publishers, 521 Fifth Avenue, New York, NY 10175
A division of Greenwood Press, Inc.

Printed in the United States of America

(∞)

The paper used in this book complies with the Permanent
Paper Standard issued by the National Information Standards
Organization (Z39.48-1984).

10 9 8 7 6 5 4 3

To Senators Jake Garn and William Proxmire of the Senate Committee on Banking, Housing, and Urban Affairs

and

To Congressmen Fernand St. Germain and Chalmers Wiley of the House Committee on Banking, Finance & Urban Affairs

Whose Committees have the awesome responsibility of determining how banks and other financial institutions are to be regulated in the future.

"Monsieur Diderot," she said to him, "I have listened with the greatest pleasure to all the inspirations of your brilliant mind; but all your grand principles, which I understand very well, would do splendidly in books and very badly in practice. In all your plans for reform, you are forgetting the difference between our two positions: *you* work only on paper, which accepts anything, is smooth and flexible and offers no obstacles either to your imagination or to your pen, while I, poor Empress, work on human skin, which is far more sensitive and touchy."
Catherine the Great by Henri Troyat

FOREWORD

For quite some time we have been witnesses of an increasing liberalization of international capital flows and of a growing interdependence among international financial markets; these changes and developments have in part been due to the response to market pressure from both inside and outside the national economies. Markets are innovative and dynamic almost by definition. Interest rate and currency swaps are booming and an indication that a truly international market is developing, increasingly sidestepping barriers between national financial systems. Growing internationalization clearly indicates the futility of trying to preserve rigid structures and vested interests in the face of powerful market forces that cannot be stemmed at will. The slow and too-often reluctant adjustment of the authorities to actions unforeseen and the consequences of these changes — often a direct result of regulatory and discretionary actions themselves — have put additional strain on the system and increased frictional losses.

Elimination of withholding taxes in major countries is the latest step toward a really global market. As it is less and less possible for national markets to insulate themselves from external competition, authorities will finally have to allow free flows of their currencies, unless they want to lose the fight with markets that increasingly and forcefully direct and control these flows. Indeed, the world has become too small a place for artificial barriers to trade, as the author of this book points out. Unrestricted international trade of goods and exchange of services are indispensable for growth and development. Liberalization of trade and of international monetary and financial relations are complementary to, and dependent on, each other. While the establishment of a new international monetary system with control of the money supply under international (or supranational) guidance might seem desirable, this would by no means guarantee the absence of political pressures.

Since monetary policy aimed at, and committed to, price stability can be efficient and successful only if it is not undercut by fiscal policy and economic policy in general, it is absolutely necessary to reconcile and coordinate monetary and fiscal policy on the national level of sovereign states. Thus problems arising from contradictory domestic policies cannot be solved by transferring them to the international (or even supranational) level, where interests tend to diverge even more. Floating exchange rates have rendered it possible to pursue — at least in principle — independent domestic monetary policies. However, national independence from the effects of monetary policies of the major trading partners in and of itself does not guarantee price stability if the central bank is not shielded from political pressures from the inside and its stability-oriented policy is not undermined by fiscal policy.

The use of monetary policy to achieve and secure long-term price stability makes it necessary that central banks abstain from activist policies aimed at short-term gains in the fields of growth, employment, and interest and exchange rates. Moreover, monetary policy is unfit to promote economic growth and employment and to smooth business fluctuations by so-called fine-tuning. Monetary policy is at its best if it tries to control what it can control best: the general level of prices. Stable and predictable evolution of the money supply of major industrial countries will lead to decreasing international portfolio shifts and therefore to a diminution in erratic short-term exchange rate variability.

Excessive exchange rate volatility has led to the proposal to coordinate (or harmonize) monetary policy internationally. Coordination is advisable if it aims at a general reduction in the rate of inflation in countries with above-average inflation rates. However, there are numerous stumbling blocks on the road to stability. Increasing competition between monetary and fiscal policy, aggravated by high and ever-rising shares of governments in national income, is the result of domestic, as well as international, struggles to redistribute income and wealth. This makes coordination of the various policies increasingly difficult even on a national level, not to mention the international level.

There are no international solutions to domestic problems. There are no global patent recipes available — nor are they necessary to enhance and secure the resilience of the international financial system. No sweeping reforms, although they would be far more spectacular, are needed but, instead, an orderly evolution in the form of continuing adaptation to a changing economic and financial environment. To put it more bluntly, there is no need for international negotiations and conferences (or even new institutions) to create a "new international monetary system," possibly headed by a world central bank. But we do need a serious commitment of sovereign nations — and above all the United States — to adhere to a policy of monetary and fiscal stability. Noninflationary monetary policy and fiscal discipline of the major countries will create a seedbed for spontaneous development of a viable international monetary order.

In this long overdue study of the Federal Reserve System in the United States, the author carefully traces the historical development of the U.S. central banking system, so different from that of other countries. He points out the recurring efforts to substitute monetary policy for fiscal policy, which has resulted in inflation not only in the United States but throughout the world. He shows clearly that fine-tuning by the Fed to smooth business fluctuations will not work. As the author stresses, the U.S. government has required the Federal Reserve to promote economic growth and employment rather than to maintain economic stability. This is the heart of the Fed's difficulties. This book not only makes clear the problems past policies have created but indicates that only close cooperation between sovereign states can solve them in a world that has increasingly liberalized capital flows and made financial markets interdependent. The role of the United States in the world economy is such that this book will be required reading not only for serious readers in the United States but for those in other countries as well.

Dr. Fritz Leutwiler
Chairman of the Governing Board
of the Swiss National Bank
and former President of the
Bank for International Settlements

PREFACE

If one adds up all the commercial banks that serve the needs of 200-plus million people in the European Common Market, the number does not begin to approach the 15,000 commercial banks that serve the needs of 200-plus million Americans. And that takes in just commercial banks; throw in close to 4,000 savings and loan associations and mutual savings banks, plus over 40,000 credit unions, and the total reaches more than 60,000 separate entities composing the depository institutions industry in the United States today.

Each and every one of those institutions is subject to some degree of federal and state regulation and supervision: directly, by the Federal Reserve System, the Office of the Comptroller of the Currency, the Federal Deposit Insurance Corporation (FDIC), the Federal Home Loan Bank Board (FHLBB) (with its subsidiary, the Federal Savings and Loan Insurance Corporation), the National Credit Union Administration (with its subsidiary, the National Credit Union Share Insurance Fund), and the 50 state banking departments; indirectly, by the Federal Financial Institutions Examination Council, the Depository Institutions Deregulation Committee, the Department of Justice, and the Securities and Exchange Commission.

Small wonder that few people understand the multidimensional structure of our financial institution regulatory system — the product of more than a century of patchwork legislation — and its impact on our economic life. The system's fundamental irrationality makes analysis and comprehension a frightening task. But that is no excuse for not making the effort.

One has to start with the realization that the three principal federal agencies perceive themselves as having quite distinct primary statutory missions, missions that drive their regulatory and supervisory decision-making processes. The Comptroller of the Currency sees himself as responsible for the safety and soundness of the national banking system; the FDIC focuses primarily on the integrity of the insurance fund; and the Federal Reserve Board is principally concerned with safeguarding its ability to execute monetary policy.

Against this backdrop of essentially conservatory mandates, how is one to view, now that thrift institutions have been given commercial bank powers, the (FHLBB), whose statutory charge under the National Housing Act is to support and encourage the growth of the savings and loan industry? Can anyone doubt that the commercial banking industry — historically the backbone of our economic system — today survives (some would say, "Is barely surviving") in spite of, rather than because of, the regulatory system under which it operates?

At the heart of that system stands the Federal Reserve, whose somewhat murky origins and inchoate history are so well described in this book. As the author makes clear, the role of the Fed does not suffer from an abundance of statutory clarity, a condition presumably most acceptable to the Board of Governors. Certainly as one reads the book, it becomes quite apparent that the Fed is not "just a central bank" as our European friends think of their central banks. Nor is it just a regulatory agency. It is both of these and more, and its effect on the nation's economic health is sometimes direct, more often subtle, difficult to measure, and always pervasive. Honest persons can have philosophical disagreements regarding the Fed's performance in any or all of its many roles, but none can question the extent of its influence in our economy.

Understanding the Fed in its entirety may by definition be an impossibility, but this book gives the reader a solid foundation of history and fact. In addition, it is flavored by the author's personal perspective, consisting of a roughly equal mix of keen intellect, wide-ranging experience, and an ever-present sense of outrage. Most important, it asks the right questions, both about our domestic banking and about the international financial and monetary systems. For this, we are all indebted to Thibaut de Saint Phalle.

Who, then, should read this book? Certainly the 535 members of Congress who will soon be forced to come to grips with the evolution of the financial services industry as an industry, a marketplace — driven evolution that in reality is a revolution for the banking industry. Fortunately for the author and the publisher, the appropriate audience is not that small (and unlikely either to buy or to read). Since the curricula of most of our primary and secondary educational institutions do not yet include such Byzantine subjects as economics or money and banking, even though the life of every American is affected by them, every high school graduate who has not had a college course in the field should read this book.

Having defined the market both narrowly and broadly, I can only hope that enough congressional members (or their staff members) and enough Americans concerned about the impact of government on the economic and banking systems will read this book so that the coming debate will be a well-informed one and so that the political process will function as it is intended to: with the broad public interest as its top priority.

Charles E. Lord
Chairman and Chief Executive Officer of
The Prudential Bank & Trust Company
and former Acting Comptroller of
the Currency

AUTHOR'S COMMENT

It is indeed very curious that we know so little about the Federal Reserve. Although it was created in 1913, no detailed book about its regulatory activities has ever been written and very little about how it controls U.S. monetary policy. Why so much mystery? Are banking and money dull subjects—to be left to the professionals? Can our future economic security be either boring or tiresome? Of course not.

Very few of us realize the extent to which all of us are dependent upon the decisions of a handful of men who act as governors of the Federal Reserve Board. Their decisions affect whether our economy grows; whether inflation reduces our standard of living; whether the interest rates on our mortgages rise; perhaps even whether our jobs exist.

It is essential that all of us understand the Federal Reserve System: how it functions, what it does, how its actions affect our lives, how it might be made to function better. This book explains why each of us *must* be aware of, and concerned with, the tremendous impact that Federal Reserve monetary and regulatory decisions have on our lives: in short, everyone who works, who spends money, who looks to the maintenance of an adequate standard of living.

All powerful organizations require continued surveillance. We can reform an organization that needs changing only if we understand how it functions and why this affects all of us. That is why this book was written.

CONTENTS

LIST OF ACRONYMS

AFL-CIO	American Federation of Labor and Congress of Industrial Organizations
ATMs	automatic teller machines
BIS	Bank for International Settlements
CDs	certificates of deposit
CSBS	Conference of State Bank Supervisors
DIDC	Depository Institutions Deregulation Committee
DIDMCA	Depository Institutions Deregulation and Monetary Control Act
FBA	Federal Bank Agency
FDIC	Federal Deposit Insurance Corporation
FHLBB	Federal Home Loan Bank Board
FHLBS	Federal Home Loan Bank System
FIDA	Financial Institutions Deregulation Act
FSLIC	Federal Savings and Loan Insurance Corporation
GAO	General Accounting Office
GDP	gross domestic product
GE	General Electric
GNP	gross national product
HHI	Herfindahl-Hirschman Index
IBFs	international banking facilities
ICERC	Interagency Country Exposure Review Committee
IMF	International Monetary Fund
IRA	individual retirement account
LIBOR	London interbank offer rate
MITI	Ministry of International Trade
MMDAs	money-market deposit accounts
NCUA	National Credit Union Administration
NCUSIF	National Credit Union Share Insurance Fund
NOW	negotiable order of withdrawal
OMB	Office of Management and Budget

| OPEC | Organization of Petroleum Exporting Countries |
| SEC | Securities and Exchange Commission |

INTRODUCTION

The Federal Reserve Board performs two essential and very different functions. First, it regulates — along with certain other agencies of the federal government — the commercial banking system of the United States. These regulatory functions are exercised not only with respect to what banks are permitted to do inside the United States but also with respect to what they are permitted to do outside the United States.* Therefore, the extent to which U.S. banks have circumvented regulation of the bank regulatory authorities through the use of subsidiaries or branches abroad is of vital interest — particularly how this has happened. Could the Federal Reserve's regulatory procedures have been made more effective? Second, the Federal Reserve acts as a central bank for the U.S. government in that it, and it alone, determines the money supply. So the Federal Reserve also determines the monetary policy of the United States. This role is especially important because the entire global economy — and not just the U.S. economy — has been operating on a *paper dollar* monetary system since 1971. Consequently, the actions of the Federal Reserve Board determine whether the global economy will function in an inflationary or a deflationary cycle; whether economic growth is encouraged or constrained; and whether, and to what extent, spending or saving is stimulated or discouraged through greater or lesser growth in the U.S. money supply.

We shall see in the course of this book just how these two diverse functions of the Federal Reserve Board have, over the years, profoundly affected each other. The reason is at once simple and perplexing: By failing to maintain a sound monetary policy (that is, one that would not allow the U.S. money supply to increase beyond carefully targeted and controlled growth) and to inform the administration and Congress of its actions on a regular basis, the Federal Reserve Board has caused great fluctuations in interest rates in recent years. In the late 1970s and ear-

---

*There are some 15,000 banks in the United States at the present time.

ly 1980s, a period of rapid inflation and rising interest rates due to Federal Reserve monetary policy, the U.S. public withdrew its deposits from the banks and sought new ways of earning a return on their savings. Here the regulatory power of the Federal Reserve played a very serious role because of Regulation Q, which forbade the banks to pay more than a token rate of interest on deposits.* In effect, the Federal Reserve, which earned over $14 billion in 1981 through its regulatory control of the banks, almost put its bank clients out of business by preventing them from paying an adequate return on their deposits while allowing interest rates to increase, thereby encouraging bank depositors to take their money elsewhere. As we shall see, the extraordinary growth in money-market funds is nothing more than a flight of depositors from the banks as a result of the interest-rate controls established by the bank regulatory authority. The current utter confusion in financial markets is directly attributable to the failure of the Federal Reserve Board to allow at least an adjustment in the interest rates payable by the regulated commercial banking system, so as to preserve its depository base. As a result of this poor monetary policy, the depository institutions have been plunged into chaos. Instead of looking at the problem from a broad perspective, there has unfortunately been a tendency on the part of the administration and/or Congress to seek partial solutions to help individual institutions rather than to examine the problem in detail and as a whole.

The current effort on the part of the Bush Task Group† and the Treasury Department to urge upon Congress legislative changes directed at the regulation of all institutions engaged in various aspects of financial services is certainly a step in the right direction. However, this is a major undertaking and should not be approached without a thorough analysis of monetary policy and realization of the fact that innovations in the development of new financial accounts and services make it essential that there be a comprehensive review of existing applicable legislation. To name but a few of the financial intermediaries that may be affected, the following are listed (but not necessarily in the order of their importance):

1. Commercial banks,
2. Savings banks,

---

*This is the Federal Reserve regulation that governs and sets the maximum interest rates that U.S. banks may pay on time and savings deposits.

†This commission, chaired by Vice-President George Bush, was appointed by President Ronald Reagan in 1982 to recommend changes in the regulatory structure of depository institutions. A detailed analysis is given in Chapter 6.

3. Savings and loan associations (stock or mutuals),
4. Insured nonmember banks,
5. Credit unions,
6. Industrial banks (state chartered with deposits in the form of passbook accounts or savings certificates),*
7. Securities dealers (investment bankers),
8. Insurance companies,
9. Nondepository financial intermediaries,
10. Bank holding companies,
11. Diversified financial services firms,
12. Industrial loan companies,
13. Investment companies (both closed and open-ended),
14. Mutual funds,
15. Money-market funds,
16. Futures and commodity brokers,
17. Investment advisers,
18. Leasing companies,
19. Real estate brokerage firms,
20. Venture capital funds, and
21. Insurance agents.

The purpose of this book is hence twofold. First, we need to determine how the Federal Reserve Board has fulfilled its congressional mandate with respect to monetary policy over the course of its existence. Monetary policy has become increasingly more difficult to control. It now affects not only the U.S. economy but also the entire global economy. Second, we need to examine whether changes should be made in the regulatory system itself. In recent years new financial institutions have been developed to compete with the banking system. Most of these financial service companies are not regulated. It has become increasingly difficult for the depository institutions to compete because the services they can offer are subject to regulation as is the extent to which they can offer services outside the state where their principal office is located. Should banking be deregulated in order to permit banks to compete more effectively? Should interstate or regional banking be permitted? To what extent should deposits be insured? We need to examine the changes that have come about in the marketplace for financial services and how such changes affect the manner in which the banks and

---

*Commercial banks, savings banks, savings and loan associations, insured nonmember banks, credit unions, and industrial banks are all depository institutions.

other providers of financial services ought to be regulated in the future. For a long time depositors in U.S. banking institutions have received special protection from the government. Has this really been necessary? How did this effort at protection of depositors come about? To what extent has it been effective? What changes, if any, should be made as a result of modification of the manner in which financial transactions are handled in our increasingly complex financial community?

The administration and Congress are on very firm ground in wanting to review this question in the 1980s from the viewpoint of today's methods of handling financial transactions without undue deference for what was legislated in the past—except, of course, to determine the extent to which decisions made, legislation adopted, and institutions created over the course of time have met the requirements expected of them. The country is fortunate because the time to make this type of legislative and regulatory examination is when—as now—there is no emergency requiring immediate governmental action. All too often the government is pressured into legislation as a result of an economic crisis. We shall see how unfortunately true this has been in the past.* But such is not the case today. The country has come through a difficult period of high inflation, recession, and substantial unemployment. So now is a time when an examination can be made without any pressure for immediate action—an opportunity for consultation with all affected parties and a process likely to ensure that the legislation finally adopted will take into account the needs of the future rather than adjust for the mistakes of the past.

---

*In Chapter 2 an analysis is made of the bank legislation hastily passed in the period 1932-1935 during the Great Depression.

PART I

REGULATION OF U.S. BANKS AT HOME

1

AN OVERVIEW
OF THE U.S.
REGULATORY SYSTEM

THE FEDERAL RESERVE SYSTEM

Structure

The Federal Reserve System was established by the Federal Reserve Act in 1913. The system consists of three components: the Board of Governors at its apex, the Federal Reserve banks, and finally, the member banks.

Board of Governors

The Board of Governors of the Federal Reserve System is composed of seven members, each of whom is appointed by the President for a term of 14 years, subject to confirmation by the Senate. The Board has several primary functions: first, to formulate and implement the monetary policy of the United States; second, to regulate and supervise the Federal Reserve banks, the member banks, and, in conjunction with other regulatory agencies, other depository institutions; third, to regulate bank holding companies; and finally, in conjunction with other government agencies having jurisdiction, to supervise the activities of member banks outside the United States. Stated in its simplest terms, the responsibility of the Board is twofold: it regulates banks* and it guides the nation's monetary policy. In the first activity its power is shared with other government agencies, but it alone is responsible for monetary poli-

---

*There are over 15,000 banks in the United States, some chartered by the federal government and referred to as *national* banks; others are chartered by the states. The regulatory power is shared by the Federal Reserve, the Comptroller of the Currency, the Federal Deposit Insurance Corporation, and the state bank superintendents.

cy. Because monetary policy involves the creation of money, this activity of the Board is described in a later section of this chapter. Even though the Board spends 90 percent of its time carrying out its regulatory role, obviously its responsibility for monetary policy is far more important.

In its regulatory role, the Board exercises functions related to both the Federal Reserve banks and the member banks. With respect to the Federal Reserve banks, the Board can examine these institutions, require reports from them, set the discount rates they allow their borrowing members, and regulate their check-clearing operations. It also has complete supervision over relations between a Federal Reserve bank and any foreign bank. In regard to member banks the Board examines them and receives periodic reports (although the Comptroller of the Currency has the prime responsibility for the examination of national banks, as opposed to state member banks where the prime responsibility for examinations rests with the Federal Reserve Board). Under the Depository Institutions Deregulation and Monetary Control Act of 1980*, the Federal Reserve Board is authorized to require nonmember depository institutions, including savings and loan associations, savings banks, and credit unions, to supply reports to the Board on their assets and liabilities. The Board also has considerable regulatory powers through its administration of the Bank Holding Company Act.

Federal Reserve Banks

The Federal Reserve Act provides for 12 Federal Reserve districts with one Federal Reserve bank in each district. These districts are presently located in Boston, New York, Philadelphia, Cleveland, Richmond, Atlanta, Chicago, St. Louis, Minneapolis, Kansas City, Dallas, and San Francisco.

Each Federal Reserve bank is an incorporated institution with its own board of directors, which consists of nine members: class A direc-

---

*The Monetary Control Act of 1980 (Public Law 96-221) was designed to improve the effectiveness of monetary policy by applying revised reserve requirements set by the Federal Reserve Board to all depository institutions including U.S. agencies and branches of foreign banks and so-called Edge Act corporations. The Act authorizes the Federal Reserve to collect reports from all depository institutions; extends access to Federal Reserve discount and borrowing privileges and other services to nonmember depository institutions; provides for the gradual phaseout of deposit interest-rate ceilings; grants broader powers to thrift institutions by allowing federally chartered savings and loan institutions to offer credit card services and to exercise trust and fiduciary powers; expands authority to make real estate loans; and authorizes federal mutual savings banks to make commercial, corporate, and business loans and to accept demand deposits in connection with such a relationship.

tors, who represent member banks; class B directors, who are not bankers, elected by the member banks in each district; and three class C directors, who are appointed by the Federal Reserve Board, one of whom is designated chairman and another vice-chairman of the district bank's board. This means in effect that the Federal Reserve Board controls the boards of the district banks. This was not always the case, as we shall see.* Historically, there was a purpose to the decentralization of the bank regulatory system represented by the creation of the Federal Reserve System.

To some the trend toward centralization of power in the Federal Reserve Board in Washington represents a step backward; to others it is a trend that has been growing in the United States since the early days of Franklin Roosevelt's presidency. There is no doubt but that we are now at one of those historical turns in the political road today—one which we seem hardly conscious of, so mixed are the apparent signals for change. The Reagan Administration wanted to reduce the size and centralization of government. To be consistent it should want to preserve our dual bank regulatory system—with both the federal government and the states playing a role. But will the Congress for other reasons want to preempt bank regulation entirely for the federal government, as is the case in other countries?

Under the close supervision of the Federal Reserve Board, the Federal Reserve banks operate the *discount window* through which member banks can borrow from the Federal Reserve bank in their district. Under the Monetary Control Act of 1980, other depository institutions may also use the discount window. It is this discount system that caused the Federal Reserve banks to be referred to as a *lender of last resort.* In point of fact, as we shall see, the contrary has been true in recent years because it is cheaper to borrow from the Federal Reserve banks than from other banks. Today it might be more appropriate to refer to the Federal Reserve as the *lender of first resort*—to indicate the extent to which the Board, perhaps against its better judgment, has sought to stimulate economic recovery and renewed consumer spending. One reason might be self-preservation; the Federal Reserve System, although purportedly independent, is under constant pressure from the executive branch, and from Congress, which created it, to maintain or restore growth in the economy.† Chairmen of the Federal Reserve will probably

---

*This topic is discussed in Chapter 2.

†The question of whether or not the Federal Reserve Board is truly independent is a most interesting one. It is discussed in detail in various contexts in Chapters 2 (in terms of history), 3 (in terms of monetary policy), and 6 (in light of current proposals for change submitted by both the administration and congressional leaders).

be remembered in history less for their understanding of economic theory than for their political acumen.

Similarly, the Federal Reserve banks, as directed by the Board of Governors, carry out other so-called open market operations—that is to say, the purchase and sale of government securities, an activity that increases or decreases the funds available for banks to lend. They also issue Federal Reserve notes (which constitute the bulk of U.S. paper currency); provide clearinghouse functions in the check-collection process; serve as principal fiscal agents for the U.S. government; and hold deposits of member banks, including their reserve deposits, as declared mandatory from time to time by the Federal Reserve Board.

Member Banks

Member banks are the financial institutions that own stock in their local Federal Reserve bank and thereby become "members" of the Federal Reserve System. National banks are required to become members of the Federal Reserve System, even though, as indicated earlier, they are regulated not by the Board of Governors of the Federal Reserve but by the Comptroller of the Currency, who is an official of the Treasury Department of the executive branch of the U.S. government. State-chartered commercial banks or trust companies may elect to become members of the Federal Reserve System but are not required to join. In 1978 only 10 percent of the state banks were members. Since the 1950s, there has been a fairly steady decline in the number of member banks and an increase in the number of nonmember banks. There are several reasons for this. The Federal Reserve is a strict regulatory body; use of the discount facility is less important today than in the past. Moreover, since the Depository Institutions Deregulation and Monetary Control Act of 1980, nonmember banks have access to some of the same services as member banks, including borrowing privileges. Nonmember banks are now subject—since 1980—to the same reserve requirements as member banks.

RESPONSIBILITY FOR BANKS' OPERATIONS ABROAD

The Federal Reserve Board of Governors has three statutory responsibilities in connection with international operations of member banks. First, it issues licenses for foreign branches and regulates their activities.[1] Second, it charters and regulates international banking subsidiaries called Edge Act corporations (after Senator Walter Edge of New Jersey, who introduced the legislation in 1919).[2] Third, it authorizes overseas investments by banks, Edge Act corporations, and bank holding companies and regulates the activities of these institutions and/or their affiliates overseas. This last function has become an increasingly important role for the Board because over the last 30 years international banking has become a vitally important operation owing to the increase in the number of international investments of U.S. companies and the very substantial growth of international trade.

Given the ingenuity of the large money center banks in the United States and the growth of the so-called Eurodollar market, have U.S. bank regulatory agencies—in particular, the Federal Reserve Board—performed their regulatory functions to prevent abuses by the banks? The current state of bank international lending makes it particularly appropriate to examine this question. By the end of 1982, large U.S. banks were operating full-service branches overseas, and a substantial portion of the deposits of the 20 largest banks were held in foreign offices. It is interesting to note that the activities of foreign banks in the United States are not subject to federal bank regulation (unless they come under Bank Holding Company legislation) but to state regulation. This is curious given the fact that foreign banks are constantly expanding their activities in the United States just as U.S. banks are becoming increasingly active overseas. On the face of it, there would appear to be an anomaly here worthy of congressional attention.

Since 1968 the Federal Reserve Board has also been responsible for formulating regulations under the Truth in Lending Act (Title I of the Consumer Protection Act). Enforcement of the Board's regulations is apportioned among some nine governmental agencies, however, and the Board's enforcement action is strictly limited to state member banks.

BANK HOLDING COMPANY REGULATION

The Board's most important regulatory activity in recent years has certainly been its role under the Bank Holding Company Act, originally adopted in 1956 and amended in 1970 to include one-bank holding companies. The purpose of this legislation was twofold. The first was to prevent bank holding companies from spreading so rapidly that bank competition would be severely curtailed. Its other purpose, however, has become much more to the fore: the Act gave the Federal Reserve Board exclusive jurisdiction to determine the extent to which Bank Holding Companies should be permitted to engage in nonbank activities related to banking while still maintaining the separation between banking and commerce thought to have been mandated by the Congress under the Glass-Steagall Act (1933) and other legislation. As financing has become increasingly important in affecting business transactions and as financial services firms have (1) proliferated in the decade of the 1970s and (2) increased the types of services offered, the activity of the Federal Reserve Board in interpreting the Bank Holding Company Act has become more and more relevant and time-consuming. Because a reexamination of controls over financial services has become so necessary, an entire section of this book* will explore just what has been determined to be acceptable in terms of services other than loans that may be "related to banking."

There appears to be no doubt whatsoever that the attitude of the Federal Reserve Board has been gradually shifting to allow banks to broaden — through the bank holding company concept — the scope of their activities so that they can compete more effectively with other firms offering financial services. The Federal Reserve is in a difficult position. It earned over $14 billion in 1981 by forcing banks to maintain reserves not required of other financial institutions. Through its regulatory powers (in particular Regulation Q), it prevented banks from paying a reasonable rate of return to bank depositors — and in this manner was responsible for the incredible growth of money-market funds (well over $200 billion) and the loss of deposits to the banks. But the Federal Reserve is reluctant to allow the banks as opposed to bank holding companies to offer other services to make up for what they cannot earn from their deposits; as a result bank depositors move to institutions that will give them a better return on their money as well as the use of checking facilities. The banks have certainly paid a heavy penalty for the privilege of paying the Federal Reserve to regulate them. What our regulators sometimes tend to forget is that unless the depository institutions can make money by accepting deposits, they will surely find themselves in deep trouble. How is this going to protect their depositors?

The original intent of the Federal Reserve Act† was to ensure that

---

*See Chapter 5.
†Chapter 2 discusses the origins of the Federal Reserve Act of 1913. It was very much the intent of Congress to make sure that banks remained profitable so that depositors would be protected.

the banks did make a reasonable rate of return on depositors' funds in normal banking transactions; otherwise they might be encouraged to take greater risks. With the onset of inflation and maintenance by the Federal Reserve of low interest rates on savings deposits, the banks became hard-pressed to maintain their domestic earnings. As a direct result, the money-center banks have moved much of their transactions outside the United States. By so doing, they have been able to earn a much higher rate of return.* Surely, this is not to the country's advantage — particularly in a period of recession. Nor can it be of any advantage to the depositors who are risking their savings in Zaire, Mexico, and Brazil rather than in the development of business (and, consequently, of employment) in our own country. There is an interesting question of government policy here.

In fairness to the Federal Reserve Board, it is necessary to examine the efforts made by the Board to apply the not-necessarily-clear mandates of the Congress with respect to permissible activities allowed the banks.† The Board, and the courts as well, have painstakingly sought to interpret the meaning of Congressional legislation. Unfortunately, in so doing, the reasons behind the Congressional intent — especially against the backdrop of today's methods of doing business — are often forgotten. The aim of Congress has been to protect depositors; practices that took place in the 1920s and that did indeed call for serious attempts to bring such practices to an end precipitated its involvement. However, some 60 years later, it is time to reexamine, in the light of today's financial environment, the manner and the extent that depositors are entitled to special protection. Should a Bank Holding Company today be permitted to undertake insurance activities; courier, brokerage, and travel services; credit cards; investment management; leasing activities; futures conversion; merchant services; operation of earnings and loans; or data processing for other than customers? Some of these activities, as we shall see, have been deemed permissible and others have not. In each case the Board has made a careful analysis and sought to interpret the intent of Congress. Whenever requested the courts have given careful judicial review. After consulting with all interested parties, the time is now right for Congress to initiate a thorough reanalysis.

---

*In Chapter 8 the risks of these foreign loans are analyzed in detail.

†The Federal Reserve System was enacted by the Congress. The Federal Reserve Board, although an independent agency of the federal government, is legally responsible to the Congress. Is the Board truly independent? Should it be? See Chapter 2.

THE FEDERAL RESERVE AND MONETARY POLICY

The Federal Reserve is expected to contribute to the nation's economic goals of growth and full employment through "its ability to influence the availability and the cost of money and credit in the economy. As the nation's central bank, it attempts to ensure that money and credit growth over the longer run is sufficient to provide a rising standard of living for all our people."[3]

It is interesting to note that, in the Fed's own words, money and credit are expected to grow over the long term. There is nothing wrong with this assumption. If the economy grows, the money supply and the amount of credit should also be expected to rise. The problem in practice has been (1) to maintain growth on some sort of a matching basis; (2) to avoid volatility in the money supply; (3) to take into account the difference between cost and availability of money and properly determine when to increase or decrease its supply; and (4) to take into account the difference between the cost and availability of credit (as opposed to money) and determine accurately when economic conditions require that credit availability be increased or decreased. As we shall see, the Federal Reserve's policy over the years has not been consistent. Again, this is not necessarily a criticism. The behavior of the economy has certainly not reflected the hoped-for consistent growth pattern Congress intended. The basic question must be whether Federal Reserve policy, on the whole, has added to, or diminished, volatility in the economy — whether such policies have contributed to, or reduced, the capacity of the economy to grow. Historical analysis can be helpful here because we can examine the behavior of the economy over the years since the Federal Reserve Act was adopted in 1913 and match this against Federal Reserve policy decisions. It is obvious that over the years the U.S. economy has grown very substantially. Our standard of living in the mid-1980s bears no comparison to what it was 70 years ago. We have indeed made very substantial, though somewhat uneven, progress. What tools has the Federal Reserve been given to govern changes in the country's economy?

Perhaps it would be helpful first to enumerate a number of simplistic assumptions regarding money and credit since these are the variables over which the Fed is given control. But are these assumptions so simple? In 1913 it could be said that money was money. We knew what was meant. People kept their savings in banks in the form of demand deposits to be withdrawn as needed. The Federal Reserve, as agent for the U.S. government, was obliged to exchange for $100 in paper money gold coins worth $100 calculated at a value for gold of $20 per ounce. U.S. currency was therefore freely convertible into gold. Although checks had existed for a long period of time, there were no credit cards to create credit, no NOW accounts, and no other unusual forms of accounts currently available today to affect either the money supply or the availability of credit. We now realize that we must ask ourselves new and difficult questions: To what extent have new substitutes for money and credit affected the capacity of the Federal Reserve to control the cost and availability of either credit or money? Is it possible for the Federal Reserve even to know how much credit or money equivalent (since we can no longer speak of money as we used to) amounts to at any given time? Is the Federal Reserve even in a position to know accurately the money supply or the availability of credit? Perhaps we had best start with cost because these figures are more readily available. We know, for example, that bank rates are spoken about in relation to a prime rate. But what is the prime rate and who sets it? Certainly not the Federal Reserve. The prime rate is that rate applied to first-class borrowers by the banks. But banks are expected to compete, and hence even the prime-rate setting by individual banks is of limited value. How then does the Fed control the cost and availability of money and credit?

The Federal Reserve has a number of tools with which to control the availability and cost of money and credit. Some are much more important than others. Some affect only money, others only credit. There are basically five means available to the Fed to control U.S. monetary policy.

The first, and most important, is the Fed's ability to increase or decrease the money supply. Put in simple terms, the Federal Reserve banks can increase the money supply by buying government securities from the banks and decrease the money supply by selling government securities to the banking system. In the first instance the banks receive a credit at their Federal Reserve bank, which can then be loaned to the public. In the second the banks are debited by the amount of the sale, and their capacity to lend is thereby reduced. When the Fed buys government securities it may be said to be monetizing the federal debt since the Fed creates money—and thereby adds to the money supply—each time it purchases government securities. The Fed handles these kinds of transactions through what is called the *Open Market Committee*. This group meets once a month and consists today (though not in the past) of the 7 governors of the Federal Reserve Board and 5 of the 12 chairmen of the Federal Reserve banks who are chosen by rotation (except for the chairman of the New York Fed, who is a permanent member). The Open Market Committee operates through the New York Federal Reserve Bank as agent for the other Federal Reserve banks. By tradition, the chairman of the Board of Governors is chairman of the Open Market Committee.

Obviously, the actions of the Open Market Committee become the key to whether credit facilities will be more or less available to the banks and, therefore, to whether the cost of credit — interest rates — can be expected to rise or fall. For this reason the decisions of the Open Market Committee are not released immediately but two or three days after the *following* meeting.

The second method used by the Federal Reserve to control the availability and cost of money and credit is the *discount rate*. The discount rate is the rate of interest charged member banks and certain other depository institutions when they borrow from their district Federal Reserve bank. In theory this rate is set by the district bank. But since the Board now controls the district banks, the Board in effect sets the discount rate that all district banks follow. Since the discount rate sets the cost of credit for the depository institution, it obviously controls the cost of money to borrowers from the banks. Curiously enough, from time to time the discount rate is lower than the rate at which banks can borrow from each other. Does this indicate that the Federal Reserve is no longer the lender of last resort, as it claims, but the lender of first resort? Banks do borrow from each other for different purposes — mainly to obtain overnight funds because some banks will have excess funds when others are short. In addition, there are penalties for excessive use of discount facilities offered by the Fed. What is important to note is that change in the discount rate is an effective means — whether through a penalty rate or not — whereby the Federal Reserve can affect the cost of credit to business or to the consumer in the United States. However, this method does not give the Fed the power to control the *availability* of money or credit.

The third device available to the Fed is the reserve requirement — a device used far more extensively in Europe and Canada — to control the availability of credit. The reserve requirement only indirectly affects the *cost* of money — by increasing the demand for credit. It does, however, directly affect the amount of loans a depository institution can support. *Reserves* are defined as the amount that depository institutions must set aside, primarily either in the form of deposits with the local Federal Reserve bank or in the form of vault cash. Under the Monetary Control Act, reserve requirements were extended to depository institutions other than banks and both the amount and method were changed.

The fourth method available, although limited in scope, is the Fed's ability to control *margin requirements* for the purchase of securities. The margin requirement is the amount of cash the customer must put up with his broker toward the purchase of a security. An increase in margin requirements creates increased *demand* for credit — and hence tends to increase the *cost* of money. This is not the principal reason, however, for margin requirements ordered by the Fed. In the 1920s, wild securities speculation was fueled by the right to purchase securities on almost no margin. In recent years margins have varied from 50 to 80 percent, but there has been relatively little market speculation. If anything, the power of businesses to raise equity capital should be encouraged, rather than discouraged, because until 1983 business was generally undercapitalized in the United States as a result of inflation and debt-equity ratios had consequently become dangerously high.

The final tool available to the Fed deals with foreign rather than domestic control and has been principally used to maintain some sort of balance between exchange rates, particularly the exchange value of the dollar. On November 1, 1978, the Carter administration completely reversed its policy of favoring a decline in the value of the dollar to encourage exports and initiated so-called swap transactions* through the Federal Reserve Bank of New York (which handles international matters for the Board of Governors) to bring about a rise in the value of the dollar. In the Reagan administration the policy of the Treasury has been not to intervene in foreign exchange markets, barring very unusual circumstances, on the theory that exchange rates should be set by the marketplace rather than by government manipulation. Under U.S. law the United States Treasury has the responsibility for any intervention by U.S. officials in the foreign exchange markets. In the years after 1971 (when the United States abandoned the gold standard) but prior to 1981, the New York Fed carried on swap operations with other central banks to maintain exchange rate relationships made necessary by the Nixon administration's abandonment of the gold exchange monetary standard and the switch in 1973 to flexible exchange rates. Therefore, in this function the Fed is acting on behalf of the Treasury pursuant to Treasury policy.† In a very real sense, however, exchange rates do affect the availability and cost of U.S. currency. In the years since the election of Pres-

---

*A *currency swap* is an arrangement between the New York Fed and central banks or other countries to lend each other foreign currencies in order to stabilize exchange rates.

†It is interesting to note that while it is the Treasury Department that controls foreign exchange intervention, the Treasury has no control over domestic market intervention in the credit or securities markets.

ident Ronald Reagan the dollar has been unusually strong (to some extent at least because of the Federal Reserve's policy from 1979 to 1982 of bringing about a decline in the constant increase in the U.S. money supply). This policy, as we shall see, brought about an increase in interest rates in the United States, encouraged foreign investors to convert foreign currencies into dollars to earn the high returns available here, and thereby brought about an increase in the value of the dollar, which has continued to make the dollar a very strong currency. In a sense the strong dollar has had a substantial effect on the availability of money and credit because it has encouraged foreign funds to be transferred to the United States and hence available here for loan purposes as well as equity investment. Has the policy of nonintervention adopted by the Treasury in 1981 been helpful or hurtful to U.S. economic policy? Investors would have one answer, exporters another; but if the conclusion is that, on balance, the policy has had a positive effect, this leads one to wonder whether the constant interference by the New York Federal Reserve in domestic money markets should be considered as positive or negative. One effect it has had, of course, is to make millions of dollars annually for bond dealers in the United States.*

The Federal Reserve Board is trying to accomplish two contradictory goals: to control the *availability* of money and credit and to control the *cost* of money and credit. If we did not understand how impossible this is, we have only to look at the experience of Saudi Arabia in trying to maintain the Organization of Petroleum Exporting Countries (OPEC) cartel in 1982/83. In order to maintain the price of oil (its cost to the buyer), the Saudis had to reduce its availability. The same rule applies in reverse. In order to maintain availability (the market for oil), price would have to be reduced. Congress has given the Federal Reserve an impossible task, which the Fed has attempted to meet by allowing a little of both or by alternately stressing either *cost* or *availability*. The compromise has resulted in inflation, and the alternate focus has resulted in high volatility, both in regard to the money supply and in regard to interest rates. As we shall see, both the executive branch and Congress avoid responsibility for the impossible mandate they created through stressing the so-called independence of the Federal Reserve Board. But what good is independence—no matter how real—if the instructions one is required to abide by are fundamentally contradictory?

*In a speech presented in July 1981, Professor Milton Friedman stated: "In the year 1980, the Federal Reserve made gross open market purchases of securities of something over $800 billion and gross transactions . . . of more than double that amount. The net change in the portfolio was $4.5 billion. . . . Why all this churning. . . . What function does it have for monetary policy and why has it occurred?"[4]

OTHER FEDERAL
DEPOSITORY INSTITUTION
REGULATORY AGENCIES

Believe it or not, there are seven regulatory agencies in the United States that have some control over depository institutions. These are:

- The Federal Reserve Board,
- Comptroller of the Currency,
- Federal Deposit Insurance Corporation, –FDIC
- The Federal Home Loan Bank System, –FHLBB
- The Federal Savings and Loan Insurance Corporation, –FSLIC
- The National Credit Union Administration, –NCUA and
- The National Credit Union Share Insurance Fund. –NCUSIF

We have analyzed the functions of the Federal Reserve Board. Each of the other regulatory agencies needs some brief introduction because each performs a different function and was created in response to a different perceived legislative need.

Comptroller of the Currency

The easiest way to understand the office of the Comptroller of the Currency is to think of the Comptroller as the official who regulates national banks, that is, those with a federal, as opposed to a state, charter. As was pointed out earlier, the Comptroller's office is part of the executive branch of the U.S. government, with the Comptroller reporting to the Secretary of the Treasury. The office was created by the National Currency Act in 1863 — at the height of the War Between the States — when the federal government found it necessary to establish a centralized banking system to cope with the financial demands of a wartime economy. Until that time there had been no centralized banking system in the United States except for two periods of 20 years each, during which the First and Second Bank of the United States came into existence. In 1832 President Andrew Jackson, a man who saw in the creation of a central banking system a method by which the bankers in the Northeast could slow the growth of the South and West by keeping interest rates high and money scarce, vetoed the renewal of the Second Bank of the United States. Jackson was a Populist who clearly did not believe in a central banking system. One finds in the House of Representatives today, interestingly enough, many political leaders who express the same distrust of centralized control banking. This includes distrust of the Federal Reserve System as a central banking system.

Jackson's veto was responsible for the dual banking system that still exists to the present day, with some banks chartered by the federal government and others chartered by the individual states. Figure 1-1 provides a graphic rendering of just how complicated the dual bank regulatory system has become. One has only to read the reports of the General Accounting Office on the subject in 1976 and 1977 to realize how much overlapping authority exists with each agency having jurisdiction requiring its own reports—though not necessarily asking for the same information.

At any rate, in 1863 it was thought that the Comptroller of the Currency under the National Banking Act would gradually come to exercise control over the banking system and that state banking charters authorized between 1837 (when the authority of the states to charter banks was upheld by the Supreme Court)[5] and 1863 would fall into disuse. In order to make sure that this would happen, the federal government even taxed the notes of state banks. But with the development of the checking account, state banks continued to flourish under a more lenient regulatory environment, which lasted until 1913 when the Federal Reserve Act gave state banks advantages to come under the control of the Federal Reserve System. At the present time a bank may elect (with regulatory approval) to convert at any time from state to federal charter, or federal to state charter. As we shall note, there have been times when banks have purposely switched in order to accomplish certain functions that were not possible under their current regulatory controls. The dual banking system has often been criticized as overly complex and burdensome. What it means is that in addition to at least three overlapping federal regulatory bodies—the Federal Reserve, the Comptroller's office, and the Federal Deposit Insurance Corporation—there are 50 state regulatory bodies, some of which, like New York, have very strict regulations, whereas others such as Tennessee or Kentucky have relatively little.

It has been wisely suggested that the Comptroller of the Currency should be renamed "administrator of national banks" because this is what the proper definition of the function has become.[6] The Comptroller is appointed by the President, subject to Senate confirmation, for a fixed term of five years and acts under the general direction of the Secretary of the Treasury, who has the right to appoint up to four deputy comptrollers. Administratively, the office of the Comptroller is divided into 1 central office in Washington, D.C., and 12 regional offices, located in different cities around the country. Each is headed by a regional administrator who has general regulatory and administrative supervision over the national banks in that area. In 1983 the 12 regional offices were

FIGURE 1-1
The Tangled Web of Bank Regulation

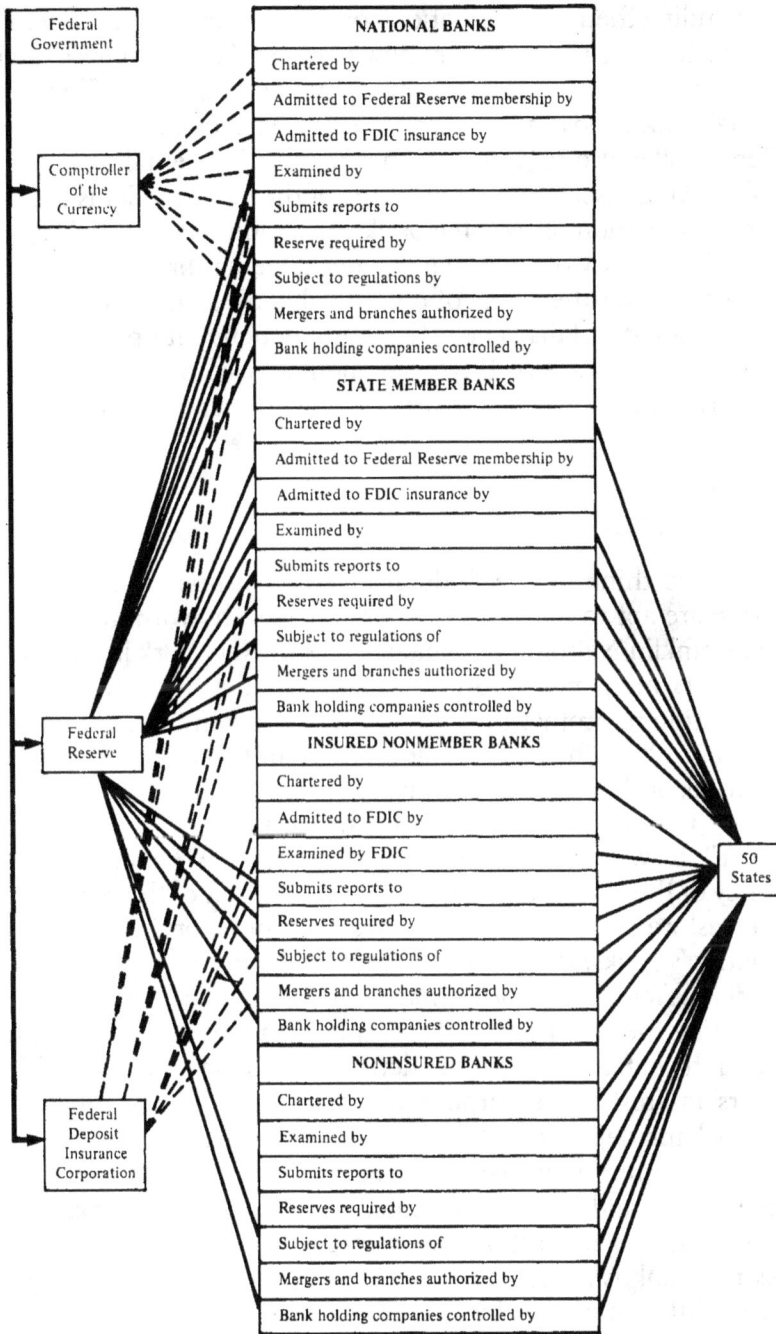

	NATIONAL BANKS
	Chartered by
	Admitted to Federal Reserve membership by
	Admitted to FDIC insurance by
	Examined by
	Submits reports to
	Reserve required by
	Subject to regulations by
	Mergers and branches authorized by
	Bank holding companies controlled by

Federal Government

Comptroller of the Currency

Federal Reserve

Federal Deposit Insurance Corporation

50 States

STATE MEMBER BANKS
Chartered by
Admitted to Federal Reserve membership by
Admitted to FDIC insurance by
Examined by
Submits reports to
Reserves required by
Subject to regulations of
Mergers and branches authorized by
Bank holding companies controlled by

INSURED NONMEMBER BANKS
Chartered by
Admitted to FDIC by
Examined by FDIC
Submits reports to
Reserves required by
Subject to regulations of
Mergers and branches authorized by
Bank holding companies controlled by

NONINSURED BANKS
Chartered by
Examined by
Submits reports to
Reserves required by
Subject to regulations of
Mergers and branches authorized by
Bank holding companies controlled by

Source: Adapted from U.S., Congress, Senate, Subcommittee on Financial Institutions of the Senate Committee on Banking, Housing, and Urban Affairs, *Hearings on Financial Structure and Regulation*, 93rd Cong., 1st sess., 1973. Cited in Murray E. Polakoff and Thomas A. Durkin, *Financial Institutions and Markets*, 2nd ed. (Boston: Houghton-Mifflin, 1981).

reduced to 6. The Comptroller has general supervision over all national banks, including their trust activities; approves their charters; and must approve both applications to form new banks and conversions of state-chartered banks to national bank status, the establishment of branches by national banks, and any merger where the survivor is a national bank. The Comptroller also regulates the permissible incidental activities of national banking associations. The office of the Comptroller is charged with the examination of national banks, the soundness of their operations, and the quality of their management. He has broad powers and may even take over the assets of a national bank or appoint a conservator to operate its affairs. The office is not dependent upon appropriated funds. Its costs are met by assessments levied on national banks and, in part, by interest earned on U.S. government obligations.

The Federal Deposit Insurance Corporation (FDIC)

When we think of the Federal Deposit Insurance Corporation (FDIC) we are apt to recall newspaper stories of how it intervened to save the Franklin National Bank depositors in New York in the 1970's by forcing its merger; or more recently, we might have read about its intervention to protect the depositors of the Penn Square Bank in Oklahoma in 1983, which had made all those unfortunate oil loans. We need to think of the FDIC as the insurance agency that is there to protect the depositors in bank and thrift institutions.

The FDIC was created by the Banking Act of 1933 as an independent agency of the federal government. The purposes of the corporation were to "restore confidence in the banking system, protect depositors in the nation's banks, and promote safe and sound banking practices."[7] The Banking Act of 1933 (otherwise known as the Glass-Steagall Act), passed during the worst part of the depression, found that banks had conducted their affairs in a manner detrimental to the protection of their depositors' interests. One purpose of the legislation was to provide insurance to bank depositors. Another (which we will examine in great detail) was to correct a severely criticized bank practice: combining commercial banking and investment banking. In investment banking, the risks to the banking institution are much greater since as a dealer in securities the bank is acting in its own behalf rather than as an agent.

The FDIC is managed by a board of three directors, one of whom must be the Comptroller of the Currency. The two other members are appointed by the President, subject to Senate confirmation, for a term of six years. Only two of the three directors may come from any one political party. The board elects one of their members to be chairman.

The FDIC serves two main purposes: it insures depositors in banks up to $100,000, and it regulates and supervises insured (primarily non-member) banks. As well as providing deposit insurance to banks (state or national), the FDIC may also insure state-chartered mutual and stock savings banks and similar depository institutions (including certain federal savings banks) that are engaged in the business of accepting deposits other than trust funds. It may also insure accounts in branches of foreign banks in the United States. Coverage is automatic for all banks that are members of the Federal Reserve System (including, of course, all national banks). Others may apply for coverage even though they are not members of the Federal Reserve System.

What happens in the event of failure of an insured bank? The FDIC will pay the depositors either in cash or by making available to such depositors a transferred deposit in a new bank or another insured bank. Although the limit of insurance is $100,000 on each account, Penn Square's insolvency was the first instance involving a major bank where the FDIC did organize a takeover by another insured institution so that all depositors and not just those with $100,000 or less were protected against loss. FDIC chairman William M. Isaac intentionally permitted this to happen to large depositors to incur losses, in this instance to signal a warning to large depositors to exercise more care in making deposits. When a bank failure occurs, the FDIC acts as receiver to wind up the affairs of the bank and pay off creditors including the FDIC. In addition to its other powers, the FDIC can, for a three-year period that began on October 15, 1982, arrange for emergency cross-industry or interstate mergers, provided that the insured bank in question has total assets of $500 million or more.[8]

The FDIC has considerable supervisory authority over insured banks, which seems only natural since it bears the consequence of any loss to depositors. It may terminate insurance coverage of any insured institution that it finds to be operating in an unsound fashion; it may also issue cease and desist orders and may even suspend or remove an officer or director of an insured bank.

Finally, note that the FDIC, like its counterparts, is not dependent on appropriated funds. It can make assessments against insured banks and can issue its own debt obligations. Furthermore, the FDIC has a line of credit with the Treasury Department of $3 billion. Its commitments are backed by the full faith and credit of the U.S. government.

The Federal Home Loan
Bank System (FHLBB)

The Federal Home Loan Bank System (FHLBB) is the federal agency that supervises *thrift* institutions: savings banks and savings and loan institutions. The federal government has a particular interest in these types of banks because they finance housing, and public policy favors financing for home buyers. This agency was created by the Federal Home Loan Bank Act of 1932. Its purpose was to encourage the financing of long-term mortgage lending as well as to provide a reserve credit system for thrift institutions primarily engaged — as opposed to banks — in long-term home finance activities. The concept was somewhat analogous to the reserve credit system established by the Federal Reserve Act for commercial banks. There are other analogies to the Federal Reserve System. At the top is the Federal Home Loan Bank Board (FHLBB), an independent agency of the Federal government that is composed of three members appointed to four-year terms by the President, subject to confirmation by the Senate. Its primary function is the supervision of the FHLBB and the chartering of federal savings and loan associations and federal savings banks. Below the Board there are 12 regional Federal Home Loan banks patterned after the 12 Federal Reserve banks. These are owned by member institutions within the region that are required to subscribe to its capital stock. Their boards are appointed in part by the FHLBB and in part by the members. They provide advances to the member institutions, accept deposits, provide technical advice, and maintain and publish statistical information of value to the members.

The FHLBB also administers the Federal Home Loan Mortgage Corporation (known as Freddie Mac), which was created by the Emergency Home Finance Act of 1970 to provide a secondary market in conventional as well as federally insured or guaranteed mortgages.

The FHLBB derives its funds from examination charges and from assessments on the regional banks and the Federal Savings and Loan Insurance Corporation. In addition, the Secretary of the Treasury is authorized to purchase and hold up to a maximum of $4 billion of Federal Home Loan Bank obligations at any one time.

Member institutions include all federally chartered savings and loan institutions and savings banks. State-chartered savings and loan institutions, building and loan associations, savings banks, insurance companies, and similar institutions — but not commercial banks — that engage in the business of making long-term mortgage loans may become members.

The Federal Savings and Loan
Insurance Corporation

The Federal Savings and Loan Insurance Corporation (FSLIC) was created by the National Housing Act of 1934.[9] It is managed by the FHLBB. Its principal functions are to insure accounts at eligible institutions (up to a maximum of $100,000) and to regulate and examine insured institutions. In effect, it does for savings and loan associations and savings banks what the FDIC does for banks. It is entirely self-supporting, with its income earned from premiums paid by insured institutions supplemented by interest earned on investments. The FSLIC may also borrow funds by issuing obligations—as is the case with the FDIC—and it has a limit of credit with the Treasury of $750 million. All federally chartered savings and loan associations and savings banks must be insured by the FSLIC. It may also if it chooses insure other eligible* members of the Federal Home Loan Bank System.

The National Credit Union Administration
and the National Credit Union Share
Insurance Fund

Credit unions are considered by the government to play an important role in U.S. financial regulatory policy because they serve as financial cooperatives, helping their members both to invest their funds and borrow when necessary. It is very much in the American tradition of community service. Hence, public policy favors credit unions. The National Credit Union Administration (NCUA) was created much later by an act of Congress in 1970.[10] The NCUA is managed by a board of three members who are appointed by the President, subject to confirmation by the Senate, for a period of six years. The NCUA is statutorily defined as an independent agency within the executive branch of government. Its functions are (1) to charter new federal credit unions and approve the conversion of state-chartered credit unions to federal status and (2) to supervise their financial condition and compliance with federal law and regulations. The NCUA board also operates a program of deposit insurance in which all accounts in federal credit unions are insured for up to $100,000. It may also grant insurance protection to state-chartered credit unions that apply.

---

*This includes savings and loan associations, building and loan associations, and cooperative banks.

Congress established a National Credit Union Share Insurance Fund in the Treasury Department to meet insurance payments and to assist credit unions in difficulty. The fund is financed through premiums charged the insured credit unions as well as interest earned on government securities. The fund has a line of credit with the Treasury Department of up to $100 million. It may also borrow from an organization established in 1978 by an act of Congress to provide loans to member credit unions to meet seasonal or emergency needs.[11] The facility is an interesting vehicle because it is a so-called mixed-ownership government corporation managed by the NCUA board. Any credit union may join by subscribing to capital stock. It obtains funds through the sale of stock, but it also can issue obligations and borrow up to $500 million from the Treasury. Furthermore, as a result of the Garn–St. Germain Depository Institutions Act of 1982,[12] the facility may also act as an agent of the Federal Reserve System to funnel funds from the Fed's discount window to credit unions in the event that the facility has reached its borrowing limits and credit unions still have liquidity needs. Such is the high regard in Congress for credit unions: to allow credit unions insurance facility advances not allowed to banks through the FDIC nor to savings and loan associations and savings banks through the FSLIC. It is interesting to note, however, that in other respects the same type of insurance coverage is afforded each of the country's varied depository institutions, whether they be banks, savings and loan associations, savings banks, or credit unions.

So ends this brief description of the regulation of depository institutions in the United States. Almost like the federal tax system in our country, the development of regulation over financial institutions that accept deposits has been gradual, haphazard, and triggered only when specific legislation has been adopted to meet a specific perceived need. If asked, most of us would say that financial institutions are regulated by the Federal Reserve Board. But the answer would be highly misleading. In the United States, in the banking sector alone there were—as of 1984—some 14,700 commercial banks and some 56 regulatory agencies that supervised them with considerable overlap: 50 from the states, 3 from peripheral geographical governments, and 3 from the federal government. To the latter had to be added 4 additional federal agencies that regulated other forms of depository institutions. At the end of 1980, out of approximately 15,330 banks in the United States over 50 percent—in terms of assets—were supervised by the Comptroller of the Currency and an additional 32.2 percent by state authorities and the FDIC. Only 15 percent of the banks' assets are currently supervised by the Federal Reserve (along with state authorities). These statistics will surprise readers who think of the Federal Reserve as the principal bank regulatory agency of the federal government.

Just how this regulatory system developed in our country, how it functions, and whether it needs modernization will be the subject of upcoming chapters. We will also examine how the Federal Reserve, which has sole control over U.S. monetary policy, is performing its function as the country's central bank and whether here, too, we should examine changes in policies or in methods of operation. Since this book is principally concerned with the role of the Federal Reserve, emphasis will be on its functions and operations. It is obvious, however, that many references will have to be made to other agencies of the federal government if only to determine the extent to which gaps have been created in the regulatory circuit and the extent to which the internationalization of banking, as well as commerce, may itself require a new look at the regulation of U.S. banks' activities outside the United States.

STATE BANKING REGULATION

We have alluded to the dual nature of bank regulation in the United States, with responsibility divided between the federal government and the states. How does a state bank differ from a national bank? Simply stated, a national bank is one that obtains its charter from the Comptroller of the Currency, that is, from the federal government; a state bank is one that obtains its charter from the authorities of the state where it intends to do business.

In effect, this regulatory division of responsibility between state and federal government exists because Congress has sanctioned it. The federal government could have preempted the field, first because so much of banking crosses state lines, and second, because the Constitution specifically delegated to Congress responsibility for the money supply. Yet throughout our U.S. history, there has been a very strong distrust among much of the general population and members of Congress towards concentrations of financial power and control by a central authority. Americans inherently believe that certain sectors of the population and the economy must have special protection, which might not be available if the economy were dominated by a few giant financial institutions. Housing, agriculture, small business, and local government are generally the sectors referred to. But many believe that the very scattering of regulatory power—not only between state and federal agencies but within the federal agencies as well—has served the country well and has permitted rather than constrained financial innovation. Since this feeling is widespread, there may indeed be much merit in spreading regulatory authority—as it has been done despite the fact (as we shall observe in the next chapter) that we are unique among the industrialized countries of the world in doing so.

Very early in U.S. history there was a split between (1) those led by Alexander Hamilton, who believed in a strong, centralized banking system to encourage the development of industry, principally in the Northeast and subsequently in the Midwest, and (2) those segments of our early society who were mostly farmers, principally in the South, followers of Jefferson, and fearful that concentration of financial assets would raise the cost of money and delay development of new sections of the country, as well as make farmers' seasonal loan needs prohibitively expensive.

These same considerations have existed throughout our history and are as real today as at the time when the First Bank of the United States was created by Congress or when President Andrew Jackson of Tennessee vetoed the renewal of the Second Bank of the United States in 1832. As noted earlier, from 1837 to 1863 when the National Banking Act was adopted, banks were only chartered by the states. Each bank issued its own notes, and this was the currency of the United States. There were 1,089 banks issuing their notes as currency when the National Banking Act was adopted; so one can imagine the difficulty in handling the simplest banking transactions. And yet Congress, throughout the years, has kept insisting on the decentralization of the banking system. The McFadden Act of 1927, the Federal Deposit Insurance Act of 1932, and the Douglas amendment to the Bank Holding Company Act in 1970 are all evidence of this very strong congressional belief in the value of a decentralized banking system.

The McFadden Act[13] and the Douglas amendment[14] to the Bank Holding Company Act helped to prevent banks from crossing state lines and thereby served to prevent the concentration of financial power in a small number of banks. The McFadden Act restricts geographical locations in which national banks may establish branches and conduct their general business. The Douglas amendment provides that the Federal Reserve Board may not approve an application of a bank holding company to acquire a bank in a state other than the state in which its banking operations are principally conducted* unless the law of the state where the bank is located specifically permits, by statutory language and not merely by implication, such an organization by an out-of-state bank holding company. Bank holding companies that already owned banks prohibited by the Douglas amendment prior to 1956 (the date of the Bank Holding Company Act) were not required to divest themselves of such banks. Since almost all states have statutes either prohibiting or severely restricting out-of-state bank holding companies from owning or controlling in-state banks, the Douglas Amendment has effectively precluded except for this grandfather provision, most post-1956 interstate acquisitions by bank holding companies.

The antitrust laws apply to banking just as they do to other industries. The Department of Justice reviews bank mergers and expresses its opinion as to whether market share will reduce competition.† In recent years, however, the Federal Reserve Board has become much more lenient about permitting large bank holding company acquisitions.[15] However, the bank merger process has received considerable criticism.

The dual banking system is valuable for a number of reasons. First, with its freedom of conversion between the two systems, the dual system creates a competitive environment containing an impetus to modernization. Second, it tends to preserve local option. For example, banking conditions differ in a primarily agricultural state from those in a primarily manufacturing state. Third, the system makes for a more equitable administration of regulation by allowing banks to convert to the other system. Finally, state banking as an equal partner in the dual banking system ensures a concentration of regulatory and decision-making authority at the local level. Regulatory judgments on most banking matters are apt to improve when those responsible are closer to the site of the actual banking services to be rendered. Local and regional perspectives permit the people to be the conscience of banking. Local needs in terms of services required will play an important role.

---

*It should be noted, however, that the Garn–St. Germain Depository Institutions Act of 1982 — Public Law 97–320 secs. 118(k), 141(a)(4) — created an exception by allowing interstate acquisitions of institutions in difficulty by out-of-state bank holding companies. This has become, as will be noted in later chapters, an important loophole towards permitting interstate banking.

†The Bank Merger Act of 1966 requires the Comptroller of the Currency, the FDIC, and the Federal Reserve to obtain competitive factors reports from the Antitrust Division of Justice before approving a bank merger. To determine concentration, the division uses the so-called Herfindahl-Hirschman Index (HHI) to determine concentration in individual markets by relative percentage share.

Local controls are exercised in two ways: through local ownership and through regulatory control at the state level. In terms of regulation, it means banning out-of-state institutions and exercising local political authority over the charters and operations of financial institutions.

The chief duty of individual state regulatory agencies is to ensure that state-chartered banks operate in a safe and sound manner and in compliance with state laws adopted to achieve this end. Supervision is carried out primarily through periodic unannounced examinations and constant monitoring of the financial condition of these banks through the information contained in their periodic reports. To ensure that the banking system serves the public interest, bank supervisors scrutinize applications for more banking activities and/or for changes in structure.

State authorities have a powerful tool in the requirement that all banks operating within a given state—be they state member banks of the Federal Reserve, state nonmember banks, or national banks—must comply with the branching regulations of that state.

THE OVERLAP OF RESPONSIBILITIES

There is of necessity a good deal of overlap between state and federal regulatory agencies. First, state member banks are subject to examination by both state personnel and the Federal Reserve; state nonmember banks, similarly, are subject to examination by both the state and the FDIC.

Second, in some states an alternating examination policy has been adopted, with each party providing the other with a copy of its Report of Examination and each agency retaining the right to examine a bank under its jurisdiction whenever deemed appropriate.

Third, there is also overlapping jurisdiction with respect to the formation of new institutions. The Federal Reserve or the FDIC will defer their decision until the state has acted. In merger decisions, approval is often required of both a state and a federal agency.

Fourth, the problem is made more complicated in the event that a bank holding company is involved. As we saw, the Federal Reserve has exclusive jurisdiction over the regulation of bank holding companies but only examines and supervises banks that are state member banks since national banks fall under the supervision of the Comptroller of the Currency. This means that a bank holding company and its bank subsidiaries may frequently be examined by different regulatory agencies. Since bank holding companies own or control 25 percent of all commercial banks, which in turn control two thirds of all assets and deposits of banks in the United States, there is a big opportunity for overlap. The problem here is clear: Will affiliated transactions between bank and bank holding companies be properly scrutinized if the two entities are examined by different regulatory agencies? We will discuss this in detail under our discussion of bank holding company regulation* because Federal examiners recognize that problems frequently occur between a bank holding company and its affiliated bank transactions to the detriment of the bank. A few specific examples are transfer of loans between subsidiaries; payment of excessive management fees by the bank to its holding company; payment of dividends from the bank to the holding company where not justified by earnings but used to offset weaknesses in nonbank subsidiaries; excessive investment in bank headquarters; insistence by the parent on risky real estate loans to be made by the bank; and self-dealing of various kinds for the benefit of the parent holding company. Whose responsibility should it be to analyze these transactions between affiliates: the regulator of the bank holding company (that is, the Federal Reserve) or the regulator of the bank, the protection of whose depositors is the reason for regulation in the first place? Unbelievable as this may sound, many of the Federal Reserve banks did not have formal holding company inspection programs in place until 1974, a full 18 years after passage of the Holding Company Act giving exclusive supervision of such institutions to the Federal Reserve. By 1975 only 13 percent of all holding companies had ever been inspected. Weaknesses in many of the holding companies were not detected by the Fed until after they had damaged subsidiary banks.

The General Accounting Office (GAO) has noted the need for better supervision of bank holding companies by the Federal Reserve Board. This is one of the weaknesses of the dual banking system, where one federal regulatory agency has exclusive supervision over the parent but a state agency may supervise the affiliated subsidiary bank. Obviously, the overlap between the three federal bank regulatory agencies is another weakness.

---

*Chapter 5 discusses the regulatory problem, whereas Chapter 2 traces the historical development of bank holding company regulation.

THE REGULATION OF
INTERNATIONAL OPERATIONS

The responsibility of the Federal Reserve Board in connection with the activities of U.S. banks abroad was briefly analyzed earlier in this chapter. Unfortunately, both the FDIC and the Comptroller of the Currency in the course of examining the banks over which they have jurisdiction—the Comptroller in the case of national banks and the FDIC because of its insurance functions—necessarily have to exercise judgment with respect to the lending practices of U.S. banks abroad and the evaluation of country risk.

The Federal Reserve and the Comptroller of the Currency have taken different approaches in evaluating loans subject to country risk, but the problem is understandable because of the political considerations involved. Federal bank regulators are, after all, political appointees regardless of declared independence or fixed terms. A finding of country risk, particularly if it involves a country (such as the case of Italy in the early 1970s) with a substantial constituency in Congress, can result in questioning before congressional committees, which bank regulators prefer, quite naturally, to avoid. On the other hand, bank examiners, particularly those sent outside the United States to review operations of U.S. banks overseas, must be given clear mandates from their supervisors in order to do their jobs properly. The problem is a delicate one and (as will be discussed in more depth later) an increasingly difficult one, as recent loans to the developing countries are becoming more questionable. It is particularly difficult for bank examiners to operate in a volatile political environment where pressures may come from foreign policy consideration in the executive branch as well as from national constituencies represented in Congress. It is clear, however, that U.S. federal bank regulators should apply, in terms of country risk evaluations, the same yardstick to all foreign loans made by U.S. banks.* The obvious solution would be to use recognized experts to evaluate economic conditions in each country, rather than to depend upon numerous bank examiners whose training is not in international economics. The GAO also recommended that to cut expenses agencies make use of each other's examiners when examining banks in the same country. The Federal Reserve commented on the GAO's recommendation, noting:

---

*Regulation of U.S. banks abroad is the subject of Chapter 7, which examines in detail the overlaps that exist in the U.S. regulatory system.

In many areas examination of foreign subsidiaries are not possible because of host country laws which preclude direct examinations by other governmental authorities of banks chartered in those countries regardless of the ownership.[16]

Surely, the Federal Reserve could either ban branches in such countries or declare "questionable" loans made to governments of such countries by U.S. banks. Either one regulates or one does not but if the Fed appears to be declaring that it is not possible to exercise your regulatory functions, it is simply inviting the banks under its control to make use of such countries to evade the normal controls applicable to banks in the United States. There are many ways for the Federal Reserve to handle this problem without publicly admitting its inability to deal with it — particularly at a time when countries are almost forced in today's global monetary environment to borrow dollars from U.S. banks or forego development. U.S. bank regulators overseas have been singularly timid in exercising their regulatory functions. Surely, one of the counterpart responsibilities for controlling the world monetary system with one's currency is to make sure that one's banks are behaving in accordance with established regulatory procedures. The same rules noted should of course be applied to the extent that such activities may affect subsidiary or affiliated banks.

ATTEMPTS TO IMPROVE BANK REGULATION IN THE UNITED STATES

In recent years there has been renewed interest in examining the steps that might be taken to simplify and/or improve the regulation of banks in the United States. Steps have been taken for this purpose not only by the executive branch of government and by Congress but by the regulatory agencies themselves, all to their credit.

In March 1970 the Federal Financial Institution Examination Council came into being. This council, an interagency committee, is composed of representatives from the Federal Reserve Board, the office of the Comptroller of the Currency, the FDIC, the FHLBB, and the NCUA. Its mandate was to provide uniform principles and standards for the federal examination of depository institutions, to make recommendations to promote progressive and vigilant supervision of depository institutions, and to conduct schools for examiners. The council established five task force groups whose purposes were (1) to establish uniform principles, standards, and report forms for examination of federally regulated financial institutions; (2) to develop uniform reporting systems for such institutions, their holding companies, and nonfinancial subsidiaries of such institutions or holding companies; (3) to make recommendations for uniformity in other regulatory matters; (4) to conduct schools for examiners; and (5) to be also open to state as well as Federal regulatory employees.

The council was created as an alternative to considering ways of merging the federal agencies regulating depository institutions in order to establish better uniformity. But it is a tall order to expect federal regulators — of whatever industry — to agree on uniformity when each agency has developed its own way of dealing with regulation over a period of many years. Whose procedures should be followed when those of each agency have been sanctified by time and experience?

In early 1983, in order to force the issue the Presidential Task Group on Regulation of Financial Services was established to undertake a detailed study of the problems inherent in federal regulation of financial institutions at present.* The mandate of the task group was a broad one, directed at achieving reductions — whether administrative or legislative — in the burden on the economy by unnecessary or inefficient regulation. While promoted as part of the Reagan administration's efforts to deregulate unnecessary activities on the part of the federal government and hence under the chairmanship of Vice President George Bush, the mandate of the Task Group was really devoted to a simplification and restructuring of overlapping regulatory agencies rather than to the elimination of regulation. Its mandate included, however, a reexamination of the extent of regulation in certain areas, the cost-benefit relationship of individual regulatory procedures, and the manner in which competition could best be encouraged among different types of financial institutions.

The time for such a task group to make this type of examination could not have been more appropriate. In the 1970s and early 1980s the structure and nature of financial institutions changed as new services were conceived of and as the line between standard banking services and those rendered by insurance companies, brokerage firms, investment bankers, and others tended increasingly to become unclear. This change was largely brought about, as noted earlier, by the large increase in inflation in the United States and the effect of Federal Reserve regulations on the ability of the commercial banking sector in the domestic

---

*See Chapter 6 for the result of the Task Group's recommendations.

market to maintain a hold on their deposits against the onslaught of new institutions that were either permitted, or could afford, to pay more for money entrusted to them by the public. The task group has wisely concentrated its efforts on asking the federal regulatory agencies for their views on changes that might be made to fulfill its mandate. It was quite evident — if the task group was to succeed in its endeavor — that it would have to present to Congress a comprehensive program of legislation to modernize or replace items of legislation adopted in the past as a result of changes in the manner in which financial services were now rendered.

The task group consisted of the vice-president (as chairman); the Secretary of the Treasury; the Attorney General; the Director of the Office of Management and Budget (OMB); the chairman of the Council of Economic Advisors; the Assistant to the President for Policy Development; the chairman of the Board of Governors of the Federal Reserve, the FDIC, the FHLBB, the NCUA, the Securities and Exchange Commission (SEC), and the Commodities Futures Trading Commission; and the Comptroller of the Currency. By its composition, the Task Group was sure to go beyond questions dealing just with the regulation of depository institutions and to review all kinds of financial services. In today's financial marketplace the decision to extend the field of coverage was obviously a wise one. Whether any proposed legislation may be forthcoming as a result of the activities of the task group is an open question — given congressional reluctance to act, where bank regulation or deregulation is concerned.

COMPARABLE BANK REGULATIONS IN OTHER INDUSTRIALIZED COUNTRIES

As was noted earlier, bank regulation in the United States differs from that of other advanced countries: first, because our system involves at the federal level three separate agencies, often with overlapping functions; and second, because we have a dual regulatory system with responsibility divided intentionally by Congress between the federal government and the states. How is the matter of monetary policy and of bank regulation handled in other countries? Let us take a brief look at four countries: the United Kingdom, France, the Federal Republic of Germany, and Japan. Each differs from the other, which is very much in keeping with what we would expect from the political and social development within each country; therefore, each is very much a reflection, just as in the United States, of the evolution of the country's political and economic development.

The United Kingdom

In the United Kingdom, in almost any activity, there has historically always been an aversion to administrative decisions by government having the force of law. Power is and has been in the hands of Parliament, which legislates relatively infrequently. The executive's power comes from Parliament and is thus (1) responsible to an organization very cognizant of its responsibility for laws within the country and (2) very jealous of its prerogatives. The same concept is true with respect to banking and the regulation of banks. While the Bank of England has, of course, the prerogative of guiding the government's monetary policy, it does not have the authority to direct it; rather, the party in power carries out this role, and it draws this right from the majority in Parliament it represents. In regulatory matters it was thought — until the 1974 secondary bank failures indicated that the former policy was inadequate — that the Bank of England should act as a consultative body (guarding, suggesting, and helping through advances in the event of need) but that bankers should, after all, know their business better than public servant regulators and be left alone except in the event of need. Like everything else in the United Kingdom, tradition is the key to behavior, and people in responsible positions are expected to behave responsibly and with moderation. The English banking system, therefore, is characterized by both a paucity of laws and an abundance of tractability, as evidenced by the workings of the Bank of England and the government.

The Bank of England was created in 1694 as the country's central bank. Its direction is entrusted to an administrative council, which includes the governor, the vice-governor, and 16 members, all nominated by the Crown. According to the Bank of England Act of 1946, control by the state is limited to allowing the treasury to give directions to the bank. This power has never had to be used; it is sufficient that it exists and is accepted. The bank has been able to work out monetary policy in agreement with the government and, obviously, in conformity with the government's policy.

In terms of regulatory authority, the bank may make recommendations to bankers and, authorized by the treasury, may convert, in a given case, its recommendations into directives that must be followed. Yet the bank's authority is limited even here because no sanctions exist in the event that its directives are not obeyed. The Bank of England has always been opposed to any system of fixed rates for banks, preferring instead to deal with individual banks on an advisory basis dictated by individual circumstances.

In the United Kingdom there is not even a legal definition of a *bank*.

Banks are simply put into categories by laws referring to particular activities and recognized as such within the limits of such laws. There is, however, a distinction between a *primary banking sector* and a *secondary banking sector.* The primary banking sector is composed of the clearing banks (deposit banks whose main activities consist of the collection of deposits and the granting of short-term credits), accepting houses, authorized banks, and banks voluntarily subject to the control of the Bank of England.

The secondary banking sector consists of a large number of bank-type enterprises that devote themselves to the collection of short-term deposits that are used in real estate investment operations, in medium- and long-term mortgage loans, and for private credits. As a result of fevered speculation in the real estate market in 1974 and a consequent severe decline in prices that brought about the downfall of many institutions in the secondary banking sector, it was realized that some action would have to be taken to prevent a recurrence of this type of activity with its consequent risk to depositors. The result was the Reform Bill presented by the government to Parliament in 1976 for bank reform. The bill requires institutions intending to accept deposits to obtain prior authorization from the Bank of England in order to ensure a minimum of capital and reserves. The bill also sets up an obligatory fund for the guarantee of deposits; reinforces the Bank of England's control powers; and provides for the fixation of capital and debt to equity ratios by the Bank of England (in agreement with the treasury).

Even with the new bill, the regulation of banks in the United Kingdom is certainly not a burdensome matter, nor does it involve any great bureaucracy to police the banking system, because it is still based on faith and the capacity of recognized experts to behave in a professional manner.

France

If there is an antithesis to the British bank regulatory system, it would certainly have to be the French. In the United Kingdom, as we saw, Parliament formulates the laws. Basically, law is custom and custom is tradition, with great deference paid to the practitioners in any activity. Since practitioners are considered trustworthy, governmental authorities need only suggest or guide, and there is little need for formal regulation. Compare our own confrontational regulatory system to that of the British. In France one finds the opposite of the U.K. system. Authority and judgment reside with the state, not with the people. This has always been the case in France: under kings, emperors, or democracies; the Right or the Left. France has always been an elitist society — even during its revolution, which depended upon chosen autocrats of the Left who ruled without question until beheaded. In recent years it is the famous schools that have produced the ruling mandarinate, and their graduates are as much at home ruling under François-Maurice Mitterand as they were under Charles de Gaulle or Valery Giscard d'Estaing. The tradition is that wisdom comes from the top down: Those considered to have superior intelligence and training propound the rules; the others obey.

It should, therefore, come as no surprise to find that the banking system was established by Napoléon Bonaparte, who created the Bank of France in 1800. While Napoléon is portrayed in history as a soldier and a conqueror, his three greatest achievements were surely his establishment of the *Code Civil,* the legal system that exists today in most of the countries of the world; his creation of a banking system; and his development of the educational system that makes the French Lycees a symbol of excellence throughout Latin America and many other parts of the world even today.

The Bank of France is characteristically affirmed by the statutes of January 3, 1973, to have "receive[d] from the state the general task of supervising currency and credit." It is therefore responsible for the application of the state's monetary policy. The bank has the exclusive and unlimited privilege of issuing bank notes. It is responsible for purchase and sale of gold and foreign currencies; for discount operations; for advances on public bills or on stocks or shares; for advances to the state; and for acquisition and sale of public and private bills on the open market, that is, for open market operations. It also operates a special service for the transfer of funds between banks. In addition, it bears the cost of the French export subsidies, which has amounted to as much as $5 billion per year. It is interesting to note that when General de Gaulle resumed power in 1958 — at the time when the Algerian crisis had almost unleashed a civil war in France and the economy was in dire trouble — he made Jacques Rueff, one of France's outstanding economic thinkers, a kind of economic czar to restore a stable economy. Rueff's first act was to inform the Bank of France that no more open market purchases of French government securities were to be made, thereby forcing a reduction of 30 percent in the following year's budget — strong but effective medicine that succeeded only because of the support of a strong president.

Except for the fact that the French have a discount window for export credits, the powers of the Bank of France in the monetary area are similar to the powers of the Federal Reserve Board. The Bank of France, however, has no direct regulatory functions. Banks in France are supervised by the National Credit Council (Conseil de Credit), composed of 45 members, mostly selected by the minister of Finance, who is president. The vice-president is the governor of the Bank of France. The Council makes recommendations to the minister of Finance on any question relating to the currency, savings, or credit. The Council controls the rate payable on bank deposits and the cost of credit (including installment sales). In addition, the Council supervises banks, approves charters, and exercises disciplinary measures. It also approves bank mergers.

A commission for the Control of Banks was created by statute in 1971 and consists of five members, with the governor of the Bank of France serving as president. The commission watches over bank legislation and receives periodic reports submitted by the banks. It makes sure that banks abide by all bank legislation, and exercises disciplinary action over both banks and banker—the commission even has the power to withdraw bank charters. In extreme cases there is a right of appeal to the commission regarding decisions of the National Credit Council; so the commission has judicial functions as well.

Under French law, a distinction is drawn between two types of financial institutions: those defined as banks, which accept demand deposits and time deposits not exceeding two years; and financial institutions, which carry out credit and financial operations without accepting deposits.

The banking system, of course, has been further centralized as a result of President Mitterand's decision to nationalize all French banks of any significant size. This move completed the action begun in 1945 when the four largest French banks were nationalized at the end of World War II. Curiously enough, even though nationalized, large French banks will open accounts for French citizens under bank secrecy laws in Switzerland or Panama or Hong Kong, regardless of legislation regarding maintenance of accounts abroad.

Incidentally, the largest bank in the world is a French bank, the Credit Agricole, which, as its name implies, was formed to finance credits to the agricultural sector. It has branches in most agricultural countries, including the United States, and actively finances the export or import of agricultural products throughout the world.

The Federal Republic of Germany

The banking system in the Federal Republic of Germany (FRG) differs again from that of the United Kingdom or France. It is helpful to think of the FRG in terms of the Germany of 1848, a collection of states making up collectively a country, much more similar to Switzerland than to France. In such a system the central bank—the Bundesbank —plays a very independent role in its relationship to the government (unlike France or even the United Kingdom). The Bundesbank only came into being in 1957, interestingly enough as successor by merger of 11 regional central banks. It is now the central institution of banking organizations in West Germany. The sole stockholder of the Bundesbank is the government. It is directed by a council consisting of representatives of the 11 regional banks and members of the directorate of the Bundesbank, with all members appointed by the president of the country. The Bundesbank issues the country's currency and has the responsibility of maintaining its stability in foreign exchange markets. It fixes the discount rate, imposes obligatory reserves on credit institutions, and conducts open market operations. Its powers are, therefore, both those of a central bank and a bank regulatory institution. It is independent of the government but has the obligation of upholding the general economic policy of the government.

In 1971 the German Parliament created the Federal Control Office to control and supervise the banking sector; the Bundesbank, however, acts as the active agent for the control office. The Federal Control Office authorizes bank activities but has no authority to prevent the opening of new branches by the bank. In 1976 the act was amended to grant the Federal Control Office some additional functions, such as the right to conduct audits of credit institutions whenever deemed desirable and to insist that all such institutions submit detailed financial statements to the Bundesbank within three months of the end of their fiscal year.

The banks in West Germany may be divided into three categories:

1. Private sector banks, which have diminished in number from over 2,000 in 1928 to only 130 in 1975. These include the three largest German banks, Deutsche Bank, Dresdner Bank, and Commerzbank, which have branches throughout the country and a large number abroad. Other private institutions include approximately 100 regional or local banks and credit institutions that specialize in mortgage financing and business loans.

2. Public sector banks, which include real estate credit institutions; some 750 savings banks; and 12 so-called *Girozentralen*, which are central bodies of the savings banks that grant large housing credits, finance industry, or form underwriting syndicates (that is, act as investment bankers would in the United States).
3. Banks created as cooperative associations either for commercial credit, of which there are over 700, or for agricultural credit, of which there are about 9,000.

German banks, particularly the three largest ones, extend very long term credits to their customers — up to 15 years. They have been able to do so because the currency in Germany has been remarkably stable and interest rates have not been as volatile as they have been in the United States. This has enabled West Germany to finance its exports (approximately 40 percent of German-manufactured goods are exported) without subsidy finance and using only a government insurance program to eliminate the risk from foreign export. As a result of interest rate stability, West Germany (and Switzerland as well) has had no need to establish an institution such as the Export-Import Bank in the United States or similar institutions in Canada, Brazil, Spain, the United Kingdom, Italy, or Japan, among the industrialized countries. France is a special case because the Bank of France, as was noted, subsidizes exports through a special discount window available to banks engaged in financing French exports.

Japan

The Japanese bank regulatory system is again different from those foreign systems we have briefly analyzed. The key to Japanese activities, whether in the public or private sector, is the search for consensus. And this applies in the bank regulatory system, as well as in other areas, except that with the importance placed on growth in foreign trade to ensure Japanese economic survival, increasing tensions have been created in the area of finance between the Ministry of Finance and the Ministry of International Trade (MITI).

In principle the Ministry of Finance in Japan exercises much more power and has much more responsibility than even our Treasury Department in the United States. It not only carries out all the functions of our Treasury Department, but there is added the functions of the Securities and Exchange Commission, state banking commissions and many of the policy-making functions of the Federal Reserve Board, as well. The ministry is divided into seven bureaus and a secretariat. Each bureau, in turn, has some 6 to 13 divisions. The newest bureau, organized in 1964, is responsible for Japan's financial dealings with the rest of the world. It is obviously in this area that the friction with MITI is generated.

Another important bureau, for our purposes, is the Banking Bureau, which regulates most financial institutions in Japan. It also determines whether any structural changes are needed in the Japanese financial system — given the problems faced by the Japanese government as a result of the structural changes insisted upon by the American occupation forces. After the close of World War II the United States set about dismantling the old *zaibatsu* system of powerful financial and commercial concentration and replacing it with a series of new institutions designed to decentralize economic power so that Japan could never again become a military threat among the weaker countries of Asia. To withstand these structural changes, the Japanese applied a combination of extraordinary discipline, even within the government itself: consensus about what needed to be done to recreate the old system on a new basis and unusual flexibility on the part of the public and private sector alike. The principles of U.S. antitrust laws, which were adopted by the Japanese government at the behest of the occupation government, have quietly disappeared; the *zaibatsu* have been recreated on a different basis of interlocking directorates and cross holdings of minority stock interests within members of a group that generally includes one or more industrial companies, a bank, an insurance company, a trading company, and possibly others, so that, in effect, the former powerful commercial, financial, and trading entities have been created anew. This does not mean that there will not be competition taking place within the group or that either MITI or the Ministry of Finance will not insist in a given case that the group forego a transaction overseas — or an investment or an acquisition — in order to maintain some agreed-upon balance of power between groups and a semblance of degree of competition. Administrative guidance, from either the Ministry of Finance or MITI, is generally verbal only, although written directions are not unknown. The verbal directive is the result of the consensus process within the ministry and with the bank or group concerned, operating from middle management up to the top. By the time the directive is issued, a full discussion of the reasons for it has already taken place.

The Bank of Japan is Japan's central bank. Its responsibilities, although limited, are fourfold: it is the sole issuer of bank notes in Japan; it is the government's bank; it is the lender of last resort to commercial banks (which are relatively thinly capitalized compared with U.S. banks); and it is the arbiter of monetary policy.

CONCLUSION

In this chapter I have sketched out in general terms how the bank regulatory system operates in the United States. It is important to re-iterate some of these points because they play a role throughout the book.

First, there is in effect in the United States a dual regulatory system divided between the federal government and the states. Through the dual system banks are given a choice as to who is to regulate them; they may — at will — switch from a federal to a state charter or vice versa. At a time like the present, when commercial banks feel very threatened by other types of financial services institutions that are either less regulated or not regulated at all, it is important to observe how the banks have tried to escape regulation in order to become more competitive.

Second, there are essentially three federal regulators of commercial banks: the Federal Reserve, the Comptroller of the Currency, and the FDIC. It is sometimes difficult to follow the logic that caused the Congress to establish so many federal regulatory agencies, particularly as the thrift institutions have their own federal regulators and the lines of authority are not as sharply drawn as one would expect. The result is overlap and conflict.

Third, the Federal Reserve is certainly not the all-powerful regulating agency one is sometimes led to believe. It does not even regulate a majority of the banks, either in numbers or in assets. Its power lies in the fact that it has sole jurisdiction over bank holding companies; and these, in turn, own banks that have a clear majority of bank assets under their control.

And fourth, what are the questions we should ask as we read the text?

1. How did we ever create such a strange statutory scheme for the regulation of the U.S. banking system?
2. Is it the result of some logical sequence over the years on the part of our congressional leadership?
3. Does it *really* work?
4. Or are we faced with the prospect of restructuring our entire regu-

latory system — if only to make it understandable to the public at large?*

NOTES

1. Section 25 of the Federal Reserve Act governs the operations of foreign branches of member banks and provides for direct investment in foreign banks.

2. Section 25 of the Federal Reserve Act provides for the establishment of Edge corporations by U.S. banks.

3. Board of Governors of The Federal Reserve, *The Federal Reserve System: Purposes and Functions*, 1974, Washington, D.C., p. 2.

4. Maxwell Newton, *The Fed* (New York: Times Books, 1983), 205–206.

5. *Briscoe v. Commonwealth of Kentucky*, 36 U.S. (11Pet.) 257 (1837).

6. James White, *Teaching Materials on Banking Law*. (St. Paul: West Publishing Co., 1976), p. 66.

7. Federal Deposit Insurance Corporation, *1980 Annual Report of the Federal Deposit Insurance Corporation*, Washington, D.C., 1981, p. 3.

8. Public Law 97–320, secs. 116, 141(a)(3).

9. Title IV, 48 Stat. 1246 (1934), 12 U.S.C. Sec. 1724 *et seq.*

10. Public Law 91–206, 84 Stat. 49 (1970).

11. Public Law 95–630 (1978).

12. Public Law 97–320 (1982).

13. 12 U.S.C. Sec. 36 (1927).

14. See 3(d) of the Bank Holding Company Act 12 U.S.C. Sec. 1842(d).

15. The bank merger process has been generally criticized. See *Report of the General Accounting Office* (GAO) dated August 14, 1982; and NOTE, "Commercial Bank Mergers: The Case for Procedural and Substantive Deregulation," 95 *Harvard Law Review* (1982). 1914. For comment and recommendations, see Chapter 6.

Figures 1–3 in the center of the book summarize asset distribution and bank holding company growth.

---

*This is discussed in detail in Chapter 6.

2
A HISTORICAL PERSPECTIVE OF BANK REGULATION

INTRODUCTION

To understand the development of the bank regulatory system in the United States, it is helpful to review those historical events that resulted in the gradual creation of regulatory institutions quite different from similar regulatory bodies in Europe or Japan. In the United States we spend little time reflecting on our past; history as a precursor of what we are today is inadequately taught in our educational system; we tend to expend considerably more effort in the study of sociology and psychology, not realizing perhaps that it might be at least important to consider that we are the kind of people we are, with the kinds of institutions we have, because of the beliefs and goals of our forefathers.

U.S. monetary and economic development can be traced back to the early days of U.S. history and the fundamental conflict between the ideas of Alexander Hamilton and Thomas Jefferson about the structure of the U.S. government. Hamilton was a remarkable financial and political genius, who stood almost alone in the early days of American independence among the leading political figures of the day in understanding the importance of a sound currency and a banking system that would fuel the country's economic growth; Jefferson, on the other hand, was a man whose base was in plantation life and agricultural development, to whom the necessity of seasonal credit was more important than the strength of a banking and monetary system established on a sound basis. Among farmers, credit was needed in good times to meet seasonal requirements; and in bad times to bear the expense of carrying land and equipment until good times returned. One understood best the need for a monetary banking and credit system that would be carefully structured to protect and reward the lenders of money; the other represented the needs of the agricultural sector for credit at reasonable rates in both good times and bad. These two men were the precursors of the Republican and Democratic philosophies of today. At least until recently, in the Northeast and Midwest were found the investors with money and their bankers while in the South and West one found the users of money with the needs to grapple with an economy alternately growing and then contracting to establish a new base for further growth. Politically, this has separated those who favor growth, full employment, and social programs from those who want to ensure control of the money supply and adequacy of interest rates and who believe in the ability of the marketplace to meet the demands of borrowers without sacrificing the interests of lenders.

The fundamental differences in banking emphasis represented by the ideas of these two great men are found today in Congress just as strongly as in the days when the United States first became a nation. Both have merit. The development of bank regulation in the United States since 1800 represents an attempt on the part of Congress to balance these two contradictory philosophies at the legislative level, where sectional needs have played a dominant role. It is not happenstance that President Andrew Jackson, who came from the farming area of Tennessee, vetoed the Second Bank of the United States in 1838 and that today the leader of those forces in the House of Representatives who wish to force the Federal Reserve Board to target interest rates rather than the money supply, Jim Wright, comes from an agricultural sector of Texas. The legislative strength of those favoring easy credit has always been in the House of Representatives where leaders such as the late Wright Patman, the Populist from Texas, spent a lifetime fighting on behalf of reduced interest rates, as opposed to such figures in the Senate as Winthrop Aldrich of Rhode Island, banker and kin of the Rockefellers, for whom the soundness of the banking system was paramount.

It is only by understanding that this strong difference in monetary philosophy has existed in our legislative branch throughout U.S. history that one can begin to understand why the regulation of banks and other depository institutions has evolved as it has and why it is that today we still have a dual regulatory system—run, in part, by the individual states and controlled, in part, by the federal government.

The attempts by the Reagan administration to initiate reform in the bank regulatory system in the United States, a step that is necessary if only in view of the changes that have recently occurred in banking methods, is bound to rekindle in the Congress the antagonisms that have existed between those who have favored lenders and those who have favored borrowers throughout U.S. history.

Few Americans are aware of how the U.S. banking system functioned before the creation of the Federal Reserve System in 1913.

EARLY ATTEMPTS AT CENTRAL BANKING

The origins of the banking system go back to Alexander Hamilton, who was generally recognized at the time of the creation of the country as the leading voice in matters of finance. He had recommended that the country create a financial institution similar to the Bank of England, a large chartered bank standing close to the government. It was clear that some steps needed to be taken: During the war the troops and the country's creditors had been paid with IOUs issued by the Continental Congress, which the Congress had subsequently disowned — hence, the phrase "not worth a Continental." The currency, therefore, had little recognized value, commercial credit was not organized since banks' bills throughout the country were not recognized as legal tender, and there was little gold or silver in the country. A centralized banking institution was clearly in order.

The First Bank of the United States was created by the Congress in 1791 with a 20-year charter. Its mandate was to handle the finances of the government, to issue bank notes, and generally to watch over the development of the country's banks. The Secretary of the Treasury was given the power to inspect all transactions with the bank except the accounts of private individuals and was authorized to call for reports as often as he liked. The bank could open branches. It also acted as fiscal agent for the government.

The First Bank proved a great success, bringing stability to the currency, supplying bank accommodation, providing a recognized currency, and supervising state banking institutions as well as assuming prompt payment of their obligations.

The capital of the bank was $10 million, divided into 25,000 shares of $400 each. Some 80 percent of the capital was opened to public subscription, whereas the balance was subscribed by the federal government and paid for over ten years. The voting power was set so that no one person could vote more than 30 shares. A large percentage of the stock was sold abroad, but foreigners were given no voting rights. The bank paid out an average of $\frac{3}{8}$ percent per annum in dividends.

Unfortunately, there were many who opposed the bank. New York objected because the bank was located in Philadelphia, no longer the largest city in the nation. State banks gradually increased their antagonism, in part because they were required to send their notes home for redemption each week. As a result of this opposition, the bank's charter was not renewed, and it went out of business in 1811 when the original charter expired. The vote on renewal was exceedingly close. The margin was one vote in the House, and the tie vote in the Senate was broken by Vice-President George Clinton because he had never forgiven Albert Gallatin, the Secretary of the Treasury, for opposing his nomination for the presidency.

As happened much later when the Federal Reserve Act was passed, it was the fear of war that brought about the creation of the Second Bank of the United States. Although war had broken out in 1812, the bank was finally created in 1816 with a capital of $35 million. Although it was modeled closely after the First Bank, in 1819 it began to apply a rigid system of control over state institutions, insisting that their notes be redeemed in coins upon presentation. The bank's own note currency rapidly became the principal medium of exchange. The bank thus performed a very valuable function.

This, however, did not stop political opposition. State banks did their utmost through their legislators in Congress to fight the bank because they objected to its control of their operations. The leader of the opposition was Andrew Jackson, who became President in 1829. In his first message to Congress he attacked the bank as "corrupt and dangerous." Since the President could not control the bank's officers or take away its charter prior to expiration in 1836, he sought to cripple it by withdrawing government deposits, thereby causing a decline in lending and a sharp increase in bankruptcies. This did not deter congressmen, principally from the West, from opposing the bank—to a large extent because the Jackson party could not control it.

In 1832 recharter of the bank nevertheless passed the House by a vote of 167 to 85, and the Senate by 28 to 20. A week later President Jackson vetoed the recharter of the bank, and in 1833 Jackson won reelection as President.

What lessons can be gained from the ultimate failure of the First and Second Banks of the United States?

The experience with a central banking system was very positive for the country. The bank managed the government's public funds well, handled transfers effectively, and proved the value of a uniform bank note currency amply secured by sound, short-term commercial paper used in the loan and discount business. On the other hand, the failure to renew either charter indicated that giving Congress control over the banking system would necessarily cause political problems, regardless of the value of a central banking system, principally because of the adversary relationship between the central bank and local banks. The failure of these two attempts at central banking has to be explained, therefore, solely in political terms. Central banking should have succeeded in the United States, as it has in other countries, had it not been for the particularities of our constitutional system that subordinated the efficiency of a central banking system to geographical or sectorial pressures at a purely political level.

What happened in the country after the veto of the Second Bank's charter by President Jackson is clear proof of the value of the bank—if any other proof was needed. After the demise of the Second Bank in 1836, the United States went through a period of chaos in its banking system. It is hard to imagine in today's world how the country could have developed in a period when some 1,400 banking institutions were in fact issuing their own notes as legal tender, and the country did not even have a national currency. Yet such was the case from 1836 to 1863. The effect was immediate because in 1837 the country suffered a severe panic due principally to the extension of credit by state banking institutions lending upon improper or inadequate security. Although there were gradual improvements in methods between 1840 and 1860, the evils of a decentralized, widely diffused, and uncontrolled banking system still resulted in bank and business failures at frequent intervals. The Second Bank had provided for a nationwide money system, managed by a central financial institution that furnished an efficient and sound payment system. After 1836, when the recharter was vetoed, the old defects of thousands of different types of bank notes, inefficient methods of making payments, and the like, reappeared. In 1860, at the beginning of the Civil War, there were more than 1,600 kinds of bank notes in circulation, and counterfeits, as can be imagined, proliferated.

A NEW START AT NATIONAL BANKING

In 1846 Congress enacted an "independent Treasury system"; and in 1862 it authorized the first issue of legal tender Treasury notes in order, once again, to meet the demands of a wartime economy.

The National Currency Act was passed in 1863 to attempt to strengthen the nation's economy by rebuilding its financial structure.[1]

This act called for a number of important steps. Provision was made (1) for the examination of banks through a currency bureau; (2) for the maintenance of reserves and the redemption of notes over the counter at the issuing banks and at agencies in certain of the principal cities; (3) for the conversion of state banks into national banks; and (4) for the deposit of public monies in banks, when necessary, upon the security of government funds. It was this act that also established the office of the Comptroller of the Currency as a bureau within the Treasury Department.

What indeed had been the role of the Treasury Department in the development of the U.S. banking system prior to 1863? The answer is none. It is true that Alexander Hamilton, as soon as the act establishing the Treasury Department had been passed on September 2, 1789, and he had been designated as its first Secretary, immediately resolved to restore the country's finances by establishing a national bank that would work very closely with the Treasury in support of its function of strengthening the public credit. Hamilton fully understood the importance of a central currency — without which it would have been necessary at great expense and considerable difficulty to transfer the limited quantities of government gold and silver from place to place.

We have seen how Hamilton's ideas failed because of the lack of any leadership in Congress to place the country's banking system on a sound footing. With the exception of the National Currency Act of 1863 brought about by the grave financial difficulties created by the Civil War, banking remained in a chaotic state long after the war. What finally brought about a change in thinking?

THE PANIC OF 1907

It must be stated at the outset that the change in thinking was very limited and came about as a result of a banking collapse that — when we look at it today — seems almost impossible to believe could have taken place in a country that regarded itself as very advanced in business and financial matters. The trigger was the panic of 1907 where, strange as it may seem, the financial well-being of the country was saved by the confidence and dexterity of one man: J. P. Morgan.

There were many causes behind the panic of 1907, but even afterward there was little thinking about either the causes or the steps that should be taken to avoid a recurrence. It was even said that the crisis had been brought about by the Wall Street bankers for their own gain.

Unfortunately, the flaws in the system were many, the principal one being the lack of a centralized banking institution able to come to the aid of any bank in difficulty. There were also more immediate causes: the San Francisco fire of April 1906 had caused enormous losses to many insurance companies; the unusually large crops that year had resulted in a shortage of freight cars and a shortage of currency to finance crop storage; and the railroads of necessity had had to borrow heavily short term in order to increase their equipment rapidly. In addition, at the end of 1906 the London banks had refused to discount any more American bills, thereby forcing the New York banks to contract their loans. At the time there were about 5,000 national banks in the United States. The National Bank Act of 1863, which provided for the chartering of national banks, allowed each national bank to issue bank notes of uniform value. But the system itself contained serious flaws. These are important to note in order to see whether they were later cured.

First, there were problems caused by a lack of any central organization: scattered reserves, lack of clearing facilities, absence of any lender of last resort. Excessive individual bank independence meant that in times of panic each bank acted independently to protect its own liquid position. If a run started on one bank, all of the others would attempt to collect large amounts of cash simply to protect themselves against a similar run. Since there was only a fixed amount of cash in the system, this necessarily meant that the banks that had not quickly increased their cash position would face default if depositors demanded the return of their cash deposits. The system totally lacked any flexibility, but this was only one of several problems.

The second involved the "pyramiding of reserves." The National Bank Act allowed banks to deposit a certain percentage of their reserve requirements with banks in major cities but to continue to list those deposits as reserves. Inevitably, in order to earn higher interest rates those funds tended to flow to New York banks to be used quite frequently as stock market call loans.* In times of panic when those loans could not be repaid because no one wanted to buy securities, this tended to destroy the liquidity of New York banks and made it impossible for them to pay back the reserves of the banks in other cities. We shall see

---

*It is important to note this because this practice played a key role in bringing about the Wall Street panic of September 1929. People purchased securities on margin; the stockbrokers borrowed the money to carry their customers' accounts from the banks; in normal times there was little risk, but if the market collapsed, no one was then willing to buy securities and hence the brokers could not repay their loans.

what happened in 1929 as a result of this practice — even after the creation of the Federal Reserve System, which was supposed to counter this very difficulty.

Third, the lack of any central check-clearing facilities made it difficult for banks in different parts of the country to transfer funds rapidly; checks took too long a time (National Banking Act). Fourth, the banks in the system were restricted in their issuance of notes to serve as currency. When times were good and both consumers and businessmen wanted to borrow, the amount of cash in the system could not expand to meet the needs because there was no elasticity in the system. Conversely, when times were bad and the demand for money was reduced, there was no way to shrink the currency supply.

In the panic of 1907, it was the failure of the Knickerbocker Trust Company on October 22, 1907, that precipitated the crisis. Knickerbocker was the third-largest bank in the country. Within a very few days the Trust Company of America, the second-largest bank in the country, closed its doors. It seemed as if many others would follow. It was then that J. P. Morgan stepped in by organizing a group of other Wall Street bankers who pledged the necessary funds to support other banks in the city. This effectively stopped the panic as depositors realized that they could withdraw their deposits if they so desired. One man, in a country with no lending institution of last resort, exercised his enormous standing within the financial community, backed by his wealth, to dissipate the spread of fear and financial panic. It was an extraordinary act on the part of one man making up for the country's failure to adopt a banking system adequate to protect its depositors.

What were the consequences of the panic of 1907? Bankers realized that some form of central bank would be required to avoid a repetition of successive runs on the banks. The politicians, however, remained unconvinced and sought, as often happens, to find other explanations to blame for what had occurred. The political result was predictable: a compromise. An act was passed in Congress — the Aldrich-Vreeland Act — that set in motion the steps that would ultimately result in the passage of the Federal Reserve Act in 1913. Aldrich-Vreeland provided a number of positive steps. First, it allowed for currency associations to issue emergency currency backed by commercial paper or certain long-term bonds. This provided an element of elasticity in banking, which we saw was so essential. Second, it established a Monetary Commission consisting of nine members of the Senate and nine members of the House to study the banking system in the United States and various European countries with a view to adopting a new U.S. banking system if advisable. The result of the inquiry was a series of 42 reports covering every phase of financial operations at home and abroad. Much of the information had never before been available to U.S. legislators. Yet the Commission failed to present any plan for bank reform.

THE JEKYLL ISLAND CAPER

The failure of the Monetary Commission to come up with any recommendations for reform of U.S. banking caused the principal New York bankers and their supporters in Congress led by Senator Nelson Aldrich to initiate discussions as to what might be done to get congressional action on a banking bill. The upshot was a secret meeting attended by several key bankers, a Treasury official, and, of course, Senator Aldrich. We know that Frank Vanderlip (head of National City Bank), Arthur Sheldon, Henry P. Davison (of Morgan), Paul Warburg, Wright Stevenson, and Aldrich were all members of the group. In order to keep the meeting secret, individual members went to Hoboken, New Jersey, in their own carriages. There they boarded a private railroad car for the trip south; each man using only his first name, and stopped only in Washington long enough to pick up a Treasury expert. From there they went to Jekyll Island, off the coast of Georgia, where for a number of days they worked on the text of a possible banking bill that would come close to creating a central bank. There was good reason for the secrecy: Congress would surely reject any proposal if it became known that Wall Street bankers had played a role in drafting it.

The product of this meeting was the Aldrich Plan. It was the first substantial plan presented to Congress on bank reform and was tailored as a general proposal defining the issues and shaping a framework so that the final bill could be modified and shaped through congressional debate. The principal architects of the proposed bill were Aldrich, Warburg, and Vanderlip.*

The plan was carefully crafted to meet congressional objections to a strong central bank. First, it created a National Reserve Association; it provided for one central bank for the whole United States, with 15 branches and all gold reserves to be kept at one location; each reserve association branch had a district, in turn divided into local associations

---

*Vanderlip had started out in life as a baseball reporter in Chicago before he moved on to banking. It was he who coined the word *southpaw*, referring to a left-handed pitcher because his left hand would face the south side of Chicago as he pitched.

of 10 or more banks. There would be a board of directors for each district and each association. Only 6 out of 46 members of the Board of Directors of the National Reserve Association were to be selected by the President. All national banks would be members of the association, and state banks, as well, if they met the capital reserve requirements outlined in the National Banking Act. The association would fix the rate of discount from time to time; it would be uniform throughout the country; reserve requirements would be left unchanged from the National Banking Act; finally, the association would be authorized to issue notes to serve as legal tender and to be issued to redeem all national bank notes. It is surprising how much of this program eventually became a part of the Federal Reserve System.

Nevertheless, the Aldrich Plan never became law. In the first place, there were significant controversial features in the Plan: the absence of any real governmental influence on the system; the proposed practice to allow the banks to include notes as reserves; a uniform discount rate; and centralization of the National Reserve Association's administration. There were also political problems: the Democrats had just taken control of the Congress, and both House and Senate were against centralized control of the banking system. Finally, many in Congress looked upon Aldrich as the spokesman for Wall Street bankers and, therefore, distrusted in advance any proposal associated with his name.

Two very different men played key roles in designing the conceptual framework that ultimately became the Federal Reserve System: Nelson Aldrich and Paul Warburg.

Nelson Aldrich

There is no doubt that Nelson Aldrich was a key figure both in the Senate and in banking. His story is an interesting one. Born in 1841 to a middle-class family in Providence, Rhode Island, his first exposure to politics came when he joined the Franklin Lyceum in Providence. It was here that he developed his skills as an orator, a debater, and a writer. In due course, he became its secretary and then vice-president. At the same time, he rose rapidly in the business world, becoming president of the First National Bank at the age of 36 as well as president of the Providence Board of Trade and a partner in various local business ventures. He was well liked and looked up to.

At 36 he ran for the House of Representatives and was elected. Shortly thereafter, he was appointed to finish the unexpired term of the late Senator Burnside, and he was himself elected to the Senate in 1886, though still under 40. He continued his business ventures, participating in a program financed by his friends to establish street car systems in Rhode Island and other eastern states; this turned him into a millionaire. It was only in 1903 when he had succeeded so well in both politics and in business that he decided to learn about the theories of banking and currency. The panic of 1907 made it clear to him that reforms were needed. He realized that without reform the value of business securities might collapse along with the banks and that there had to be adequate money in circulation to meet emergency needs. It was in 1908 that he submitted the Aldrich-Vreeland Bill, which, in addition to creating the Monetary Commission we spoke of, allowed currency associations to issue emergency currency backed by commercial paper or long-term bonds.

Paul Warburg

Paul Warburg was born into a German international merchant banking family, M. M. Warburg and Co. As a young man he was sent around the world to observe how international banking transactions were handled. Paul's younger brother, Felix, had, in 1894, married the daughter of Jacob H. Schiff, head of the New York investment banking house of Kuhn, Loeb, who had himself married the oldest daughter of Solomon Loeb of Worms, Germany, one of the founders of the firm. At his brother's wedding, Warburg met Schiff's youngest daughter, Nina, whom he married a year later and took back to Hamburg. All his life Paul was torn between being a banker in his native Germany and responding to the appeals of his wife to move to New York and take the partnership that awaited him at Kuhn, Loeb. Paul finally managed to do both, spending half the year in Germany and half in New York. He brought to the Jekyll Island discussion not only a thorough understanding of U.S. bank practices but also a knowledge of European banking and relations with central bank systems, which were of enormous value to a definition of what was essential to a centralized banking system. Of particular importance were the two concepts he persuaded the others to adopt: (1) a central organization that controls all reserves and performs check-clearing functions and (2) a discount market through which credit facilities could be generated by banks in need.

If Nelson Aldrich played the key role in getting legislation through the Congress because of his understanding of the legislative process,

Paul Warburg played the key role in making his American counterparts understand what was so important about a central bank system along European lines.

It is interesting to note that Warburg was named a member of the first Federal Reserve Board by President Woodrow Wilson.

THE PUJO COMMITTEE

While the bankers and their advisers were trying to find a means to adopt legislation so as to avoid a repetition of the panic of 1907, the chairman of the House Banking Committee, Arsene P. Pujo of Louisiana, was heading in 1912 an investigation of the so-called "Money Trust." There was a strong movement in Congress, as often happens after a crisis like the panic of 1907, to investigate what had happened for the purpose of identifying culprits abusing the system so that appropriate legislation would prevent any recurrences. The purpose of the investigation was "to obtain full and complete information of banking and currency conditions of the United States for the purpose of determining what legislation is needed."[2]

In fact, the investigation had been principally prompted by violations of the National Banking Act by National City Bank through the creation of National City Company and by the Chase Bank's creating Chase Securities. The Pujo Committee found that J. P. Morgan and Company partners held 72 directorships in 47 of the country's largest corporations; that Morgan owned a large part of the stock in First National Bank and National City Bank, which in turn owned stock of other large banks and trust companies; and that through interlocking directorships with insurance companies and savings banks, Morgan was able to control in large measure the flow of capital to the country's principal industries. The committee also found that tightly held bank control had been instrumental in bringing about large corporate mergers at the turn of the century and that these mergers had resulted in further adding to the strength of the banks responsible for bringing these about.

The committee came out with a series of recommendations: clearinghouses should be incorporated; interstate commerce transactions should be illegal between stock exchanges unless regular reports were required and stock exchanges be subject to margin requirements; interlocking directorates among banks should be prohibited; and commercial banks should not engage in underwriting.

Ferdinand Pecora, who became so well known in the investigation of banking practices in 1933, was counsel to the Pujo Committee. While no legislation resulted from the work of this committee, many of its conclusions had an impact on the presentation of the Federal Reserve Act and perhaps even more on the Glass-Steagall legislation some 20 years later.

PASSAGE OF THE
FEDERAL RESERVE ACT

How did it happen that the Federal Reserve Act was passed in 1913 when we consider that the Aldrich Plan had failed and that Congress was investigating bank practices of which it disapproved? This is an interesting question because the act's passage was the result of compromises worked out among leaders in the Congress who approached the idea of centralized banking from totally different points of view and a Democratic President who might never have agreed to such legislation if he had not thought that war was imminent and that the United States therefore needed to have in place a strong banking system, even though he would have preferred that the central bank be under government control.

During the negotiations leading to the passage of the Federal Reserve Act, Senator Robert L. Owen was appointed chairman of the newly formed Senate Banking Committee, whereas Carter Glass of Virginia had become head of the House Banking and Currency Committee. These two men worked closely together to produce the Glass-Owen Bill, which was to become the Federal Reserve Act of 1913. In preparing the bill, constant use was made of the Aldrich Plan, which had already received support from the Republicans in Congress; and to a substantial extent, from both the President and the Secretary of the Treasury participated as well. The President was working on a free-trade tariff bill, and he saw the necessity of having at the same time a banking system that might increase the competitiveness of U.S. business through appropriate credit facilities. The act was finally signed by the President on December 23, 1913, a few months after the death of the man who had saved the country in the panic of 1907, J. P. Morgan. Many said it was fortunate that a new banking system was now in place because Morgan would no longer be available should another panic occur. As it was, the beginning of World War I in 1914 gave the new system its first test. In July 1914 individuals and banks began to hoard some $600 million, and the stock market, which had remained open during the financial crises of 1893 and 1907, now closed. Within two weeks from the start of the war, $89 million was withdrawn from New York banks, and the country was faced with a liquidity crisis. Before the Federal Reserve System began operating, more than $35 million in bank notes was issued. Together with over $20 million of clearinghouse certificates, it was estimated that $575 million of new notes was injected into currency circulation within a short time.

PARTICULARS OF THE FEDERAL RESERVE ACT

The purpose of the act, as stated in its preamble, was clear:

> To provide for the establishment of the Federal Reserve Banks, to furnish an elastic currency, to afford means of rediscounting commercial paper, to establish a more effective supervision of banking in the United States, and for other purposes.[3]

1. Provision for an elastic currency was important because a system was needed in order to allow for the money supply to expand as business activity grew seasonably or cyclically and to contract as the need for currency diminished, thus avoiding periodic crises where the public wanted to withdraw more currency than the banking system could provide.
2. Centralization of bank reserves was necessary to pool the system's reserves for common use in periods of credit stringency. Previously, when there was even the slightest suggestion of a tightening of credit, each bank felt obligated to hoard reserves, thereby helping to intensify deflationary pressures.
3. Establishment of an effective interregional check and currency clearing system was essential in view of the country's growth and regional development.
4. Provision of adequate banking facilities for the federal government — which had previously used nine such treasury offices and some 1,500 depository banks under a system that was also subject to political favoritism in the deposits of public funds — was also crucial.

The act provided for 12 regional reserve banks to be located in Boston, New York, Philadelphia, Cleveland, Richmond, Atlanta, Chicago, St. Louis, Minneapolis, Kansas City, Dallas, and San Francisco.

Each district bank was to have a board of directors with staggered terms over three years. The board of directors of each of the 12 district banks was to select one person to be on the Federal Advisory Board, which would meet in Washington four times a year.

The Federal Reserve Board was to have seven members, two of whom would be the Secretary of the Treasury and the Comptroller of the Currency. One board member was to be designated by the President as Governor and one as Vice-Governor. The Board of seven, all appointed by the President for 14-year terms, were to supervise the 12 district banks.

Section 16 of the act delegated to the Federal Reserve Board the power to issue currency without limit:

> Federal Reserve notes to be issued at the discretion of the Federal Reserve Board for the purpose of making advances to Federal Reserve Banks through the Federal Reserve Agents as hereinafter set forth, and for as other purpose, are hereby authorized. The said notes shall be legal obligations of the U.S. and shall be receivable for all taxes, customs, and other public debts. They shall be redeemed in gold on demand at the Treasury Department of the U.S. in the City of Washington, D.C. or in gold or lawful money at any Federal Reserve Bank.[4]

Section 14 of the Federal Reserve Act states that every Federal Reserve bank shall have the power from time to time to establish "notes of discount to be charged by the Federal Reserve Banks for each class of paper."[5] Discount rates could vary among the districts because it was believed that a regional bank would be more competent to judge the credit situation in its district. All discount rates, nevertheless, had to be approved by the Board first.

In the open market, the Federal Reserve Board was authorized to buy and sell acceptances and government securities. The act also provided for the gradual withdrawal and cancellation of the notes issued by national banks.

It is curious that the original Federal Reserve Act paid little attention to the establishment of a national monetary and credit policy conducive to maintenance of general economic stability. Instead, the act was mainly concerned with what we now consider "service" functions, that today we simply take for granted, not realizing the difficulties faced by banks before the adoption of the Federal Reserve Act.

It is true that the act did provide for some powers—including discounting and changes in discount rates, open market operations, and examinations of member banks—that were aimed at promoting sound credit conditions. Yet these were secondary considerations.

Determination of the proper amount and use of currency and bank credit was felt to be provided by adherence to the gold standard and by insistence upon sound banking procedures.

It is important for us to understand just how limited the powers initially granted to the Federal Reserve Board by the Congress were. We will want to determine just how in the course of time these powers were extended. Was this due to additional legislation? Or has the Federal Reserve Board on its own converted its original very limited function (for example, the maintenance of a bank credit system in difficult periods) into a full-fledged power of control over the monetary system of the United States? From where comes the mandate of the Federal Reserve Board to encourage growth in the economy regardless of the inflationary consequences of so doing?

Similarly, we want to examine with great care the extent to which the Federal Reserve Board was directed to function as a regulatory agency in view particularly of similar powers granted other agencies of the government dealing with depository institutions.

One thing is clear: Today the Federal Reserve Board is not acting very much in the manner anticipated by the Federal Reserve Act of 1913. It is no longer a mechanism mandated to make the banking system function better through new tools but rather a most powerful quasi-independent agency of government subject to no control or even audit. Was this power acquired over the years by self-interpretation of statutes or by specific grant of Congress to control the monetary system of the United States and the activities to be permitted to banks?

There was nothing in the Federal Reserve Act of 1913 that gave the Federal Reserve Board the vast powers it has today.

EARLY DAYS OF THE SYSTEM: REGULATION BY THE REGULATED

The early days of the Federal Reserve Board covered the period of World War I, the postwar recession, the growth of stock market investment followed by speculation, and the stock market crash of 1929. These events centered around a concept and a man. The concept was that the Federal Reserve Board should function in such a way that bankers would be protected by adequate rates of interest. The bankers controlled the Board, and they interpreted the act as a device to make the banking system function more effectively, thus reducing the risks to the banks and their depositors. The man was the extraordinary Benjamin Strong, Governor of the Federal Reserve Bank of New York for many years, who developed the role of the Federal Reserve so that its activities became centered in New York (which, after all, was the financial capital of the United States) and not in Washington, which in time of peace then bore the same political relationship to New York on a national scale as Albany did within the state.

During this period there were no attacks on the Federal Reserve Board as having failed to perform the functions mandated to it by Congress. It must therefore be assumed that the manner in which the banking system was being governed generally met the test imposed by Congress in the passage of the Federal Reserve Act in 1913. There was a central system, as the Republicans and the bankers had wanted; it respected geographical dispersion, as the Democrats from the South and West had insisted; and it was performing the services required by the act to maintain the solvency and health of the country's banks. Was that not what the act was intended to accomplish?

The power of the bankers in this period of self-regulation* came from their control of the district banks. The Federal Reserve Board had made the mistake of allowing the directors of each district bank, controlled by local bankers, to elect a chief executive officer and call him a "governor," when the statute only provided that each bank should have a chairman who was also the fiscal agent. By doing this the Board allowed the bankers at the district banks to head the banks with a highly paid governor designated by them, whereas the chairman and fiscal agent were simply government employees drawing government salaries and having little power.

In February 1915 the Board suggested lowering interest rates. Governor Strong of the New York District Bank argued that this might have adverse consequences on member bank balances held in New York City banks. The Board submitted to the bankers' arguments as expressed by Strong. The bankers were in favor of tight money and high interest rates and insisted successfully on such a policy. This policy continued after the war was over at a time when there was (exactly as happened after World War II in 1946) a surge in consumer spending, expansion of credit, speculation, and rising prices. The Federal Reserve was thus faced with

---

*The reader is invited to refer to the English system as cited earlier in Chapter 1. Were we not borrowing, at least in principle, the English concept during this period?

two contradictory policy options. First, it wished to keep interest rates from rising in order to help the Treasury both finance new borrowing and prevent the cost of the war-increased debt from increasing. Second, it wished to control consumer borrowing while avoiding curtailing credit for "legitimate" business expansion as industry converted again to consumer products. The Treasury needed low interest rates, yet high rates were required to prevent a too-rapid consumer boom. In early 1920 the Treasury announced that debt management problems were sufficiently well in hand for a discount rate policy to be directed toward other objectives. As a result the discount rate was increased sharply, with the final increase to 7 percent by some district banks taking effect by the middle of 1920. This caused the postwar boom to peak and was followed by recession and falling prices. As was predicted by a member of the Federal Reserve Board as far back as 1917:

> The most serious part of inflation is, after all, the aftermath. We sow the wind to reap the whirlwind. Somehow or other, we have to come down off that perch.

Where was this sage among the governors of the Federal Reserve Board in the 1970s? In the 1920s bankers and academicians were far more cautious than they are today. Professor M. W. Sprague of Harvard, for example, one of the most highly esteemed economists at the time, stated in reference to the depression of 1920/21:

> A period of readjustment and liquidation was inevitable. Liberal credits at low rates in 1920 would have deferred its advent somewhat, but with certain consequence that the difficulty and losses incident to readjustment would have been materially enhanced.

The question arises, Did we really do any better in 1974/75 or in 1981/82 when the Federal Reserve exercised enormous power over monetary policy?* Nevertheless, even in 1921 the Congress deemed it advisable to open an inquiry as to whether the Federal Reserve policies might have been responsible for the postwar recession.

The 1920s was an interesting period in the history of the Federal Reserve for other reasons besides the failure to halt the essentially agricultural depression of 1920–22. In many ways the United States was faced in international economic and financial terms with a situation very

---

*The question is considered in great detail in Chapter 3, which deals with Federal Reserve control over monetary policy.

similar to the one it faced in 1946–50. The gold standard that had been in place since the days of Isaac Newton (he of the apple who was not only a scientist but also head of the English Assay Office) in the eighteenth century became a victim of the war. By 1927 the United States had approximately half of the world's gold stock. It was necessary, therefore, that U.S. monetary policy take into account during this period its economic and financial relationships with other countries. This became one more reason why the New York Fed was able to seize a special niche in the bank regulatory system.

In the period following the postwar depression (1923) and the onset of international monetary problems (1927), the Federal Reserve focused on domestic policy, and the Board of Governors stated that accommodation to business needs should be the principal objective of open market operations. In 1925, for example, the Federal Reserve banks resorted to balancing the sales of government securities to tighten the money supply and gradually raised the discount rates. But the index of wholesale prices did not increase, so there was relatively little concern about inflation. What was occurring even as early as 1925 was something quite different: a flow of credit into the New York stock market financed for the customers and their brokers through the New York banks was gradually syphoning money from banks in other sections of the country by paying more for their deposits. This phenomenon created a totally new problem for the Federal Reserve. Should money be tightened to discourage speculation, or should, on the contrary, money be loosened to encourage agricultural recovery and further business investment? At a conference of central bankers in New York in July 1927 Governor Strong agreed that the New York Fed would take the lead in reducing U.S. interest rates in order to aid foreign currencies. Both England and France faced the prospect of further devaluations if U.S. assistance did not discourage capital flows to the United States.* The Federal Reserve Board put pressure on the district banks to lower their discount rates, but this did not last long, and by 1928 the district banks had raised their rates progressively from 4 percent to 4.5 percent to 5 percent. As the rates increased, the stage was gradually being set for the Great Depression of 1929.

We shall see what the Federal Reserve did when this event occurred by way of a disastrous policy. But first it would be helpful to say a word

---

*The reader will note that the same phenomenon has been occurring in the period from 1981 to 1984. Does this mean that we will see the same parallel of boom to depression that we saw from 1927 to 1929 in the period from 1984 to 1986?

about Governor Strong because without a doubt he was *the* key Federal Reserve official of this period and placed a lasting stamp on the development of the Fed and its subsequent policies.

Benjamin Strong

Benjamin Strong is the proof that intelligence, perseverance and courage, personal charm and warmth, administrative ability, and a capacity to make friends of enemies can carry a man very far indeed. It seems clear that over a long period of years Strong modified the Federal Reserve into the mold both nationally and internationally that he felt it should occupy, even against the wishes both of the Federal Reserve Board in Washington and the district banks in other parts of the country. Although without a college education—losing his first job in finance because his handwriting was so poor—by 1907 Strong had worked his way up to being secretary of Bankers Trust Company; and at the time of J. P. Morgan's efforts to save the country's financial system during the panic of 1907, it was he who was responsible to Morgan and his associates as head of the committee that determined which banks could be saved and which would have to be closed. In 1914, shortly after becoming president of Bankers Trust, he was reluctantly prevailed upon to become Governor of the New York Federal Reserve Bank.

From 1914 to 1917 Strong took it upon himself, as a first task, the job of strengthening the U.S. banking system internally and externally, by introducing currency reform, increasing the number of banks in the system, amassing gold reserves in the Federal Reserve banks, and developing a major money market in New York. It must be remembered in connection with Strong's leadership activities that there was really no Federal Reserve System when Strong and his colleagues took office; the Federal Reserve Act only authorized the establishment of new institutions; it was purposely vague because of a conscious desire to make the system flexible and adaptable and because of the prevailing ignorance among both the bankers and members of Congress about just what kind of a banking system the country needed. This is important to keep in mind. All of a sudden from their marble palaces the members of the Federal Reserve Board are trying to tell the administration and Congress that their prerogatives and their activities were mandated in detailed form by Congress and have since been enshrined by custom. Nothing could be further from the truth. Hence comes the necessity to understand what the Federal Reserve Act said and how the powers of the Board have grown—in part through legislation but more often through the necessary filling of a vacuum through the intelligence and perseverance of men such as Governor Benjamin Strong.

It was Strong and his colleagues who turned a passive structure designed for a service function only into an active force as an instrument of monetary, and later regulatory, policy. Strong clearly became the world's most influential leader in the fields of money and finance. Yet he was not even a member of the Federal Reserve Board in Washington. How did this happen? The Federal Reserve Act did not provide for control of the banking system by the Federal Reserve Board. The directors and officials of the district banks were opposed to the exercise by the Board of policy-making functions; the location of the Board in Washington away from the centers of finance was not helpful; New York was so obviously the center of national and international banking (especially after World War I); in particular, Governor Strong realized early in his career that the money supply of the United States (and perhaps of the world as a result of the events outlined of 1925 to 1927 as to England and France) could be controlled by the Federal Reserve. He understood for the first time that the scope of this power came from the Fed's ability to add to or subtract from the reserves available to the banking system of the United States* by buying or selling government securities.† Because of the power this represented, Strong used the New York Federal Reserve Bank to carry on these activities. In effect the power of the Federal Reserve Board over the U.S. monetary system was not in the hands of the Federal Reserve Board in Washington but under the control of Governor Strong in New York.‡ Even during World War I nearly half of all securities offered by the Treasury were distributed in New York; it handled most of the Treasury's foreign exchange business, dealt with other central banks, acted as a central depository of funds from other Reserve banks, and was the principal purchaser of acceptances. Indeed, the Treasury used the New York Fed as the channel for communicating with other Reserve banks. When Strong managed to persuade the other Reserve banks to allow all open market transactions to be handled by the New York bank, both the power of the Board and the power of the other Reserve banks were very

---

*Just how the Federal Reserve controls the monetary system through the actions of the Federal Open Market Committee is spelled out in detail in Chapter 3.

†If the Fed buys government securities from the banks, it increases their power to lend.

‡In Chapter 3 I show just how this is in effect still true at the present time. This explains Governor Anthony Solomon's extraordinary power and that of Paul Volcker before him.

much reduced. In effect the New York Fed, through its open market operations, determined bank reserves, and hence interest rates, throughout the country.

RELATIONS BETWEEN THE FEDERAL RESERVE AND THE TREASURY

In 1921, when Strong realized what could be accomplished for the economy through the buying and selling of government securities, the New York Fed began making large purchases of government securities. In 1922 an ad hoc "Government Committee" was created by Strong and Andrew Mellon, then Secretary of the Treasury. It included the heads of the five Eastern Reserve banks and thus created a direct challenge to the Federal Reserve Board. The Board disbanded the committee as a threat to its power but then immediately reappointed the same members to a new committee called the Open Market Investment Committee of the Federal Reserve System. It was to operate under the supervision of the Federal Reserve Board and act according to its regulations. For the first time the open market purchases and sales of securities came under the control of a central committee.

Strong's position, however, was in no way reduced. In 1923/24 he used open market operations to buy government securities contracyclically and thereby saved the country from another recession by lowering interest rates. Then in 1925 Strong saw the value of using the discount rates to exercise positive control over the volume of credit and force changes in interest rates. To do this he abandoned the idea that discount rates should be penalty rates. He also found that open market operations were an excellent instrument for bringing about changes in market rates, which in turn would justify changes in the discount rates.

Until Governor Strong realized the implications of buying and selling government securities, neither the Board nor the Reserve banks paid much attention to this question. The Board regarded this as a matter for the Reserve banks; and indeed during the war years they had supported the Treasury by purchasing Treasury issues, but after the War the banks principally purchased government securities as a way of increasing Reserve bank earnings. This policy was condemned by both the Treasury and the Board. The Treasury in particular was concerned about this practice and had urged in 1921/22 that the Reserve banks substitute acceptances as a way of meeting their earnings targets.

Andrew Mellon as Secretary of the Treasury had no great admiration for the Federal Reserve Board. His sympathies lay with the bankers and the District banks, although he cooperated closely with Strong in operating the open market account, thereby giving a strong indication that open market operations were to be handled quite independently of any supervision by the Federal Reserve Board — or even by the Administration or Congress. As was stated earlier, the Federal Reserve Act had done little to indicate what relationship should exist between the Secretary of the Treasury and the Federal Reserve Board. Discussions, of course, had taken place in Congress before passage of the act. In general the banking community had urged complete independence for the Board, whereas many in Congress had urged that the Board be subordinate to the Secretary of the Treasury in the same manner as the Comptroller of the Currency. The compromise, in naming both the Secretary and the Comptroller as ex officio members of the Board, clearly indicated the desire of Congress for a close working relationship between the Treasury and the Board.

At any time when the Treasury was funding federal deficits — such as in periods of war or national emergency (to say nothing of the current federal deficits) — it was obvious that formulation of credit policies by the Federal Reserve Board should be closely coordinated with the Treasury's needs for funding. Again in World War II (as in World War I), the Federal Reserve purchased large amounts of government securities so that banks would be in a position to extend credit to the government. During World War II the banking system bought roughly $95 billion of government securities (40 percent of the total amount borrowed), thereby facilitating government borrowings from the banks and making it impossible to pursue an anti-inflationary credit policy. The Korean War was the great exception because President Harry Truman, with rare courage, refused to allow the Fed to monetize the government deficits created by wartime expenditures. In any dispute between the Secretary of the Treasury and the Fed, the Treasury has enormous leverage because (1) the Secretary is a member of the President's Cabinet and generally one of his closest advisers; (2) it handles very large balances with commercial and Federal Reserve banks; (3) it invests government trust funds and (4) it handles the foreign exchange stabilization fund.

EFFECT OF THE GREAT DEPRESSION

The depression of 1929 brought about a second major test for the U.S. banking system. We saw how in 1922–23 Governor Strong had purchased government securities through the New York Federal Reserve Bank in order to increase bank reserves and lower interest rates to avoid a new recession. In 1929, at the time of the stock market crash, the Federal Reserve unfortunately did not move fast enough to increase bank reserves. Given the extent of the crisis, such a policy might only have helped to defer the depression because the pressures were much too great. We saw how since 1925 the banks outside of New York had been transferring their reserves to the New York banks to make call loans on the purchase of securities. As was noted, the collateral ceases to have any real value if buyers of stock are no longer willing to buy. In September 1929 liquidity in the U.S. banking system was destroyed because stock market customers could no longer reimburse their brokers, and these could no longer reimburse the banks. Stock as collateral had simply lost its value.

There was at that point an immediate need to restore liquidity through Federal Reserve action. It was not forthcoming. The Federal Reserve discount rates were not adjusted to reflect the inordinate demands for money until much later; and by that time no matter how low the interest rates had become, there was no longer any demand for credit because consumers had ceased to buy and business needed neither new equipment nor plant facilities. Chapter 3 makes the point that once the velocity of money has been sharply reduced in a period of rapid disinflation, it no longer makes any difference as to how low interest rates may be or how much money is available to borrow; the demand for credit has ceased.

In 1933 the Federal Reserve Open Market Committee had pledged to keep on increasing bank reserves, but the time when such reserves could have been helpful had long since passed. In 1933 alone, in the hope of stimulating revival of demand for credit, the Federal Reserve banks pumped $600 million into the money markets through open market purchases of government securities, but the demand was not forthcoming. By early 1934 the discount rate at the New York Federal Reserve Bank was down to 1.5 percent, but even this rate did not stimulate member bank borrowing. As a matter of fact, had there been any renewed demand for money, this could well have been met without the help of an easy-money policy because with the rise in the price of gold from $20 to $35, and the difficulties experienced in Europe, money was beginning to flow into the United States in very substantial amounts. The Hoover administration had not moved fast enough; and with the onset of the depression it was no longer of any value to inaugurate a program of increasing bank reserves on a massive sale because there was no longer any demand for credit.

The amendments to the Federal Reserve Act adopted in 1932/33 1) to make government securities eligible as collateral against the issue of Federal Reserve Notes so as to stimulate credit expansion and 2) to make loans to member banks in collateral previously considered ineligible, failed to stimulate credit demand. By 1936 Federal Reserve authorities felt obliged to try to reduce member bank excess reserves by doubling the previous reserve requirements against demand deposits to 14.20 percent and 26 percent, and to 6 percent against time deposits. Unfortunately, the Open Market Committee neglected to sell government securities on balance to absorb excess member bank reserves. On the contrary, Federal Reserve credit outstanding increased slightly under a special grant of authority to make loans directly to individuals who were unable to borrow from the banks. As a result of these inconsistent Federal Reserve policies, excess reserves of member banks reached a peak of nearly $7 billion in late 1940.*

CONGRESSIONAL INTERVENTION
IN THE ROOSEVELT YEARS

One of the great functions of Congress is to carry out investigations. We saw how the panic of 1907 led to the Pujo investigation of the so-called Money Trust, which was in fact helpful to the more serious efforts made by the House Banking Committee to solve some of the problems unearthed by Pujo and hence led to the Federal Reserve Act of 1913.

Although President Franklin Roosevelt did not take office until March 1933, Congress had already begun in January 1933 an investigation of New York Stock Exchange practices that led to the stock market crash of September 1929. Its counsel was Judge Ferdinand Pecora, who had been counsel to the Pujo Committee of 1912. The judge was now old and the investigation was not as searching as it might have been. Most people remembered the investigation principally because of the press photograph of J. P. Morgan sitting on a member's knee. Nevertheless, some horrifying stories of bank practices were unfolded that shocked the nation: endless self-dealing and conflicts of interest were revealed, involving the heads of our leading banks and their friends and relatives. Equally shocking were the revelations regarding foreign lending. National City Bank and National City Co. were selling bonds to Peru, for example, even though they had received adverse information

---

*It must be remembered that in 1940 this figure was approximately equal to the entire budget of the U.S. government.

regarding the country's broken pledges and the Treasury's inability to collect on Peruvian government loans. Three issues of Peruvian bonds had gone into default in 1931, yet the large U.S. banks continued to make new loans: Wells Fargo, National City, Chase, and others, lured by the 13 percent interest return. One can compare, for example, the similarity in the speeches made at the time by the chairmen of National City and Chase with the speeches of their successors in regard to Brazil, Argentina, or Mexico in 1982 to the effect that: "No country goes bankrupt; this is a temporary phenomenon; all we need to do is advance a little more money: etc."* While the declarations the leaders of the money center banks today are thus similar to those made by their predecessors in the early 1930s, there is, of course, a big difference today. The Federal Reserve now stands behind the banks, and there is an International Monetary Fund (IMF) in place, but the risks to the depositors are essentially the same.†

The effect of this investigation, which lasted from January 1933 to July 1934 (a period of 17 months), was the passage of two important pieces of legislation: the Glass-Steagall Act (the Banking Act of 1933) and the Banking Act of 1935, which reformed the Federal Reserve Act of 1913 to take away control from the bankers and give it to the board of government appointees in Washington.

THE GLASS-STEAGALL ACT

Three fundamental questions are presented today in regard to Glass-Steagall. First, do the same conditions exist today that required the enactment of Glass-Steagall in 1933? Second, did Glass-Steagall hit the right target or should it have covered other aspects of banking that are even more important today? And third, in view of the changes that have recently taken place in the services that banks and other financial institutions perform, should Glass-Steagall be modified to meet competitive conditions in the financial services industry today?

Because of the importance of this legislation, which was enacted

---

*We examine in Chapters 5 and 8 just how the U.S. regulatory authorities have allowed these risks to grow by paying little or no attention to foreign lending by U.S. banks. Yet until very recently Congress seemed more interested in preventing rescues by the IMF than asking why U.S. bank lending abroad was permitted to get out of hand.

†See the detailed discussion in Chapter 8 on foreign lending in the late 1970's and early 1980's and the consequent risks taken by Citicorp, Chase, and other large U.S. banks and bank holding companies.

hurriedly as a result of an investigation made in the middle of a terrible depression that revealed unusually bad banking practices, it would appear very important for Congress to review what happened then and why, and what changes in legislation might be appropriate today in the light of current methods of rendering financial services to the public.

The Glass-Steagall Act has certainly become one of the two linchpins of federal regulation of the commercial banking system.* It adopted five changes to the Federal Reserve Act of 1913:

1. It created the FDIC to protect bank depositors through insurance.
2. Section 16 restricts the investment banking activities of national banks (later extended to member banks) to three functions only: acting as an agent, making restricted purchases for its own account, and dealing in certain government securities.
3. Section 20 prohibits the affiliation of any member bank (including national banks) with any business entity engaged *principally* in investment banking activities.
4. Section 21 makes it illegal for any depository institution to engage in investment banking and receive deposits at the same time, except as permitted under Section 16.
5. Section 32 prohibits interlocking directorates and certain other links between member banks (including national banks) and firms or individuals *primarily* engaged in investment banking.

Because there have been so many judicial interpretations of the Glass-Steagall Act and so many attempts on the part of depository institutions (as well as securities firms and other business concerns) to get around the wording of the act, it seems important to explain in simple terms what the Congress was trying to accomplish and why. It should also be noted that in the course of trying legislatively to bring about an end to the abuses that the congressional investigations of 1931/32 had turned up, Congress focused on only one part of the problem, that is, the relationship between banks and their securities affiliates, while not addressing other problems endemic to commercial banking practices.

It is not to be expected that legislation can perform an adequate surgical operation. That is why so much time is later spent in determining through a study of the legislative history what the intent of the

---

*The other is the McFadden Act of 1927 as extended by the Douglas Amendment to the Bank Holding Company Act of 1956, which prevents interstate banking. This question is discussed in detail in Chapter 5.

drafters was and why judicial interpretation is required to find out whether the legislation applies to a set of circumstances that could not have been foreseen at the time. It is, however, exceedingly important to examine what the act was trying to accomplish because it has now been so twisted by judicial interpretation and by attempts to find loopholes in the language that it is almost impossible to remember its original intent and whether the act still has much real meaning, given the way in which banking activities are conducted today.

It must be remembered that Glass-Steagall was adopted at a time of wholesale bank failures. The basic intent of the act was therefore to ensure that such failures would be avoided in the future in order to protect bank depositors. That is why the FDIC was created as part of the act to insure bank depositors. Congress also decided that to protect depositors it was necessary to separate the functions of an underwriter (investment banker) from that of a commercial bank. Banks could, and did, fail because the securities affiliates of banks had made bad investments (including the purchase of the banks' own shares), and this practice should cease.

The act itself represented an important departure from prior legislative thinking. The Federal Reserve Board had at least tacitly allowed member banks to carry on the securities business since banks engaged in such business were quite freely permitted to become member banks. And in 1927 the McFadden Act specifically reaffirmed the authority of national banks to engage in the underwriting of investment securities. By 1930 commercial banks had become dominant in the investment banking field.

Glass-Steagall did not go beyond this simple separation of functions between investment and commercial banking. Even this limited functional separation has, however, been circumvented. The act purported to bar investment banking by U.S. banks anywhere — even outside the United States. Yet U.S. banks or their holding companies have freely been acting as underwriters outside the United States in carrying on, for example, the syndication of long-term credits to developing nations without any complaint by the regulatory agencies.*

Glass-Steagall could certainly have taken action in 1931/32 on other banking practices where conflicts of interest existed. One of these inherent conflicts of interest is that among the trust departments of banks,

---

*This phase of bank regulation, by the Federal Reserve in particular, is examined in detail in Chapter 7 and its effect on developing country borrowers in Chapter 8.

the banks, and their securities affiliates.* Congress did not address this problem. What it did do has only been given limited application; what it did not do is still cause for concern. Some years ago the author defended the trust department of one of the leading New York banks for failure as trustee to sell the controlling block of a large company's shares listed on the New York Stock Exchange. The bank was also depository of the company's funds, its lender, and its principal transfer agent. Clearly, and quite understandably, the commercial side of the bank would have been reluctant to see the block sold. Yet over the years the shares declined constantly in value, and the trust department took no action to register the shares and sell them despite the urging of the trust beneficiaries. In a highly competitive world, should trust departments of banks be separated from the commercial banking operations to avoid this type of problem? Glass-Steagall does not address this question. Had the principal purpose of the act not been to protect bank depositors, the act might also have added provisions to protect the bank's customers. In addition, the act did not limit the extent of bank participation in the stock brokerage business.

What then did Glass-Steagall accomplish? In a 1981 decision the Supreme Court had this to say:

> It is familiar history that the Glass-Steagall Act was enacted in 1933 to protect bank depositors from any repetition of the widespread bank closings that occurred during the Great Depression. Congress was persuaded that speculative activities, partially attributable to the connection between commercial banking and investment banking, had contributed to the rash of bank failures. The legislative history reveals that securities firms affiliated with banks engaged in perilous underwriting operations, stock speculation and maintaining a market for the banks' own stock often with the banks' resources. Congress sought to separate national banks, as completely as possible, from affiliates engaged in such activities.[6]

It must be remembered, in connection with the passage of Glass-Steagall, that this was a period in the nation's history when the economic

---

*For example, it was for a long time the almost universal practice to use trust department commissions to obtain deposits from securities firms. This benefited the commercial department but not the trust department. Because of the growth in pension fund business in the last 20 years—a trend that will continue—there is a need to expand trust company competition and perhaps allow money managers to acquire trust companies without having to acquire banks, given the difference in function.

problems facing the nation were so great and so diverse that it appeared to those in power (most of whom were highly gifted young graduates of Harvard Law School with little or no political, economic, or business experience) that action — any action — was preferable to no action and the most important criterion was taking *some* action, regardless of the advisability of modifying it later after review.

Reference was made to the role of Senator Nelson W. Aldrich in the discussions and studies that led to the passage of the Federal Reserve Act of 1913. The part played by his son Winthrop W. Aldrich in connection with the passage of the Glass-Steagall Act is an unusual story, particularly so because at a time when the excesses of many top commercial bankers made headlines day after day, here was a man who stood out as an outspoken, responsible banker clearly aware of the problems in the banking system and dedicated to bringing about change.

Winthrop W. Aldrich

The son of Nelson W. Aldrich, Winthrop, born in 1885, was at Harvard Law School in 1907. The panic of 1907 was significant to him because the work his father was doing at the time not only shaped his ideas about monetary and financial matters but gave him his first contacts with financial leaders. As a young lawyer he began working with John D. Rockefeller, Jr., who had married his sister Abby in 1901. Through his work for the Rockefellers, then the greatest fortune in the United States, he became directly interested in banking and in 1929 became president of Equitable Trust Company. Six months later Equitable was merged into Chase National Bank, and Aldrich thereby became president of the world's largest bank.*

Coming to the banking world as a lawyer, it was only as a result of the Pecora investigation that he realized what the Chase Bank had been doing with its securities affiliate. He immediately took the lead in criticizing the practices that had now been shown to exist in his own bank as well as many others. In his testimony before Congress as president of the nation's largest bank, he stressed the need to prevent a repetition of the abuses engaged in by commercial banks as revealed by the Pecora investigation. His recommendations for reform caused a bombshell in the financial community.

It was he who recommended that commercial banking and invest-

---

*See Appendix A for an analysis of the 43 bank acquisitions made to create Chase National Bank by 1930.

ment banking be separated, carefully explaining, as a banker and a lawyer, the fundamental difference between the two functions. He stressed that the basic function of a commercial bank consisted of short-term loans against good collateral. Commercial banks as an essential part of the monetary and credit system must be able to meet their deposit liabilities on demand. Investment banks, by comparison, are involved in long-term loans where the risk is necessarily greater. In a public statement on March 8, 1933, Aldrich called for five reforms:

1. Any entity that takes deposits should be subject to the same regulations as commercial banks.
2. No business dealing in securities should be permitted to take deposits even subject to regulation.
3. No officer or director of a commercial bank should be an officer or director of a securities firm, and vice versa.
4. Boards of directors of commercial banks should be limited in number so that directors can be fully aware of the affairs of the bank.
5. Commercial banks should not be allowed to underwrite securities except those of the U.S. government and of states, municipalities, and other U.S. public bodies.

This was the essence of Glass-Steagall as recommended by the president of the nation's largest bank. Aldrich served Chase for 23 years, 5 as president and 18 as chairman. He retired in 1952, aged 67, leaving his bank in excellent condition. The son had thus played a role equally important to that of his father in U.S. legislation relating to bank regulation.

THE BANKING ACT OF 1935

The Banking Act of 1935 changed the structure of the Federal Reserve Board. It was the result of suggestions made by another remarkable banker, Marriner S. Eccles, followed by lengthy debate in the Congress. It provided for staggered membership of 14 years for members of the Board of Governors; it provided for a president and a vice-president of the district banks; and it changed the composition of the Federal Open Market Committee (which had been given statutory recognition by Glass-Steagall) by making membership consist of the seven members of the Federal Reserve Board and five representatives of the Federal Reserve district banks selected annually—one by Boston and New York;

one by Philadelphia and Cleveland; one by Richmond, Atlanta, and Dallas; one by Chicago and St. Louis; and one by Minneapolis, Kansas City, and San Francisco. This transferred control of the Federal Open Market Committee from the district banks to the Federal Reserve Board, an important forward step. Finally, the reserve banks were required to establish the discount rate every 14 days with the approval of the Board of Governors. The effect of these changes, in particular the transfer of control over the Federal Open Market Committee, was to create a central bank in Washington from a 12-bank regional system.

These two great banking acts left a number of wide-open gaps in the banking system: no separation of trust from commercial banking functions; the opportunity for interlocking of management between investment banks and commercial banks, both national and state, and between commercial banks themselves, so long as they were not national banks; and the opportunity for an individual engaged in the securities business through a corporation to act as a director of a commercial bank without even obtaining a prior permit from the Federal Reserve Board. Congress undoubtedly did not go further because it was asked to pass on only one problem and in the course of the massive legislative agenda of the New Deal could give only a limited amount of time to the deficiencies in the banking system.

Constituent priorities in banking are necessarily low. It is only at a time of great crisis that the public becomes interested in bank legislation—and then only to the extent that a very specific abuse is shown to exist, as was done by the Pecora Commission. The administration's attempt in 1935 to gain control over the Federal Reserve Board failed; and as a result the Board and the Federal Open Market Committee were further removed from control by the executive branch. The failure of Congress to act more effectively has to be ascribed (1) to a failure on the part of the membership to understand fully the nature of banking and finance as well as (2) to the persistent influence of New York banks. The problem has not changed in the intervening period since 1935.

THE FEDERAL RESERVE SYSTEM IN THE POSTWAR YEARS OF ECONOMIC GROWTH: 1950s AND 1960s

While the New Deal, as Arthur Schlesinger, Jr., has pointed out, "made the economy relatively depression-proof, we made it at the same time inflation-prone."[7] The period between the Roosevelt years and the

Reagan counterreformation (1981–84) in economic terms must be understood in the light of this quotation. The intervening years were years during which the economy seemed to grow with only a minimum of government interference until inflation took hold in the 1970s. Then, in order to solve the problem of inflation, the country returned to a reduced increase in public expenditures, a recession in the classic mold, and a new beginning of monetary expansion certain to bring back a new inflationary cycle. We passed through a period when we first believed that economists did indeed have the power to direct and control the economy, as Walter Heller believed in the early 1960s, only to realize in the 1970s that this was not so and that we had yet to find out how to control the cycle between recession and inflation. The Federal Reserve Board played an important role over the economy. It did this through gradually asserting its control over monetary policy.* Until the 1970s there was little need for Federal Reserve action because economic growth continued without inflation.

In his second inaugural address, Roosevelt could say:

> The test of our progress is not whether we add more to the abundance of those who have much, it is whether we provide enough for those who have too little.[8]

In 1984 we are questioning whether it is the role of government to redistribute wealth if by so doing it takes away the incentive of producers to increase the country's wealth.

One of the best of Roosevelt's many good appointments to positions of responsibility in the federal government was the appointment of Marriner S. Eccles, governor of the Federal Reserve Board in June 1934. Although he was then relatively unknown in Washington politics, he played a most important role in the passage of the Banking Act of 1935. His background is very much worthy of mention.

Marriner S. Eccles

Marriner was the son of Mormon, David Eccles, a Scotsman, who grew up in the slums of Glasgow, Scotland, and emigrated with his family to the United States in 1863. Becoming one of the earliest settlers of Utah, David fathered 21 children by his two wives; Marriner was the thirteenth and the eldest of 9 by David's second wife. He went to work

---

*This is discussed in great detail in Chapter 3.

at the age of eight, although his father was already a millionaire and controlled some 27 companies. When he had saved $100, his father sold him a share of stock in an Oregon lumber company and told him: "Son, you are now a capitalist because you have saved more money than you have spent. That is how capital is created."

In 1934 Marriner was invited to testify before the Senate Committee on Finance on how to rescue the country from depression. He came with a challenging program of government action that included implementation of the Federal Reserve Board's powers as one of five principal recommendations. He would not accept appointment as Governor of the Federal Reserve Board unless the administration endorsed the following changes: conscious control and management of the monetary mechanism and reliance on monetary control to ensure that economic recovery would not bring about inflation, to be followed by a new depression.* Eccles's program was to become Title II of the Bank Act of 1935, finally adopted against the opposition of the country's bankers. Title II was to include a specific direction to the Federal Reserve to use its powers over the country's monetary system "to promote conditions conducive to business stability."

Eccles conceded that monetary policy alone was insufficient to prevent alternate cycles of boom and depression. He wanted a properly managed plan of Government expenditures and a system of taxation conducive to a more equitable distribution of income. In other words, Marriner Eccles, in 1935, foresaw exactly the problem that the Reagan administration, Congress, and the Federal Reserve have been trying to solve without success by agreement in 1983/84. Eccles also believed strongly that the monetary power in the nation should be held by men representing the public interest and not by the bankers who had controlled the Federal Reserve System from 1913 to 1935.

Eccles was appointed chairman of the Board in 1936 after passage of the act, which gave effect to his ideas. Unfortunately, in the Truman administration he found himself at odds with the Secretary of the Treasury, opted for the independence of the Federal Reserve in order to follow the policies he believed best for the nation, and was replaced as chairman by President Truman at the end of his 14-year term. Truman appointed Thomas McCabe to take his place.

---

*The others were adoption of the administration's economic policies, supervision of investment banking and stock exchange, a large public works program, and an outline of the objectives of the National Industrial Recovery Act and the Agricultural and Adjustment Act.

The Early Postwar Years

The period immediately following World War II found the Treasury and the Fed frequently at odds on monetary policy. The Treasury wanted low interest rates to manage its high war debt; the Fed wanted to let short-term rates rise to keep the economy from overheating in the wake of enormous demand for consumer goods after four years of wartime pent-up demand. The matter came to a head when the Korean War broke out in 1950. The Fed deemed it important to control excesses in the money supply, which would enable the Treasury to fund the increase in the federal debt at low interest rates but would ultimately bring inflation. Truman sided with the Federal Reserve and forced the Treasury, on March 4, 1951, to recognize that monetary policy would be set by the Federal Reserve and that the debt would not be monetized by the Fed. This was a courageous act on the part of the President. It enabled the country to make expenditures needed for the war without creating inflation. Had President Lyndon Johnson acted in the same manner at the time of the Vietnam War in 1967, the inflation of the 1970s might have been reduced, if not altogether avoided. In World War II the Fed had monetized the increase in the federal debt by increasing bank reserves and enabling the banks to buy some $95 billion of government securities. At the end of the war, Eccles and the Fed believed that the controls had to be maintained to reduce the threat of inflation and that the money supply had to be reduced. President Truman, supported by the Treasury, wanted controls removed in order to spur the economy and maintain low interest rates.

Did the accord of March 1951 between the Treasury and the Fed really affirm the independence of the Fed as is sometimes stated? In a sense, yes. But it was largely a promise by the Fed of "cooperation" with the Treasury rather than a "declaration of independence." It certainly gave the Fed a voice in the management of monetary affairs and took away its obligation to monetize the debt in order to maintain low interest rates on Treasury borrowings. It required the Fed, however, to maintain "orderly conditions in the government security market." This did not mean, however, "maintenance of fixed prices for government securities." The accord therefore can hardly be said to reaffirm the independence of the Fed as "suggested" by the Banking Act of 1935. At any rate, immediately thereafter, Chairman McCabe resigned and was replaced by William McChesney Martin. He had been under secretary of the Treasury and had negotiated this accord.

FEDERAL RESERVE INDEPENDENCE

When President Dwight D. Eisenhower came into office in 1953, he stated with characteristic simplicity:

> The Federal Reserve Board is setting up no separate agency of government. It is not under the authority of the President and I personally believe it to be a mistake to make it definitely and directly responsible to the political head of state.

The Fed has since exercised this independence at odd times:

1. In December 1965 Chairman Martin raised the discount rate from 4 to 4.5 percent when President Johnson was opposed to a tightening of credit.
2. In 1968, alarmed that the antiinflationary tax hike passed by Congress would throttle the economy, the Fed increased the money supply, thereby nullifying the intent of Congress.
3. In 1975 the Congress, at President Gerald Ford's urging, passed a $12 billion tax cut for both individuals and corporations. Before the cut could take effect, the Fed slowed the growth in the money supply, thereby causing interest rates to rise even though there was little demand for credit.

There are many other instances when the Fed has followed monetary policies requested by the administration:

1. Under Eisenhower, policy was in favor of reduced inflation. The Fed obligingly increased the discount rate from 1.77 to 2 percent in January 1953. The cost of maintaining stability at the end of the Eisenhower administration was an increase in unemployment and a recession.
2. Under John F. Kennedy the Fed loosened control over the money supply in order to help "get the country going again." The President was unwilling to accept the cost of high unemployment that came with the low inflation rate. Furthermore, the decade and a half since the war that had seen high U.S. exports to aid in the reconstruction of Europe was now over. The dollar remained overvalued, but the reasons for this had disappeared. Imports from new European plants were pouring into the United States, and the large U.S. multinational companies were finding it advantageous to establish new plants in

Europe not only to take advantage of lower labor rates but to establish new market penetration. The postwar period was over, but the administration preferred to increase the money supply rather than begin a drive for exports, which might endanger the political stability in Western Europe achieved as a result of the massive U.S. aid effort of 1945–60.

3. In 1966/67 the Fed allowed the money supply to increase under pressure from President Johnson, who did not want to increase taxes to pay for an unpopular war in Vietnam.

4. In 1972 Chairman Arthur Burns held the discount rate to a low 4.5 percent, kept the prime rate under 6 percent, and increased the money supply at a very rapid rate. Then in 1976 Burns again sharply increased the money supply to accommodate President Ford's election chances.

5. In May 1980 the Fed reversed its tight money policy established in October 1979 as a result of strong pressure from the OPEC countries who were paid in dollars and hence wanted to see its value maintained. From May through September 1980 the money supply was sharply increased to accommodate not only President Carter's new social programs but also his election chances.

6. Shortly before the elections of 1982, the Fed again reversed its tight money policy to spur economic recovery prior to the November elections.

While the Fed is independent from direct control, either by the administration or by Congress, it was created by Congress, and the Fed is fully aware that Congress can at any time change its mandate, responsibilities, or powers. It is also very much aware that it must cooperate with the Treasury, particularly at a time when federal deficits are out of control and must be funded by constant new Treasury issues. Interest rates are vital to the size of the deficit because on $1 trillion every 1 percent of rate increase means $10 billion a year in higher federal deficits.

The targeting of interest rates by the Fed (as will be noted in the detailed discussion in Chapter 3) can only result in increased inflation and thus higher interest rates. The experience of the 1970s and early 1980s amply demonstrates this. In 1983/84 the refusal on the part of the administration and the Congress either to cut spending or to raise taxes has placed the burden of managing the rapidly increasing federal deficit solely on the monetary policy of the Federal Reserve. This is not only unfair but quite impossible. If the debt is monetized by the Fed, the money supply will increase sharply; inflation will return, worse than ever; and interest rates will rise higher than 1981 levels. If the debt is not monetized, interest rates can still be expected to remain high. They would have been much higher in 1982/83 had it not been for the enormous capital flows to the United States from other parts of the world fleeing political instability or socialist governments.

The last ten years has brought about a great change in methods of banking, again as a result of inflation and the Fed's refusal to allow the banks to pay commensurate interest on deposits. This has encouraged new financial service institutions that are not banks and therefore not regulated but that are making available checking and other services that banks historically performed for their customers. The banks, in turn, have tried to find new ways around Federal Reserve regulation in order to protect their deposits by broadening their services. The vehicle banks have used for this purpose is the bank holding company, permitted by the Bank Holding Company Act of 1956, as amended.

BANK HOLDING COMPANIES
AND THEIR REGULATION

A *bank holding company* is simply any business entity that owns or controls a bank. The definition therefore does not include the so-called chain banks that were popular 100 years ago—banks owned or controlled by one or more individuals. These were considered to have performed a useful function because they were small, located in rural areas, and serviced the needs of people in remote areas. In 1889 New Jersey became the first state to allow one corporation to own stock in another. In banking parlance this became known, where bank ownership was concerned, as "group banking," as opposed to "chain banking." In our more sophisticated language of today we speak of *bank holding companies* instead of *group banking.*

Why did Congress believe there was a need to regulate bank holding companies in 1956? A number of different reasons have been advanced. In the 1920s bank holding companies began to proliferate as the general merger movement in industry required bigger banking institutions to handle the financing needs of bigger corporations. It was also a way of getting around limitations on interstate banking or branching restrictions as people began to move to the suburbs of our largest cities. Furthermore, expanding sections of the country no longer wanted to be dependent on the large eastern banks for their financial needs. This was particularly true in the West.

As bank holding companies grew in size and number in the late 1920s, Congress began to show concern but it was not until the Banking Act of 1933 (the Glass-Steagall Act) that Congress began to control the activities of holding companies by requiring that they register with the Federal Reserve Board to obtain a permit in order to vote their stock in the election of board members of controlled banks. They had to submit to examination by the Fed and dispose of interests in securities companies. The legislation, however, only applied to holding companies controlling a member bank of the Federal Reserve, and *control* was defined as majority stock control. The legislation did not apply to the registration of nonbanking interests by the holding companies, nor did it affect the ability of holding companies to expand. In 1938 President Roosevelt, in a special message to Congress, asked for additional legislation to control the expansion of bank holding companies and gradual divestiture of banks held by holding companies.

It was only some 18 years later, however, that Congress finally took action — some say because of the failure of the administration and the courts to break up Transamerica on antitrust grounds. In 1948 the Federal Reserve bank had issued a complaint against the Transamerica Corporation, the holding company established by the Giannini family to control the Bank of America and numerous banks in California, Oregon, Nevada, Washington, and Arizona. After hearings the Board had ordered Transamerica to get rid of all its banks except the Bank of America within two years. Transamerica appealed to the U.S. Court of Appeals for the Third Circuit, and the Court in 1953 upheld the company despite the fact that it controlled 645 banking offices in the five-state area, some 41 percent of the total. The result triggered congressional action.

What did the Bank Holding Company Act of 1956 do? First, it redefined a *bank holding company* as a company that owns 25 percent of the voting shares of two or more banks. It thus contrived exemption from federal regulation of one-bank holding companies. Bank holding companies were required to register with the Fed; and Fed approval was required for a new bank holding company, for acquisition by a bank holding company of a new bank, or for merger with another bank holding company. The so-called Douglas amendment, which became a part of the act, prohibits any interstate acquisitions of banks by a bank holding company unless such acquisitions are specifically authorized by the statutes of the state in which the banks are located.*

Section 4 of the act required bank holding companies to divest

---

*The Garn–St. Germain Depository Institutions Act of 1982 created an exception to this restriction by allowing interstate acquisitions of failed or failing institutions by out of state bank holding companies. The exception expires in 1985. It did permit the acquisition by Bank of America of Seafirst, a Washington bank holding company, in

themselves of nonbank affiliates and prohibited affiliations with non-banking entities. (Under this section Transamerica spun off all its banking interests and became a commercial conglomerate.)

The act was amended in 1966 and 1970. The 1970 amendment revised the definition of a *bank holding company* to include one-bank holding companies. There was reason to do so. From 1955 to 1968 the number of one-bank holding companies had grown from 117 to 783, and their deposits increased from $11.6 billion to $108.2 billion (approximately one third of all commercial bank deposits). Furthermore, these banking entities were engaging in a wide variety of commercial activities ranging from agriculture, mining, and oil and gas to various types of manufacturing, real estate, and wholesale and retail distribution. The amendment of 1970 therefore provided that the Fed could only permit bank holding companies to own shares in companies (including companies operating in other states) whose activities were "so closely related to banking or managing or controlling banks as to be a proper incident thereto."[9] The act also included a "public benefits" test. With such language it was obvious that constant court interpretation was in store; and this has indeed turned out to be the case.

What does *closely related to banking* mean? And how is the public benefits test to be interpreted even where great deference is given to findings by the Federal Reserve Board, particularly in the light of today's banking practices? Not only the Board of Governors, in exhaustive hearings, but the courts as well have devoted enormous time and effort to develop a rationale over the years. For example, some insurance activities have been found to be permissible; others not. Finally, the Garn–St. Germain Depository Institutions Act of 1982 provided that — except for certain exceptions — providing insurance as principal, agent, or broker is not an activity closely related to banking. The act severely curtails expansion of bank holding companies into the insurance area; on the other hand, it allows some insurance activities previously prohibited by either the Fed or the courts.[10] Courier services are prohibited; so are travel agency services; and so is operation of a savings and loan association unless necessary to save it.* But full pay-out leasing is per-

---

1983. The Douglas amendment also contained a grandfather clause to protect interstate holdings acquired prior to the effective date of the act. In *Lewis v. B. T. Investment Managers, Inc.*, 447 U.S. 27 (1980), the Court added another exception by holding that the Douglas amendment did not cover the acquisition of companies performing bank-related services, such as investment advisory and trust services.

*Under Garn–St. Germain a bank holding company may acquire even an out-of-state thrift if it is in trouble. On September 28, 1982, the Federal Reserve Board ap-

mitted, as are investment advisory services, brokerage services, futures commission merchant activities, and data processing for others (under the Fed's amended Regulation Y). With the passage of the 1970 amendments, the two major objectives of bank holding company legislation had been achieved: most bank holding companies were subject to regulation; and statutory and regulatory controls had been placed on the expansion of bank holding companies into other businesses.

As competition from other types of institutions rendering financial services to the public increases, there will certainly be increased pressure to liberalize the interpretation of the Bank Holding Company Act or to pass additional legislation. The difficulty is that—as in the case of Garn–St. Germain—Congress tends to legislate a specific problem that it perceives to require action without standing back and taking action on the fundamental relationships between the various types of institutions engaged in financial services. Congress is understandably reluctant to take the broader look because it makes the passage of any legislation much more difficult. Like our tax code that cries out for general overhaul but is politically impossible to accomplish, there is now a real need for a comprehensive review of banking legislation in terms of today's financial services activities and the current manner in which such activities are regulated. Congress senses the need because by the close of its session in 1984 many bills had been introduced; the administration is trying on its side to recommend regulatory modifications, with both the Bush Task Group* and the Treasury working hard to develop recommendations to Congress to simplify the regulatory structure.

Even under current restrictions, bank holding companies have continued to proliferate. As of December 31, 1980, there were 3,054 bank holding companies of which 429 were multibank companies. The 3,054 bank holding companies had 4,940 bank subsidiaries with consolidated assets of $1,453 billion, or 78 percent of all commercial bank consolidated assets.

The Bank Holding Company Act has become particularly important† in recent years for two reasons. First, although the Federal Re-

---

proved an application by Citicorp, a bank holding company, to acquire Fidelity Federal, a California savings and loan association in severe financial difficulty.

*The vice-president heads a task group focusing on bank deregulation. The conclusions of the task group are discussed in Chapter 6.

†This whole question of recent interpretation of the Bank Holding Company Act is analyzed in detail in Chapter 5, which deals with the application of federal bank regulations under today's circumstances.

serve Board has added numerous extensions to the Douglas amendment, the states through their own laws have enabled banks to extend their activities across state lines in spite of the Douglas amendment restrictions. Second, banks have sought to avoid the Bank Holding Company Act through the acquisition of so-called nonbank banks. The act contains a very large loophole: A bank that does not *both* accept demand deposits and make commercial loans is not a bank under the definition of a *bank* in the act. This means that a commercial firm that acquires a bank that either does not accept demand deposits or does not make commercial loans has not acquired a "bank" and therefore is not subject to regulation by the Federal Reserve under the Bank Holding Company Act.

What are demand deposits? What are commercial loans for purposes of the act? These are some of the difficult questions touched on in Chapter 4 and examined in detail in Chapter 5. The Federal Reserve does not like nonbank banks because it loses jurisdiction; so it interprets the act very strictly. The Comptroller and the FDIC take the liberal view because they do not favor the limitations on banking activities insisted upon by the Federal Reserve. This results in a fundamental conflict among the federal regulatory authorities that Congress alone will be able to clear up. It also makes a complicated subject even more complicated. Nevertheless, it is important for the reader to understand these intricacies because the eventual determination of these differences will surely affect the future appearance of the U.S. banking system and who the key players will be.

CONCLUSION

This chapter has traced the historical evolution of bank regulation in the United States. The reader will reach a number of conclusions.

1. In the United States there has always been a division of responsibility between the federal government and the states — a division still not resolved today.
2. There is a fundamental distrust of strong central government control even when it affects something as fundamental as the nation's currency.
3. The congressional attitude has been to take action only when an emergency situation occurs — and then only to the extent of taking

care of that particular problem; when there is no strong public pressure to act, the legislature takes no action.

4. The regulatory system has, therefore, been allowed to develop with every little executive or legislative interference and with mandates that are generally unclear and overlapping.
5. The notion of a strong central bank has been totally absent from the American system.

In the next chapter I will examine how the failure of a central banking system similar to that found in other countries has affected the development of U.S. monetary policy. It is a particularly interesting story because it reveals how power develops where a vacuum has been allowed to exist and yet action must be taken. This analysis is all the more important because in monetary policy the Federal Reserve Board does act as the central bank. Moreover, its actions affect not only the U.S. economy but — since the end of the gold standard in 1971 — the economies of the entire world, as well.

APPENDIX A

Banks Merged into
The Chase National Bank of the City of New York, 1921–1930

Metropolitan Bank (1921)
- Shoe and Leather Bk. National Shoe & Leather Bk.
- Metropolitan Bank
- Hamilton Trust Co.

Mechanics & Metal National Bank (1926)
- Mechanics Nat'l Bk. (1865)
- Leather Manuf. Nat'l Bank (1904)
- National Copper Bk. (1910)
- Fourth National Bk. (1914)
- New York Produce Exchange Bank (1920)
- Lincoln National Bank (1922)
- Lincoln Trust Co. (1922)

Mutual Bank (1927)

Garfield National Bank (1929)

National Park Bank (1929)
- American Deposit & Loan Co. (1895)
- Bowling Green Trust Co. (1909)
- Madison Trust Co. (1911)
- Trust Co. of America (1912)
- North American Trust Co. (1912)
- Importers & Traders Bank (1923)
- Colonial Trust Co.
- Produce Exchange Trust Co.

Equitable Trust Co. (1930)

Interstate Trust Co. (1930)
- Franklin National Bk. (1927)
- Bloomingdale Bros. (1927)
- Hamilton National Bk. (1928)
- Century Bank (1929)

Van Norden Trust Co.
City Trust Co.
New York Real Estate
  Guaranty Co.
Citizens Loan Agency
  & Guaranty Co.
International Banking &
  Trust Co.
American Bond &
  Mortgage Guaranty Co.

Seaboard National Corp.
Seaboard National
  Bank (1929)

Seaboard Bank (1883)
Mercantile National
  Bank (1922)
Mercantile Trust Co.
  (1922)
Mercantile Trust &
  Deposit Co. (1922)
New Netherlands Bank
  (1928)

Sources: Trust Companies Magazine, July 1925, pp. 45–46; Chase National Bank, *Annual Reports*; Aldrich papers.

NOTES

1. 12 Stat. 165 (1863). This act is also referred to as the National Bank Act of 1863.

2. Resolution adopted February 24, 1912, by the Committee of the House of Representatives Committee on Banking and Currency.

3. *The Statutes at Large of the United States of America from March, 1913, to March, 1915* Vol. XXXVIII, part 1. Washington, D.C., 1915, p. 251.

4. *The Statutes at Large of the United States of America*, Vol. XXXVIII, p. 265.

5. Ibid., p. 265.

6. Board of Governors v. Investment Co. Inst. 450 U.S. 46 (1981).

7. Arthur Schlesinger, Jr., "The Hundred Days of FDR," The New York *Times*, April 10, 1983, p. F8.

8. Ibid., p. F9.

9. The Bank Holding Company Act Amendment of 1970. Public Law 91-607, Section 103.

10. See U.S. Congress, Senate, S. Rep. 97536. 97th Cong. 2d sess., 1982, p. 3642. See also U.S. Congress, House, Committee on Banking, Finance and Urban Affairs, *Committee Print 984*, 98th Cong. 1st sess., May 1983, pp. 5-66.

3

THE FEDERAL RESERVE
AND MONETARY POLICY

Between the Idea and the Reality, Falls a Shadow.

— T. S. Eliot

In the area of monetary policy the role of the Board of Governors of the Federal Reserve System must be considered absolute if we are to believe in the independence of the Board — a belief so often reiterated by Presidents and Congressmen alike.

This chapter concerns itself with how the Federal Reserve Board has managed this independence over the years and poses several questions. How has the Federal Reserve Board exercised this powerful function? Has it been helpful in generating economic growth and increased employment in the United States? Has the growth in the money supply been kept within targeted areas? Have interest rates remained constant, or are they becoming increasingly volatile? In short, has the Federal Reserve done the job mandated to it by the Congress in this area? If the answer to the last is no, or partially no, is it the result of uncontrollable events or the result of outside pressures to adapt to changed circumstances? If the answer here is that the board might have taken different steps to meet changes in the economy, is this a matter that requires congressional or administrative action? And if so, what kind of action might be helpful to accomplish the board's congressional mandate? These are difficult questions that should be examined — as the Courts have suggested — with respect for, and acute awareness of, the Board's regulatory functions and the men and women of the utmost integrity and impressive professional experience that have served on the board over the years.

Since not even our foremost economists have agreed upon what the U.S. monetary policy, as articulated by the Federal Reserve Board, should be, we can judge in advance how difficult it is to understand what monetary policy is all about and just how it can be controlled by the Fed. The purposes then, of this chapter are: first, to describe the purpose of monetary policy; second, to show just how it is affected by the Federal Reserve's actions and what those actions might be; and third, to explain how various steps taken by the Fed over the years may have affected the U.S. economy (although, here again, we must realize that there are other important factors that may affect the economy — such as economic cycles, OPEC's action, congressional or administrative budget policies, and the like) that have to be weighed to determine their effects, quite independently of anything the Fed did do or could have done had it had better forecasting powers concerning global economic or political change. A final purpose is to draw some tentative conclusions. These conclusions must take into account the fact that the Federal Reserve, although repeatedly said by successive administrations and by Congress to be an independent agency of the federal government, is still an agency of the government; and from time to time it is subject to intense pressures from the administration and Congress because the economy is not behaving as some think it should. This political pressure has been much greater in the last few years than in past decades. For one thing, each economic cycle since World War II has tended to be shorter, showing deeper troughs and higher peaks with each successive cycle. Is there a link between the steps taken by the Federal Reserve and the changing nature of our economic cycles? Many economists think so. Others are not so certain, preferring to think that it is natural for the economy to go through these cycles and that there is relatively little the monetary policies of the Federal Reserve Board can do about it.

THE FORMATION OF
MONETARY POLICY

What interests both the administration in power and Congress, quite naturally, is that the economy continues to grow and that people seeking a job are able to find employment, preferably in the private sector, since the public is against the growth of government bureaucracies whether at Federal or State levels. This political ideal has been repeated by Congress at various intervals since the end of World War II, beginning with the Full Employment Act of 1946 and concluding with the

Humphrey-Hawkins Act in 1977. Various other bills are pending to direct the Federal Reserve's monetary policy to better effect the mandate of Congress.

For its part the Reagan administration is considering the advisability of either administrative or congressional action — supposedly to deregulate the banking system but in reality to go beyond that and reinstate the responsibility and functions of the various regulatory agencies (including the Federal Reserve Board and the Federal Reserve System) to increase competitiveness within the financial services industry (including, but certainly not limited to, banks) and, one would also think, to make monetary policy function better. It is obvious that during the tenure of the Reagan administration there has been friction at times between the White House and the Secretary of the Treasury, on the one hand, and Chairman Paul Volcker of the Federal Reserve, on the other. In mid-1983 the President recommended that Volcker be reappointed for another term, and Congress confirmed the appointment. By summer 1983, therefore, all major differences of opinion between the Fed and the administration seemed to have been resolved. But if the economic recovery should slow down before the 1984 elections, it is likely that there will be renewed pressure on the Fed to increase the money supply again.

THE FED'S METHODS OF CONTROLLING MONETARY POLICY

The Federal Reserve controls U.S. monetary policy, as we noted earlier, by increasing or decreasing the growth in the money supply or by increasing or decreasing the cost and availability of credit. The Fed utilizes three tools to accomplish this, putting aside its power to regulate foreign credits in U.S. banks or its power to increase or decrease credit to purchase securities. These three tools involve manipulation of the discount rate, changes in reserve requirements, and purchase or sale of government securities in the open market. They are designed either to affect interest rates (the cost of credit) or to affect the growth in the money supply (the availability of money), which, of course, will in due time also affect the cost of money to borrowers.

The fundamental difference of opinion between the monetarist economists, who are generally conservative in their political views, and academics or members of Congress, who are more concerned about economic growth than the fear of inflation, is that the former stress the importance of maintaining a constant increase in the money supply, which can be targeted in advance depending upon the condition of the economy, whereas the latter want the focus to be upon maintenance of low interest rates without which, they say, the economy cannot grow. The difference of opinion is a very fundamental one. It is very much the same difference of opinion that we observed earlier between those who have always been in favor of a strong central bank in order to maintain the value of money and those, essentially and historically from the South and West, who believe that the central bank should have very little power and that what is needed is a focus on maintaining an ever-growing supply of money with resulting low interest rates. Conservative Republicans in the Congress are generally found in the first group, whereas the second is apt to include Democrats of the Left. It is not surprising, therefore, to find Jim Wright of Texas, the majority leader in the House, to be the leader of a group of 100 congressmen who would like to see the Federal Reserve announce in advance its interest-rate targets for the year rather than the targeted increase in the money supply. We will come back to this important difference in political opinion later in the chapter.

It need only be noted here that the Federal Reserve did in fact change its monetary policy — or at least its methods — in October 1979 when Chairman Volcker came to the conclusion that the Fed's attempts to control interest rates had resulted in constant, very large increases in the money supply and that this was the reason why inflation was also continuously increasing in the United States. As a result, from that date on the Federal Reserve Board decided to focus on money aggregates rather than on maintenance of constant interest rates. Unfortunately, as we shall see, the two are inextricably linked. If the money supply is increased to make interest rates decline, rates will indeed decline over the short term. But, as the money supply continues to increase, it will fuel a boom in the economy and bring about increased inflation; this will, in turn, cause interest rates to rise — until the economy turns downward again.

Essentially, the Fed controls monetary policy by controlling bank reserves. The more reserves a bank has, the more money it has to lend. This will also affect the cost of credit, that is, the interest rates. Bank reserves are the key to Federal Reserve monetary policy. The Fed controls bank reserves in one of three ways: through the discount rate, through reserve requirements, or through buying or selling government securities in the open market.

The Discount Rate

The *discount rate* is defined as the rate at which the Federal Reserve lends funds directly to banks that are in need of money. While some economists say that the Federal Reserve uses this control tool only very infrequently, it has at times, nevertheless, played a very prominent role in Fed policy. Furthermore, it is very important psychologically. From October 1982 to July 1983, the money supply increased very rapidly (over 13 percent at an annual rate). It was thought that in July or August 1983 the Fed would increase the discount rate — which had been reduced from 9 percent to 8.5 percent in December 1982 — in order to assure the public that the Fed was really serious about making sure there would be no renewal of inflation. Supposedly, the presidents of three Federal Reserve banks had recommended an increase in the discount rate. President Reagan, on the other hand, and Democratic members of Congress were urging that the Fed not increase the discount rate, apparently in fear that the banks might be led to increase their interest rates to the public further. So what happened? The discount rate was kept at 8.5 percent by the Fed, but the banks raised their prime rate anyway.

The discount rate is not very significant in amount loaned. In 1980 the amount outstanding varied from $500 million to $3.5 billion. When compared with total bank reserves of $40 billion, this amount is not significant. However, what has happened is that instead of being the lender of last resort, as it claims, the Fed, through its repeated recent reductions in the discount rate, must be regarded as lender of first resort. Of course, the Fed has other controls over the use of the discount rate since it penalizes frequent users. For example, in May 1981 the Fed not only raised the discount rate to 14 percent in a move to curb increases in the money supply (M1-B had increased $4.8 billion in the previous week), but it also raised the surcharge it applied to frequent users to 4 percent from 3 percent. This meant that frequent borrowers from the Fed were paying 18 percent to borrow from the discount facility. However, the Fed's action followed an increase in the prime rate to 19 percent and a sharp decline in the stock market. The effect of the Fed's increase in the discount rate in May 1981 was a sharp increase in the Treasury bills rate. This particular increase in the discount rate was the fourth since September 1980 but the first since December 1980. The reason for the Fed's action in 1981 with respect to the discount rate is easy to understand: Use of the discount facility increased bank reserves and increased the money supply since the Fed issued new money by creating credits on its books in the name of the banks.

And by July 1984, with the discount rate at 9.0 percent and the rate at which banks lend to each other (the federal funds rate) at 12.38 percent, there was a large spread in rates; banks therefore had an earning advantage in borrowing from the Fed to lend to other banks. This spread makes the Fed's efforts to check increases in the money supply, through use of the discount facility, a difficult task. In July of 1983, when the discount rate was 8.5 percent and the federal funds rate at 9.14, President Reagan urged the Fed to maintain a low discount rate. This has not been possible. The demand for credit since the summer of 1983 has been rising rapidly. The Treasury has to raise ever larger amounts to pay for the federal deficits; consumers are coming back to the retail stores causing a sharp increase in consumer debt; and the capital needs of business are growing because of growing consumer demands. Curiously enough, during this 1983 to 1984 period, most corporate treasurers still appeared to expect interest rates to stay constant or go down slightly. As a result, they have not been in a hurry to borrow long or short term. But as the economy picks up, this is likely to change because corporate inventories are low and very little capital investment was made by business over the 1981–83 period. Bank rates are not likely to go down further in 1984, but Treasury bills hit their low in August 1982 and federal funds in January 1983.

In recent times the discount rate policy of the Federal Reserve has been very volatile. In February 1980 it was 13 percent. Continuing to be reduced gradually, it reached 10 percent in July 1980. Then it was gradually increased until it was set at 14 percent in May 1981. After that it was reduced again, hitting 8.5 percent in December 1982. The Federal Reserve's discount rate is likely to rise again if the velocity of money, contrary to Federal Reserve predictions, increases again as the economic recovery continues into 1984 and threatens to turn into a boom.

The discount rate is not a very good tool. A useful policy instrument should lead and not follow the market.

Reserve Requirements

Change in the reserve requirements of the banks is also a tool that has been relatively seldom used by the Fed to control bank reserves. A small change in percentage requirements can obviously mean a massive change in the amounts of dollar reserves that financial institutions must keep at the Federal Reserve. Until 1984 there was a two-week time lag in accounting to meet reserve requirements, so that banks could anticipate their needs and then borrow from the discount window at concessionary rates. This is no longer true. But control over reserve requirements has never proved to be a very useful tool — probably because if reserves were sharply increased at any time, there would be a political uproar in Congress.

Increasing or Decreasing Bank Reserves through Open Market Transactions

Controlling bank reserves by buying or selling government obligations in the open market is obviously the Fed's principal tool to control the growth in the money supply and, more important, the bank's capacity to lend and at what rate. If the Fed buys securities in the open market, it can do so either from an individual or a corporation or from a bank. If it buys from a bank, it creates a credit on its books in the bank's name. The bank thereupon has that much additional reserves to lend. When it lends, it adds to the money supply funds that did not exist before. If the Fed buys from a source other than a bank, the net result is the same: the individual or corporation transfers the credit issued by the Fed in payment for the securities to a bank; so the bank has additional money to lend. The deposit creates an increase in the money supply since the transaction takes place with money that did not exist before.

If the Fed, instead of buying, decides to sell government securities in the open market, the reverse takes place, and the money supply is reduced by the sales transaction since the Fed acquires in effect the money it issued earlier. By preventing reserves from increasing, the Fed can keep interest rates higher than normal for a short period. Similarly, as happened in the period from October 1982 to August 1983, the Fed can lower interest rates for a period of time by regularly on balance buying government securities increasing the level of bank reserves. We say *for a relatively short period of time* because under normal circumstances an increase in bank reserves (which creates an increase in the money supply as soon as the bank loans the money) will bring about a temporary decline in interest rates, leading to increased consumer spending and capital investment by business — in other words, growth in the economy.

Why then is it not a good policy to increase the money supply in this manner continuously? Unfortunately, in due course as the economy heats up, inflation comes about and the demand for credit keeps on increasing. People develop the attitude that if they put off buying, prices will go up; so they borrow more to buy more, particularly capital assets, land, collectibles, and the like. At this point interest rates climb on a steady basis, while the Fed — in trying to bring about a decline in the inflation that accompanied the rise in interest rates—reverses course and tightens up on the reserves available to banks. This ends the economic boom. The change of policy now brings about a deeper recession than should have occurred. Does this mean that Fed policy is always applied too late?

There are, of course, important other factors to consider, such as the velocity of money and the necessity of banks to roll over bad loans, as the money-center banks had to do with their foreign loans in 1982/83 (so that they were not disposed to make new loans). The effect of this, as happened in the last half of 1982 and the first half of 1983, was that while the Fed made reserves available to the banks, the banks did not use more than a portion of these additional reserves to make new loans to domestic borrowers that would add to the money supply. (Nevertheless, the money supply did grow at a very substantial rate.)

An increased money supply leads the public to believe that inflation will resume and leads the banks to maintain a higher-than-normal spread between their cost of money and the interest rate they charge to their borrowers. As the big banks became increasingly less liquid in the 1979–82 period, a curious phenomenon occurred. Depositors at the banks withdrew their money because the Fed had imposed a ceiling—Regulation Q—on what banks could pay for deposits.* Through its policies the Fed in effect, created money-market funds, which pay the investor more and can be turned into cash at any time. Money-market funds, however, are generally invested in certificates of deposit (CDs),† some 40 percent of which are issued by banks. What this has meant is that banks could no longer rely on their depositors for money to lend but had to purchase their money in the marketplace through the issuance of CDs just as any other financial services company would have to do. Furthermore, it was discovered that some well-known industrial firms dealing in credit—such

---

*This ceiling was not relaxed until authorized by Congress in the Monetary Control Act of 1980 (Public Law 96–221), which provided for the gradual phaseout of deposit interest-rate ceilings.

†CDs are instruments made generally by banks in other banks in denominations of $100,000 or more. There are no ceilings set by the Federal Reserve on interest rates, and the maturity may vary. Commercial paper is a short-term security issued by both financial and nonfinancial corporations. It is uninsured and generally issued by corporations with a very high credit standing like General Motors or General Electric. Banks invest in CDs rather than commercial paper because CDs at banks pay higher rates of interest. Commercial paper competes with bank loans as short-term loans for corporations. From 1963 to 1979, for example, commercial paper increased in volume from $6 billion to $92 billion because corporations can often borrow more cheaply through the issuance of commercial paper than through bank loans. The maturity of commercial paper issues is generally 60 days or less.

as General Motors Acceptance, Ford Motor, General Electric Credit Corporation, and others — could borrow on their commercial paper at a better rate than the banks could on their CDs. The low rates on commercial paper are essentially due to the fact that banks are bypassed as intermediaries. (In 1982, IBM made a loan in the Eurocurrency market at a better rate than did even the U.S. Treasury.) Recently, the rate payable by some banks for CDs has risen because questionable foreign or domestic loans made by some of the bigger money-center banks such as Continental of Illinois and Manufacturers Hanover, caused these banks' securities to represent increased risk.

The system is said to be in a *free position* when the Fed provides more reserves than banks need, so that they need not borrow from the central bank; the system is in a *borrowed position* when there are not sufficient reserves in the system, and banks are obliged to borrow from the Fed. The rate charged by banks to one another is referred to as the *federal funds rate.* Commercial banks usually sell federal funds to other banks, and they purchase CDs from other banks. The Federal Reserve banks can affect the federal funds rate, that is, the rate charged by banks for transfers to other banks. If the banks buy sufficient government securities, they will reduce the rate; the lower rate will cause a more rapid rate of growth in the money supply; this in turn is expected to stimulate demand and consequently reduce the rate of unemployment.

In the early 1970s the Fed made use of both the level of the funds rate and the rate of expansion in the money aggregates in its monetary policy. The dual policy has proved to be a difficult one because the Fed does not know how fast it must lower the funds rate to achieve the desired expansion in the monetary aggregate. The federal funds rate rises as reserves become scarce relative to demands for credit. With borrowed reserves in July 1983 ranging only from $50 to $100 million, the federal funds rate varied from 8⅞ to 9 percent. If borrowed reserves were to go to $200 million, the federal funds rate might rise to 9¼ percent; or to 9½ percent, if borrowed funds should reach $300 million. The federal funds rate is very important in understanding the Federal Reserve's control over monetary policy.

THE FEDERAL FUNDS RATE

For a long time the Federal Reserve Board directed monetary policy with reference to the federal funds rate because this rate indicated how tight the banks were for money and what the likelihood might be for increases or decreases in interest rates charged to borrowers. Until the

Fed policy changed in October 1979 it concentrated on trying to keep the federal funds rate within a predetermined range, on the theory that this would in turn keep the interest rates charged by the banks to their borrowers at a constant, predictable level. The Fed can, in the short run at any rate, control the federal funds rate quite precisely by carefully raising or lowering bank reserves through its purchase and sale of government securities. For a long time the Shadow Open Market Committee, made up of monetarist economists, has been urging the Fed to abandon attempts to control the federal funds rate and instead to monitor the growth in the money supply. A number of presidents of Federal Reserve banks believed, just as the monetarist economists did, that the Fed should adopt a monetary policy based on control of the money supply. One of the principal proponents of this view within the Federal Reserve System has been Lawrence K. Ross, president of the Federal Reserve Bank of St. Louis. When the Federal Reserve Board changed its monetary policy in October 1979, there were articles and speeches made by monetarists, such as Milton Friedman of Chicago, applauding the change in policy on the assumption that now the Fed would allow the federal funds rate to find its own level and concentrate its efforts on limiting the growth in the money supply.

It is true that since that time, interest-rate movements have become much more volatile. But has the growth in the money supply really been brought down? And has the Fed's new policy really brought about the desired growth in the economy? It is highly questionable that the new Federal Reserve monetary policy has been any more successful than the former policy. The Shadow Open Market Committee claims this is so because it has been impossible for the Fed to change its policy in practice, regardless of any formal decision of the Board. Nonmonetarist economists are no more satisfied with the Fed's new policy. Benjamin J. Friedman, professor of economics at Harvard, has charged, for example, that the Fed's operating procedures between October 1979 and October 1982 led to a big increase in the volatility of interest rates without any improvement in control of the money supply—"nor for that matter, any other apparent gain." Interest rates were certainly more stable in 1983 than in 1982 but only at the cost of rapid growth in the money supply (13 to 14 percent, as we noted earlier). And in 1984 interest rates have had a tendency to rise as demand for money has grown and the Fed has been reluctant to increase much further the rate of growth in the money supply.

In mid-1983 there was a hue and cry almost worldwide about the U.S. interest-rate situation. President Mitterand of France says to anyone who will listen, including the heads of state at the economic summit that took place at Williamsburg in May 1983, that the United States is using a policy of high interest rates to siphon savings out of the other industrialized countries to pay for the huge federal deficit that should be paid for not by foreign savers but by U.S. taxpayers. Günther Schleiminger, general manager of the Bank for International Settlements (BIS) in Basel, Switzerland, has asserted: "The most important and the most urgent task for policy is to exert downward pressure on U.S. interest rates. . . . [This falls] fairly and squarely on the shoulders of those in charge of fiscal policy." As noted earlier, in mid-1983 both President Reagan and Jim Wright, Democratic majority leader in the House, had joined the chorus of pleaders to the Fed to get interest rates down. The Federal Reserve Board is quite conscious of the Democratic move in the House to require the Fed to target interest rates again. In fact, has the policy of the Federal Reserve Board really changed since October 1979, or are we talking of an announced policy change that has little substance to back it up? This brings us to an examination of just how the Federal Reserve's open market operations function in practice.

THE FEDERAL RESERVE
OPEN MARKET COMMITTEE

Already back in 1964, at a time when Congressman Wright Patman was very much head of the House Banking Committee (and no friend of the Federal Reserve Board), Allan Meltzer of the Carnegie-Mellon Institute in Pittsburg and Karl Brunner of the Graduate School of Management at the University of Rochester published a study entitled *The Federal Reserve's Attachment to the Free Reserve Concept*, which was written on behalf of the Subcommittee on Domestic Finance of the House Banking Committee.[1] This study, written during a period when U.S. economic growth was still very much in full swing, indicated that sooner or later Federal Reserve policy would bring about grave difficulties because there was, in fact, no systematic policy other than that developed on a very short-term basis by the manager of the Federal Reserve System Open Market Account and that the Federal Open Market Committee actually responded much later to actions already taken by the "Desk" official at the New York Fed. David Meiselman, a monetarist economist and former official of the U.S. Treasury in the area of monetary policy, has said: "The people on the Desk then go and work for the dealers. So they can't afford to offend the dealers too much because they won't get jobs. It's the same fraternity, at somewhat different stages of the game."[2] What he and others have been talking about is the constant *short-term* buying and selling of government securities handled by the "Desk" officer at the Federal Reserve Bank of New York, acting as agent for the Open Market Committee during the intervals between its meetings.

When one considers that the Open Market Committee meets some eight times a year, this means that day-to-day policy is taken over by the Fed officials in New York. As we noted in Chapter 2, this was not the way the mechanism was mandated to operate following the changes made in 1933 in the power of the New York Fed.* What has happened is that the role that President Benjamin Strong had reserved for the New York Fed in the early days of the Federal Reserve System is now necessarily executed by a permanent staff official who, while he communicates daily with members of the Open Market Committee, has to make the decisions on his own because he is *constantly* buying and selling government securities. On June 6, 1981, Fernand St. Germain, chairman of the House Banking Committee, wrote President Anthony Solomon of the New York Fed to ask him why, to increase the money supply by $25 billion, the Fed had handled repo agreements (99 percent of the New York Fed's transactions are repos) totaling $1.67 trillion over the year. The purpose of the exercise, of course, was to control short-term changes in the banks' monetary reserves.

A *repo* is an agreement to buy and sell very short-term (generally five days) on the basis that the seller or buyer from the Fed will take back the securities within the agreed-upon time. On the face of it, it is hard to see that these repo agreements make much sense except to enrich the bond dealers with whom the New York Fed deals on a regular basis. On a purchase of government securities by the Fed, the buyer has five days of interest-free funds even though the rate to dealers is set by competitive bidding. Surely, if Open Market Committee policy is based on increasing reserves within the period between meetings, the Fed should, on balance, buy securities because it knows that this is Open Market Committee policy. Is there really any reason for the constant trades that take place both ways several times a day?† It does indicate clearly, however, that the Board, regardless of its policy decision to con-

---

*See Chapter 2.

†Presumably, the enormous number of trades is made to mask the Fed's current policy, whether to buy or sell on balance, in order to prevent market speculation.

centrate on monetary aggregates rather than on the maintenance of steady interest rates, is still focusing on hour-to-hour interest-rate variations and that this kind of a policy can only be carried out by officials who are on the spot, that is, the "Desk" officials in New York.

EFFECT OF THE REAGAN ADMINISTRATION

With the election of President Reagan in 1980, and the appointment of the monetarist commercial banker Beryl Sprinkel as undersecretary of the Treasury for Monetary Affairs (a position occupied earlier in the Carter administration by Anthony Solomon, current president of the New York Fed, and still earlier in the Nixon administration by Paul Volcker, now chairman of the Federal Reserve Board), it was to be expected that pressure on the Fed to relax its day-to-day concern with interest rates and really focus on bringing about a decline in the growth of the money supply would increase sharply. Did this indeed happen? In July 1982 the outgoing chairman of the President's Council of Economic Advisors, Murray Weidenbaum, told the author:

> In late 1981, we eliminated the supply-siders from the Administration. Now we are quietly eliminating the monetarists. Those who stay, including Sprinkel, are going to be very quiet indeed, because the Administration's policy is mainly concerned with economic recovery, and if this requires increasing the reserves available to the banks dramatically, then so be it.

Indeed, it appears that whether because of fears of some major bank disaster as a result of the purchase of Penn Square loans by such major banking institutions as Seafirst, Continental Illinois Bank, and Chase Manhattan Bank or because of the sudden realization by the Federal Reserve Board that the large money-center banks were greatly overextended in their foreign loans, particularly to South America, the Board in the summer of 1982 abruptly abandoned the tight-money policy favored by the monetarists and began supplying the banks with massive increases in reserves.

This was the start of a new policy that the experts on Wall Street (who deal with the New York Fed on a daily basis, as we pointed out, and hence are almost necessarily privy to changes in policy) immediately saw would result in a decline in interest rates. Institutional clients were immediately advised to buy, and the result was the biggest rise in Wall Street history from August 1982 to July 1983. It is noteworthy that the biggest holder of securities in the world is the trust department of Morgan Guaranty Bank as was noted in Chapter 2. There has seldom been a more spectacular turn-around in the history of investment psychology. One minute the business world was facing increased numbers of bankruptcies, and many banks were coming under severe liquidity stress; the next minute, the pattern of economic recovery was clearly forecast by the change in policy at the Federal Reserve. As has been so carefully noted, such massive injections of reserves will bring down interest rates for a period of time but must in due course, unless reversed, result in renewed inflation. The only question in dispute is when such an inflationary cycle will start again.

The monetarist position was, to a large extent, followed from the time of Reagan's election until summer 1982. Sprinkel had wanted the Fed to reduce the growth in monetary aggregates to reduce the growth in the money supply. To do that, he wanted the Fed to stop trying to keep the federal funds rate within a predetermined range. He also wanted a flexible discount rate policy that would allow for fluctuations in the Fed's discount rate. We saw, however, that this was not the President's wish in July 1983, when he urged the Fed to maintain the rate at 8.5 percent. In addition, Sprinkel wanted the Fed to calculate reserves on a day-to-day basis — rather than with a two-week time lag for execution. He wanted the Fed to halt its focus on M1-B and focus instead on the adjusted monetary basis (bank reserves plus currency in circulation). It is true that ever since October 1979 the Fed has allowed wider limits for the funds rate. By March 1981 it could move as much as 4 percentage points, whereas before it was confined to as narrow as 0.25 percentage points.

Nevertheless, as has been pointed out, it is clear that the Fed— through its system of buying and selling securities on a daily basis — is still fighting to maintain the level of interest rates rather than controlling the growth in the money supply. Certainly, this has been true since August 1982. In 1980, supposedly at the height of the Fed's tight-money policy but in an election year, the federal funds rate had been on a real roller coaster path. Between February and May the rate shot up from less than 13 percent to over 19 and fell to 9 percent in June after the President pointed out to Chairman Volcker that unless there was substantial growth in the economy by September, his chances for reelection would decline sharply. By December 1980, after the election, the rate shot back up to 20 percent. In 1984, the same pressure will be put on the Fed to increase the money supply. If the economic recovery, which began in 1982, shows signs of slowing down, there will be a good deal of pressure on the Fed to loosen the money supply to stimulate the recovery again.

After the 1982/83 increase in reserves, however, it would have seemed better politics, as well as better economics, to let the federal funds rate rise moderately. Bank economists such as Leif Olsen of Citicorp and Norman Robertson of Mellon Bank think that rates will go up but that if they do, there is enough momentum in the economy so that the recovery will be only slightly slowed but not halted. Olsen notes that in May 1983 personal income alone grew by 1.2 percent. If income rises, rates become less important. But housing starts are bound to slow down appreciably if mortgage rates continue to rise during the balance of 1984. In part, they did *not* rise more in 1984 because the adjustable rate mortgage (ARM) became popular. Mortgage rates are adjusted by the lending institutions, generally after a year's grace, to conform to actual rates. This is a very dangerous idea as house buyers are led to believe interest rates will go down when the opposite may well be true. Jerry Jordan, former member of the Reagan Council of Economic Advisors, notes, however, that with interest rates on mortgages and other loans *tax deductible* in the United States, high interest rates are less a factor than is the case in Canada, for example, where one cannot deduct interest on a mortgage on one's home. The deductibility of interest, to the extent it is allowed in the United States, is one of the reasons why interest rates are apt to rise again. Although Congress might well allow deduction for interest payable on one home and one car, its current deductibility policy would suggest encouragement for consumer borrowing and higher interest rates.

A rise in the federal funds rate would encourage banks to borrow elsewhere, presumably through the sale of Treasury bills or CDs. Eventually, this would result in lower prices and higher interest rates for Treasury bills and CDs.

BANKS AND NEGOTIABLE CDs

The role of negotiable CDs has become a very important one for banks and may become more so in the future. As was noted earlier, banks lost deposits because—under the Fed's Regulation Q—they were limited in what they could pay to depositors. This was one more attempt on the part of the Federal Reserve to control interest rates—this time through the control of what banks could pay for money. As a result of the Fed's policy, and with the rise in inflation in the late 1970s, the public began to withdraw its money from banks to invest in money-market funds sponsored by brokers and investment bankers who had set out to give investors the same advantages of instant cash when needed and true checking accounts while earning a much higher return than could be obtained through a bank deposit (or an investment in Treasury bills). The idea grew like wildfire until money-market funds had reached over $200 billion and forced the Fed and Congress to come to the aid of the depository institutions in 1982 — first in favor of the thrifts, many of which were facing bankruptcy, and then the banks — by allowing new accounts (NOWs [negotiable order of withdrawal] and super-NOWs), which could pay increased rates of interest to depositors. In the meantime the banks had to replace their lost deposits by selling their short-term CDs to the money-market funds. The money-market funds spent approximately 40 percent of their reserves by purchasing the bank CDs. Negotiable CDs have thus enabled the banks to expand their loan volume despite the Fed's attempts to tighten credit.

Negotiable CDs started in 1961 in very large denominations, and the idea grew over the years. In 1969 the Fed imposed a rate ceiling on what the banks could pay on their CDs, but this simply encouraged the banks to bring back the deposits they had in the Eurodollar market in London. The Fed then removed the rate ceiling in 1973. In the last quarter of 1980, and the first quarter of 1981 when money was very tight, the banks used CDs to raise additional funds and thereby meet their loan commitments despite the Fed's tight-money policy. It is interesting that CDs show up as time deposits on bank balance sheets, enhancing the banks' deposit pictures favorably.

In the future we may well see the banks purchasing the funds they need just as other financial services institutions do. As competition continues to increase among financial intermediaries, it is quite possible that brokerage houses, such as Merrill Lynch who deal with individual investors constantly, may find themselves increasingly packaging investments for the benefit of the depository institutions — the banks and the thrifts — who are better at making, respectively, commercial loans and real estate mortgage transactions than they have proven to be at encouraging deposits. The Fed has hurt the depository institutions by its policies in two ways: by limiting through Regulation Q what banks can pay their depositors;* and by limiting the services depository institu-

---

*In all fairness, it must be admitted that this policy was set by Congress. Nevertheless, many will argue that the Federal Reserve might have anticipated the problems inflation would cause the banks and made adjustments accordingly in their policies.

tions can render their depositors. The latter, of course, was done not so much because of Federal Reserve regulations but because of those limitations imposed on banks and bank holding companies under the Glass-Steagall Act and the Bank Holding Company Act, as amended.

The mandate of Congress to the Federal Reserve Board and other federal agencies regulating depository institutions has been a severe one. In Chapter 5 we will examine in detail the mandate of Congress to the regulators and the changes gradually taking place in the regulation of depository institutions.

WHAT CONSTITUTES MONEY OR CREDIT TODAY

The question, What constitutes money or credit? is becoming an increasingly perplexing one even to the Federal Reserve Board. We have seen an explosion in the last 20 years of new methods of extending credit such as leasing programs, the rapid growth in installment sales, and the credit card programs established by banks to supplement the old standby cards of American Express and Diners Club. There is now no way that the Fed can know the volume of credit extended at any one time as a result of these new methods, which are not included in any of the Federal Reserve M's and yet constitute the issuance of "money" since these instruments are clearly a form of credit that is just as effective as money and accepted as the equivalent of money in the country's commercial transactions. More confusing yet, since 1980 we have a new proliferation of special accounts: NOW accounts, super-NOW accounts, individual retirement accounts (IRAs), and so on. Should NOW accounts, for example, be included in the Federal Reserve's definition of M1-B? They are included, but the Fed does not take into account seasonal factors, as it does for other components of M1-B: currency in circulation and all money in checking accounts.

Given all these recent changes in the character of money and credit, what measure is the Federal Reserve to use in deciding on the trends of money supply growth? In 1983 the Fed indicated in one of its releases that M1-B was headed in one direction, whereas M-2 and M-3 were headed in the opposite direction. The Federal Reserve Board itself says that the public should no longer pay a great deal of attention to weekly reports on the growth or decline of the money supply as indicated by M1-B movements. In reading the various pronouncements of Federal Reserve officials and others regarding the significance of the various M reports released by the Fed, one is reluctantly led to believe that the effect of new sources of money and credit have either so confused the situation that our officials do not really trust what the figures say or that there is a desire to confuse the public further as to what the figures mean so that they will not be able to draw any conclusions as to the meaning of the rapid increase in the money supply, no matter which M is used. Increases in the money supply at the cadence of the 12-month period between August 1, 1982, and August 1, 1983, can only be expected to increase the public's expectations of renewed inflation at some time in the future. The only question is when. Necessarily, increases in the money supply at an annual rate of 13 to 14 percent must produce a new inflationary cycle at a later date.

Here again, our most prominent economists are not in agreement. James Tobin, professor of economics at Yale and Nobel Prize winner, finds that inflation cannot come back so long as the economy is operating at 20 percent below capacity. But this is true in part only, because certain basic industries such as steel and automobile manufacture require a vast capital investment to be made to become competitive again, given the wage-scale burden they carry competing against foreign competition. Rudy Oswald, director of economic research for the AFL-CIO (American Federation of Labor and Congress of Industrial Organizations), finds that any return to a tight-money policy would make inflation worse because high interest rates will increase financing charges, inventory costs, and production costs, which are all passed on to the consumer. His answer: Monetary policy should be geared to encourage higher productivity; cost-cutting technology cannot be introduced if financing costs are high as a result of high interest rates. Gar Alperovitz, codirector of the National Center for Economic Alternatives, a research group, claims that steel companies have had to hire more workers because they cannot afford to install modern machinery due to financing costs. Pressures are obviously exercised, as noted before, both ways.

The division of economic thinking continues to be split between the monetarist and other conservative thinkers, who maintain the importance of continuing to reduce the growth in the money supply, and the labor and liberal economists of the Left, who see the necessity of reducing interest rates as the main effort required of monetary policy. As stated earlier, the Reagan administration, faced with an election in 1984, often appeared to be very concerned with high interest rates, echoing the sentiments of the Democratic leaders of the House although President Reagan himself carefully refrained from attacking the Fed's policies. It is difficult for Chairman Paul Volcker and other members of the Board of Governors of the Fed not to be responsive to pressure from both the administration and the majority party in the House. This put the Republicans in the Congress in a difficult position, and they reflect the split in ideological views within their party.

THE INTEREST-RATE FACTOR

What of interest rates? Should the Fed return to its pre-1979 policy, assuming for the sake of argument that such policy was in fact changed to some degree after October 1979 and at least until August 1982? As we have shown, the change of policy in October 1979 was more a change of method than a real change in policy, regardless of what was said at the time. The Federal Reserve officials in New York who are in charge of implementing the Open Market Committee's targets have not changed their viewpoint or their method of operation. They are still targeting interest rates, although this method of control of monetary policy has not worked out well in the past. As has been said, the result of Federal Reserve policy has been a roller coaster of interest rates since 1979. We will examine just why this has happened because it seems likely to continue so long as Fed policy remains in the future what it has been in the 1979–84 period.

The Federal Reserve cannot and will not be able to control interest rates and keep them constant, no matter how much Congress would wish it to do so. The Fed can, however, as we shall see, keep the swings very much more in line than has been the case during the last few years. Interest-rate movements are an integral part of the control mechanism that allows for a certain amount of play in the economic system. Left to market forces, these swings will reduce the size of booms and the depth and length of time of recessionary periods. It would seem, in fact, that almost any policy would be better than the interest swings we have had since 1979:

- Between the announcement in October 1979 of the Fed's change in monetary policy and the end of the month, the Fed funds rate went from 12 to 16 percent.
- In 1980, the federal funds rate went from less than 14 percent at the beginning of the year to over 19 percent in May to 9 percent in June then up to 20 percent in December.

- The Monetary Control Act of 1980 was adopted by the Congress. Its passage meant the gradual elimination of Regulation Q, which set the price banks can pay for their deposits. This was a great step forward, but its full effect was not being registered until 1984.
- In 1981 the rate peaked again in July at 20 percent, went down to 15.5 percent in August, and moved downward again for the balance of the year. The Fed's excessive efforts to slow the interest-rate decline in early 1981 by denying reserves to the banks caused the economy to decline sharply in 1981 and 1982. This was a typical case where the Fed, in order to limit the swings in interest rates as well as slow down the increase in the money supply, brought about a recession longer and deeper than need have been.
- In 1982, as the recession really hit the economy, the federal funds rate went down again.
- In 1983 the federal funds rate was still down. In July 1983 it was around 9 percent.
- By July 1983 economic forecastings were ambivalent about the trend in interest rates. Robert J. Egypt, a consultant in Sedona, Arizona, sounded out 41 forecasters in a survey and reported that the consensus indicated that interest rates would remain steady, although there was an unusually wide range of individual forecasts. As noted earlier, business economists in 1983 and 1984 had generally, on balance, the impression that interest rates would trend downward and their business clients therefore often tended to postpone borrowing for capital expenditure programs.

It is clear that as the money supply is increased, interest rates have an immediate tendency to go down. But, as noted by Governor Henry Wallich of the Federal Reserve Board, "a reduction in interest rates achieved by a sustained acceleration of money growth eventually has to be paid for by higher inflation."[3] How long a period of time is meant by "sustained"? As of August 1983 the sharp increase in the money supply had been occurring for approximately one year at an annual rate of almost 14 percent. It is hard to see how Governor Wallich's prediction could fail to come true sometime in 1984 or 1985 unless the Fed should have decided to return to a tight-money policy—thus incurring the displeasure of the administration, Congress, and heads of state from abroad since the effect must surely be to bring about an increase in interest rates. Would Paul Volcker have the courage to reverse course under these circumstances, particularly when 1984 was an election year? A study of the actions of past chairmen of the Federal Reserve, as well as his own in 1980, would indicate that such action would not take place.

It is much more probable that even if the increase in the money supply is slowed, money growth will continue to be substantial and will have the effect of fueling the boom more rapidly than it should and carrying the boom for a much longer period than expected—but with a return to inflation as demand for credit continues to increase with the growth in the economy. The Fed has no direct control over the demand for credit, which increases with an economic recovery. The events of April 1980, when Chairman Volcker suddenly announced that the Fed was going to limit the use of such credit instruments as credit cards, brought an immediate sharp reduction in consumer buying and a just-as-immediate significant one-month drop in interest rates. This experience has not been repeated since, but it does indicate that the Fed has power here that it has never before or since used.

While the Fed cannot control the demand for credit, it can clearly control the supply of credit. It does so, as we have seen, merely by changing the amount of the banks' excess reserves (over what the banks are required to hold at the Fed) through purchases or sales of government securities in open market transactions. When banks have excess reserves because the Fed has been buying government securities on balance, they step up their lending, thereby increasing the supply of credit (as well as the money supply). When banks' excess reserves decline because the Fed has been selling government securities on balance, they naturally cut their lending.

One last important point needs to be made about Federal Reserve policy and the rise or fall of interest rates: the question of inflationary expectations, which in summer 1983 was playing an important role in interest rates charged by the banks. One of the most frustrating phenomena that year was the failure of real interest rates to decline further. *Real interest* can be defined as the interest rate adjusted for the rate of inflation. By summer 1983 inflation was down to an annual rate of about 4 percent, yet interest rates charged by the banks varied between 12 and 16 percent, even though their cost of money at the discount window was only 8.5 percent and the federal funds rate about 9 percent. The reason why interest rates stayed high is important: it was the bankers' interpretation of Governor Wallich's statement about the effect of a sustained increase in the money supply that produced their consequent expectation of a return of inflation. For many years (during the period of high inflation) real interest rates were negative. It is not unexpected to find banks—despite the fact that they are in competition with one another—trying to rebuild an earnings position seriously weakened by years of inflation and risky lending both here and abroad.

The factor of inflationary expectations for the future clearly plays an important role in interest rates. It is unfortunate that in the United States as soon as a problem is thought to have been temporarily solved, it is dismissed as a problem and replaced in the public's mind by another. In 1981 the fear of continued rising inflation preoccupied the public most. As soon as inflation declined, the public, encouraged by the media, found the problem of unemployment of much greater concern than the fear of renewed inflation. Economic recovery at any cost became the concern of the day by 1982, and government, the media, and the public alike appeared to be convinced that inflation would not return no matter how continuous and sustained an increase in the money supply generated by the Federal Reserve Board. Regardless of the consequences, the administration, Congress, and foreign officials pressured for reduction in interest rates. Under these circumstances it is not surprising to find members of the Federal Reserve Board saying one thing in warning about renewed inflation and yet doing what is sure to rekindle inflation, that is, a continuous rapid growth in the money supply.

In Chapter 2 we commented on how often in the past this has been true: the chairman of the Federal Reserve Board warning the administration and Congress of the probability of an increase in inflation unless budget deficits were met through tax increases and yet adjusting monetary policy to increase the money supply, which was the one sure way of bringing about increased inflation. William McChesney Martin did this during the Johnson administration in 1967 because President Lyndon Johnson did not want to raise taxes to pay for an unpopular war in Vietnam. Arthur Burns, in particular, repeatedly warned Congress of the perils of inflation while continuously stoking the fires of inflation almost from the time he became chairman in October 1969 until he failed to secure reappointment in 1978. When President Richard Nixon first came into office in 1968, he was determined to return to what he called the sound monetary policy of the Eisenhower years, yet he requested Chairman Burns to loosen credit in March 1970 to avoid possible bankruptcies of certain overextended industrial firms such as Lockheed and the Penn Central Railroad. Subsequently, Burns increased the money supply again in 1972 to aid Nixon's reelection chances and once again in 1976 to assist the election campaign of President Gerald Ford. Again, under a different President, Jimmy Carter, and a different chairman, Paul Volcker, the Federal Reserve Board, in the six months prior to the 1980 presidential election, added considerably to the money supply.

This does not auger well for 1984. It has seemed quite evident—if the past behavior of the Federal Reserve Board is any indication—that monetary policy in 1984 would be based principally upon one criterion: the maintenance of economic recovery through steady or declining interest rates regardless of how much an increase in bank reserves—and hence an increase in the money supply—this effort might take.

If government officials did not understand before 1982 how short a memory the public has about the ravages of inflation, the reaction of the public to disinflation in 1982/83 should clearly convince them that in today's economic environment voters are less unhappy with inflation than with recession, which is a necessary consequence of the correction of inflation. The middle class, the elderly, the poor, and the young are the losers in an inflationary environment, but they, curiously enough, do not seem to be fully aware of it. Increase the paycheck, Social Security and Medicare, college tuition grants, and social programs, because these balance the effects of inflation but keep the economy growing with low interest rates, regardless of the inflationary effect of the monetary policy required to accomplish this. Why should this not in fact be a satisfactory monetary policy? Unfortunately, as was shown in 1981/82, the boom eventually must subside, but then if the excesses have been too great, the recession comes without a decline in real interest rates.

This is what has happened in the United States in this last recession. The BIS analysis of real hard yields in the United States has indicated: an average of 7.5 percent during 1983; 8.5 percent in 1982; 3.2 percent in 1981; and a negative net return of 1.5 percent in 1980. Over the prior decade from 1972 to 1983 real bond yields in the United States averaged 2.7 percent. By 1983 the real bond yield in the United States was much higher than rates in other industrialized countries. This is one of the principal reasons why foreign funds are attracted to the U.S. bond market and why foreign government leaders and economists keep urging the United States to reduce its budgetary deficit and bring interest rates down.

THE EFFECT OF BUDGETARY DEFICITS

This brings us to an examination of an increasingly important question: To what extent should we be concerned that our continued high federal budgetary deficits (1) will bring about a renewal of inflation, (2) preempt American savings so that funds will neither be available to meet consumer needs for money or for business borrowings for plant and equipment or to rebuild depleted inventories, or (3) cause interest rates to rise again? Many economists, both here and abroad, have urged that the administration and Congress address this question with the utmost urgency.

The President, however, has often indicated that he is opposed to increasing taxes further, estimating that the government is already taking too large a proportion of gross national product (GNP) in taxes. Nevertheless, he is also opposed to any reduction in military expenditures. Congress, on the other hand, is opposed to any further cuts in expenditures for social programs. In the meantime, the costs just of federal support programs for health care keep growing at a rate of almost 20 percent annually with no end in sight for such percentage annual increases in expenditures. While the economic recovery, if sustained, will enable the government to collect much more in income taxes than annually forecast, nevertheless, the country faces $150 to $200 billion deficits for many years unless either taxes are increased or social or military programs are readjusted downward. The President's proposal of transferring most responsibilities to the states for various social programs has raised such an uproar from the states, Congress, and the federal bureaucracy that it has been quietly shelved. So the problem is likely to continue.

What are the consequences of these continued deficits? Here again, we run across a variety of different opinions. At one end are those who see no negative consequences to continued budget deficits. At the other end are those who say that if the deficits continue, the economic recovery must eventually be aborted; interest rates will then rise sky-high; and we will find ourselves again in recession with declining tax revenues, thereby increasing the deficits even further. This must end in a return to inflation. This would result in a massive stagflation scenario with a declining economy accompanied by rising prices. Where does the truth lie? When might such a scenario occur? As early as 1985 or 1986?

Since this is a book about the Federal Reserve Board, its policies, and its powers, let us start with the Fed's point of view, so frequently expressed in Chairman Volcker's testimony before the Congress. It is Volcker's thesis that monetary policy can accomplish much but that the budgetary deficits require solutions other than dependence on monetary policy. The problem must be handled through a reduction in the deficits—either by fiscal policy, that is, raising taxes, or by a reduction in expenditures.

Volcker has repeatedly warned about what he calls the "crowding out" process. That is, the annual rate of savings, although growing in the United States, is still only so much, and the federal government of necessity has a priority on savings because its credit is better than any individual's or corporation's; therefore, if the Treasury is willing to pay the market price for money, it will always find it, whereas other borrowers will have to wait. If the Treasury's demands for money continue to rise, there is no way that private savings can supply its needs without crowding out taking place. This phenomenon threatens to jeopardize the economic recovery because the flow of savings is insufficient to supply consumers and business after the government has taken care of its needs. Furthermore, with the demand for credit—what it must be in the light of government's need to borrow—there is no way that interest rates can come down further or that monetary policy can ensure that they will come down. Governor Henry Wallich says it this way:

> Reducing the deficit will make a large contribution toward reducing real interest rates as the government's demands on the national supply of saving diminishes. . . . It is fiscal policy, not monetary policy, that can lastingly change real interest rates.[4]

Federal Reserve officials also frequently make the point that the large budgetary deficits of the 1981–84 period necessarily "nourish the fear of inflation." But is this argument sound? It appears only to be valid if the Federal Reserve decides to monetize the federal debt, not otherwise. Budget deficits will not create inflation unless the Federal Reserve decides to monetize the debt by buying government securities. As was mentioned earlier, when the French government was faced with a similar runaway deficit situation and an economy in difficulty, General Charles de Gaulle's economic adviser, Jacques Rueff, notified the Bank of France not to purchase any more government securities in order to halt the inflation and force the ministries to lower their budgets. The result was a decline in budgetary expenditures of 30 percent the next year and 10 percent the following—strong medicine, but certainly within the power of the Federal Reserve Board to do if it is truly independent and not just pretending to be.

In an earlier day in the United States, the attitudes of the Board, the administration, and Congress were all quite different. In 1951 President Harry Truman was fearful that if the Federal Reserve were pressured into monetizing the federal debt—which was growing because of the Korean War's financial burden on the government—the prime rate would rise from 1⅞ percent to 2¼ percent and this would bring about a recession. The result of Truman's concern was a compact—insisted upon by the President—between Secretary of the Treasury Murray Snyder and Chairman Thomas McCabe of the Federal Reserve Board under the terms of which the Treasury Department recognized the independence of the Federal Reserve Board and the policy of the Board not to monetize the Federal debt. As a result of this courageous action by President Truman, and by the Federal Reserve observing his mandate, the Korean War did not result in a recession and only in temporary inflation. The Federal Reserve wanted to let interest rates rise. There was a temporary period of inflation, but the Fed adopted two regulations —Regulation W and Regulation X—to bring the inflation under control. It succeeded. However, the Fed did not use this type of regulatory credit control again until spring 1980. In that year the same medicine worked again. President Carter, unlike President Truman, called it off.* There were lengthy hearings on the whole subject held by a subcommittee of the House Banking Committee,[5] which might be read today with profit by members of the administration, Congress, and the Federal Reserve Board. The Federal Reserve Board and the Treasury Department and the Congress came then to the correct manner in which federal expenditures should be financed in a crisis period. In subsequent years, all three parties have failed to recognize the clear national priority of lowering interest rates while avoiding inflation. There is no more reason to monetize the federal debt in the 1980s than there was in 1951, when at least justification could be found in the fact that the country was at war.

In other countries the same problem of high budgetary deficits has been faced. We spoke of France in 1958/59. In Japan there have been recurrent large budgetary deficits during the 1980–83 period, yet interest rates have been about 8 percent and the inflation rate has been very low. The debt has not been monetized by the central bank. Of course, in Japan the rate of savings is very much higher than in the United States. Industrial production is maintained, despite a comparatively much lower rate of domestic consumption because the share of production for exports is so much higher than in the United States. The same policy is followed in Germany where the inflation rate and interest rates are both low, 40 percent of manufactured goods are exported, and domestic consumption is not stimulated by adding to the money supply through operations of the central bank. Perhaps the situation in Ger-

---

*Regulation W placed controls on mortgages; Regulation X restricted installment credit. Credit controls will work in the United States as they have elsewhere. The Federal Reserve has, however, only used credit controls in these two instances. Effective action takes combined presidential and Federal Reserve courage. Where is it today?

many is affected by the fact that twice within the last 60 years — in 1923 and again in 1932 — the middle class was almost wiped out because of hyperinflation.

Toward the end of the Carter administration, the U.S. policy of maintaining a weak dollar to stimulate exports was abandoned. A poor policy that only increased domestic inflation, it was revised in November 1978. Thereafter, Paul Volcker was appointed chairman of the Federal Reserve and adopted a tight-money policy in 1979. As a result of this Federal Reserve tight-money policy, interest rates tended to rise, and this attracted a strong flow of foreign savings into the United States. The formerly weak dollar became an increasingly strong dollar during the Reagan administration. While this made it difficult for exports, and the U.S. trade balance faced increased annual deficits each year, nevertheless, the trade deficit was balanced by capital inflows, so that the U.S. balance of payments remained positive and the inflow of money from abroad made it unnecessary for the Federal Reserve to monetize the debt. This has been true throughout President Reagan's first term. As President Mitterand of France correctly perceives the situation: the huge deficits of the U.S. government are being financed through the purchase of U.S. treasury securities by savings from other countries flowing into the United States, attracted by high interest rates and the strong dollar.

There has, therefore, been no reason for the Federal Reserve to monetize the federal debt. The deficit issue, as far as monetary policy is concerned, is what is referred to in Washington as a "red herring," an issue that Federal Reserve officials like to raise with the administration and Congress as though it *necessitated* unsound Federal Reserve monetary policy. As has been indicated, the budget deficits do not and need not require the Federal Reserve to monetize the debt. It cannot serve as justification for the Federal Reserve's actions to increase bank reserves, and hence the money supply, by buying Treasury securities. It certainly is true that the constant increase in the federal debt is unhealthy because we are passing on to our children and grandchildren the necessity of repayment as well as the cost of servicing this huge debt; nevertheless, neither the debt nor the budgetary deficits have anything to do with maintaining some sound monetary policy.

Expanding budgetary deficits create a demand for credit; therefore, they tend to raise interest rates. In asking the Fed to reduce interest rates while expanding the budgetary deficits, Congress should be aware that it is asking the impossible. Nevertheless, if the supply of money is kept from expanding rapidly through the Federal Reserve's refusal to monetize the growing federal deficits, there will be an increase in interest rates and a slowing of the economy, but inflation will remain under control. So long as the dollar remains strong and foreign savings continue to flow into the United States, these savings from abroad might even keep U.S. interest rates within bounds for a time despite federal deficits.

The ultimate answer to U.S. exports, which are being sacrificed to the current strong dollar and high interest rates, should in time be found in the renewed competitiveness of U.S. industry. With the value of the dollar high and, consequently, imported manufactured goods very competitive in U.S. markets, U.S. manufacturers must first regain their competitiveness at home. Then they will, once again, become competitive abroad. This is exactly the lesson the U.S. auto manufacturers have so painfully learned since 1978 and why in 1982–84 they are investing massive amounts of capital into restructuring their methods of manufacture. The adjustment is a very painful one because it requires difficult shifts in employment. With time, however, the restructuring of American industry will create a much stronger U.S. economy.

THE VELOCITY OF MONEY

This brings us to a discussion of the last important facet of our analysis of monetary policy as practiced by the Federal Reserve Board: the effect of the velocity of money on monetary policy.

The *velocity* of money can be defined as the number of times in the course of a year that the money supply is spent and respent. Economists can monitor this turnover-of-money rate by simply dividing the GNP by the money supply, using as the denominator any one of the *M's* the economist wishes to use. Since World War II the velocity of money has on average increased by approximately 3 percent per year. This is probably due to the development of more efficient monetary exchange mechanisms—the use of credit cards, for example—as well as to understandable efforts to hold down financial assets and buy tangibles in a period of worldwide inflation. What is surprising is that there has been no greater bidding up of assets as the value of keeping money and other financial assets has continued to decline. The oil industry mergers are, of course, one prime example of asset speculation involving the expenditure of billions of dollars without creating any increase in assets, productivity, or national wealth.*

---

*These oil mergers, financed by the banks, are but one more indication that money in the United States is ceasing to be a store of value. There is much to ponder here for our future.

A few years ago I remember trying to answer the question of a young couple from Iowa who explained to me that they had been told by both sets of parents never to borrow and to save regularly what they could. Their friends had all borrowed to the hilt and were deeply involved in tax shelters and real estate speculation. As a result they were becoming wealthier, whereas this couple earned nothing in real terms on their savings. What should they now do, they asked? It was a difficult question to answer when the period of excess had already been going on for so long. I wondered whether it was better to agree that we had indeed become a nation of borrowers rather than savers or to reassure them that their parents had been right and that sooner or later the savers would prove to be correct. I told them to continue to save as disinflation must necessarily follow an inflationary cycle. The major problem, of course, is that the government itself is the biggest beneficiary of inflation through the ratcheting effect of shifts into higher tax brackets brought about by increases in nominal income for individuals; similarly, income taxes increase for businesses because of inadequate replacement cost allowances on inventories and inadequate depreciation allowed on plant and equipment

Generally, during periods of economic growth, the velocity of money increases more than normally, whereas in a period of recession, the velocity of money declines as people buy less and, hence, the turnover shrinks. The rationale is simple. When the economy is headed toward a boom, public confidence increases and people spend more. At the onset of recession, conversely, velocity slows as the public rebuilds its financial assets, and the value of the currency strengthens, until confidence returns and people start buying goods again. Similarly, capital expenditures by businesses are tied to the business cycle, with expenditures increasing as economic recovery begins and, conversely, declining substantially at the end of the boom. How does the monetary policy of the Federal Reserve adjust to the changes in the velocity of money?

Changes in the velocity of money are linked to changes in the money supply and changes in interest rates. This means that Federal Reserve monetary policy should take into account changes in the velocity of money. Gordon Ackley intimated that velocity varies as changes in interest rates occur. Changes in velocity also occur unsystematically with new kinds of financial instruments and new kinds of accounts such as NOW accounts and money-market funds. It is these unsystematic movements that make the task of taking into account the velocity of money so difficult for the Fed in adjusting its monetary policy. This is why some economists claim that monetarism will not work. The monetarists believe in a steady, targeted, and small annual growth in the money supply. But the velocity of money that affects the demand for credit from the banking system is never stable, since it varies both systematically as interest rates vary and unsystematically as the mechanisms of money and credit evolve and take new forms.

Some economists say that monetarism cannot work because the Fed must manage the growth of the money supply in such a way as to offset consciously changes in velocity, whether systematic or irregular. For example, as Ackley points out, since velocity is speeded up by a rise in interest rates and rises in interest rates increase the demand for credit that occurs as an economic recovery matures in the form of a boom, the Federal Reserve's monetary policy should take this into account and adjust monetary growth downward earlier in a recovery period. Conversely, as the boom falters, the velocity of money will slow as interest rates decline, and monetary policy should earlier adjust the growth in the money supply upward. As we noted in Chapter 2, for example, the Great Depression was made deeper by the Federal Reserve's insistence on a tight-money policy as the economic depression began.

Despite this horrible example of mistaken policy, what happened in 1981? The tight-money policy was maintained long enough to ensure a major recession in 1981/82. The downturn in interest rates in mid-1981 was accompanied by a reduction in the velocity of money, indicating that the Fed's monetary policy should have been adjusted accordingly and that reserves should have been made available to the banks to increase the money supply in spring 1982 rather than late summer. It would appear that in 1983, in a period of economic recovery, the Fed again misjudged its timing because of a failure to take into account changes in the velocity of money.

The 1983 economic recovery, however, has posed an unusual problem (1) because interest rates have been steady and have not increased and (2) because an increase in velocity has been unusually slow in coming. What the monetarists fear is that there will be a sharp increase in the velocity of money sometime in due course and that this will accelerate the recovery into a boom with a substantial increase in demand for credit and sharply higher interest rates. Since this will have happened after a prolonged period of increase in the money supply by the Fed, it will mean a return of inflation much more rapidly than anticipated (and presumably at a much higher rate). The Fed is trying to avoid this by keeping increases in the money supply as low as possible without bringing about an end to the economic recovery. It is obvious, therefore, that an increase in velocity means an increase in inflationary pressures, whereas a slowdown in velocity tends to ease inflationary pressures. In both instances it would appear advisable for the Federal Reserve Board to take into account changes in the velocity of money in adjusting the monetary policy. If it does not, it will be several months too late in responding to changes in economic conditions and will once again exaggerate the economic cycles through its monetary policy adjustments made at the wrong time. Only if velocity does not increase quickly in the economic recovery of 1983/84 will the Federal Reserve Board's monetary policy of sustained increases in bank reserves from mid-1982 to mid-1983 have been proven correct. This would be contrary to the long-term trend of increases in the velocity of money since World War II. In 1984, the velocity of money has tended to increase substantially as consumer purchases have risen dramatically.

CONCLUSION

The Federal Reserve Board, as manager of the central bank function of the U.S. government, is wholly responsible for the country's monetary policy.

In this chapter I have analyzed the function of monetary policy in the United States, how the Federal Reserve has operated in its control of monetary policy, whether or not it has been effective, what pressures it has had to contend with from the executive and legislative branches of government, and what changes in economic conditions have occurred that have affected the Federal Reserve's role in monetary policy. Before passing to some conclusions regarding the analysis made, it might be helpful to summarize briefly what the record of Federal Reserve management of monetary policy shows.

The analysis may be divided into a number of different topics:

1. The formation of monetary policy;
2. The methods or tools available to the Federal Reserve in controlling monetary policy;
3. The federal funds rate and the role it has played in control of interest rates by the Federal Reserve;
4. The role played by the Open Market Committee and the implementation of its monetary policies by the staff of the Federal Reserve Bank of New York;
5. Changes sought by the administration of President Reagan in the Federal Reserve's monetary policy through the influence of monetarist philosophies in the Treasury Department as well as contrary

pressures from the Democratic leadership in the House of Representatives;

6. Attempts made by the banks to get around the monetary policies of the Federal Reserve through negotiable CDs in order to replace deposits lost to new institutions created by the securities brokerage industry;

7. The difficulty for the Federal Reserve Board to determine what constitutes money and credit in view of new types of accounts created and new methods, such as credit cards, of creating credit and money equivalents;

8. The interest-rate factor and the role it has played in monetary policy even after the changes in policy and methods adopted by the Federal Reserve Board in October 1979;

9. The effect of large budgetary deficits prevalent since the fiscal year ended September 30, 1981 (and expected to continue through the mid-1980s at least), on the monetary policies of the Federal Reserve Board; and

10. The effect of the velocity of money on monetary policy and the extent to which the Board takes this factor into account.

This analysis is essential in order to determine how the Federal Reserve Board has handled its mandate from Congress and successive administrations in the conduct of monetary policy. What does the record show?

For whatever reasons, the conclusion has to be that the U.S. economy has continued to move in cycles from recession to boom to renewed recession; that interest rates have been exceedingly volatile, particularly in 1980 and 1981; that the 1979–82 tight-money policy has yielded to a sharp increase in reserves made available to banks and in the money supply during the mid-1982 to mid-1983 period; that inflation was increasingly severe from 1979 through 1981 and only declined when the country was plunged into a severe recession in 1981/82 — in brief, that monetary policy has been singularly ineffective in maintaining stability for any length of time. Since 1983 the Federal Reserve has been exercising great care to maintain the economic recovery without letting interest rates decline so rapidly as to produce a boom or bring back a new inflationary cycle. It is unlikely that interest rates can decline under such a policy.

The analysis shows that the Fed has three basic ways of controlling the reserves available to the banks by which they increase the money supply and the availability of credit: (1) the discount rate, that is, the rate at which the Fed itself advances money to the banks; (2) changes in reserves required to be deposited by the banking system with the Federal Reserve; and (3) the purchase and sale of government securities. This last method is the one most frequently used by the Federal Reserve Board's Open Market Committee, which operates, as was noted, through the Desk officer of the Federal Reserve Bank of New York, acting through recognized bond dealers located in New York.

The Board's method of handling monetary policy was changed in October 1979 from the targeting of interest rates to maintain them as nearly constant as possible to control of the monetary aggregates as recommended for some time by the so-called Shadow Open Market Committee. This committee is made up generally of monetarists (economists who believe that monetary policy should consist solely of a gradual targeted small annual increase in the money supply to accommodate growth of the U.S. economy). Nevertheless, it seems clear that the permanent officials of the Federal Reserve Bank of New York, charged with implementing the policies of the Open Market Committee, have continued to use interest rates as targets through their historic method of operation rather than by controlling the growth of the money supply. It also seems clear that Federal Reserve monetary policy changed abruptly in August 1982 to make reserves once again freely available to the banking system. Was the Fed influenced because of its discovery of poor domestic lending practices by some of the larger money-center banks (particularly in buying loans to gas drillers from such small banks as Penn Square Bank in Oklahoma) or because of shaky foreign loans to governments through their foreign branches? Was it concern that many manufacturers faced bankruptcy because of excess nonliquidity in the banking system? It is not clear. What is certain is that from mid-1982 to mid-1983 the money supply increased by almost 14 percent even though the velocity of money did not increase and that while bank reserves were significantly increased, bank lending remained, on the whole, very cautious. It also seems evident that the Fed's tight-money policies were allowed to go on beyond the time when bank reserves should have been increased, probably in spring 1982, thereby undoubtedly deepening the recession. It is similarly likely that the Fed allowed the growth in the money supply to continue for too long a period in 1983, with the result that as the velocity of money finally picked up with the economic recovery in 1983/84, the demand for credit increased considerably. The recovery will turn into a boom, inflation will return, and interest rates will go up again, perhaps even more strongly than in early 1981, given the sustained increase in bank reserves and the money supply.

The factor of money velocity was perplexing in 1983 because with the economic recovery the velocity should have increased by mid-1983 as it had in previous upward turns in the economy. This did not happen, as noted earlier, until 1984. In any event, ever since World War II, on average, there has been a growth in money velocity averaging 3 percent per year. So the trend is distinctly upward. If the money velocity continues to increase, in 1984 and 1985 it will be said that Fed monetary policy will have once again turned out to be tightened too late. The velocity factor also raises serious questions as to the monetarist view, since it does not take into account that money velocity decreases in a recession and increases in a recovery, thereby overaccentuating the downward or upward trend in the economy.

Another factor that has played an important and very negative role in monetary policy has been the efforts of Congress and the Federal Reserve Board to control what banks can pay for money. Regulation Q (the control over the interest rate that banks can pay on deposits) was finally phased out by the Monetary Control Act of 1980, but the impact has been only gradual. It was also noted how the Federal Reserve Board, under Arthur Burns, attempted in 1969 to control how much the banks could pay in interest on their CDs. This forced the banks to bring back dollars from their overseas branches in lieu of issuing CDs. The regulation was finally rescinded in 1973. But as a result of congressional and Fed action in restricting what banks could pay to depositors and for CDs, the role of banks and other depository institutions was gradually taken over by innovative securities brokerage and similar financial services companies including big industrial firms such as Sears, General Motors Acceptance Corporation, General Electric Credit Corporation, Merrill Lynch, and Prudential Insurance Company. The competition from these unregulated financial services companies and its meaning to the depository institutions will be examined in greater detail in Chapter 5, which specifically analyzes the role of the Federal Reserve Board as a regulatory agency. The Board, of course, has enormous power here because it is the regulatory agency of government with exclusive jurisdiction over bank holding companies. The fact remains that as a result of these new competitors for the public's savings the competitive position of banks has been changed—and not for the better.

It has been repeated throughout this book how Federal Reserve monetary policy has been responsible for the growth of inflation in the United States. Yet, at the same time, the Fed was preventing the institutions it regulated from paying the kind of interest rates that depositors and savers felt entitled to demand in an economy where the real rate of return was constantly being reduced by the rate of inflation. The banks have paid an undue price in terms of reserve requirements for the privilege of being regulated in such a way that they are both losing their deposits and experiencing difficulty in selling their CDs. It is no wonder that so many of our money-center banking institutions are fleeing Fed reserve requirements through the transfer of funds to their foreign branches and, through such branches, making loans abroad. It is hardly in the interest of the U.S. economy for the Federal Reserve Board to be encouraging even indirectly the transfer of U.S. financial assets abroad and the making of very large loans to foreign governments. To the extent possible, the Fed should be stimulating lending in the United States to American industry, which is in such need of modernization. Will we eventually be required to consider credit allocation to accomplish this? This would be a method used only under unavoidable circumstances.

The new competition from other types of financial services institutions and the new accounts permitted banks to meet this competition have created a situation where it has become increasingly difficult for the Federal Reserve Board to determine what constitutes credit or money equivalents and what accounts or credit instruments should be included in calculating the money supply. The Fed itself has continuously been warning the public not to pay undue attention to its weekly published figures regarding the increase or decrease in M1-B, which consists of what people used to accept in payment for goods and services: currency, demand deposits in commercial banks and other checkable deposits of depository institutions (such as thrifts and credit unions), and travelers' checks, all adjusted on a seasonal basis; also, more recently, the so-called NOW accounts included on a nonadjusted basis. Whether the system used to determine the amount of credit outstanding for reporting purposes should be changed certainly is worthy of the most careful consideration because in the increased competition for the public's savings, it is certain that innovation will continue — particularly if there is a return to the inflationary cycle as a result of the sharp and sustained new increase in the money supply in 1982/83. The role of depository institutions and the regulation of these institutions has certainly become an increasingly important subject for examination by both the executive and the legislative branches of government.*

Successive chairmen of the Federal Reserve Board since 1967 (par-

---

*The necessity of a rescue of the Continental Illinois Bank (the 8th largest in the country) by the federal regulatory agencies in June 1984 indicated that many of the large money-center banks had not been managed as they should have been. Yet the banks are asking for deregulation. Should Congress allow the banks additional powers under these circumstances? The analysis in Chapter 8 would indicate the need for caution.

ticularly Arthur Burns, who was chairman from 1969 to 1978) have continuously warned of the dangers of inflation while repeatedly increasing bank reserves and hence the money supply, which is the mechanism by which inflation is created. In 1967, 1970, 1972, 1976, 1980, and 1982/83, there have been sharp and sustained increases in the money supply, in each case greater than in the preceding instance. In at least three such instances—1972, 1976, and 1980—such increases in the money supply took place in election years, leading one to the conclusion that the chairman of the Federal Reserve Board, who is appointed by the President, can be pressured by the President to use monetary policy to create, in an election year when the person who appointed the chairman is running for office, an economic climate in the country that is positive, regardless of resulting inflationary consequences at a later date. As indicated, the Fed has been trying to avoid such a policy in 1984. There is nothing unusual about this. In a period when economic cycles have tended to be shorter, it is to be expected that a President running for reelection will do everything to ensure that the economy will be healthy at the time the election takes place. The economy grows when interest rates are low; monetary policy can certainly affect interest rates; inflation historically in the United States has never had the effect in the public mind that rising unemployment, for example, has had. The public is constantly made aware of the importance of interest rates to the growth of the economy by the press, by liberal economists, and by influential members of Congress who are themselves running for reelection. Unfortunately, while the immediate effect of increasing bank reserves and the money supply has been to lower interest rates, we have now learned that this ultimately brings about the reverse effect. It eventually increases the demand for credit; and this, in turn, brings about in due course much higher interest rates and the return of inflation. It is, therefore, clear that the Federal Reserve Board chairman, who is appointed by the President but whose mandate and the mandate of his Board come from the Congress, must at all times be acutely aware of the political necessity of keeping interest rates low.

The public cannot grasp money supply figures, particularly with all the current discussions of which M should be used; but all of us understand the importance of interest rates on the loans we need to make, whether auto loans, mortgages, or other consumer borrowings. In a democratic society the voter is very much aware of the cost of money, and the rate of interest has to be an issue that affects the voter.

Under these circumstances, can the Federal Reserve Board pursue a monetary policy that is truly free of political considerations? The record since the mid-1960s certainly does not indicate that the Board has followed an independent course. Quite the contrary. Given the fact that the Federal Reserve Board cannot act independently as it did during the Truman and Eisenhower era, with the blessing of the then administration and the Congress, would it not be better today for the Board of Governors of the Federal Reserve to implement monetary policy as directed by the administration, as is done by central banks in other countries? It is only in this way that elected officials can be held truly accountable for monetary policy and its effect on interest rates and inflation. Today it is too easy for both the administration and Congress to shield themselves from public criticism of the effects of poor monetary policy behind the myth of Federal Reserve independence. The alternative would be to have the President insist, as President Truman did in 1951 during the Korean War, that the Federal Reserve and the Treasury agree to recognize the independence of the Federal Reserve to the extent that the Federal Reserve Board would not be required to monetize the federal budgetary deficits. This, too, would be a wiser solution than our current one because it is the monetization of budget deficits by the Federal Reserve's open market buying of Treasury obligations that creates renewed inflation.

With respect to the effect of budgetary deficits on the monetary policy of the Federal Reserve Board, the analysis shows that while large budgetary deficits for prolonged periods are bad, they need not in any way affect the Fed's monetary policy. It is entirely within the Federal Reserve Board prerogatives to refuse to monetize the deficits by buying Treasury obligations. In 1951 President Truman urged the Federal Reserve Board to avoid doing this because he feared that it would cause interest rates to rise and affect the economy adversely. It appears that the Fed is trying to hold Congress responsible for its own action in 1983/84 in monetizing the debt by buying Treasury obligations by blaming its action on congressional reluctance to lower the federal deficit. The increase in the money supply resulting from the Federal Reserve Board's expansionary monetary policy has nothing to do with the amount of the federal deficits, nor is Paul Volcker's crowding out argument valid so long as interest rates do not go up sharply and the dollar remains strong. Foreign savings flowing to the United States during the Reagan administration's strong dollar policy have indeed, as President Mitterand of France charges, been financing U.S. government deficits.

Finally, the analysis discusses the effect of the velocity of money on the Federal Reserve's monetary policy. The Fed must take money velocity into account in adjusting its monetary policy; otherwise its actions will be taken too late and will accentuate alternate periods of boom and recession. The Board appears to have adjusted its policy of tight money too late in 1982, as in 1930. It may well have made the same mistake in the other direction in 1983. The interest monetary phenomenon of 1983 was that as the economic recovery took hold, the velocity of money did not increase as rapidly as it had in past turnarounds — businessmen and consumers other than home buyers remained cautious despite the recovery and the returns of business and consumer confidence. Does this indicate that the inflationary impact of the last boom has now so frightened the public that it does not want in a period of high budgetary deficits to do anything to bring back inflation? Have we in effect learned a valuable lesson from the terrible inflationary cycle of the late 1970s?

It is unfortunately more likely that the reason why the velocity of money had not increased markedly by the end of 1983 was that the economic recovery of 1982/83 was spotty at best. In the basic industries structural problems persisted and wage rates tended to decline or at least remain steady, whereas prices increased only moderately. In the agricultural sector, prices remained steady and conditions for farmers remained precarious; in deregulated industries such as trucking and the airlines, fierce competition brought about steady or declining wages and cut-rate prices resulting in near bankruptcy of such marginal carriers as Eastern, Continental, and Republic. There were even efforts on the part of labor unions in the air carrier industry to urge Congress to bring back regulation, a sure indication of the value of competition to control both wages and prices. The media, in publishing the difficulties faced in certain basic industries, has made the public much more aware than in past recoveries of the very fragile nature of this upturn in the economy and the necessity of maintaining U.S. competitiveness against imports.

The result has been that inflation by the standards of the 1970s, if not the 1950s, has been relatively low and increasing only very slowly. Pressure on domestic producer prices brought about by the high value of the dollar has also continued to be a major factor in controlling inflation. This, again, represents a change from prior recovery periods. Management will not be disposed to grant wage increases so long as it faces strong competition from imports, and labor is no longer strong enough to force Congress to pass domestic-content legislation in the face of consumer resistance to halt competition, for example, from imported automobiles; the public is well aware today that wage rates in both the steel and automobile industries have played a major role in making U.S. autos (particularly the smaller cars) noncompetitive against Japanese imports which cost $1000 to $1500 less to manufacture. Can the Federal Reserve claim that these events are the result of its monetary policy? The rapid increase in the money supply in 1982/83 did help to bring about the economic recovery and obviously was the key factor in reducing interest rates somewhat. Will this monetary policy eventually, necessarily, bring about increased inflation once again in the future, however, as it always has in the past? This has not happened in 1984, but if the recovery turns into a boom, it is likely to occur in 1985 or 1986.

What prognosis can we make for the future? The past behavior of the Federal Reserve Board in an election year would lead one to believe that in 1984 if the recovery shows any sign of slowing down, monetary policy will again be loosened to bring about an upsurge in consumer buying. This is what happened in 1968, 1972, 1976, and 1980 under various chairmen of the Federal Reserve Board. Will the federal debt be monetized as well? Given the size of the federal deficit for the fiscal year beginning October 1, 1983, it seems obvious that the Federal Reserve will have to increase bank reserves by monetizing the debt if it is to keep interest rates from going up, not down, and avoiding the crowding out process. It is quite possible to finance a $200 billion deficit, increased capital spending by business, and the financing of rising consumer expenditures without a further increase in bank reserves and hence the money supply. But this can only happen if the dollar remains strong, if interest rates remain approximately as they were in early 1984, and savings from abroad continue to flow to the United States. It should be obvious at the same time that the elements of an incipient boom will be in place once again, that the stock market will be uncertain but looking for reassurance until election time, and that inflation will temporarily appear to be under control. The consequences of such a monetary policy will be deferred until 1985, when we would then return, as we did in 1981, to a period of rising interest rates, renewed inflation, and a peak in the boom to be followed once again by a recession. How can such a scenario be avoided?

One way, of course, would be to take the pressure off monetary policy through a combination of reductions in federal expenditures and tax increases to reduce the federal budgetary deficit sharply. This is almost impossible to do in an election year and particularly difficult in 1984 inasmuch as the president has expressed his opposition to tax increases and the Congress will not cut expenditures further. A change in fiscal policy would have the advantage of cutting consumer expenditures, whereas its effect in lowering interest rates would be inclined to stimulate both investments in housing and capital expenditures by business firms.

By stressing monetary rather than fiscal policy the government has consciously or otherwise affected the structure of the economy: it has paid for the decline in inflation through reduced business investments rather than through reduced consumer spending. In the long run this has to be a bad policy because it sacrifices the future for the present. It favors short-term goals over the long-term increase in those assets of the nation—that is, business investment in plant and equipment—that will result in new jobs in the future. This will accomplish exactly the reverse of what the Reagan administration has been trying so hard to accomplish: an increase in business investment. Such an increase in investment is a highly laudable goal essential to the recovery of U.S. productivity and competitiveness. As the economy recovers, it is all the more important that increased savings be encouraged and that they flow into business investment rather than into increased consumer spending. This is the only way to prolong the economic recovery. But to accomplish this, budget deficits would have to be reduced through a change in fiscal policy and much tighter control over government expenditures.

So long as budget deficits continue to remain as high as they will be in fiscal 1983 and 1984, so long as fiscal policy is ignored, and so long as the government continues to rely unfairly on monetary policy to control the economy, how can monetary policy succeed any better in the future than it has in the past? Two suggestions are worthy of mention, coming from economists with very different viewpoints:

> Stable money growth is not the solution when deregulation of the banking and financial sector is changing the nature of money altogether, blurring the distinction between checking accounts and long-term investments.
>
> A principle with wide and growing support among economists of all ideologies is the following: the Fed should conduct monetary policy so as to keep the dollar value of total output in the economy on a prescribed growth track. In short, it should set a course for growth in the nominal gross national product.
>
> If a boom pushes the dollar value of output above the track through a combination of higher prices and more physical output, then the Fed would step on the brakes, contract the money supply and raise interest rates. In case of a recession the Fed would accelerate money supply growth and bring down interest rates . . . One of the mistakes of past monetary policy has been its focus on annual

rates of growth rather than levels of the monetary targets . . . Starting at the beginning of 1982, the depressed level on the dollar value of output should have told the Fed to turn expansionary.[6]

The Federal Reserve's 1983 game plan reveals two important changes in monetary policy making. First, along with its familiar monetary targets, the Fed will use a new yardstick, the growth of total credit, to gauge monetary policy. But second, the Fed will adhere less rigidly to any mechanical targets, for either money or credit — What is clear today is that attention to the monetary aggregates alone is insufficient, and sometimes dangerously misleading.[7]

Second-guessing Federal Reserve monetary policy has become an intellectual pastime — and with good reason, in view of the inadequacy, regardless of explanation, of past Fed monetary policy. Unfortunately, while interest rates decline with the growth in the money supply and the economy is stimulated, the historical record shows that the inevitable consequence is an expansion in the business cycle, which causes interest rates to rise, inflation to increase, and attempts by the Federal Reserve Board to halt the boom with tight money, which then brings about a recessionary cycle once again. An increase in the money supply growth by the Fed, as a result of the experiences of the late 1970s, also brings about public expectations of a rise in inflation, which results in a self-fulfilling prophecy.

What, then, are the options available to improve monetary policy if one concludes that the Federal Reserve Board has neither brought the country reasonable interest rates nor halted the economic cycles of expansion and contraction, inflation and disinflation, or the volatility of interest rates? Would the situation be improved if the Federal Reserve Board were to be made truly independent? Is it even possible to do so? Or should the lack of true independence of the Fed be freely admitted and monetary policy controlled by the executive or legislative branch, as is the case in other developed countries? These are difficult questions to answer, especially because the United States is the only advanced developed country where the executive and legislative branches of government can be, and frequently are, under control of different parties. This makes the role of a supposedly independent federal agency like the Federal Reserve Board particularly difficult. It must satisfy not only the mandate of the government in power but also both the administration and Congress, who may each have different policies they wish the Federal Reserve to pursue.

The author's criticism of Federal Reserve past policies therefore has to be tempered by a realization that the role of the Fed, and particularly that of its chairman, is quite impossible under current conditions. It has been amply demonstrated that although stated to be independent, the chairman of the Federal Reserve Board—at least since the presidency of Lyndon Johnson—has been under frequent pressure from the President to take action for political rather than economic reasons. This has been true regardless of who has been chairman or whether the individual was appointed by a Democratic or a Republican President. At the same time, the chairman of the Fed has not hesitated to recommend policies to Congress with respect to the necessity of controlling inflation, for example, which he then contradicts through his own actions taken on behalf of the President. Arthur Burns, in particular, constantly exhorted Congress about the dangers of inflation while following monetary policies at the Federal Reserve Board that could only increase inflation.

Would it be possible to ensure that the Federal Reserve Board be totally independent? The answer is probably yes, since the third branch of our government, the Supreme Court, has managed to maintain its independence successfully throughout American history even though each member is appointed by the President and confirmed by the Senate. One option clearly could be appointment for life of Federal Reserve Board members numbering at least seven persons. This would ensure, presumably, that no one President could appoint a majority of the Board. The best argument in favor of such an option is: If the Board is not to be independent, how can it be responsible to both the executive and the legislative branches of government? Is monetary policy too important to be left under the control of the executive branch, with the chairman appointed by the President and serving at the pleasure of the President, even though as in the case of other agencies that are part of the executive branch confirmation by the Senate would be required?

There is much to be said for the proposition that monetary policy is just as important as foreign policy and that it is an integral part of an administration's domestic economic policy. Hence, at least the chairman of the Federal Reserve Board should be appointed by the President, subject to Senate confirmation, with his or her term of office not fixed but at the discretion of the President in the same manner as members of the Cabinet. In this way monetary policy would clearly be administration policy because the Board's independence would then be laid to rest once and for all and monetary policy would unmistakably be the responsibility of the administration in office. At the same time, the special role of the New York Fed in its execution of monetary policy would be ended. The administration would set credit policy that would loosen or tighten credit in accordance with administration policy and be in no way subject to manipulation by staff officials in New York, no matter how competent or educated. Concurrently, the whole system of separate Federal Reserve banks might also be considered redundant in today's world of instant communication in financial transactions.

Changes that have been occurring in the marketplace have made the role of the Federal Reserve Board infinitely more difficult. With the new accounts devised either by Congress or by the banks, and the competition to banks now created by other financial services companies, we are led to wonder, Just what is money and what is a bank? Monetary policy cannot control what it can no longer understand or statistically evaluate. Have we reached the point where money, as we thought of it, requires a redetermination because it includes new forms of credit instruments? Is a bank today something quite different from that imposing building in the center of town where we kept our excess funds and negotiated loans? In the next chapter, I will briefly analyze what seems to be occurring. The meaning of what is happening to money, credit, and the very concept of banking is enormously important. It not only affects monetary policy, but it must also profoundly alter our whole system of regulation of banking institutions.

NOTES

1. House Banking Committee, Subcommittee on Domestic Finance, *The Federal Reserve's Attachment to the Free Reserve Concept*, 88th Congress, 1964.

2. As quoted in Maxwell Newton, *The Fed* (New York: Times Books, 1983), p. 90.

3. Henry Wallich, "The Search for Stable Money." Remarks to Cato Institute, Washington, D.C., January 21, 1983.

4. Ibid.

5. See "Monetary Policy and the Management of the Public Debt: Their role in achieving price stability and high level employment," 82nd Congress, 2nd Session Joint Committee Print (1952); also, "Hearings before the Subcommittee on General Credit Control and Debt Management of the Joint Committee on the Economic Report," Congress of the U.S., 82nd Congress, 2nd Session (1952). The accord between the Treasury and the Federal Reserve is dated March 4, 1951.

6. Hall, Robert E. "A Bid for Tracking Nominal G.N.P." New York *Times*, February 27, 1983, p. 2F.

7. Friedman, Benjamin M. "Applause for A Credit Guideline." New York *Times*, February 27, 1983, p. 2F.

4

CHANGES IN
THE MARKETPLACE:
WHAT IS MONEY AND
WHAT IS A BANK?

It seems surprising to ask, What is money and what is a bank? in a book on the Federal Reserve System. Nonetheless, it is a relevant question. The concept of money has been changing rapidly in the past four years and will continue to change as electronics increasingly revolutionizes cash transfers and methods of payment in our society. As the notion of money changes, so do the services that the public expects to get from those institutions in which they have deposited their cash resources, primarily the banks. Because of these changes, of necessity banking will change. As banks feel the need for change, our regulatory institutions must also adapt. What was true in 1913 when the Federal Reserve System was created or in 1933 when Glass-Steagall was passed or even in 1956 when the Bank Holding Company Act was adopted may have little relevance to the problems facing the depository institutions in the mid-1980s.

Above all, it is important to understand that money is no longer a store of value as well as a medium of exchange. The implications of this have hardly been understood in the United States because we have only recently experienced inflation. When inflation returns, Americans will flee the dollar as other nations have fled from holding their currencies as a store of value and buy assets — almost any assets.

THE CHANGING CONCEPT OF MONEY

The History and Development of Money

The first coins are reported to have been used around 700 B.C., but gold and silver were used by the Babylonians as early as 2000 B.C. In these early days monarchs had not learned that the gold or silver content of coins could be debased so that devaluation of the currency could match the inflation rate. This was discovered in the later days of Roman civilization when the emperors gradually reduced, over some 300 years, the gold and silver content of the currency to finance rising expenditures for wars, lavish courts, and the building of monuments to honor their predecessors and themselves. Devaluation of the currency became the counterweight for rising inflation as the Roman Empire gradually lost its strength and capacity to produce while the demands of its citizens continued to grow.

As trade began to flourish again after the dark period of the Middle Ages, banks in Italy across the trade routes between Western Europe and the East began to accept deposits of coins to be repaid upon demand. This was the beginning of demand deposits at banks. Deposits were then loaned out and new deposits taken in to offset withdrawals. Interest was paid on the deposits. Subsequently, the English goldsmiths became predominant in banking by developing the idea of bank note currency, that is, the issuance of interest-bearing receipts for deposits that could then be freely transferred by the depositor to anyone else through endorsement. Eventually, these receipts were made payable to bearer, and this convenience often made it no longer necessary to include interest. Paper money had arrived in primitive form to be replaced in time by engraved notes issued by the banks and including a promise to exchange the note for gold coin upon presentation. Eventually, monarchs took over the issuance of bank notes through a central banking institution they established. This did away with the risk of loss if a private note issuer had insufficient gold to repay the note holders. This often happened in the United States, for instance, because the country had no central banking system from 1836 to 1913 and no national banks from 1836 to 1863. The important consideration in the bank note system was, of course, the promise to redeem for gold upon demand because gold was still considered real money—paper only the commitment to exchange for gold.

In the United States the federal government began to mint gold and silver coins after the adoption of the Constitution. The Coinage Act of 1792 provided for the establishment of the U.S. mint and a bimetallic monetary standard. It did not, however, issue paper money until after the Civil War except for temporary issues during the War of 1812, the Mexican War of 1846, and, of course, the Civil War. When the National Bank Act was passed in 1863, the federal government, to discourage further issuance of notes by state banks, simply taxed state bank notes. Following the Civil War, as the country expanded rapidly, it was essential that there be a growing supply of paper money to meet the rising demand for payments in trade transactions.

It was only 14 years after the Civil War, however, in 1879, that a de facto gold standard was established in the United States. The Gold Standard Act of 1900 officially placed the United States on a gold standard. The standard lasted until the Gold Reserve Act of 1934 took away the right of U.S. citizens to own gold (restored in 1974) and made the Treasury the official dealer in gold at $35 per ounce. Foreign official holders of dollars could still convert into gold until President Richard Nixon closed the gold window in 1971. Since that time, particularly during the Reagan administration, the government has considered, but so far rejected, any decision to return to a gold standard. At the end of 1983 the world remained essentially on a paper dollar standard, but this has not discouraged foreigners from continuing to exchange their currencies into dollars. In a world with flexible exchange rates and great political instability, capital flows have continued to move toward the United States since 1981, making the dollar a very strong currency.

At the end of 1984 — and forseeable future — there was no metallic cover for U.S. currency, and the size of the U.S. money supply was governed essentially, as was noted in Chapter 3, by the degree to which the Open Market Committee chose to increase the reserves available to the banking system by net buying or selling of U.S. Treasury obligations. The Federal Reserve Board is obviously very much concerned with the money supply because the extent of its increase determines whether or not the economy is stimulated, whether inflation will or will not return.

As late as 1958 the government had no agreed-upon definition of the *money supply*. In the 1970s, when Arthur Burns was chairman of the Fed, there were at least seven definitions of *money aggregates*, of which five were regularly published. In 1979, in response to the development of new kinds of bank accounts, the Fed published a proposal for redefining the monetary aggregates, and in early 1980 it announced new definitions. Today, the Fed defines and then measures three different combinations of monetary units — M-1, M-2, and M-3:

- M-1, published weekly, is the narrowest measure of the amount of money available for public spending. It consists of coins and paper currency and demand deposits at all U.S. commercial banks. Also included are demand deposit types of accounts in thrift institutions. Basically, M-1 is meant to include all forms of money that can be spent without first being converted into another type of account.

- M-2, published monthly, includes all components of M-1 plus savings and small denomination time deposits, money-market funds, savings accounts, small certificates of deposit, and overnight Eurodollar deposits.
- M-3, also published monthly, includes all components of M-2 plus time deposits over $100,000. It also includes near monies held by businesses.

The basic definition used by the Fed and business economists who follow the money supply is M-1, published every Thursday (formerly Friday). However, its measurement value has necessarily been affected by new types of accounts and the movement of funds from one type of account to another. For example, M-1 includes NOW accounts but not MMDAs (money-market deposit accounts); NOW accounts were designed by the banks to get back funds transferred to money-market funds at a time when the Fed's Regulation Q placed a ceiling on the interest rate that banks could pay on their deposits. If, for example, funds in money-market accounts are transferred into NOW accounts at banks or thrifts, M-1 will increase and M-2 will decrease. It does not necessarily indicate that the Fed will conclude that the money supply has increased too rapidly and that a tighter money policy is required. But it makes it much more difficult to calculate the money supply accurately and leads to inaccurate assumptions. Since 1975 the Fed has been required by law to give Congress annual money supply growth targets; so it is particularly important for the Fed to monitor the monetary aggregates accurately, and this has become increasingly difficult to do. Furthermore, if the public believes the money supply is increasing too rapidly, interest rates will have a tendency to rise very gradually, and bond prices will fall as the public foresees an increase in the rate of inflation. This happened in spring 1984 even though there was little statistical indication that prices were in fact rising. Public perception of events to come can, in this manner, often result in a self-fulfilling prophecy.

The problem was compounded by the 1981–83 growth of money-market funds and large CDs in addition to NOW and Super-NOW accounts, the short-lived All-Saver accounts,* and the Individual Retirement Account (IRA)-Keogh accounts. (The IRA-Keogh accounts are no longer included in the monetary aggregates, and, therefore, M-2 and M-3 have been reduced by about 1 percent. See Table 4-1.) The Super-

---

*Some $35 billion of "All-Savers" certificates are starting to expire, and no one knows whether the runoff will go into checking accounts, included in M-1, or move into savings accounts, included in M-2 or M-3.

TABLE 4-1

Monetary and Credit Growth Ranges for 1983

Monetary Unit	Percentage Growth
M-1	4–8[a]
M-2	7–10[b]
M-3	6.5–9.5
Total credit[c]	8.5–11.5

[a]This range allows for a modest amount of shifts from sources outside M-1 into Super-NOW accounts. Thus far, growth in those accounts has been relatively small. The range also assumes that authority to pay interest on transactions accounts is not extended beyond presently eligible accounts.

[b]This range represents the annual rate of growth from the average level of M-2 outstanding in February-March 1983 to the fourth quarter of 1983. The February-March 1983 base was chosen, rather than the fourth quarter of 1982, so that the growth of M-2 would be measured after the period of highly aggressive marketing of MMDAs has subsided. These accounts, introduced in mid-December, rose to over $230 billion by early February, with a substantial amount of funds transferred into them from sources outside M-2, such as market instruments and large CDs. The 7–10 percent range for M-2 allows for some residual shifting from market instruments and large CDs into MMDAs over the balance of the year.

[c]"Total credit" represents domestic nonfinancial debt.

Quarter to quarter basis, except as noted.

Source: Compiled by the author.

NOW accounts are $2,500 minimum deposit savings accounts at market interest rates offered by the depository institutions.* The purpose of these accounts was to allow banks and particularly thrifts (which faced great financial difficulty because of the transfer of their savings deposits to money-market funds) to retrieve at least a portion of their deposits. It has worked out well. The MMDAs became the most successful bank product in history,† despite the fact that they are limited to three third-party transfers per month. Within six weeks of their creation, money-market deposits grew to $114.2 billion at commercial banks and $74.9 billion at thrift institutions. After May 1983 they began to stabilize at $220 billion in banks and $150 billion in thrifts. Meanwhile, the money-market funds had declined from about $231 billion in November 1982 to $167 billion in November 1983. They have a tendency to rise again as interest rates rise. The Super-NOW accounts are also $2,500 minimum at market interest rates but have no restrictions on the number of transactions by check or transfer. (With the NOW accounts, the banks are required to maintain a 12 percent reserve if there are more than six transactions a month in the account; in the Super-NOWs there is automatically a 12 percent reserve requirement.) CDs — generally in very large amounts — were used by depository institutions in the 1980–82 period before they were permitted to use the new money-market savings deposits to try to substitute funds for the loss of their deposits to the money-market funds organized by the securities industry. When interest rates reached 20 percent in 1981, banks and thrifts found that they were

*The Depository Institutions Deregulation and Monetary Control Act (DIDMCA) of 1980 authorized the introduction of NOW accounts by all depository institutions in 1981 and stipulated that all interest-rate ceilings on all time and savings deposits, including NOW accounts, be phased out by 1986. The similarity between NOW accounts and demand deposits prompted a redefinition of M-1.

†The public sometimes asks whether there is any connection between interest paid by banks and that charged by banks to their customers. The answer is that there is a real effect but only for a time. Banks count on the public's natural apathy in shifting funds to another bank to earn more interest. That is why payments to depositors tend to decline sharply, whereas loan rates do not decline. It should be noted that there is also very little meaning to the words *prime rate*, the rate that banks supposedly charge to their best customers. The use of *prime rate* began in the 1930s when there were many lenders but few credit-monthly borrowers. The New York banks then agreed to set a floor under interest rates charged business customers in order to avoid competing with each other into insolvency. In the recent 1982/83 economic recovery, banks were discounting prime deeply and often, because they had more money than good credit risks to borrow. As the recovery continued in 1984, however, and consumers increased their purchases, the prime rate rose! Because the base rate during the recession was so high, we can expect to see unusually high interest rates if this economic recovery continues to grow.

losing their deposits very rapidly to these funds, which then invested in CDs issued by the banks paying as high as 15 percent interest. In 1983, sales of the big certificates had declined to $225 billion, a decrease of $45 billion from just the previous year. Bank money-market deposits do have one great advantage: they are insured to $100,000.

All of these difficulties can be easily traced to one source: the 1980–82 high inflation rate compounded in the case of depository institutions by the Federal Reserve Board's ceiling on the interest they could pay on their deposits. Had it not been for the Fed's Regulation Q mandated by Congress, the depository institutions would not have seen their deposits disappear, the housing and mortgage market would not have undergone the shakeout it did, and, in particular, the thrift institutions would not have had the difficulties they faced in 1982/83. Now the balance has been reestablished, but at what cost! The Federal Reserve Board might well have foreseen the dilemma its tight-money monetary policy would precipitate.

It must be understood that in the 1981–84 financial marketplace, the competition for money between the depository institutions and the securities industry centered around two conflicting efforts:

1. The effort on the part of depository institutions to get around Regulation Q; and
2. The effort on the part of the securities firms to maintain their advantage by having their accounts insured in the same manner as the bank and thrift money-market savings deposits. Perhaps the extreme instance illustrating this effort was the securities firm in Toledo, Ohio (since bankrupt), that encouraged the opening of accounts – not to buy stocks but to invest in CDs and money-market funds, claiming that such accounts were entitled to the stock exchange firm $500,000 protection. The attempt on the part of securities firms to acquire non-bank banks is just one more instance of an effort to acquire government insurance for investors.

Human ingenuity being what it is, we can expect both industries to continue to exercise their best efforts to develop new types of accounts that will result in a flow of depositors in their direction. As capital needs in our highly technologically-oriented society continue to grow, this competition can be expected to increase.

To attempt to cope with the growing difficulty of determining how the money supply should be calculated, Chairman Paul Volcker announced in 1983 that although the Federal Reserve would continue to set and monitor various targets for the growth of the money supply, it would also monitor a new guideline: the growth of total domestic nonfinancial debt. For the first time the Open Market Committee announced its expectation of the growth of total domestic debt for the years ahead. Volcker said a range of 8.5 to 11.5 percent would be appropriate for 1983, as for 1984. This was almost sure to prove low for 1984 because the velocity of money hardly increased in 1983 but increased dramatically in 1984 as consumers began to buy heavily.

What Is a Bank?

Changes in the definition of *money* to calculate the growth in the money supply accurately have been due to the creation of new depository and savings accounts developed first by the securities industry to take the deposits away from the banks and then by the banks with congressional authorization to get their deposits back by paying a reasonable rate of interest on new types of accounts. These new types of accounts in both industries have not only brought about a redefinition of *money*, but they have also brought into question what is meant by a *bank*, particularly for regulatory purposes. In Chapter 5 we will analyze carefully how regulation has become increasingly difficult as the services rendered by regulated and unregulated financial institutions have become increasingly blurred. Here, we look at how changes in the definition of *money* affect the definition of a *bank*.

Financial services have been provided traditionally by depository institutions: commercial banks, savings and loan associations, savings banks, and credit unions. In the last ten years, however, a number of new players have entered the game: brokerage houses, investment bankers, insurance companies, real estate services firms, and even nonfinancial companies such as retailers (Sears) and manufacturers (General Electric).

If banks are deemed to render financial services to their customers, why should other companies that render some financial services as an adjunct to their normal business activities not also offer to invest the public's savings in their own broadened enterprises, particularly if they can afford to give a higher return to their investors than the banks can give their depositors? Why should the banks not buy their money from a Merrill Lynch through its money-market funds or through its distribution of the bank's municipal bond portfolio to its retail clients if it can thereby raise money for the banks and thrifts more effectively and efficiently than the banks can do on their own? Why is this increased competition for the public's savings not a better way of serving the public than having capital lying idle in the banks with little or no return to the savers? Why are we not better off as a nation if we encourage increased returns on savings when our proportion of savings (5 percent) is so much lower than it is in Germany (12 percent) or Japan (24 percent)? These are indeed very pertinent questions for our government to examine.

In my discussion of money I pointed out how and why these non-banking financial institutions developed new types of accounts to entice deposits away from banks that were limited by the Fed from paying adequate interest on their deposits in the middle of a severe inflationary cycle, at least to some extent created by Federal Reserve monetary policy. Many examples of what has happened since 1980 can be cited:

- Prudential Insurance Company first acquired the Bache Group (an investment bank and stockbrokerage house); then in 1983 it acquired a bank in Atlanta, Georgia, that was to be operated as a nonbank bank under the name of The Prudential Bank and Trust Co., using the Prudential agent network to solicit bank-related business throughout the country.
- American Express, a nonregulated insurance, credit card, and international banking conglomerate, first acquired Shearson, Loeb Rhodes, Wall Street's second-largest investment bank and stockbrokerage firm; then in 1983 it purchased a large international bank, Trade Development Bank of Geneva, Switzerland, which has acted as banker, underwriter, and trust company in many countries.
- Merrill Lynch, using Banc One as the key bank in its plan, devised its very successful cash management account, which permits the customer to use his or her account to buy securities, to write checks, and to channel idle funds daily into Merrill Lynch's money-market funds to earn additional returns. More recently, Merrill Lynch has created a series of funds that buy from banks at par their holdings of municipal securities subject to a "put" back to the bank at any time. The customer is protected by the put for which the individual sacrifices the higher rate of interest he or she would get if the bonds were purchased by the individual at the current rate of discount; the bank gets immediate cash; Merrill Lynch collects a fee and a commission on sales.
- Sears first acquired Dean Witter Reynolds, the nation's fifth-largest brokerage house, giving it more offices nationwide than the country's four largest bank holding companies, Citicorp, BankAmerica, Chase, and Manufacturers Hanover. It then added Coldwell Banker, the large institutional real estate sales company, and Sears Bank (a savings and

loan institution). It has also now created what may turn out to be a most successful international trading company. Sears had already established a strong insurance arm in Allstate Insurance Company. Its retail marketing power — to which has now been added credit sales, insurance, real estate, international trading, investment banking, stockbrokerage, and money-market funds — makes it well on its way to becoming able to cover all aspects of the financial services industry.

- The 1983 acquisition of Fidelity Savings and Loan in San Francisco by Citicorp gives that bank holding company the first merger of a savings and loan with a bank holding company across state lines.
- Security Pacific of Los Angeles and Union Planters National Bank of Memphis have so far unsuccessfully sought to acquire discount brokerage firms, whereas BankAmerica Corporation succeeded in so doing by acquiring Charles Schwab and Co.*
- Comerica Incorporated, of Detroit, a Michigan bank holding company, has been permitted by the Federal Reserve Board to set up a credit card bank in Ohio despite dissent by two governors and the banking superintendent of Ohio.† The Ohio credit card bank will not accept demand deposits, offer any type of transaction account to any person, or make commercial loans. It will be a nonbank bank under the Bank Holding Act definition of a *bank*, which says that a bank is not a bank if it does not make commercial loans or take demand deposits. Why has Ohio been picked for purposes of setting up nonbank banks to engage in credit card operations? That state has a very liberal 25 percent revolving credit rate and no limit on annual fees. In this instance the Ohio institution will offer revolving personal loans in connection with its credit card operations.
- In November 1983 Templeton Management and Trust Co. of Fort Lauderdale, Florida, obtained a national bank charter from the Comptroller of the Currency to operate a trust company in all 50 states to provide investment management and advice to employee benefit plans, endowments, and other large institutional investors; to attract overseas investors desiring a "veil of secrecy"; and to operate a common trust fund for smaller investors. The charter must, however, be

---

*These cases will be examined in more detail in Chapter 5, which deals with the regulation by the Fed and other agencies of depository institutions. In July, 1984, the U.S. Supreme Court upheld the right of BankAmerica Corporation to acquire a discount brokerage firm.

†The Fed rejected the superintendent's objections on interstate grounds, stating that the act's bar against interstate banking does not apply since Comerica is not a "bank."

approved by the Fed, which has already opposed the granting of a similar charter in two other similar cases. The Templeton Trust, according to the Comptroller of the Currency, is not a bank because it will neither take deposits nor make commercial loans. It is true that the Federal Reserve had control over the trust activities of national banks for 50 years—from 1913 to 1962—but in 1962 that section of the Federal Reserve Act was repealed and the Board's authority transferred to the Comptroller of the Currency. From a regulatory standpoint, it is clear that it is easier to do business as a trust than as a mutual fund because reporting requirements are simpler and a trust company can operate throughout the country without separate individual state registration.

The Comptroller of the Currency has granted on two occasions, in 1983 and 1984, a moratorium on allowing banks and other financial companies to combine. This was wise. Members of Congress are beginning to focus on bank regulation as a result of efforts on the part of the Reagan administration to hasten bank deregulation.* But lawmakers do not like to be pushed into shaping legislation rapidly. The questions at issue are indeed much too important not to consider all aspects of regulation very carefully; and, normally, an election year is not the best time for Congress to apply itself to a careful and complete review of regulatory legislation going back many years and affecting many industries and, ultimately, both the rate of savings in the nation and the requisite protection of depositors and savers. Certainly, the answer is not to allow financial institutions, as the Comptroller has done, to take advantage of loopholes in the Bank Holding Company Act, regardless of the merits of his position on the matter. It is obvious that the Federal Reserve Board is very unhappy about the Comptroller's action in the past and that among lawmakers there is a wide range of opinion on the whole question of bank deregulation. This goes far beyond the issuance of nonbank bank charters to enable bank holding companies to get around congressional restrictions on interstate banking as interpreted and applied by the Federal Reserve.

Who are the winners and who are the losers in the recent deregulation of interest rates charged by depository institutions and the increased competition coming from other types of financial service institutions?

Individuals and small businesses have received an estimated $40

*The various deregulation plans supported by the administration and/or pending in Congress are outlined and discussed in detail in Chapter 6. If Congress has not taken action in 1984, the Comptroller warned that his embargo would be lifted.

billion more than they did from ordinary passbook savings accounts. On the other hand, they must pay more when they borrow. Also, since the cost of bank services has risen, low-balance depositors are paying relatively more for such services than the increased rate of interest received. The winners have been high-balance depositors who earn more interest; money-market mutual funds operated by securities firms free of government regulation; buyers of financial services who find, for example, that there are now many more discount brokers; and convenience seekers who at best can do all their financial transactions at a one-stop financial supermarket. In time other winners will turn out to be those banks that finance, for substantial fees, company acquisitions or so-called leveraged buyouts of commercial businesses. In this area the bank can avoid the restrictions of Glass-Steagall while rendering services ordinarily provided by an investment banker. As deregulation becomes more extended, additional competition in bank services will undoubtedly benefit those persons in our society who save rather than spend.

CONCLUSION

In this chapter I have indicated how increased competition between depository institutions and other providers of financial services has resulted in new types of interest-paying savings deposits at banks and thrifts and new efforts on the part of commercial firms to furnish financial services formerly provided by banks. The effect of these developments—all during the late 1970s and early 1980s—has made the already-difficult task of bank regulation very much more arduous.

In the next chapter we will examine the efforts of the federal regulators to maintain their control over the activities of the depository institutions both in terms of allowable product and in terms of limitations on geographical extension, that is, interstate banking. It is a complicated subject, with the states playing an active role in order to help their own banks or to increase local employment. It is a political battle between the federal government and the states. It is also a jurisdictional battle among the federal regulatory agencies themselves. Eventually, Congress will have to decide the extent to which it wishes bank regulations to be shared with the states and the extent to which federal bank regulation should be modified to meet the economic conditions of the next 10 or 20 years. In dealing with this second very important question, Congress will also have to restructure the federal bank regulatory system, including the role to be played by the current Federal Reserve system.

5

DOMESTIC BANK
REGULATION BY
THE FEDERAL RESERVE
AND OTHER AGENCIES

*We cannot all live better by borrowing from each other. Unfortunate-
ly, it is not obvious that this trend will not continue. The reason is that
discussions of financial reform are rarely conducted in terms of the
needs of the economy and its beneficiaries. Now, as in the past, discussions of the role of particular financial institutions deal largely with
the subject of turf—its conquest, its protection, its sharing. . . . That
is also what gives discussions of banking reform so unattractive a flavor
and makes them so unpopular in the Congress. Economic considerations are in danger of being neglected in this process. . . . The impression is left that the industry is looking out for itself instead of focusing on how best to serve the customer. The customers' yachts are
nowhere in sight.*

—Governor Henry Wallich of the Federal Reserve Board

As was noted in Chapter 1, contrary to popular opinion, the Federal
Reserve Board is not the principal federal agency involved in the regulation of the activities of depository institutions within the United States.
Because the Fed does, however, have exclusive jurisdiction over bank
holding companies under the Bank Holding Company Act, its regulatory
activities are very important. It has been said that 90 percent of the Fed's
time is spent on regulatory matters.

One of the principal questions in this chapter is how the regulatory
activities of the Federal Reserve mesh with those of other federal and
state agencies: the SEC; the Comptroller of the Currency; the state
superintendents; the FDIC; the FHLBB and its sister insurance agency, the FSLIC; and the NCUA. To what extent is there overlap that
could be usefully eliminated? How does the regulatory system work in
practice? How can this ponderous, burdensome, turf-conscious, and po-

litically motivated method of supervision mandated by Congress be simplified so that competition can be increased among those who render financial services to the public, some regulated and others not?

It has become obvious both to the administration and to Congress that developments in the marketplace have moved far ahead of changes in the regulatory system. By 1984, instead of playing a lead role, the regulators were busily trying to determine the extent to which their regulations should be adapted to conform to changes already brought about by financial institutions that had taken the initiative to give the public what it obviously wished to have: a higher return on savings, greater convenience in withdrawing or depositing money, and the right to transfer from one type of account to another at one institution to avoid having idle funds earning an inadequate return during a period of unusually high interest rates. If we assume that the violent inflationary cycle of the late 70s and early 80s will not return, interest rates should not climb to their level of only a few years ago. The trend toward a greater return on savings can be expected to continue, however, encouraging an increase in the very low rate of savings in the United States. An important question becomes: How soon will the government revise the current regulatory system so that it satisfies the public's demand for a simpler financial services mechanism?

To analyze in some methodical way just how the regulatory process works today and the extent to which there are both overlaps and gaps in the system, it is essential, first, to distinguish those financial institutions that are not subject to regulation from those that are; second, to define which regulatory agencies are empowered to regulate those regulated institutions; and third, to determine the extent to which regulation limits the capacity of that institution to compete effectively or encourages it to modify itself to become more competitive.

Government regulation in a democratic society is necessarily complicated by public policy, which plays a very important role in the regulatory system. Congress may want to encourage the use of funds for housing, for example. It is also important to stimulate savings, since the rate of savings in the United States is so very low compared with the rate in countries such as Japan and West Germany. Public policy also demands that speculation or risk taking with bank deposits be discouraged; that is the reason why deposits are insured. In part our very safeguards encourage what we wish to avoid: Since bank deposits are federally insured, this encourages the innovative financial services company entrepreneur to earn a higher return for the customer or depositor by taking greater risks, if the individual can bring the activity within the insurance protection afforded to certain types of depositors or customers

by the federal government. Financial services companies are constantly seeking to bring their activities under the government insurance um-
brella, whether or not truly justified. Adaptation on the part of government to changes in the marketplace is cautious, slow, and sometimes
ineffective.

Innovation in the rendering of financial services is here to stay. It
must be considered a positive development, but it may involve risk to
the depositor. Government is therefore faced with a real challenge: to
force itself to adapt to change while seeking to minimize the risk to those
who cannot afford the loss. At the same time, it must continue to make
it advantageous for the public to save more and to encourage that savings flow into areas deemed to be important for public policy reasons,
such as housing and municipal improvements. On the other hand, there
is also a need to effect reductions in the burden of regulation so that
competition can be stimulated.

NONREGULATED FINANCIAL
INSTITUTIONS

As the cost of credit has increased during the last few years and
its availability at times has been reduced, the value of credit has of course
increased. Firms such as Sears and General Electric (GE), which had
been extending credit to their customers, began to see that credit itself
was what made it possible for the customer not only to buy at Sears but
to buy at all. The same phenomenon is true with respect to credit cards
and why banks have increasingly adopted either VISA or Master Charge
to compete with the American Express credit card. American Express,
through its travelers checks, has over the years developed its banking
(credit) operations by means of the huge (several billions of dollars)
amount of unused cash locked up in its travelers checks outstanding
throughout the world.

Increased demand for credit generated new providers of credit; at
the same time, the normal providers of credit sought new ways of obtaining the public's savings so as to have additional sources of funds available for loans. The power to extend credit is directly linked to the sources
of savings. Since savings were traditionally the prerogative of depository
institutions, it became necessary for the new financial services companies to entice these savings away from the banks. With the aid of the
Federal Reserve's Regulation Q, they succeeded only too well. One successful way of doing this was through the establishment of money-market

funds. Today the depository institutions are facing a challenge they cannot meet unless government restores the competitive balance, either by loosening controls over the depository institutions or by restricting the new financial services companies' ability to secure savings. The Garn–St. Germain Depository Institutions Act of 1982 was an attempt on the part of Congress to restore the balance. Unfortunately, at the Federal Reserve and other regulatory agencies there is pressure to try the other method: to extend the scope of regulation to apply to institutions that are not banks and that do not have demand deposits. This would reduce competition and increase regulation, a highly inadvisable program. Recent Federal Reserve attempts to redefine a bank are a step in this direction.*

What other kinds of commercial companies have access to inexpensive sources of funds? Because of the risky loans made both domestically and internationally by larger banks – such as Chase Manhattan, Seafirst, and Continental Illinois in the domestic energy market or Citicorp, Manufacturers Hanover, and Bank of America, among others, to Latin American or Communist bloc countries – the money-center bank holding companies may find themselves having to pay more on their commercial paper than the large, well-managed industrial companies such as IBM, GE, General Motors Acceptance Corporation, Sears, and J. C. Penney. GE, for example, is very active in the field of financial services. In May 1984 it purchased a large insurance company. Earlier, it had entered the business of financing to international trade operations by creating an Export Trading Company.† Other large generators of cash such as insurance companies, financial conglomerates such as American Express, and large brokerage houses are in the same position. These companies are well managed, venturesome, and international as well as domestic, and they have no real need for government insurance on funds entrusted to them by the public because of their intrinsic financial strength. Since these institutions are not subject to regulation as banks even though they obtain funds from the public, they are grad-

---

*Until the regulatory authorities were required to advance billions of dollars to save Continental Illinois Bank of Chicago in June, 1984, there appeared to be a trend in Congress to reduce bank regulation and allow the banks to engage in additional activities in order to remain competitive with the non-regulated financial services companies. Particularly in the House of Representatives a contrary trend has now appeared. See Chapter 6 for a detailed analysis of this whole question.

†The Export Trading Company Act, passed in 1982, was designed to encourage the financing of U.S. exports. Bank holding companies and even competing commercial firms may participate.

ually forcing banks and thrift institutions to change their way of doing business in order to compete effectively.

What have the nonregulated institutions done to increase their financial services activities? Stockbrokers and mutual fund companies such as Merrill Lynch and Dreyfus Corporation have formed, or are proposing to form, state-chartered banks and nonbank financial companies. Merrill Lynch is competing with banks in consumer lending by offering unsecured lines of credit through the Visa cards it offers to more than 1 million customers. E. F. Hutton formed E. F. Hutton Bank in Wilmington, Delaware, in 1983 and avoided becoming a federally controlled bank holding company by not offering checking accounts.* Among mutual funds, FMR Corporation, the parent of Fidelity Investments, formed a New York City bank through which Fidelity will offer fiduciary services to pension funds and other institutional investors. It will also offer banking services to its other mutual fund clients through a bank it owns in New Hampshire. Several brokerage firms, including Merrill Lynch, sought federal approval to buy or start savings and loan associations. Sears talked about acquiring as many as 50 banks to broaden its ability to acquire deposits.

The insurance companies — usually conservative — are stirring. Travelers owns Keystone Massachusetts Group mutual fund. It owns a trust company, Massachusetts Co., that offers federally insured deposits. It also owns Securities Settlement Corp., a brokerage firm dealing only with other securities houses. It has also begun asset management functions through broker dealers. Prudential bought a bank in Georgia, now Prudential Bank & Trust Co., to tap into the consumer credit market by joining a major credit card network. It offers "jumbo" CDs through the bank to get funds. These are insured up to $1 million, $100,000 through the FDIC and the balance through Prudential Insurance Company. As one banker says: "If I could start again, I'd start over as an insurance company. They can do just about everything."[1] Even conservative John Hancock bought Tucker, Anthony, the securities firm that now owns Julia Walsh and Sons of Washington, D.C., an expanding securities market. Why would the insurance companies want to expand their activities? The answer is simple. Maintaining a force of insurance agents nationwide is a very expensive proposition. Those agents need to be able to sell more than insurance in many cases. They can sell real

---

*An institution, as previously noted, is not a bank for purposes of the Bank Holding Company Act if it does not both take demand deposits *and* make commercial loans.

estate, credit cards as part of a package of financial services, and consumer loans. Prudential, for example, has 22,000 independent agents. Its capital is $500 million; its portfolio is $4 billion. It also issues commercial paper. Its assets to equity leverage is 9 to 1. A bank can have higher leverage, as much as 12 to 1 in most instances. The Prudential bank in Georgia can go to 16 to 1 (6 percent capital to assets ratio). So there is every reason for insurance companies to want to acquire banks to increase their leverage and to provide their agents with bank-related services to perform to increase their income, as well as reduce the company's cost of its agent network.

The depository institutions, both banks and thrifts, are limited by government regulators in the services they can render, in the places where they can do business, and in the return they can give depositors for use of their savings. This is making it increasingly difficult for the banks and thrifts to compete with unregulated financial services companies. The activities of the depository institutions are constrained (1) by congressional mandates enacted many years ago; (2) by decisions of the regulatory agencies, principally the Federal Reserve; and (3) by the courts, which, while paying deference to the regulatory agencies, have a tendency to interpret congressional mandates strictly and without regard for economic considerations. As was noted in Chapter 2, the McFadden Act of 1927 and the Douglas amendment to the Bank Holding Company Act of 1956 are both aimed at preventing interstate banking. The Export Trading Company Act of 1982 limits bank participation in export trading companies to bank holding companies and then only to a portion of the bank holding company's assets. The Glass-Steagall Act prevents banks from acting as underwriters of securities. Although the Federal Reserve and the courts have recently ruled that the act did not prevent the acquisition by a bank holding company of a discount brokerage firm,[2] a District U.S. Court has subsequently ruled that while this activity was not barred by Glass-Steagall, nevertheless the geographical limitations of the McFadden Act did apply and limited the business of a national bank's discount brokerage activities to the bank's central office and chartered branches within the state where its principal office was located.[3]

In applying "the letter of the law" the courts do give deference to the decisions of the bank regulators but, nevertheless, interpret the words of the applicable statutes without any concern for consistency or any obligation to take into account changes in the manner in which business is carried on today. It is not the function of courts to take change into account but the obligation of the legislative branch, which established the limitations on permissible activity in the first place. The Congress's understandable reluctance to take any action — because the matter is highly technical, does not particularly interest the media or the public, and involves strong lobbies in multiple directions — does not excuse its reluctance to act. The result of legislative inaction encourages banks to explore the possibility of converting into savings and loans or to urge state legislatures to adopt laws that will permit bank entry into nonbanking activities such as securities brokerage, credit card operations, or even insurance. This will only cause additional confusion in an already confused regulatory environment.

NATIONAL BANKS

In looking at those institutions that are subject to regulation, we turn first to national banks. Their activities are very much controlled by both statute and regulation. National banks are authorized to discount notes, drafts, and other evidences of debt; to receive deposits; to buy, sell, and exchange coin and bullion; to lend money; to underwrite and deal in the general obligations of U.S. and state and local government (but not state and local revenue bonds);[4] and to exercise "all such incidental powers as shall be necessary to carry on the business of banking."[5] This limited authority to act is even further reduced by the Glass-Steagall Act, which provides in Section 16 that national banks may only purchase and sell securities for others "without recourse, solely upon the order, and for the account of, customers" and that they may trade investment securities for their own account only "under such limitations and restrictions as the Comptroller of the Currency may by regulation prescribe."[6] Glass-Steagall goes on in Section 20 to prohibit applications between banks that are members of the Federal Reserve System[7] and any firm "engaged principally" in the underwriting of securities.[8] Finally, as noted earlier, Section 21 of Glass-Steagall prohibits all depository institutions from underwriting securities.[9]

Over the years the Comptroller of the Currency has had considerable trouble with the application of Glass-Steagall provisions to national banks. In the 1960s, interpretation by the Comptroller that the language of the act, particularly the "incidental powers" clause, would permit national banks to perform travel services, to underwrite municipal revenue bonds, and to sponsor mutual funds was struck down by the courts.[10] On the other hand, the courts have permitted activities such as issuing credit cards and letters of credit and engaging in leasing transactions on the grounds that these activities are "incidental" to banking.[11] In recent years the Comptroller appears to be much more disposed to extend the permissible activities of national banks even at the cost, as was noted in the Security Pacific and Union Planters cases in 1983, of having his authorizations struck down by a court on highly technical grounds. In 1982 North Carolina National Bank received preliminary authorization to establish a futures commission merchant subsidiary within certain limitations; in 1983 Provident National Bank was authorized to engage, through a discount brokerage subsidiary, in the trading of foreign currency options for itself as well as agent for its customers; in October 1982 Citibank was authorized to offer IRAs invested in common trust funds maintained and managed by the bank.[12] There was an interesting question here. The Comptroller treated Citibank's activity as an extension of its traditional trust activities since IRAs are really trust accounts. The Investment Company Institute has challenged the Comptroller's decision in the courts.[13] Are we dealing here with an extension of traditional banking services, the normal function of a bank acting as trustee, or the marketing of interests in bank common trust funds directly to the public? The latter would be subject to the prohibition on distribution of mutual fund shares to the public as an underwriting activity banned by Glass-Steagall.

Two conclusions are apparent from this discussion. First, when faced with statutes that are not explicit, it is unfair to ask the courts to decide which side of the line a bank business activity will fall, particularly if the regulatory authority entrusted with the initial decision has already ruled. Second, with financial practices constantly changing to meet market demand, it can only become increasingly difficult to make hairline distinctions between permissible and prohibited conduct in a given instance without first asking whether in today's business environment the conduct in question is truly likely to cause the problem that legislation enacted 50 years ago was trying to correct. The philosophers and clerics of the University of Paris at the time of St. Thomas Aquinas could argue for months about the type of question now being presented to bank regulators and to the courts, but it seems highly doubtful that there is any real need to draw such a fine line on individual cases. It would be far better for Congress to review carefully whether and to what extent Glass-Steagall is still applicable today, given changes in bank methods and other safeguards established by government.

The long-standing belief of bank regulators and the courts that national banks should have only very limited powers was changed through legislation by the passage of the Garn–St. Germain Depository Institutions Act of 1982.[14] The act expands the potential activities of national banks (and state banks as well) through the establishment of bank service company subsidiaries. Since the act reduced the statutory limitations on bank activities, what becomes important are the limitations established by Federal Reserve regulations on activities permissible for subsidiaries of bank holding companies under the Bank Holding Company Act.* The Fed may deny a bank holding company application on several grounds, including a finding that such activity would constitute an unsafe or unsound banking practice.[15] So the regulatory power of the Fed was further enhanced by this act even though its purpose was to extend the deregulation of banks.

STATE-CHARTERED BANKS

What about the regulation of state-chartered banks? As noted in Chapter 1, these banks are subject to regulation by their respective state bank superintendents. But they are also subject to federal regulation. The Fed is the primary regulator of the approximately 1,000 state-chartered banks that are members of the Federal Reserve System, whereas the FDIC is the primary regulator of over 8,000 insured nonmember banks — those state-chartered institutions that have federal deposit insurance but are not members of the Federal Reserve System. Just to confuse things further, note that the FDIC is also the primary federal regulator of state-chartered savings banks, which for historical reasons have the same regulators as insured nonmember banks. Since federally chartered savings banks and all insured savings and loan associations are regulated by the FHLBB, it would have been logical to have the same regulator for state-chartered savings banks and have them insured by the FSLIC, which, as noted in Chapter 1, is managed by the FHLBB.†

Both the Fed and the FDIC apply federal laws, including Glass-Steagall, to the state-chartered banks they regulate. They approve mergers and changes in control of banks subject to their supervision (except in the case of bank holding companies, where the Fed has exclusive jur-

---

*This enormous power given the Federal Reserve plays an important role in the Fed's continued pressure on the banks to maintain the Fed's regulatory role. This is discussed in detail in Chapter 6.

†This puts state-chartered savings banks at a disadvantage as compared with savings and loans and federally chartered savings banks because such federal laws as Glass-Steagall apply to these state-chartered savings banks.

isdiction). More important, each regulatory agency has the power to prohibit "unsafe and unsound banking practices."* This power, while not exercised lightly, is considerable.

The application of Glass-Steagall raises special problems where state-chartered banks are concerned. Sections 20 and 32 of the act† do not apply to insured nonmember banks (or savings banks) regulated by the FDIC, although they do apply to national banks and state member banks. The FDIC has taken the position that insured nonmember banks and savings banks are therefore free to affiliate themselves with firms engaged in all aspects of securities activities. For example, in 1982 the FDIC permitted both the Boston Five Cents Savings Bank and the Washington Mutual Savings Bank to engage in securities activities — the Boston bank to sponsor, underwrite, and advise a mutual fund; the Washington bank to acquire a full-service securities broker-dealer. Securities industry trade associations have challenged the FDIC's decision in court actions.[16] Both cases have been dismissed.

In September 1982 the FDIC went further by issuing a policy statement[17] in interpreting Section 21 of Glass-Steagall to apply only to a bank, ruling that insured nonmember banks and savings banks may own subsidiaries engaged in any kind of securities activity, including acting as dealers and underwriters, without violating the act. Finally, in May 1983, after asking for public comments on the issue, the FDIC proposed a regulation that would allow bona fide subsidiaries of nonmember banks to engage in all forms of securities dealing and to underwrite, on a "best efforts basis," any kind of security; on a best efforts or firm basis, debt securities that banks are already permitted to underwrite under Glass-Steagall and debt securities given one of the four top ratings by "a nationally recognized rating service"; and the shares of a money-market mutual fund. Since securities dealing is more risky than underwriting, this policy-making of the FDIC hardly appears consistent with the intent of Glass-Steagall.‡ Nevertheless, the FDIC is obviously leaning to-

---

*In Chapter 6 the possible solutions to these problems of overlapping jurisdictional powers are examined in detail. The Treasury, the Bush Task Group, and the Senate Banking Committee all have devoted considerable time to an examination of such questions.

†These sections prohibit affiliations between underwriting firms and banks.

‡The arbitrary nature of the FDIC statement may be seen in the limitation that investments in securities subsidiaries must be restricted to 20 percent of equity capital, that the subsidiaries must be "adequately capitalized" (whatever that means), and that they must be operated separately from the bank, that is, under a different name and in separate offices. Is this regulation solely for the sake of regulation?

ward the position that under appropriate supervision depository institutions should be able to invest a substantial proportion of their capital in nonbanking enterprises.

This regulatory agency has come a long way toward eliminating the restrictions on permissible banking activity established many years ago by the Glass-Steagall Act. The FDIC has given considerable encouragement to state nonmember depository institutions, broadening their activities. This is important because it is — and will increasingly be in the future — difficult for state nonmember lending institutions to compete against the bank holding companies regulated by the Federal Reserve. The large money-center banks are gradually circumventing the limitations on interstate banking established by the McFadden Act and the Douglas amendment to the Bank Holding Company Act.* Some state legislatures have responded to the pressure of the money-center banks. The FDIC in its recent actions has tried to maintain the balance so that the regional state nonmember banking institutions can survive.

---

*Citicorp, the world's largest banking institution, with assets of $136 billion, has, for example, been allowed by the Federal Reserve Board to purchase or establish industrial banks in five states. In February 1984 the Fed approved applications by Citicorp to set up industrial banks in two more states: Kentucky and Tennessee — this despite the fact that Tennessee gives industrial banks broad powers in other areas of banking, such as accepting federally insured time deposits and making commercial loans. If industrial banks can obtain FDIC insurance on their deposits, are they not banks and hence subject to the restrictions on interstate banking of the Bank Holding Company Act? It is increasingly difficult to follow the Fed's distinctions. The Fed has also permitted Citicorp to acquire ailing savings and loans in Florida, California, and Illinois in addition to the industrial banks. Its chairman, Walter Wriston, was determined to get around the limitations on interstate banking. It has used two principal methods to build its nationwide consumer business. First, Citicorp has blanketed the country with credit cards; Citicorp distributes MasterCard and Visa and owns Diner's Club and the Washington area Choice card, among others. Second, Citicorp builds lending and deposit-taking offices. This is the reason for the acquisition of the now-seven industrial banks (Utah, Nebraska, Minnesota, Kansas, Colorado, Kentucky, Tennessee), with more to come; it is also the reason for the acquisition of ailing savings and loans. In addition, Citicorp, in order to get around New York usury laws, persuaded South Dakota to pass a law permitting Citicorp to establish Citibank South Dakota to process credit card loans. South Dakota has no usury ceilings, so all Citicorp credit card accounts have been shifted to South Dakota. It then opened a bank under Delaware's new law encouraging outside banks to establish branches in Delaware to engage in out-of-state operations. In 1984 Citicorp pushed hard to get Maryland to allow it to establish a full-service bank there but failed. It also has acquired a bank in Maine. It is at the same time fighting regional banking in New England by bringing suit against Massachusetts and Rhode Island. It does not want to allow regional banking to get in its way to becoming the first *national* interstate bank. If Congress continues to do nothing, this will happen regardless of past legislation forbidding interstate banking. Citicorp already does business in 41 states and, as will be seen in Chapter 7, in over 100 foreign countries.

It is curious that members of Congress who are normally in favor of regional development have allowed the Federal Reserve to secure more and more power for the bank holding companies over which the Fed has exclusive jurisdiction at the expense of regional institutions, which have done so much more to develop small- and medium-sized businesses in their areas. Are we gradually going to reproduce the same type of bank regulatory system in the United States as exists in Canada or West Germany with a handful of powerful banks determining who will have access to capital, thereby throttling the ability of small regional businesses to develop through local sources of funds? Much more than the dual system of regulation would appear to be at stake here. Are we prepared to see an ever-increasing concentration of capital because the central bank wishes to extend its regulatory control, a control never intended by the Federal Reserve Act of 1913?

The problem is a complex one. If states are to pass laws enabling state-chartered banks to exercise activities not formerly considered to be appropriate for banks, what will stop the money-center banks from acquiring such entities or taking advantage of such statutes to extend their own activities not only in terms of geography but also in terms of additional activity not previously permitted? South Dakota, for example, recently enacted a law that permits banks chartered in that state to engage in "all facets of the insurance business."[18] California has enacted a law allowing banks, savings and loans, credit unions, and industrial loan companies in that state to "organize, sponsor, operate, control or render investment advice to, an investment company, or underwrite, distribute, or sell securities of an investment company."[19] The state of Washington enacted a law in 1982 allowing commercial banks to engage in any activity permitted to bank holding companies under the Bank Holding Company Act. Minnesota recently postponed consideration of a law that would allow state-chartered commercial banks to engage in all types of insurance and securities activities through bank subsidiaries. Pierre duPont, governor of Delaware, proposed that banks chartered in Delaware be allowed to serve as travel agents, to provide investment and tax advice, to engage in data processing and transmission, to underwrite and sell insurance, to serve as futures and commodities brokers, to sponsor and manage mutual funds, and to control or manage a corporation engaged in issuing, underwriting, or dealing in all types of securities.

It is evident that the states — on the pretense of creating new jobs in the growing service economy — are prepared to change federal regulation of financial services. This is a particularly interesting phenomenon because just as 50 years ago agricultural employment declined consistently in favor of jobs in industry, today in the United States white-collar jobs in the services industries tend to replace the jobs of blue-collar workers in the basic industries such as steel, automobiles, and tires. In all industrialized countries we observe the same phenomenon: the basic industries, unless they acquire new technologies, tend to shrink their production and create unemployment, as the United States specialty steel companies continue to compete successfully while basic steel plants lose employment.

How will the Federal Reserve react to the permissiveness of the FDIC and the new state statutes? At least one governor of a Federal Reserve Bank has expressed decided alarm at the banks' straying from activities not strictly related to banking.[20] Nonetheless, the Federal Reserve Board has not opposed all expanded activities of state-chartered banks.[21] It is clear that there is a widening difference of opinion between the FDIC and the states, on the one hand, and the Fed, on the other. At the least this means that state nonmember banks will be treated differently from state-chartered banks that elect to retain their membership in the Federal Reserve System; this is hardly a helpful regulatory split. National banks are also thereby encouraged to convert to state charters. Surely this difference in regulation, unrelated to any difference in the nature of the institution regulated, should be eliminated by congressional action.

Since the Fed has exclusive jurisdiction over bank holding companies and these institutions continue to grow and acquire a preponderant position in the banking system, it is conceivable that a bank holding company might choose to acquire a nonmember state bank with broad powers permitted by the FDIC or that such a bank might choose to form a bank holding company. Each such transaction would require approval of the Fed, and it is not likely that such approval would be forthcoming despite the fact that the FDIC would have approved the extension of the bank's activities into nontraditional banking functions. The reason, of course, is that the Fed has been much more reluctant than the FDIC or the Comptroller of the Currency to extend the powers of banks.

REGULATION OF
THRIFT INSTITUTIONS

The traditional separation of functions between banks and thrift institutions (savings banks and savings and loan associations) has had a tendency to disappear. Originally, thrifts handled personal time deposits and used these for mortgage loans—an activity deemed essential for public policy reasons as an encouragement to more housing. The prohibition on reasonable interest payments to depositors under Regulation Q of the Federal Reserve brought about the Super-NOW accounts and the MMDAs for both thrifts and commercial banks.[22] However, Federal thrift institutions would not take the risk of making mortgage loans to match short-term funds, and hence Congress in 1980 authorized thrifts to make consumer loans.[23] In 1982, by the Garn–St. Germain Depository Institutions Act, Congress further expanded the authority of federal savings banks to make commercial loans and granted the same authority for the first time to federal savings and loans.* The act also allowed commercial leasing and increased the limits for commercial real estate lending. The net effect is that a federal thrift institution can now place up to 75 percent of its assets in commercial-type investments despite the public policy importance of mortgage lending by thrifts.[24]

The distinction today between commercial banks and thrifts has virtually disappeared. In Massachusetts, for example, the law gives both institutions the same powers.[25] What is the effect of the elimination of any distinction in powers between banks and thrifts? It gives thrifts an important advantage because they do not function in the same regulatory straitjacket, particularly since they are not subject to regulation by the Federal Reserve Board.

The FHLBB, as noted earlier, is the primary federal regulator of the thrift industry. Through its subsidiary, the FSLIC, it also regulates state-chartered savings and loans (although not savings banks) that obtain federal insurance.[26] Unlike other regulatory agencies, the FHLBB has a mandate from Congress to promote the growth of the industry it regulates.[27] So the FHLBB has moved aggressively to broaden the range of nonbanking services that thrifts can offer. Through services corporation subsidiaries, federal thrift institutions can develop and manage real estate, broker most forms of insurance, issue credit cards and extend credit by means of such cards, prepare tax returns, and provide certain fiduciary services. If the Conference Report on the Garn–St. Germain Depository Institutions Act had not expressed strong opposition, the FHLBB would have adopted the rule it had proposed, to allow thrift services corporations to go so far as to manufacture mobile homes, underwrite insurance, serve as securities broker, sponsor and operate mutual funds, lease business and consumer goods, and serve both as real estate broker and developer. In 1982 the FHLBB did allow a jointly

---

*As of January 1, 1984, the limit was increased to 10 percent of assets.

owned services corporation to serve as a securities broker for several savings and loans from offices located in their branches. The Securities Industry Association has challenged this FHLBB decision in a court proceeding.[28]

Federal savings and loans and savings banks, through services corporations, may therefore now offer nonbanking services that are prohibited to national and member banks. Since the FHLBB has a mandate to encourage the business of the thrifts it regulates, it will surely enable them in time to offer through subsidiaries the broad range of services needed to compete with diversified financial services institutions such as Sears and Merrill Lynch. It is surprising that only Citicorp appears to be aware of the opportunity presented here and that Canadian and other foreign institutions have not taken advantage of the opportunity to extend the range of the financial services they offer in the United States through the acquisition of a federal thrift institution organized as a stock corporation. It is, of course, also true that state-chartered savings banks may, depending upon state legislation, be able to match this same competitive advantage by offering nonbanking services through subsidiaries with the approval of the FDIC. Unfortunately, these advantages are denied to national banks by law and to member banks by Federal Reserve Board policy. It is surprising that commercial banks have not tried to convert to a federal savings charter.[29] Savings and loans, however, have tended to convert from mutual to stock form. Some 186 such conversions have already taken place in the year since passage of Garn–St. Germain, and many others are in process. Use of the stock form allows thrifts to form holding companies, thereby further broadening the services they can offer.

REGULATION OF HOLDING COMPANIES

The Bank Holding Company Act limits the activities of companies that control banks, thereby complementing the limits on the activities of the banks themselves. Since the depositors of the controlled banks are supposedly unaffected by the outside activities of the parent, there is some question as to whether the parent should be controlled as though it were also a bank; but in 1956 Congress feared that bank holding companies would become too powerful, and they were therefore put under the exclusive regulatory control of the Federal Reserve Board. Why this was done must remain somewhat of a mystery, but the Fed is not about to relinquish this power without a battle in Congress — regardless of the merits of its case in today's business environment.* In the bureaucratic world, turf commands loyalties without any regard for logic.†

The important language in the Bank Holding Company Act is that which limits the activities of companies that control banks to those that are "so closely related to banking or managing or controlling banks as to be a proper incident thereto."[30] One of the purposes of the legislation — as was hinted in Chapter 2 — was to reduce the power exercised by the Giannini family through its control of both banks and commercial firms in the West through ownership of Transamerica Corporation. The act effectively accomplished that.‡

The Fed used its regulation to control bank holding companies. Its regulation permits bank holding companies: (1) to make loans; (2) to operate an industrial bank or similar institution that does not both accept demand deposits and make commercial loans (a so-called nonbank bank); (3) to act as an investment adviser; (4) to produce certain leasing services; (5) to provide limited data processing services; (6) to act as an insurance agent or broker under certain circumstances;[31] (7) to underwrite credit life and health insurance directly related to its lending activity; and (8) to engage in real estate appraisals. In 1982/83 the Fed did take a number of steps to enable bank holding companies to broaden their activities. They are now permitted to engage in: (1) data processing and transmission services;[32] (2) futures commission merchant activities;[33] (3) operation of a savings and loan under very limited circumstances;§ (4) arranging equity financing for real estate development;‖ and (5) discount brokerage.[34]

In essence, the Fed has regarded the Bank Holding Company Act as an expression of congressional desire to limit the activities in which bank holding companies may engage. It will be interesting to see the extent to which the recommendations of the Bush Task Group with respect to deregulation of depository institutions will ultimately influence

---

*See Chapter 6 for an explanation of the Fed's tenacity in insisting on control over the major bank holding companies, supposedly in order to control monetary policy.

†The Fed's position will be examined in detail in Chapter 6, which deals with proposed changes in bank regulation and suggests some solutions for the future.

‡Transamerica chose to remain a commercial conglomerate and spun off its banks.

§Operation is permitted only when the savings and loan is in danger of failing. This is what has enabled Citicorp to acquire one in California, Illinois, and Florida, thereby neatly circumventing the limitations on interstate banking, at least in these states.

‖But the Fed has prohibited bank holding companies from developing or syndicating real estate, from listing or advertising properties for sale, or from holding themselves out as a real estate broker or developer.

Congress to enlarge the powers of bank holding companies as a means of expanding competition in the area of financial services. Changing regulators will not accomplish this purpose. A clearer expression of the intent of Congress is very much needed here. This is particularly true because, as a result of the Garn–St. Germain Depository Institutions Act, thrift institutions can generally now exercise—at least indirectly—all the functions of banks without many of the regulatory limitations applicable to banks and bank holding companies.

Federally insured savings and loans and federal savings banks (whether these are insured by the FDIC or the FSLIC) are subject to the Savings and Loan Holding Company Act.[35] Under this act a company that controls only one savings and loan or federal savings bank may engage in any other type of business activity without any restriction, provided it qualifies for domestic building and loan tax status under the Internal Revenue Code.* This was the means used by Sears to operate a retail business, a securities firm, an insurance company, and a savings and loan, all under a single holding company. It has given enormous value to such an institution because it quite effectively gets around all the limitations of federal banking regulation while maintaining the advantages of having a federally insured depository institution in the holding company. It will be difficult for the reader to understand why the federal government has devised a complicated regulatory system to control the activities of bank holding companies while making it so easy to get around all such carefully designed limitations through the use of a federally insured thrift institution that can exercise not only banking powers but any other activity forbidden to bank holding companies regulated by the Federal Reserve Board. It is no wonder that Merrill Lynch and Thompson McKinnon, Inc., both full-service broker-dealers; Kemper Corp., a leading financial services holding company with its principal base in insurance; and others are seeking to acquire a savings and loan.

Even multiple savings and loan holding companies are far better off than bank holding companies because the pertinent language of the act simply requires that the outside activity be a "proper incident" to the operations of a thrift rather than the language "closely related to banking" that appears in the Bank Holding Company Act.

Why is a thrift not also a bank holding company since it can now

---

*The code requires that the thrift must invest at least 60 percent of its assets in residential housing mortgages, government obligations, or certain other instruments. See 12 U.S.C. 1730a(n) for the application of their test under the Garn–St. Germain Act.

accept demand deposits and make commercial loans under Garn–St. Germain? That act specifically states that federally chartered and FSLIC insured thrifts are not "banks" under the Bank Holding Company Act.[36] However, the exemption does not apply to state-chartered savings banks that convert to stock form. Under Garn–St. Germain these will be deemed to be banks under the Bank Holding Company Act if they take demand deposits and make commercial loans. A state-chartered savings and loan can, however, take advantage of the Garn–St. Germain exemption because it is FSLIC insured.

NONBANK BANKS

Perhaps most indicative of the anomalies contained in the U.S. bank regulatory system is the phrase *nonbank banks*, which to both laymen and professionals must indicate that the regulatory system is indeed inconsistent and guilty of hairsplitting. A nonbank bank is a depository institution holding a federal or state bank charter that can provide federal insurance to its bank depositors but is not a bank as that term is defined under the Bank Holding Company Act.[37]

This important definition has allowed institutions that could not otherwise meet the restrictions of the act on nonbanking activities to establish or acquire insured banks and combine their banking services with other financial services that otherwise would not be permitted.

In late 1982 the Dreyfus Corporation, an investment adviser and mutual fund operator, applied to the Comptroller for permission to establish a national bank subsidiary and to the FDIC under the Change in Bank Control Act[38] for permission to acquire an insured nonmember bank. In both cases Dreyfus contended that the subsidiary would not be making commercial loans after acquisition and hence would not be a bank for purposes of the Bank Holding Company Act. The Fed urged the Comptroller and the FDIC not to approve the applications by stating that it proposed to change the definition of the term *commercial loans* as used in the act to include "the purchase of such instruments as commercial paper, bankers acceptances, and certificates of deposit, the extension of broker call loans, the sale of Federal funds, the deposit of interest bearing funds and similar lending vehicles."[39] Both the Comptroller and FDIC rejected the Fed's stand as inconsistent with its previous position, and both agencies have approved Dreyfus's applications. Since then, the Comptroller has approved a similar application from J. W. Seligman & Co., Inc.[40] Such firms as Prudential, J. C. Penney, Merrill Lynch,

Aetna Life & Casualty, and Beneficial Corporation have all acquired or announced their intention to acquire nonbank banks.

Because neither the Comptroller nor the FDIC heeded the Fed's notice that it intended to close the nonbank bank loophole, at the end of 1983 the Fed announced a redefinition both of *deposits* and of *commercial loans* as defined under the Bank Holding Company Act and issued a lengthy explanation for its decision.[41] It is clear that the Fed has no intention of permitting nonbanking institutions to enter banking through the acquisition of nonbank banks and thereby offer a full range of financial services when it does not allow these activities on the part of bank holding companies within its exclusive jurisdiction. Whether or not the courts will permit the Fed to modify the Bank Holding Company Act and extend the Fed's jurisdiction by regulatory interpretation of the laws of Congress in such a way as to give the Fed additional power remains to be seen. It is certain that the Fed's action will be attacked in the courts, and the conflict will probably have to be resolved ultimately by the Supreme Court unless Congress in the meantime decides to amend the Bank Holding Company Act. In today's very different environment involving the rendering of financial services, with competition to banks and bank holding companies coming from several new directions, it appears clear that the Fed should allow bank holding companies to furnish much broader financial services to their customers while insulating bank activities from the remainder. If the Fed is unwilling to do this, Congress should by legislation modify the Bank Holding Company Act to specifically permit bank holding companies to exercise these additional powers free of Fed interference or control except for those activities specifically related to banking — and then only to the extent of ensuring the protection of bank depositors.

How does the change in interpretation by the Fed of the Bank Holding Company Act affect the question of nonbank banks? The acquisition of existing banks that have divested or will divest their commercial loan portfolios or cease to accept deposits is exempt from Fed approval under the act. Such acquisition still requires approval of the Comptroller for national banks and by the FDIC for insured nonmember banks, but the regulatory body has only 60 days to act and can disapprove only on limited grounds. So we can expect acquisitions of existing banks to continue, pending a court test of the Fed's revision of Regulation Y to redefine *deposits* and *commercial loans*.[42]

In 1984 committees of both houses of Congress adopted legislation to do away with the nonbank bank loophole. Given the mood of Congress, it is likely that such legislation will be adopted even in the shortened sessions resulting from 1984 being an election year.

NECESSITY FOR
CONGRESSIONAL ACTION

The inconsistencies and irrationalities of current regulatory stand-ards governing the different regulatory agencies having jurisdiction over depository institutions indicate how important it has become for Con-gress to clarify the situation as soon as practicable. Regrettably, past leg-islation does not help us very much in today's environment. At a time when massive federal deficits presage a return of inflation sooner or later, the public is entitled to a better return on its savings than has been per-mitted by the Federal Reserve Board's Regulation Q and its restrictive controls over bank holding companies. Under the guise of protection of depositors, the Fed under the mandate of Congress has not only dis-couraged bank deposits but led the banks to try by every means possi-ble to circumvent the Fed's regulations in order to remain competitive. Unfortunately, the Fed's policies have encouraged the banks to lend abroad rather than in the United States to be better able to match the earnings of other institutions rendering financial services demanded by the public. Why should Congress not mandate the bank regulators — as it did in the case of thrifts, for example — to promote as well as to reg-ulate banking? The well-being of banks is essential to the protection of depositors.

While the Comptroller has shown more flexibility than the Fed, he is operating under the statutory restriction that gives national banks only such powers "as shall be necessary to carry on the business of banking"[43] — highly restrictive language. Furthermore, national banks remain cov-ered by the severe limitations of Glass-Steagall.

State-chartered member banks are also governed by Glass-Steagall and are unable to expand their nonbanking activities because of the re-strictions imposed by the Fed and the courts.

Insured nonmember banks and state-chartered mutual and stock savings banks are — subject to state law — able to offer significant secur-ities services through subsidiaries. The FDIC has given these institu-tions broad leeway to offer almost all the financial services, including insurance, that their customers may require.

The FHLBB and the FSLIC have been very conscious of their man-date to promote as well as regulate the thrift industry and have acted accordingly in allowing federally chartered thrift institutions maximum leeway under the restrictions of the Home Owners' Loan Act. The Fed-eral Savings and Loan Holding Company Act places no restrictions on the nonbanking activities of holding companies that control a single savings and loan if that savings and loan qualifies for building and loan tax status. Since the enactment of the Garn–St. Germain Act, there has been very much increased interest on the part of nonbanking financial services companies to acquire thrift institutions. Why should the two holding company acts, one for banks and one for thrifts, continue to remain so at variance with each other at a time when Garn–St. Germain has, as a practical matter, removed the distinction between the activities in which a bank and a thrift institution may engage? If narrow limits on bank activities still reflect congressional policy as the National Bank Act, Glass-Steagall, and the Bank Holding Company Act (as interpreted by the Fed) seem to suggest, then why is the federal government through the FDIC or the FSLIC insuring thrifts that are not subject to the limitations on banks?

If congressional reform is not forthcoming reasonably soon, there will be even greater pressure for depository institutions to modify their status to avoid the restrictions applicable to banks and bank holding companies. Whether this is in the nation's interest is highly questionable. But before Congress can act, it needs to answer the fundamental question posed in this book: Is a federally insured depository institution so different from other kinds of business enterprises that its activities need even now be severely controlled and limited? Or should such an institution be permitted, directly or indirectly through subsidiaries, to engage in activities not formerly associated with banking but today demanded by its customers for both a fair rate of return on savings and maximum investment flexibility?

The Reagan administration, in its initial proposal for deregulation of bank holding companies,[44] took the position that depository institutions should not engage, directly or through subsidiaries, in activities not traditionally associated with banking. However, bank holding companies should be permitted to engage in a wide range of activities so as to compete effectively with other financial intermediaries while keeping depository institutions under a comprehensive system of regulation justifying the special advantages granted to them: deposit insurance, access to liquidity assistance, and exemption from securities laws in connection with their issuance of CDs.* In effect the administration was saying that depository institutions were special but bank holding companies need not be prevented from offering a full line of financial serv-

---

*A detailed analysis of the Bush Task Group recommendations agreed upon in 1984 is to be found in Chapter 6.

ices because the depository institution subsidiary can be protected independently. The idea is sound, but the regulatory system must be modified accordingly. It is only through changes adopted by Congress after careful consideration that a new comprehensive system of bank regulation can be enacted.

The administration's proposal would attempt to insulate the depository institution as an intermediary between users and savers of capital. But suppose the depository institution subsidiary fails because it has advanced moneys to its parent that the parent has invested in risky ventures and cannot repay, thereby causing both parent and depository sub to fail. How will this scenario be avoided unless the parent is itself regulated or the dealings between the parent and sub are subject to supervision? The administration would handle the matter through a series of restrictions on the transactions between banks and their affiliated holding companies. Only the bank would be subject to regulation by banking authorities; the holding company would be subject to whatever regulations were applicable to its type of industry: the SEC would treat it like a commercial firm; the Superintendent of Insurance, like an insurance company; and so on. The aim here would be to avoid overlap of regulation by placing an effective screen between bank and nonbank activities.

The holding company's capacity to raise capital on its own would enable it to fund its depository institution if the depository institution were ever under some strain, thereby making the latter more stable as a result of its affiliation with a holding company. This is fine in theory. When one looks, for example, at foreign lending by bank holding companies in the last few years, however, one is led to question the extent to which the depository institution has been protected by its affiliation with the holding company or indeed whether the Federal Reserve Board —which is charged with regulating the holding company under current law—has indeed been exercising its functions adequately.* Perhaps by allowing bank holding companies to engage in all manner of financial services, this very diversity will better protect the bank affiliate than the current narrow limitations on its activities so unsatisfactorily "controlled" at present because this will tend to increase as well as diversify bank holding company revenues.

---

*The nine largest U.S. bank holding companies, for example, made loans to Latin American countries between 1980 and 1983 in excess of their combined capital funds without any interference by the Federal Reserve. See Chapter 7.

CONCLUSION

It is clear from the discussion in this chapter that the present bank regulatory system is no longer adequate to meet the needs either of borrowers or of depositors in the regulated depository institutions. Changes in methods of rendering financial services now require that Congress take action to change the system of bank and thrift regulation. Banks must be allowed to compete more effectively with commercial firms rendering financial services. This means that at least bank holding companies should be allowed to broaden the products they may offer their depositors. It also means that at least bank holding companies, if not banks, should be permitted to extend their activities across state lines.

It will surprise the reader to note that the trend in banking has been in exactly the opposite direction of current commercial firm movement. In business, firms are encouraged to become national, if not international, in their scope. In banking it is the reverse. The Federal Reserve and the courts have continued — supposedly under mandates from Congress — to construe in narrow terms the power of banks to render services outside the state where they are principally based. The result has been to encourage banking institutions to pressure the states to allow bank affiliates located there to carry on peripheral activities outside the state. In this manner the states both protect their domestic banking institutions and increase their financial services employment. The result, however, is ever-increasing chaos in our national banking system. Action by Congress is now long overdue.

In the next chapter I will analyze the various recommendations that have been made by the Reagan administration to Congress, and within the Congress itself, to restructure the bank regulatory system in the United States and, at the same time, to restructure the regulatory agencies themselves to simplify regulation and to get rid of overlapping authority and inconsistent rulings. There is no excuse — even allowing for the deliberate pace at which legislation moves in Congress — for the present chaotic bank regulatory system to continue any longer.

NOTES

1. See "Financial Fracas — Banks and Rivals Push into New Business as Congress Dawdles," *Wall Street Journal*, March 23, 1984, p. 1.

2. This involved the purchase by BankAmerica Corporation, the holding company of the Bank of America (then the country's largest bank), of Charles

Schwab & Co., the country's largest discount brokerage firm. After extended hearings the Federal Reserve approved the purchase. 69 Fed. Res. Bull. 105 (1983). The Board's opinion was affirmed by the U.S. Court of Appeals, Second Circuit, in *Securities Industry Association v. Board of Governors of the Federal Reserve System*, 716 F. 2d 92 (2d Cir. 1983); aff'd by U.S. Supreme Court in June 1984, 52 U.S.L.W. 4962. In 1983 Schwab almost doubled the number of its customers—to 600,000. It had revenues of $117 million, compared with $43.5 million in 1982, and pretax profit of $25 million, compared with $3.5 million in 1982. Its link to Bank of America has proved highly beneficial. The Supreme Court, however also ruled in July, 1984, that commercial paper issued by companies had to be regarded as a security. See note 21, *infra*.

3. In 1982 the Comptroller of the Currency approved the acquisition by Union Planters National Bank of Memphis, Tennessee, of Brenner Steed and Associates, Inc., a discount broker in Memphis, and the application of Security Pacific National Bank to establish a new subsidiary to engage in discount brokerage activities in California and eventually in other states. The U.S. District Court for the District of Columbia reversed the Comptroller's decision— *Securities Industry Association v. Comptroller*, 577 F.Supp. 252 (D.D.C. 1983)— holding that an office of a national bank for the conduct of discount brokerage is a "branch" subject under the McFadden Act to state law limitations on the establishment of bank branch offices. It will be interesting to see whether this court's holding will eventually be reversed on appeal. The appeal was docketed No. 84-5026 (D.C. Civ., Jan. 13, 1984). Union Planters, one of the applicants, had proposed to carry on discount brokerage activities at its branches in Tennessee, at affiliated banks in Tennessee, and at correspondent banks in Tennessee and six other states. The Court did not discuss whether its opinion would have differed if bank holding companies, rather than banks, had made the application.

4. (D.C. Cir. 1968).

5. U.S.C.A. Title 12, Sec. 24.

6. Id.

7. National banks are required by statute (12 U.S.C. 222) to be members of the Federal Reserve.

8. 12 U.S.C.A. 377.

9. 12 U.S.C.A. 378a.

10. *Arnold Towns v. Camp*, 472 F.2d 427 (1st Cir. 1972)—travel service; *Port of N.Y. Auth. v. Baker, Watts & Co.*, 392 F.2d 497 (D.C. Cir. 1968)— municipal revenue bond underwriting; and *Inv. Co. Inst. v. Camp*, 401 U.S. 617 (1971)—de facto mutual funds.

11. *M & M Leasing Corp. v. Seattle National Bank*, 563 F.2d 1977 (9th Cir. 1977), cert. den., 436 U.S. 956 (1978)—leasing; 12 C.F.R. 7.7378—credit cards; and 12 C.F.R. 7.7016—letters of credit.

12. Fed. Banking L. Rep. (CCH) par. 99,339 (1983).

13. *Investment Co. Institute v. Conover*, No. 83-0549 (D.D.C. filed Feb.

24, 1983). This case was still pending as of July, 1984.

14. Public Law 97–320, (1982), 12 U.S.C. Sec. 1861–1867. See further, Hawke, Sweet, and Mierzewski, "Revised BSC Act Offers Banks New Opportunities," *Legal Times*, December 20, 1982, p. 17.

15. 12 U.S.C. 1864, 1865.

16. *Investment Co. Institute v. FDIC*, no. 82-1321 (D.C. Cir. 1982) dismissed without prejudice on June 7, 1984; and *Inv. Co. Inst. v. United States*, no. 82-2532 (D.D.C. 1982) case dismissed with prejudice July 6, 1984.

17. 47 Fed. Reg. 381984 (1982).

18. 1983 S.D. Sess. Laws (Sen. Bill no. 256, Sec. 5), enacted March 4, 1983, to amend Ch 51-18 of the laws of South Dakota.

19. 1982 Cal. Stats. Ch 1050, Sec. 1-5.

20. See E. Gerald Corrigan, "Are Banks Special?" in 1982 Annual Report of the Federal Reserve Bank of Minneapolis, 12 C.F.R. Sec. 208.7 and 208.8.

21. The Fed declared, for example, that commercial paper was not a "security" within the language of Glass-Steagall and that member banks could underwrite these short-term promissory notes. Fed Banking Law Rep. (CCH) par. 98,435 (1980) aff'd, *A. G. Becker Inc. v. Board of Governors*, 693 F.2d 136 (D.C. Cir. 1982); reversed by the U.S. Supreme Court on June 28, 1984 in a 6 to 3 decision declaring that commercial paper is a security and therefore is covered by the Glass-Steagall prohibition on bank's underwriting of securities.

22. Depository Institutions Deregulation and Monetary Control Act of 1980, Public Law 96–221, Sec. 303, 12 U.S.C., Sec. 1832.

23. 12 U.S.C. Sec. 1464 (c)(2)(B).

24. See Thomas P. Vartanian and Randall H. McFarlane, "FHLBB Helps Bring About Major Changes in Thrifts," *Legal Times*, November 1, 1982, pp. 16, 22, 23 and 28.

25. Mass. Ann. Laws, Chs 167–170, and 172.

26. The FSLIC was established in 1934 under Title IV of the National Housing Act 48 Stat. 124b (1934) (12 U.S.C. 1724, *et seq.*).

27. 12 U.S.C. 1465.

28. *S.I.A. v. FHLBB*, no. 82-1920 (D.D.C., filed July 12, 1982).

29. See Thomas Vartanian and Jerry Hawke, "It Sounds Like a Banker's Fantasy, But It Isn't," *American Banker*, April 13, 1983, p. 4; idem, "Conversions May Spur Thrift Industry Rebirth," *American Banker*, April 14, 1983, p. 4.

30. Section 4(c)(b) of the act. See Note *The Bank Holding Company Act Amendments of 1970* Geo. Wash. L.R. 1200, 1207 (1971) for an analysis of the Federal Reserve's narrow interpretation of this language.

31. These are permitted activities of Bank Holding Company subsidiaries. Public Law 997–320, see 601, 12 U.S.C. 1843(c)(8).

32. 47 Fed. Reg. 37368-37373 (Aug. 26, 1982) amended. Regulation is to include these activities as closely related.

33. See *J. P. Morgan & Co. Inc.*, 68 Fed. Res. Bul. 514 (1982).

34. See note 2 regarding the acquisition of Charles Schwab & Co. by BankAmerica Corporation. See also 48 Fed. Reg. 7746 (1982) for a proposed

amendment by the Fed to a regulation permitting Bank Holding Companies to invest in discount brokerage firms.

35. 12 U.S.C. 1730a(1)(A) and (D).

36. Public Law 97-320, sec. 333. But banker's banks (chartered by the Comptroller to perform services solely for other depository institutions) are specifically included within the definition of bank. See Public Law 97-320, sec. 404(d)(1).

37. Section 2(c) of the Bank Holding Company Act—12 U.S.C. 1841(c)—defines a *bank* as an entity that "(1) accepts deposits that the depositor has a legal right to withdraw on demand, and (2) engages in the business of making commercial loans." If it does not meet both tests, it is not a bank, and therefore the institution that controls it is not a bank holding company under the act.

38. 12 U.S.C. 1917-8.

39. See letter of William W. Wiles, secretary of the Board, to William M. Isaac, chairman of the FDIC, dated December 1, 1983.

40. Fed. Banking L. Rep. CCH par. 99,463, (1983); par. 99,464, (1983).

41. See 12CFR Part 225, and especially 225.2(a)(1) published in Federal Register, Vol. 49, No. 3 (Jan. 5, 1984) p. 818. This section redefines a "bank" to include new definitions of demand deposits and commercial loans in order to make it more difficult to create a nonbank bank. See also Federal Register Vol. 49, No. 49 (March 12, 1983). The Board proposes therein to amend Regulation Y, 49 FR 794 (1984) to add certain proposed nonbanking activities as permissible for bank holding companies. On July 10, 1984, in a press release dated that day, the Federal Reserve Board announced it was delaying for five months the effective date of Regulation Y revisions designed to close the nonbank bank loophole.

42. Idem.

43. 12 U.S.C., sec. 24. The leading case interpreting the powers of national banks is Arnold Towns v. Camp 472 F.2d 427 (1st cir. 1972) where the circuit court decided that a national bank could not operate a travel agency as an activity necessary, useful, or convenient to its banking business.

44. "The Bank Holding Company Deregulation Act" introduced in the 97th Congress as S. 2490 and H.R. 6762 in 1983.

Figure 1
Total Private Financial Assets Percent Held by Different Financial
Services Firms
(As of 12/31/83; $ in billions)

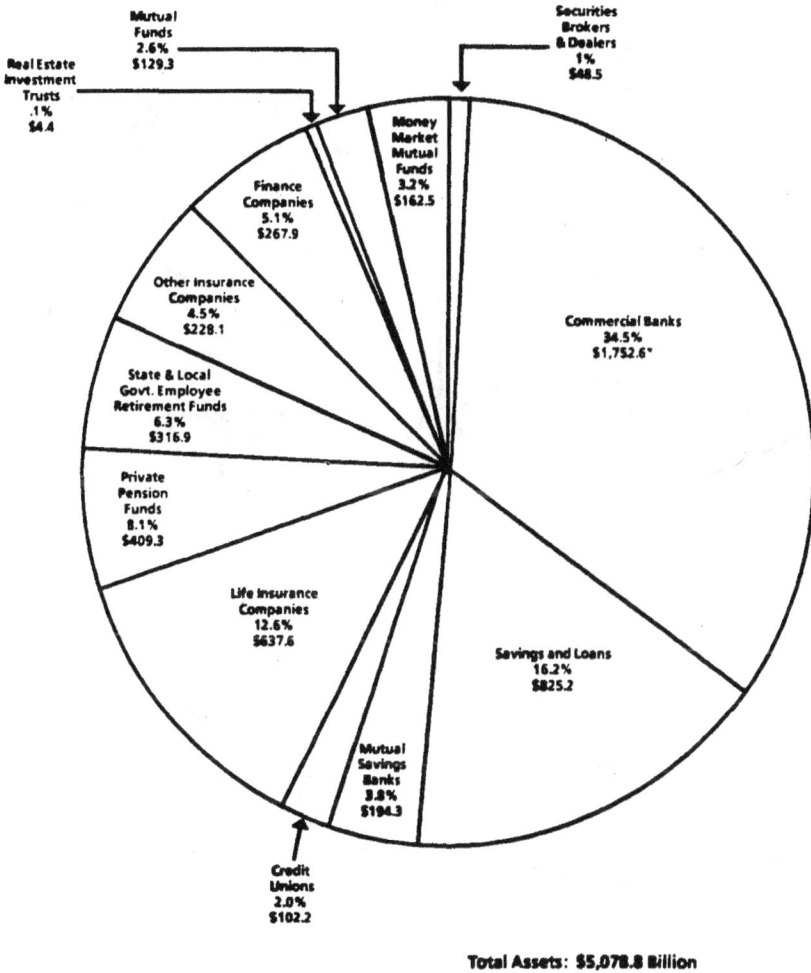

Total Assets: $5,078.8 Billion

*This figure does not include international banking facilities, and is net of inter-
bank liabilities.

Source: Blueprint for Reform: The Report of the Task Group on Regulation
of Financial Services, July 1984, p. 17.

Figure 2

Distribution of Assets and Numbers of Banks
(As of 12/31/83; $ in billions)

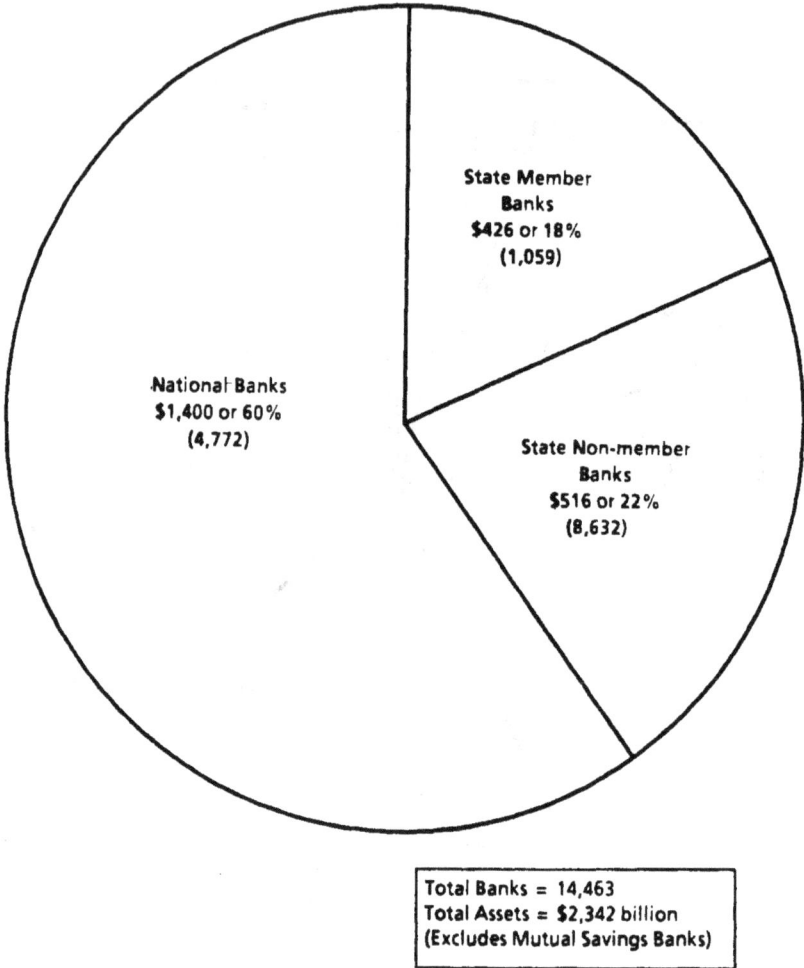

State Member
Banks
$426 or 18%
(1,059)

National Banks
$1,400 or 60%
(4,772)

State Non-member
Banks
$516 or 22%
(8,632)

Total Banks = 14,463
Total Assets = $2,342 billion
(Excludes Mutual Savings Banks)

Source: Blueprint for Reform: The Report of the Task Group on Regulation of Financial Services, July 1984, p. 100.

Figure 3

Growth of Bank Holding Companies and Banks Held by Holding
Companies
(As of 12/31/83)

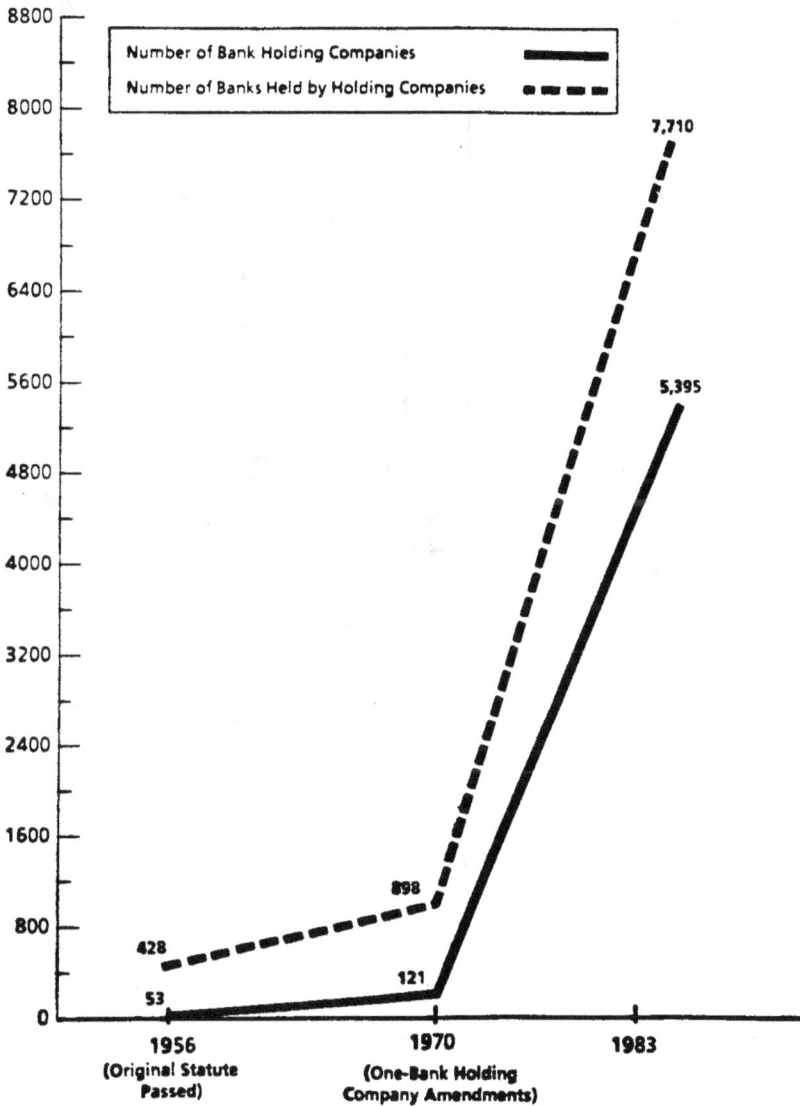

Source: Blueprint for Reform: The Report of the Task Group on Regulation
of Financial Services, July 1984, p. 21.

Figure 4
Existing Regulation of Banks and Their Holding Companies

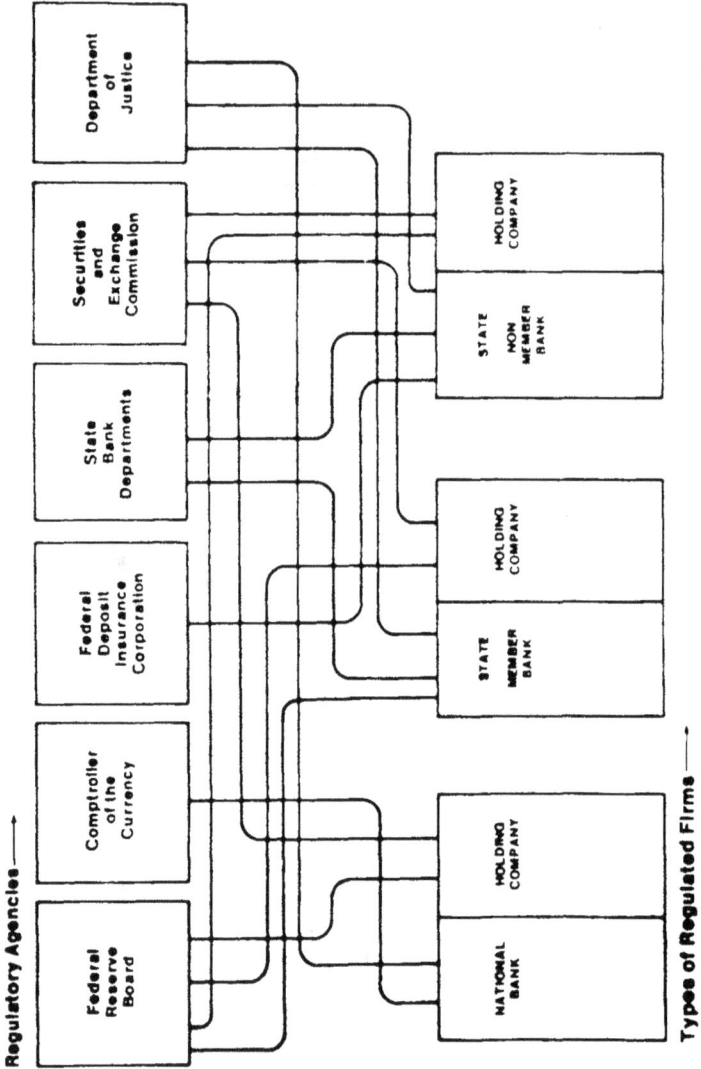

1. Antitrust Enforcement Only.

Source: Blueprint for Reform: The Report of the Task Group on Regulation of Financial Services, July 1984, p. 19.

Figure 5
Proposed Federal Regulation of Commercial Banks and Their
Holding Companies
(Excludes Purely Insurance Functions of the FDIC)

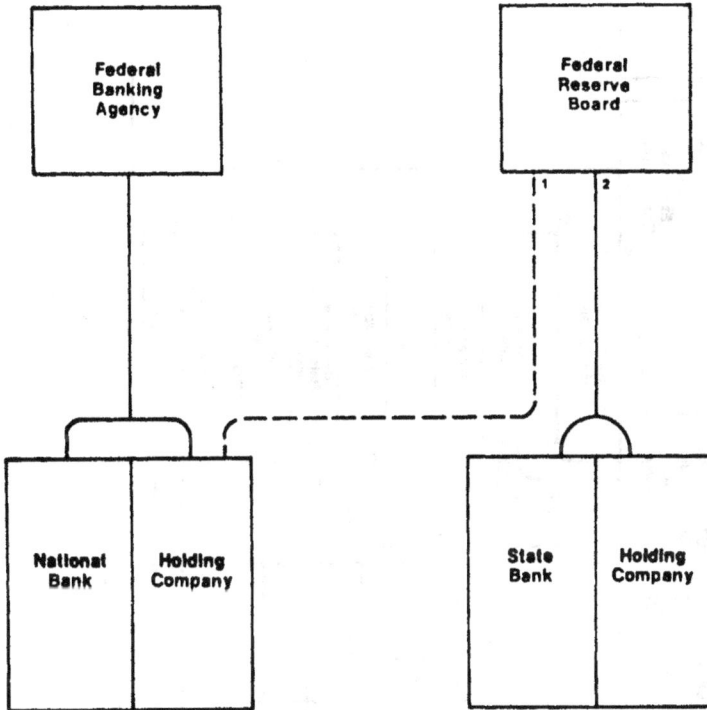

1. Only for those holding companies of national banks (35) which qualify as an "international class" holding company.

2. To the extent responsibilities are not transferred to the states.

Source: Blueprint for Reform: The Report of the Task Group on Regulation of Financial Services, July 1984, p. 55.

Figure 6
Functional Analysis of Existing Federal Bank Regulation

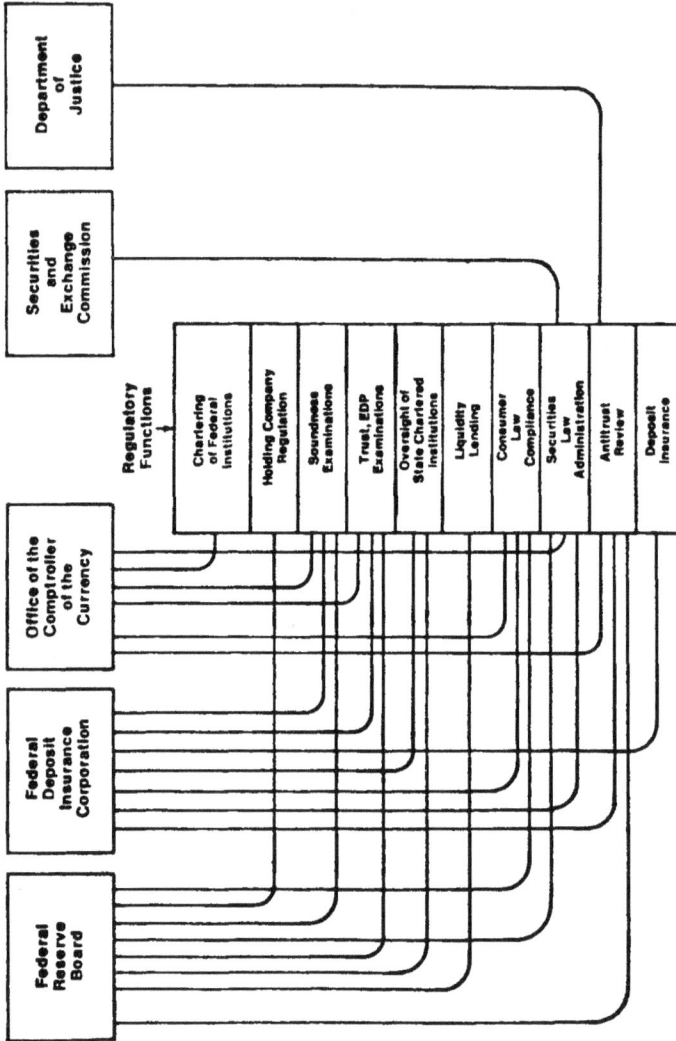

Source: Blueprint for Reform: The Report of the Task Group on Regulation of Financial Services, July 1984, p. 51.

Figure 7

Regulatory Reveiw of Proposed Merger of Two National Banks and Their Holding Companies

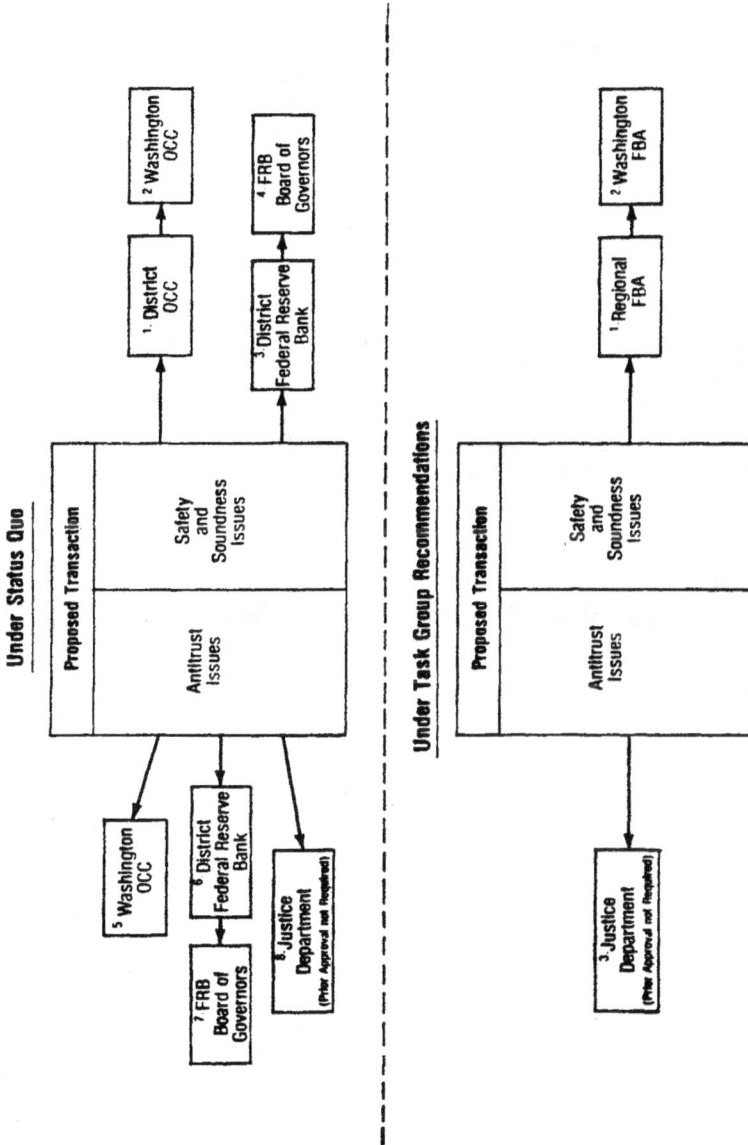

Source: Blueprint for Reform: The Report of the Task Group on Regulation of Financial Services, July 1984, p. 61.

6

MOVES TO
MODERNIZE THE
REGULATORY SYSTEM

Two separate questions will be examined in this chapter. The first is, What should depository institutions be allowed to do to become more competitive with financial services companies? Initially, we will look at their authority to act beyond the confines of one state despite the prohibitions of the McFadden Act and the Douglas amendment to the Bank Holding Company Act. This we call *geographical* expansion to regional or interstate banking. Then we need to consider which activities depository institutions should be allowed to engage in despite the prohibitions of the Glass-Steagall and the Bank Holding Company acts. The first act separates banks from securities underwriting distribution; the second limits the activities of bank holding companies to those "so closely related to banking—as to be a proper incident thereto after considering public benefits and possible adverse effects."* What we are talking about here is the abrogation of statutory limitations on product.

The second question is really dependent upon the answer to the

---

*Sec. 4(c)(8) of the Bank Holding Company Act. By its terms, this section contains no geographical limitations. Permissible activities permitted by the Fed have included mortgage banking, consumer finance, commercial finance factoring, credit card lending, operating industrial banks, "nondepository" trust companies, giving investment advice, full payout leasing, limited credit insurance agency and underwriting, data processing courier services, management consulting for banks, sale of money orders, savings banks and travelers checks, real estate appraisals, real estate equity financing, securities brokerage (but not combined with investment advice), underwriting and dealing in securities to the same extent as a state member bank, foreign exchange advice and transactions, acting as futures commission merchant, tax preparation, commodity trading advisory services, check guaranty, and consumer finance counseling. The Fed has not permitted—because of perceived risk—real estate development, unlimited life insurance underwriting, real estate syndication, or acquisition of savings and loans (except in emergency situations).

first. If it appears advisable to Congress to extend the activities of depository institutions in terms of geographical area and/or product so that they may better compete with other financial services companies, what kind of regulatory system should the country have to supervise better the expanded activities and areas open to the depository institutions?

Although some would urge that a review of the regulatory system is in any event overdue, it makes more sense to address the question of expanded permissible activities first and then to determine which regulatory structure will fit the requirements of these extended banking powers. With this in mind, the chapter is divided into two parts. First, I will address the question of new permissible activities. Second, I will discuss the changes in the regulatory structure that appear to be called for by such new powers.

The Reagan administration has addressed both these issues: the first through the Secretary of the Treasury's deregulation plan; the second through the report of the Vice-President's Task Group on Regulation of Financial Services chaired by Vice-President George Bush (the Bush Task Group).

EXTENSION OF PERMISSIBLE ACTIVITIES

The Reagan Administration's Plan

On March 28, 1984, Secretary of the Treasury Donald T. Regan appeared before the Senate Committee on Banking, Housing and Urban Affairs, chaired by Senator Jake Garn, to comment on various bills introduced in the Senate to deregulate the banking system in the United States.

There were then three principal proposals pending before the Senate: the administration's Financial Institutions Deregulation Act (S. 1609), commonly referred to as "FIDA"; Senator Garn's Financial Services Competitive Equity Act (S. 2181), the "Garn bill"; and Senator William Proxmire's Depository Institutions Holding Company Act Amendments of 1983 (S. 2134).

Under the theme of the disarray in the marketplace, Regan said:

> Until very recently, the activities of banks, thrifts, investment banks, insurance underwriters, and securities brokers were all separate and clearly defined. However, under the competitive pressures of today's financial services marketplace, the old structure is breaking down,

thus creating inequities in the system and regulatory disarray. The number and type of direct competitors to depository institutions has increased dramatically. Unregulated financial services firms have responded innovatively and rapidly to market changes, offering consumers effective substitutes for traditional banking services as well as other financial services that banks by law or regulation are forbidden to offer. Today there is virtually no major bank or thrift-like product that is not available from a diversified financial services firm, and there is no bank or bank holding company that can offer the range of services that more sophisticated consumers are demanding from their financial intermediaries.[1]

The Secretary went on to cite a number of instances:

- Sears, Roebuck's offering the equivalent of banking (through a savings and loan association); insurance and securities underwriting; mortgage banking; and insurance, securities, and real estate brokerage.
- Prudential Life Insurance Company's offering securities brokerage through Prudential-Bache and now in banking through the acquisition of a nonbank bank.
- American Express Company's offering securities brokerage through Shearson/American Express; trust services through Boston Safe Deposit Trust Company; and now insurance, investment products, and mutual funds through its acquisition of most of the assets of Allegheny Corporation, including Investors Diversified Services operating nationwide.

While industrial firms and insurance companies were diversifying into other financial services, bank holding companies were trying to extend their range of products and remain competitive by trying to exploit loopholes within the statutory framework of bank regulation; for example, BankAmerica moved into the insurance business by announcing a plan to allow Capital Holding Company of Louisville, Kentucky, to sell insurance at its branches; Citicorp was operating savings and loans in California, Florida, and Illinois; many banks, holding companies, and savings and loans offered discount brokerage services. The FDIC had even proposed a rule that would allow state nonmember banks to underwrite investment-grade corporate securities. The FDIC was also considering two additional proposals: variable insurance premiums, depending upon risk; and classification of different kinds of deposits.

Regan urged Congress to take statutory action to bring bank regulation up to date and to accommodate the "market dynamics in the future":

> By doing nothing, Congress makes a very unwise decision—to endorse haphazard and chaotic deregulation by court interpretations of existing laws that were not meant to cope with a new economic environment, by actions of states anxious to assist their depository institutions and create jobs, and by the Federal regulators. Moreover, consumer demand for innovative services and greater convenience will not abate. Competitive pressures fed by consumer demand will continue to create upheaval in the marketplace unless a structure is adopted to rationalize it.[2]

In the last chapter I referred to many of the court interpretations to which Regan was referring. The principal loophole in the Bank Holding Company Act, as noted in Chapter 5, has been the definition of a *bank* as an institution that *both* accepts demand deposits and makes commercial loans. While the Fed has tried to close this loophole by regulation, a federal appellate court recently ruled that an industrial bank offering NOW accounts was not taking demand deposits.[3] Unitary thrift institutions (if their assets are sufficiently concentrated in housing-related loans) may engage in almost any kind of activity. State savings and loans and nonmember banks can conduct unlimited securities activities to the extent permitted by state law and deposit insurance regulations.* Finally, the states—under the dual banking system—can decide the activities in which their banks and bank-operating subsidiaries may engage. The states have been very active in giving their depository institutions new powers because this creates new jobs and additional financial reserves within the state.

Remember that our society is becoming more and more service oriented and that this trend will continue in the future. Financial services companies are growing employers, particularly since services companies are notoriously labor-intensive. This explains why a temporary New York State commission has proposed that beginning on January 1, 1985, New York banks be authorized to engage in insurance brokerage activities directly or through subsidiaries. The commission also recommended that New York banks be permitted through their holding companies to underwrite both life and property and casualty insurance. Since insurance operations would not be limited geographically, New York banks would

---

*The FHLBB, however, is charging extra insurance premiums, or refusing insurance coverage to state savings and loans that engage in activities beyond those permitted by the Garn–St. Germain Depository Institutions Act of 1982.

gain a substantial competitive advantage over banks in other states.* How long will it take other state banking centers such as California, Illinois, Pennsylvania, and Ohio to do the same? In 1984 banks in at least three states—California, Massachusetts, and North Carolina—were permitted to invest all or a specified portion of their capital or assets in just about any activity in which they wished to engage. It is a foregone conclusion that competition among the states to extend the powers of their own financial institutions will keep on growing unless and until Congress takes action to preempt the field.

The Reagan administration has opposed extending the powers of banks through state action largely because it believes nonbanking activities should be carried on not by the banks but by their holding companies, thereby insulating the banks' depositors from activities that carry greater risk. As spokesman for the administration, Secretary Regan, who clearly understands and approves increased competition among banks and other financial services organizations, has been urging Congress to adopt a comprehensive program of deregulation that will permit bank holding companies to compete within the financial services industry while still protecting the special responsibility of depository institutions to their depositors. The Secretary knows the industry well. He was, after all, chief executive officer of Merrill Lynch, perhaps the most competitive and innovative financial services company in the field.

Congress has given depository institutions very meaningful advantages. They can offer deposits that are federally insured, and they have access to a lender of last resort through the Federal Reserve's discount window. In return they are subject to federal supervision through the regulatory authorities. The other financial services organizations want freedom from regulation, but they would also like to use the existing regulatory loopholes to obtain federal insurance for their customers. At the present time federal insurance appears to be going beyond its traditional role of protecting bank depositors. Where should the protective line be drawn?

The essence of the Reagan administration's proposed deregulation plan was two pronged: (1) to insulate banks by maintaining tight regulatory controls over their permissible activities but (2) to allow their holding companies much more leeway to engage in activities enabling them to compete effectively with other financial services companies.

---

*As one banker explained it to me: "Financial institutions are to New York what high technology is to California."

The Garn Bill

The Garn bill differed in certain respects from the administration's deregulation plan. It would create an exemption from bank holding company regulation for a limited-purpose depository whose commercial loans did not exceed 5 percent of assets and whose activities were restricted to small business lending and financing of consumer goods inventories. This gave the appearance of being a worthwhile proposal. But it would permit nonfinancial conglomerate firms, through ownership of a consumer bank, to have access to federally-insured credit to finance their sale of goods and services. Would this not distort the competitive balance that deregulation legislation must seek to achieve between depository institutions with access to federal insurance and other financial services firms? In effect the administration has been saying: "Let the bank holding companies compete freely with other providers of financial services, and vice versa, but keep the depository institutions to one side, since they must remain under federal control because their depositors must, as a matter of public policy, be protected. They can, therefore, borrow funds more cheaply because their risks are covered by federal insurance."

The Treasury subscribed to the notion that a *bank* should be defined as any insured depository institution. The Fed persuaded the Treasury that it should be any institution eligible for insurance. Any final bill adopted by Congress will have to redefine a "bank" for purposes of the Bank Holding Company Act.

The Garn bill also proposed to exempt certain thrifts from restrictions on their activities those that would have at least 60 percent of their assets invested in residential mortgages or not more than 25 percent in commercial loans. At present, unitary thrift holding companies (if they meet minimal tests) and thrift services corporations remain potentially unrestricted in their activities. FIDA, the administration bill, proposed to eliminate these exemptions in order to ensure equal treatment for banks and thrifts.

Was the Garn bill correct in maintaining some form of inequity between banks and thrift institutions? The qualified thrift lender under Garn would have the advantage of the liberal liquidity assistance, capital requirements, and banking authority generally available to the thrift industry, as well as freedom from the Glass-Steagall limitations applicable to banks. The reason for encouraging thrift institutions is clear: Public policy wishes to encourage lending to the housing industry. Nevertheless, some sort of equitable competitive relationship between banks and thrifts should be maintained. The Garn–St. Germain Depository Institutions Act of 1982 had allowed thrifts to exercise the same prerogatives as banks. Their special advantages were to be limited except to the extent that they act as housing lenders; otherwise banks would be likely to change their charters and become thrift institutions. Traditional savings banks presumably were to be treated in the same manner as other thrifts, with the same portion of their loans in residential real estate as savings and loans.

What was the purpose of Garn's services corporation exemption for thrifts? The administration urged that this exemption be eliminated so that thrifts as well as banks would be required to use holding companies to carry on activities unrelated to banking. It does appear sound to restrict the depository institutions from expanding their activities through the use of services subsidiaries to minimize the risk to depositors' assets. One of the purposes of changing the regulatory system should be to take away any current inequities among depository institutions as well as between them and other financial services organizations.

Another provision of the Garn bill would have limited combinations, through holding companies, between large depository institutions and substantial firms engaged in nonbanking financial services. These restrictions on further concentrations were to be aimed at approximately 25 of the largest depository institutions. The question here is, Are the antitrust laws sufficient to prevent an undue concentration of power?

At present three federal regulatory agencies, including the Federal Reserve, decide whether bank or thrift mergers create antitrust problems.* The Justice Department reviews the question independently and gives its advice. But the regulators are apt to be too lenient whenever they see a risk to the survival of a bank if they do not give their consent. Obviously, the bigger the depository institution, the safer it will appear to be. I do not believe that antitrust laws should be interpreted by the bank regulators.

Remember that the purpose of the Bank Holding Company Act of 1956 was to prevent "undue concentration of resources." The problem is just as important now — if not more so. The major money-center banks, as will be seen in the next two chapters, did not behave particularly responsibly with respect to their foreign loans in the late 1970s and early 1980s. Nor have some of them handled energy loans with any acumen. The country would be much better served if there were some limitation

---

*Each agency has its own interpretation of the antitrust laws. The Comptroller's office, which has a more liberal attitude, has won 14 times in court against the Federal Reserve.

on concentration of power in the financial area. Historically, the development of the U.S. economy has clearly not been due to any concentration of financial power but, on the contrary, to the multiplicity of business firms and the support they received from their local banks.* We have only to look at Europe's development since World War II to observe how the concentration of financial power tends to discourage the financing of new enterprises in favor of old, more established firms. The development of entrepreneurial initiative in business depends upon the availability of local sources of capital willing to take risks. One of the reasons why Europe—and West Germany, in particular—has not kept up with the development of technology in the United States and Japan in the last 20 years is the concentration of financial power in a handful of institutions closely allied with the major business firms. The same might just as well be said of Canada or Switzerland or France. Wherever there is a high concentration of financial power through a handful of national banks, the individual entrepreneur has almost no chance of obtaining capital.† One will find almost no venture capital firms in either Europe or Canada and very few new, rapidly growing small enterprises as are so frequently found in the United States. The large bank deals with large companies. It has little interest in the development of new businesses because these require time, constant attention, and necessarily a high degree of risk. Whether the Garn bill properly provided for limitations on financial industry concentration can be debated. It is, however, sound that there be some limitation on the concentration of financial power if we wish to continue to develop our smaller industries.

The Garn bill also attempted to prevent bank holding companies from tying their banking services to other services such as insurance and real estate. A simple way of handling this problem would be to prohibit tie-in sales and to allow trade associations for the aggrieved to bring treble damage suits if tying practices were indeed taking place. In addition the law could require that a bank credit customer be advised that he or she may purchase insurance through an independent broker if the individual so desired. While the insurance companies were demanding antitying

---

*There is, of course, a very important philosophical question at stake here. Conservatives will point to the development of the country in the nineteenth century by men such as John D. Rockefeller, J. P. Morgan, Andrew Carnegie, and Henry Clay Frick who created vast enterprises as a result of concentration of power. The Sherman Act of 1890, which established antitrust concepts for the country, is the result of public questioning of their activities.

†But note that Citicorp, today the world's largest bank holding company, has been very active in the venture capital business.

provisions applicable to banks, no one was asking that insurance companies affiliated with depository institutions, like Prudential and Allstate, be also prevented from tie-in sales. These were merely efforts to maintain competitive advantage to which Congress should not pay undue attention.

The Proxmire Bill

What was the difference between the administration's bill — FIDA — and the Proxmire bill — the Depository Institutions Holding Company Act Amendments of 1983? The Proxmire bill did not go as far as FIDA presumably because Senator Proxmire believed its limitations gave his bill better chances of passage. There were three basic differences between the two proposals. First, the Proxmire bill limited permissible activities by not authorizing bank holding companies to engage in new insurance activities, real estate activities, or activities determined not to be "of a financial nature." This last proviso might limit the development of a regulatory framework by which banks could keep pace with future developments in the financial services industry. Second, Proxmire's bill did not provide for parallel treatment of bank and thrift holding companies or services corporations. This seemed to run counter to Garn–St. Germain, which sought to eliminate any regulatory imbalance among depository institutions.* Third, the Proxmire bill proposed to extend coverage of Glass-Steagall to nonmember banks. It also prohibited state-chartered institutions after January 1, 1983, from initiating any activities not permitted by the Bank Holding Company Act to be performed outside the state. Senator Proxmire was thereby proposing to close a loophole used by banks to extend their powers both in terms of product by engaging in investment banking activities and in terms of geographical extension by getting around the limitations of the McFadden Act and the Douglas amendment. In effect the Proxmire bill intend-

---

*Savings and loans have become increasingly banklike in recent years. The Housing and Urban Development Act of 1968 authorized savings and loans to accept both time and savings deposits. The Depository Institutions Deregulation and Monetary Control Act of 1980 authorized federal savings and loans to exercise fiduciary powers to the same extent as national banks and gave them commercial lending authority. The Garn–St. Germain Depository Institutions Act of 1982 permitted federal savings and loans to accept some demand deposits and broadened their commercial and consumer lending powers. The powers of some state-chartered savings and loans also have been broadened through state code parity clauses that provide state-chartered savings and loans with the same powers as federal savings and loans.

ed to preempt bank regulation by the federal government, thus restricting the federal-state dual banking system. It raised a difficult question: In trying to structure a "level playing field" between different depository institutions and between these and other financial services organizations, to what extent are state laws that extend specific powers to a given group going to be subordinated to federal preemption? The Reagan administration's view has been to foster de facto deregulation by its declared respect for states' rights, in this instance. To do so it is violating its own premise of the "level playing field" since state nonmember banks would continue to have a distinct advantage over national banks.

View from the House of Representatives

There appeared to be no reason why the three proposals pending before the Senate in 1984 could not be compromised to a consensus satisfactory to a majority of the Senate Banking Committee and in fact this is what eventually occurred. In the House of Representatives, however, the problem seemed more difficult. On February 29, 1984, Chairman Fernand St. Germain of the House Committee on Banking, Finance and Urban Affairs gave a speech on the floor of the House entitled "It's Time for a Rational Look at Deregulation."[4] To Chairman St. Germain the deregulation fever gripping financial institutions ignored the fact that depository institutions had been given broad support by the federal government because

> they have a unique place in the economy and their money and credit powers give them leverage not matched by any other industry. Credit, like air and water, is an item of survival in today's economy.[5]

To St. Germain the demise of Regulation Q has meant that banks are charging the poor, the elderly, and military personnel large fees to cash their checks or handle their accounts. In the competitive world of which bankers speak, their desire, in his opinion, was to serve the affluent, not the community, and deregulation means the avoidance of service to those depositors in the community whose deposits were too small to provide sufficient earnings for the bank. St. Germain saw the need to halt deregulation—even to force divestiture, as was done in amending the Holding Company Act in 1970—without regard to grandfather clauses. To St. Germain, government insurance for depositors required a counterpart duty on the part of the depository institutions to provide banking services at reduced fees and to serve all members of the public, as a public utility does. He has wanted a moratorium on deregulation until Congress has had a chance to make a thorough review of the need for further deregulation. St. Germain can be considered as the philosophical as well as the linear successor to Representative Wright Patman of Texas, who was chairman of the House Banking Committee for so many years and a true Populist.

We have here a sure confrontation — between the administration and the Senate, on the one hand, and members of the House who believe as St. Germain does that bank regulation is not to be discarded except after the most careful consideration. Once again the United States faces the classic argument that has existed throughout our history between those who believe in economic growth through the power of large financial institutions and those, on the contrary, who distrust any concentration of financial resources, whether it be through a central bank or through the interstate banking efforts of major financial conglomerates. Change has certainly occurred in the manner in which financial services are provided, but the fundamental dichotomy in philosophical outlook is as alive today in the Senate and House as it was in the days of Thomas Jefferson, Alexander Hamilton and President Andrew Jackson. The confrontation will most likely not be resolved unless, and until, banking ceases to be a national issue and becomes instead a question of international regulation.*

The Views of Interested Parties on Deregulation

The importance attached to the administration's proposed bank deregulation bill — FIDA — and the Senate hearings on this and the Garn and Proxmire bills could be deduced from the organizations and individuals asking to be heard. These included, in addition to individual consultants and academics, the regulators: the Comptroller of the Currency, the chairman of the FDIC, the chairman of the FHLBB, the chairman of the SEC, the deputy assistant attorney general of Justice, consumer groups, the real estate industry, the securities industry, insurance agents and underwriters, state financial institution regulators, finan-

---

*We have progressed from county banking to state banking. We now speak of moving on to regional banking as a step to interstate banking. But in an age of electronics no artificial barriers are recognized either in commerce or banking. It is highly possible that very shortly we will discuss limitations on banking activities in international rather than national terms. See Chapter 10.

cial services firms, mutual savings banks, savings and loan associations, and, of course, commercial banks. The American Bankers Association opposed interest on demand deposits, but if interest was to be paid, it wanted usury ceilings to be removed, interest paid on reserves, expanded assets to be authorized, and bankruptcy abuses to be corrected. The savings and loan institutions opposed legislation that would attempt to deprive the thrift industry of its services corporations. They did not like the idea of consumer banks because they did not see any public policy objective as being as important as housing finance. Savings and loans also did not like the Proxmire bill's restrictive approach to new activities of state-chartered institutions. In addition, savings and loans believed that new antitying provisions were unnecessary and merely conducive to increased litigation. They supported interest on demand deposits and equally on reserves. Savings and loans were concerned that securities firms are not prohibited by statute from acquiring savings institutions and nonmember banks. They appeared convinced that securities firms only wanted depository institution subsidiaries in order to obtain federal deposit protection for securities investments.

Mutual savings banks opposed the Fed Regulation Y revision that would classify savings banks as banks for purposes of the Bank Holding Company Act. They opposed regulation that would apply Glass-Steagall to savings banks and savings and loans so as to limit their securities activities to discount brokerage. The mutuals wanted savings bank life insurance to be available nationwide—not just in Connecticut, Massachusetts, and New York. They also supported interest on demand deposits and reserves. Finally, mutual savings banks wanted regional branching.

The financial services companies—represented by the American Financial Services Association and the American Retail Federation—favored the consumer bank exemption proposed in the Garn bill and also an industrial bank exemption. These companies believe strongly that future options for retailers to enter into the financial services industry should be preserved. They particularly want automatic teller machines (ATMs) in grocery chains to help consumers cash checks, make deposits, and so on. They also favored the Garn bill's experiment in interstate banking (Title X) and objected to any moratoriums or piecemeal closing of loopholes in the regulatory system.

The securities industry—represented by the Securities Industry Association and the Investment Company Institute—was opposed to any attempts on the part of the depository institutions to expand their activities in the underwriting or distribution of securities, at least unless securities firms were given banking powers. The securities industry representatives were clearly against the provisions of both the Garn bill and the Proxmire bill permitting underwriting of mortgage-backed securities through bank subsidiaries. They stood squarely against any weakening of the Glass-Steagall Act. The securities industry representatives believed that the government's efforts at deregulation were contradictory because the government was trying to ensure a safe and sound banking system while at the same time allowing banks to engage in all phases of the financial services industry.* They feared that corporations would give their pension funds to banks to manage in order to create a willingness on the part of the banks to give them new or bigger loans.

The real estate industry preferred the Proxmire bill to Garn's. The industry greatly fears the growth of vertical integration in which financial institutions would set up companies to buy land, develop it, build on it, market the product, finance the acquisition, and then insure the mortgages. It sees a great increase in concentration of power by the financial institutions as a result of deregulation proposals.

As might be expected, consumer groups — represented by the Consumers Federation of America, the American Association of Retired Persons, the National Federation of Independent Business, and the AFL-CIO — came out against deregulation because they believed it would result in further concentration of financial power against the interests of home buyers, small depositors, and small business in general. They see the winners as big business and especially the big banks. Consumer groups were strongly in favor of provisions to accelerate check clearance, including disclosure of check-clearing periods by banks.† Finally, these groups favored Title IX of the Garn bill regarding elimination of credit card fraud. This section proposed to extend the definition of credit card fraud to include any misuse of an account number.

Academic witnesses expressed widely different views. One would severely curtail deposit insurance coverage and increase the cost of FDIC insurance. Another found it unnecessary to restructure financial institution regulation, claiming that the Federal Reserve had simply been too timid to exercise the powers given to it by Congress under the Bank

---

*The Investment Company Institute points out, in addition, that banks now have 44 percent of institutional holdings of stock through their management of corporate retirement funds.

†The Interagency Task Force on Small Business Finance found that three quarters of small business credit comes from small and medium-sized banks and that small banks and banks in limited-lending states provide better interest rates on loans to small business than larger banks. This is an important finding that should encourage further congressional attention for public policy reasons already referred to.

Holding Company Act of 1970, which effectively allowed the Fed to permit bank holding companies to engage in insurance and real estate activities. This professor had also found that the Fed and the FDIC did not need congressional authorization in 1980 and 1982 to allow them to eliminate deposit rate ceilings; they already had the power to virtually remove them. The witness found little need for congressional action; it was simply that the Fed had been too cautious. Still another witness was concerned that the drive for deregulation came from the excess lending of the major banks to developing countries: The banks now wanted to cut their capital risk by merging with other financial institutions. Radical restructuring, he thought, should be avoided: Computer technology had made it possible for banks to adjust to any market structure; so there was no need to permit additional concentration of financial power.

Academics generally favored the payment of interest on demand deposits as well as the payment of interest on reserves deposited with the Federal Reserve. One witness favored allowing the banks to broaden their activities without using the bank holding company mechanism on the premise that insulating the bank would not work and that it was preferable to monitor bank activities directly, with control or risk handled through adjustment in the insurance premiums charged by the FDIC.

What about the views of the regulators? The Comptroller of the Currency came out strongly in favor of comprehensive deregulation because removal of Regulation Q ceilings made it necessary for the banks to develop additional sources of earnings. He also supported regional interstate banking arrangements.

The chairman of the FDIC also gave strong support to the general framework of the deregulation bills. The FDIC did not believe it necessary to segregate underwriting or brokerage of insurance and securities through a holding company separate from the bank. The FDIC, however, would define a *bank* as any institution that has the word in its name and that has FDIC-insured deposits. The FDIC would permit the underwriting of securities by a bank but would favor stronger application of the antitrust laws to prevent undue concentration of financial power. The FDIC would also favor payment of interest on all reserves, whereas the administration appeared very hesitant to do this if it would result in any budget impact. Remember here that the Federal Reserve by not paying interest on bank reserves is able to pay the Treasury at the end of each year in excess of $15 billion, a painless way of reducing the deficit through indirect taxation of banks.

The chairman of the FHLBB was principally concerned with not losing his power over thrift institutions and with ensuring that there would be no limitation on the powers of thrifts and thrift holding companies as part of any deregulation plan. He favored the broad services corporation authority permitted by the Garn bill. (The administration's bill would have eliminated this on grounds of maintaining competitive equity between banks and thrifts.) Interestingly enough, the FHLBB does not favor the extension of interstate banking because it did not want to reduce potential bidders for ailing thrifts. (Remember how Citicorp purchased ailing savings and loans in California, Illinois, and Florida as a means of getting a foothold into interstate banking.)

The chairman of the SEC strongly supported the provisions of the Garn and Proxmire bills that related to the SEC's areas of responsibility. He wanted the securities activities of banks in separate affiliates, opposed the proposal to permit banks to underwrite and make a market in mortgage-backed securities as much riskier than state or federal obligations, and thought it too permissive to allow bank trust departments to purchase securities or assets from their own securities affiliates. He also, understandably, wanted bank holding companies that serve as advisers to affiliated investment companies to register under the Investment Advisers Act, since this would come under the SEC's jurisdiction.

The Antitrust Division of the Department of Justice supported the Garn bill as a positive step toward needed reforms. Justice disagreed with provisions to control size, however, believing that the antitrust laws could handle competitive concerns better. (It is never surprising to find an agency of government satisfied with both its actions and its prerogatives.) Justice also believed in eliminating geographical restrictions on expansion of depository institutions. It therefore proposed repeal of both the McFadden Act and the Douglas amendment. It also opposed the extension of existing restrictions on the interstate acquisition of banks by bank holding companies and favored as an interim measure the proposal to allow regional banking pacts.

In effect, each of the regulators had been taking this position with Congress: "Deregulate, but don't interfere with our own prerogatives. If you don't take action, the depository institutions will continue to get around the antiquated statutory structure established many years ago to meet needs that no longer exist. They will do this by continuing to expand loopholes in the regulatory system, or they will prevail upon certain states in our dual regulatory system to allow for expanded activities. Once one state has done this, others will follow. This will give the depository institutions an expanded product base and the capacity for geographical expansion into interstate banking, which they have for years been trying to achieve."

To complete the impact of the proposals presented to the Senate in 1984, it is only necessary to discuss three additional areas: the Garn bill's proposal to allow so-called consumer banks to be treated as non-banks for purposes of the Bank Holding Company Act; the likelihood of continued deregulation through state action if the Congress did nothing; and the problem of broker's deposits, that is, what they are and what will probably be done about them.

Two Exemptions Under the Garn Bill

It would hardly seem necessary to create additional exemptions to the Bank Holding Company Act. Yet this is what the Garn bill proposed in order to encourage the creation of consumer banks to meet a perceived public need. A consumer bank would be a special kind of insured depository institution authorized to make only noncommercial loans and would not be a "bank" for purposes of the act, hence free of Federal Reserve control. The idea was intriguing: Garn saw in the consumer bank idea, and its counterpart for thrifts, an opportunity to give some advantages to securities firms; in practice, however, it would permit unregulated firms to own or control banks insured by the federal government.

For thrift institutions, the Garn bill added a similar exemption—the "qualified thrift lender." The thrifts, as was noted, already had an escape hatch through use of the unitary savings and loan holding company. This is how Sears Roebuck has used an insured savings and loan, which carries on the activities of retailer, insurer (Allstate), securities underwriter (Dean Witter Reynolds, Inc.) and real estate broker-manager (Coldwell Banker). The administration proposal was to eliminate this unitary savings and loan advantage for thrifts in order to redesign "the level playing field" between banks and thrifts; Garn's proposal of a consumer bank represented another exemption from the act to give banks the same advantage as thrifts. But Garn also then proposed to allow a new special purpose thrift that would be owned by a holding company but that would still be free of regulation. In Garn's proposal a qualified thrift lender would have to meet either of two tests: (1) at least 60 percent of its assets to be invested in residential mortgage loans or (2) no more than 25 percent of its assets could be invested in commercial loans. In effect these tests would mean that a thrift could by satisfying the second test, be a consumer bank but with five times more commercial lending authority. This would tend to make a bad situation worse. The qualified thrift lender would be able to do everything a consumer bank could do, would have five times the commercial lending power, and would be able to take advantage of the other benefits generally made available to thrifts under current law — including medium-term loans from the Federal Home Loan banks, lower capital requirements, more liberal branching authority, and extensive nonbanking powers through the use of services corporations.

Since both consumer banks and qualified thrift lenders would be able to make consumer loans without restriction, it was easy to see what would happen: Commercial retailing firms would use this device to obtain access to federally insured funds to finance purchases by consumers of goods or services sold by the retailer's parent or affiliated companies. Just take the case of an automobile manufacturer that today uses an affiliated credit company to finance the purchases of its cars. Ownership of a consumer bank or qualified thrift lender would allow the auto manufacturer access to low-cost federally insured deposits for the purpose of financing automobile sales. How could such use of taxpayers' funds possibly be defended? These exemptions would allow retail firms to compete directly with bank holding companies on their traditional turf, whereas bank holding companies would remain barred from offering nonbanking services. A level playing field indeed!

If such exemptions were to be adopted, this would only result in increased pressure to eliminate any bank holding company limitations whatsoever. Indeed, this seems to be the likely trend. This is particularly true when one considers that insurance companies (which are major commercial lenders) are not prohibited from affiliating with securities firms. Prudential-Bache and Shearson/American Express are but two examples of this type of financial services institution. The more one closely studies these congressional proposals, the more one becomes convinced that the whole regulatory scheme needs to be reexamined totally and probably from a fresh perspective. Like the tax code, it is high time that the bank regulatory system ceased to be subject to constant patching. It is the whole regulatory scheme that needs a fresh look, an up-to-date philosophical analysis, resulting in a wholly new statutory framework. This is not said in criticism of those who have tried so hard to improve the system to meet changes in the way bank transactions are handled and to make the system more responsive to public demands. Our method of statutory compromise simply does not function effectively in the dynamic world of today's developing methods of providing financial services.

States Will Deregulate Banking
if Congress Does Not

It is difficult to foresee what action Congress will take with regard to changes in bank regulation. It is faced with not one but many problems: the extent of regulatory control, to whom such controls should be applied, how extensive federal insurance should be, what agencies should regulate, and how they should interface. Congress would prefer not to examine these questions in an election year such as 1984. But in the meantime the depository institutions remain under ever-increasing pressure to increase their earnings, now that they must pay market-related interest rates to their depositors and their cost of money is rising. The simplest way out for these institutions in our dual banking system is to go to the states for assistance. The banks have a strong card to play: Their employment, as in any services industry, is high. Any state quite naturally wishes to entice additional banks to domicile themselves there; those that are already domiciled are encouraged to offer new services. Above all, states do not want their depository institutions to move elsewhere, which would reduce employment and local sources of credit. But this is necessarily a "beggar thy neighbor" policy. The chairman of the House Banking Committee, Fernand St. Germain, has said:

> The dual depository system now in operation in this country has produced what is better described as a "competition in laxity". It is a system measured by the looseness with which the Congress and state legislative authorities have chosen to treat the regulation of financial institutions.[6]

State banking statutes generally authorize banks to engage in other-than-traditional banking activities if these are "incidental" or "closely related" to banking.[7] Five examples will suffice to show how broadly state statutes can be interpreted: (1) Florida authorizes banks to own subsidiaries "engaging in any activity (except certain insurance activities) that is related or incidental to the business of a financial institution;[8] (2) Indiana and Wisconsin statutes permit banks to engage in certain insurance activities[9] and South Dakota allows banks to engage in both brokerage and underwriting;[10] (3) in at least four states, including California as of July 1, 1984, banks are authorized to engage in securities activities beyond discount brokerage;[11] (4) at least seven states (including New Jersey, New York, and Ohio) allow banks to operate travel agencies;[12] and (5) eight states specifically allow banks to engage in data processing activities.[13]

The trend toward state deregulation has been accelerating rapidly. Delaware, as was mentioned in Chapter 5, is an interesting case in point. In 1981 Governor Pierre duPont IV, encouraged by Chase Manhattan Bank and Citicorp, persuaded the state legislature to enact a package of new banking laws. The key was to let new state-chartered subsidiaries of out-of-state banks sell credit and services nationwide under the state's unlimited interest law while sharply restricting their right to compete with established banking institutions within Delaware. The Delaware Financial Services Development Act would have allowed state banks to underwrite and sell insurance and corporate securities, operate mutual funds, act as real estate brokers, and engage in other activities generally closed to banks elsewhere. While this act was not adopted because of insurance agents' complaints, nevertheless, the Delaware Consumer Credit Bank Act was passed. Within 24 hours some 70 percent of the credit card portfolio of 200 Midwest banks was moved from Detroit to Delaware. Might Delaware become the Luxembourg of the United States, supplanting South Dakota? Incoming banks have to guarantee at least 100 jobs in Delaware within a year; banking associations, 250. It is easy to see how legislation to increase employment in services industries can spread from one state to another. It is certain that state innovation will continue to grow in the absence of congressional action. It is only a question of time before enterprising state governors raise their sights from taking domestic bank lures to starting their own export banking institutions to encourage the financing of international trade transactions for the benefit of local manufacturing plants!

It is clear that at some time the federal government will have to decide whether to exercise preemption. But this would mean abandoning the dual regulatory system, which so many observers claim has worked so well over the years. Recently, New York has proposed to enact legislation granting broad insurance and real estate powers to state-chartered banks. If New York takes this action, other states will be sure to follow.

The FDIC, which regulates state-chartered banks that are not members of the Federal Reserve System, has taken a very tolerant view of state deregulation moves. Chairman William Isaac has made clear his view that for competitive reasons banks must diversify into such activities as securities brokerage and insurance.[14] For member banks the story is different. The Fed—in applying Glass-Steagall—has imposed limitations on the nonbanking activities of state member banks. Here again, however, the tendency has been to relax the rules.[15] The Fed is the exclusive regulatory agency dealing with bank holding companies. But under the Bank Holding Company Act, the states retain the authority to prescribe the powers of state-chartered banks owned by holding companies even if such powers go beyond those permitted the holding company. Indeed, the Fed has never claimed otherwise.[16]

In regulating bank holding companies in 1956 and 1970, Congress clearly had no intention of preempting the rights of states to determine what activities would be permissible for state-chartered banks even though they were subsidiaries of bank holding companies regulated by the federal government. The dual regulatory system can result in some odd interpretations of federal versus state regulation. The McFadden Act, for example, has been found by a court to apply to nonbanking activities of a bank or bank subsidiary.[17] This may make it impossible for a state-chartered member bank to engage in nonbanking activities outside of its home state. But insured nonmember banks are not covered by the McFadden Act, and hence the restriction would not be applicable to them. State-chartered insured nonmember banks can thus avoid the Bank Holding Company Act, the Glass-Steagall Act, and the McFadden Act in engaging in nonbanking activities to the extent permitted by state law and the FDIC. Since the FDIC shows no inclination to limit the scope of state-permitted activities by such banks, it will be up to the Congress to determine whether the federal government will, to any extent, preempt bank regulation. For reasons previously outlined, this appears quite unlikely.

The administration could, of course, also appoint a new FDIC chairman who would apply federal regulation of state-chartered nonmember banks insured by the FDIC much more strictly. In the alternative the Congress could adopt the provision in Proxmire's bill amending the Glass-Steagall Act to eliminate the loophole through which the FDIC has asserted that state nonmember banks can have affiliates and bona fide subsidiaries if they are not part of a bank holding company. The administration, in attempting to stay clear to states' rights problems, has not supported Proxmire's proposal. It certainly would, however, eliminate an inequity between state and national banks—something that the administration favors.

The Problem of Brokered Deposits

In Chapter 4, which deals with conceptual changes in both banking and money, I pointed out how savings have had a tendency in recent years to flow to money-market funds controlled by securities brokers or directly to brokers, then to be used to a great extent to purchase CDs issued by banks and thrift institutions. Merrill Lynch, in particular, has specialized in making these so-called brokered deposits. The deposits are federally insured either by the FDIC or the FSLIC. Since 1982 the brokers are entitled to charge finder's fees for placing these deposits. Since the taxpayer indirectly bears the risk of loss, there is a tendency on the part of some brokers to take greater risks in order to earn a greater return. The insuring agencies, faced in recent years with increased failures on the part of depository institutions, have sought limitations on brokered deposits. In March 1984 the FDIC and the FHLBB voted to limit the availability of insurance placed in any one institution by any one broker to $100,000, regardless of the number of individuals whose money was being placed. The agencies contended that this practice was a misuse of federal deposit insurance, which was intended to protect small savers who lacked the means to obtain sophisticated investment advice. Too many institutions on the brink of failure were offering high rates of return to obtain these insured deposits.

The administration, the Department of Justice, the Comptroller of the Currency, and the SEC have all expressed opposition to the rule promulgated by the FDIC and the FHLBB. The Fed has come out in favor.

In defense of the rule, it must be admitted that between 1982 and 1984 some 35 institutions that required FSLIC assistance or liquidations had utilized brokered funds, and in 11 cases such funds exceeded 10 percent of deposits. Unfortunately, a great many large American Indian loans were involved. The FDIC claims that 16 percent of total deposits of 72 failed banks were brokered funds. The problem is that the rule hurts smaller institutions that have to rely on retail brokered deposits. A better rule would have been merely to place a percentage cap on brokered deposits at institutions deemed to be in difficulty. This may, however, have required legislation.

It is very curious that the two agencies that have now severely limited brokered deposits — thereby preventing the smaller institutions especially from obtaining funds — are the very federal regulatory agencies that have been most willing to expand the nonbanking activities of the depository institutions. Why? The amounts involved are not great. The

FHLBB estimates that as of June 30, 1983, only $16 billion of the total $620 billion in deposits insured by the FSLIC had been placed by brokers. The FDIC has made no analysis of brokered deposits held by institutions that it insures. Merrill Lynch, the principal broker dealing in these deposits, estimates that as of October 31, 1983, total brokered deposits in banks and thrifts amounted to some $80 billion, of which $22 billion was insured, or 1.2 percent of total insured deposits of $1.8 trillion.

There is a need to realize better the seriousness of the problem represented by brokered deposits. The banks and thrifts must now compete for deposits not only with each other but with financial services companies which, unlike the depository institutions, can raise money all over the country as Merrill Lynch and Sears, for example, are doing so well. Just as a tree will die if it cannot get sunlight and moisture through its branches and leaves, or stay standing if it lacks an extensive root system, so do the large banking institutions suffer from their inability to gather deposits through an extensive branching system. Continental Illinois Bank and Trust is the classic but by no means the only case. Under Illinois law it could not have branches even throughout Illinois. As a result Continental was forced to buy its funds through CDs — brokered deposits raised in the United States and even more so abroad. When the extent of Continental's dubious energy and foreign loans became known its cost of brokered deposits increased. Then large foreign depositors of funds became frightened by its questionable foreign and domestic loan exposure and withdrew their funds. Since these deposits tended to be very large, Continental immediately faced a situation *not* of a classic run on the bank with small depositors withdrawing their money, but of a much more alarming situation, where very large foreign deposits handled through other banks were suddenly withdrawn. Veritably, a tree with no branches and no root system, overwhelmed by a sudden storm. What is the lesson to be learned? Large banks making large loans inadequately supervised will necessarily fail if they are not permitted to develop a very extensive branch system supported by masses of small depositors less likely to panic suddenly. I wonder to what extent the lesson of Continental Bank has really been learned either by our regulatory agencies or by the committees of Congress charged with the responsibility of protecting the banking system. Continental is not an isolated case. Its ultimate cost and that of other banks similarly situated risks being very large indeed. How much attention is being paid to the reasons for Continental's rapid demise or how to avoid a similar fate for other large money-center banks that are not permitted an extensive branching system? We must either reduce the exposure of our money-center banks or allow them to develop regional or interstate branch banking systems to reduce the risk represented by massive withdrawals of large brokered deposits.

Proposals for Interstate Banking

In FIDA the administration proposed that interstate banking be approved. The Garn bill proposes an experiment in regional banking to be reviewed after five years. The administration goes along with this, although it sees two difficulties:

> 1) It is discriminatory to those financial organizations which are precluded from participation due to the arbitrary drawing of state boundaries, and 2) it raises the prospect of regionally dominant institutions increasing the concentration of regional financial resources.[18]

The question of regional banking is currently in the hands of the courts. In April 1984 Northeast Bancorp asked the U.S. Court of Appeals for the Second Circuit to stop the merger of the Bank of New England Corp. with CBT Corp. until it could review the Federal Reserve's approval of the merger. Citicorp also asked the same court to enjoin two other regional bank mergers. The Fed's action in approving the mergers upheld the constitutionality of the regional interstate banking compact laws of Massachusetts and Connecticut. Citicorp is appealing in order to itself acquire New England banks.

Extension of Bank Holding Company Powers in Terms of Product

The administration has been seeking to extend the powers of bank and thrift holding companies as a way of extending the activities permitted to depository institutions to make them more competitive while at the same time keeping them separate from their bank or thrift affiliates. Senator Proxmire's bill differed from the administration's proposal with respect to (1) the extent of permissible activities; (2) parallel treatment of bank and thrift holding companies and services corporations; and (3) limitations (as was just noted) on state law provisions. Proxmire would limit the right of bank holding companies to engage in new securities activities. He would not authorize bank holding companies to engage in new insurance activities, real estate activities, or activities deemed to be "of a financial nature," as would FIDA. The Proxmire bill, in not limiting the broader thrift services corporation powers, would tend to allow the kind of comparative, competitive disparity between banks and thrifts that the administration's bill was trying to avoid in order to discourage the pressure on banks to convert their charters to thrifts.

The Service Fee Problem: Administration and Senate versus States and House

It was noted how service fee charges rankled Chairman St. Germain of the House Committee on Banking. House Consumer Affairs Subcommittee Chairman Frank Annunzio is equally concerned. The question of consumer safeguards was exacerbated in November 1983 when the Comptroller of the Currency ruled that states could not limit national banks' efforts to collect service charges on savings deposits because banks needed flexibility in developing pricing policies to meet their corporate and competitive needs. Most states believe they have a right to enforce consumer safeguards. The Conference of State Bank Supervisors (CSBS) contends that the Comptroller's interpretive ruling overturns nearly a century of case law giving the states the right to regulate the contracts of national banks. The banks' view is also understandable. Now that they must pay for deposits with interest at market rates, it is necessary for them to charge at least cost price for services. Smaller depositors are apt to need complete bank services, and yet their deposits earn very little. One of the reasons bankers are so anxious to expand their activities is that this would enable them to earn fee income, rather than income tied to interest-rate spreads. On this issue the administration takes the position that its deregulation program helps small savers and should allow banks to keep their service fees to a minimum if they are allowed to earn a fair degree of fee income. This is a delicate issue, and hopefully it will not become mired in politics.

Divestiture of Nonbank Banks as a Means of Limiting Deregulation

The Federal Reserve is determined to do away with nonbank banks despite the clear provisions of the Bank Holding Company Act. The Fed considers that the congressional language has created a loophole that should be done away with. The congressional language was clear, and the courts will presumably rule against the Fed's efforts to reinterpret congressional intent.* Congress, however, is aware of the ludicrous result of its exemption and is more than likely to do away with the loophole. The very expression *nonbank bank* invites ridicule. The problem would be solved effectively by any of the bills pending in 1984 before the Senate. In addition Senator John Heinz submitted S. 2071 in November 1983 to limit the acquisition of depository institutions by nonbanks. Senator Heinz would not only close the nonbank bank loophole; but he would also favor federal preemption to halt the type of legislation passed by South Dakota to extend the nonbanking activities of banks. The senator would like to have a moratorium on any future acquisition of nonbank banks until Congress has had a chance to come up with appropriate legislation to determine what should be the relationship between banking and commerce. The administration would grandfather existing nonbank banks. Paul Volcker, for his part, would like to end once and for all this way of avoiding bank regulation through a congressional technicality. We shall see how Volcker triumphed through the Bush Task Group compromise he was able to insist upon.

The History of the Administration's Efforts to Deregulate the Banking System

The Reagan administration has been singularly consistent in its efforts at bank deregulation. In 1980 the Depository Institutions Deregulation Committee (DIDC) was created as a result of the Depository Institutions Deregulation and Monetary Control Act of 1980[19] which called for the phaseout of depository interest-rate ceilings. The purpose of the DIDC was to phase out Regulation Q interest-rate controls. The DIDC took its mandate seriously. In 1981 it converted the low, fixed-rate ceiling on the 2.5 year small saver account to a variable-rate ceiling indexed to market rates. In 12 months $140 billion flowed into these accounts. It also, in 1981, established an 18-month ceiling-free account exclusively for IRA-Keogh depositors in order to increase its attractiveness for small depositors; this account received $25 billion in 6 months.

---

*In 1984, presumably as a means of putting increased pressure on Congress, the Federal Reserve permitted the U.S. Trust Company's Florida Trust Company to take consumer deposits in Florida, in effect adopting the Comptroller's definition on interstate banking. The Fed's decision has resulted in a flood of new applications by banks to acquire nonbank banks. It will be interesting to see whether the Fed's new policy brings about congressional action to do away with nonbank banks. It is hard to believe that the Fed's action was not taken for the purpose of increasing the pressure on Congress to adopt legislation removing this loophole in the Bank Holding Company Act even in an election year.

In 1982 the DIDC established a short-term money-market deposit account, the so-called MMDA. In one year it garnered $380 billion in deposits. The basis for this DIDC action was the Garn–St. Germain Act of 1982, whose avowed purpose was the rescue of thrift institutions.

In 1983 the DIDC deregulated all time deposits of over 31 days maturity. It also took steps to eliminate minimum denomination requirements on MMDAs, Super-NOWs, and short-term accounts for IRA-Keogh investors. All these steps by Congress and the administration did a great deal to restore the thrift industry to financial stability.

In 1983 the DIDC also recommended to Congress that depository institutions be permitted to pay interest on demand deposits. After a careful study it found that banks were furnishing free customer services in substitution for interest payments, that the market had developed substitutes outside of banks in money-market mutual funds and sweep accounts, and that legislative and regulatory changes allowing NOW and Super-NOW accounts at banks meant paying interest on bank deposits that were almost the equivalent of demand deposits. At the same time, the Treasury submitted to Congress a draft bill entitled the Demand Deposit Deregulation Act, which was accompanied by a lengthy staff memorandum in support.

In October 1983 the commission on deregulation established under the chairmanship of Vice-President Bush (the Bush Task Group) presented its initial recommendations to reform the federal regulation of banking services. The report proposed a revision of bank and thrift regulatory agency responsibilities but provided a series of alternative proposals as well as favored recommendations.

In March 1984, after several months of turbulent negotiations among the various members of the Bush Task Group — but principally between the senior aids of Chairman Paul Volcker of the Federal Reserve, the Secretary of the Treasury, and Vice-President Bush — a final agreement was reached among the members of the group and reduced to writing. It was a compromise reached with difficulty. The principal stumbling block, as may be surmised, involved the role of the Federal Reserve Board. Chairman Volcker insisted that the Fed continue to have regulatory authority as well as control over monetary policy even though all other group members had come to the conclusion that there was no need for the Fed to be both regulatory authority and central banker.*

---

*In other countries this combination of powers would be regarded as unusual. I have pointed out that 90 percent of the Fed's time is spent on regulatory matters. Indeed, monetary control takes place in New York rather than in Washington.

Nevertheless, the chairman of the Fed pointed out to the administration that if it wanted a battle before Congress, the Fed expected to win and that this would ensure that no deregulation program would be adopted. To support its argument, the Federal Reserve Board went to the extraordinary extent of circulating a document[20] supporting the thesis that without regulatory power over the largest bank holding companies and those banks that did substantial overseas lending the Fed would be unable to exercise properly its function over monetary policy. While the argument may not have been altogether convincing, the administration was not prepared in an election year to take on before Congress the chairman of the Federal Reserve. It depended too much on his help not only to convince the Congress to reduce the budget deficit but — almost more important — to keep interest rates from rising through an accommodative policy in regard to the money supply.

Volcker is certainly an astute politician. He made it clear to the Secretary of the Treasury, who had worked very hard to bring about a carefully constructed deregulation bill (which he saw as one of the crowning achievements of his term at Treasury), that there would be no deregulation unless the Fed retained its regulatory power. Furthermore, Volcker used the very banks he regulated to indicate to Congress that it would be a mistake to reduce the Federal Reserve's power. In doing this there was little need to use pressure because banks are well aware that if they wish to extend their activities, merge, or expand into regional or interstate banking, the Fed's approval is all-important. How has Paul Volcker been able to exercise such power?

Paul Volcker

Paul Volcker brings to an impossible job as Chairman of the Federal Reserve Board certain very great assets: Extraordinary intelligence, an imposing physical presence, a capacity for hard work and intense concentration, perhaps most important of all, the capability of understanding just how the political system operates in the United States and how to manipulate it to achieve his ends. Volcker has grown immensely in the job and is undoubtedly the best of Chairmen of the Federal Reserve since Marriner Eccles. As a former undersecretary of the Treasury for Monetary Affairs, he knows the Washington political scene intimately; as a former President of the Federal Reserve Bank of New York, he fully understands how the mechanism of monetary policy is operated; more importantly, that job gave him an opportunity to get to know the heads of other central banks and to look upon regulation in international not just American terms. That is undoubtedly why he has been able to play such a key role since 1982 in helping to prevent the overlending by commercial banks to the developing countries from developing into an uncontrollable monetary crisis. He has helped the commercial banks weather the storm by promptly allowing them at the end of 1982 to avoid writing down questionable loans too quickly. On the other hand he intervened in negotiations between the U.S. banks and the Mexican government to insist that the banks make more of an effort to adjust downward their interest rates and fees for rescheduling.

During the Reagan Administration, he has been frequently attacked by Administration spokesmen for not increasing the money supply faster in order to bring interest rates down. Yet he was renominated in 1983 with the support of the financial community. He has also been the target of members of Congress, yet there is no doubt that the leaders of Congress hold him in high respect. When the Bush Task Group and the Treasury Department had reached the conclusion that the Federal Reserve Board should lose its regulatory authority, Volcker was able to make clear that in any battle between the Administration and Congress on the role of the Fed, he would prevail. As a result, the Bush Task Group modified its recommendations and the Fed maintained a strong regulatory role.

Volcker will undoubtedly have the opportunity, if he chooses to take it, to play a very major role in bringing about an internationalization of U.S. monetary policy and of central bank supervision of individual country banking systems. He has the standing, the authority, and the power to bring about great change for the better in international monetary policy. Will he decide to do this? He has been Chairman since 1979 during a period of great crisis where he has been under enormous strain; his wife has not been well and remains in New York where he joins her every weekend. It would be good for the country if Paul Volcker decided to play the much broader leadership role that the international financial situation demands. He is only 61 and at the peak of his intellectual powers.

RECOMMENDED CHANGES IN THE REGULATORY STRUCTURE

The Bush Task Report

The Group duly produced a compromise satisfactory to Volcker, and in April 1984 its report was finally announced[21] though not published in final form. It must be considered as a series of recommendations agreed upon by the administration and the regulatory agencies. Publication of the full report was said to be expected sometime in 1984. Although the Federal Reserve did give up a portion of its power for the first time, Volcker had won his principal aims. The Fed was now permitted to retain regulatory control over the 50 largest bank holding companies, well over 50 percent of all bank deposits in the United States, as well as bank holding companies owning state-chartered banks. The earlier draft of the Bush Task Group report had taken away the Fed's regulatory powers altogether.

Even though the final report resulted in a compromise, leaving much of the regulatory overlap intact, it is worth a detailed examination because it represented many months of careful effort on the part of many knowledgeable and capable people and it was a first step toward much-needed regulatory reform. Sometimes in the course of time a bad compromise becomes justified as a step on the road to an eventual satisfactory solution. Everything I have described in this book indicates the clear need for Congress to enact legislation to provide the United States with a new bank regulatory system. The current recommendations are not satisfactory, and they may not constitute the final solution, because credit, money, and the monetary system are far too important matters to be settled by a compromise based upon the preservation of regulatory turf. In recommending its report to the Congress, the administration proposed that product deregulation should receive priority consideration and only after that was done should the question of regulatory reform be addressed.

At the end of 1983 a program had been approved by most of the staff of the Bush Task Group. Yet in late January 1984 a totally different program was said to have received unanimous consent from the Task Group members. What happened in the meantime? What was finally accomplished? Unfortunately, in terms of deregulation there is not much to show. None of the regulatory agencies are gone, although the office of the Comptroller of the Currency has been expanded, becoming the Federal Bank Agency (FBA). The dual regulatory system remains in place and is strengthened through the transfer of part of the regulatory burden from the Fed to the state superintendents of banks. Like all attempts at compromise, the proposals could create more confusion rather than less; only time will tell. Here is a summary of the Bush Task Group draft agreement as announced:

1. A new agency is proposed to be created—the FBA. It would be part of the executive branch, nestled in the Treasury, with its princi-

pal component the Office of the Comptroller of the Currency. It would regulate national banks (as has its predecessor). It would also regulate some 1,400 national bank holding companies (other than the 25 largest bank holding companies and the 25 principal bank holding companies that engage in international lending; both include foreign banks). Right there is an opportunity for untold future problems as banks grow or shrink to pass from one regulatory agency to another. The Federal Reserve also would hold veto power over the list of permitted activities allowed by the FBA to bank holding companies.

2. The FDIC would continue its insurance activities but lose all of its regulatory authority not directly related to insurance. It would be able to increase premiums where the risk is high; it would even be able to refuse or revoke insurance or take other enforcement action where it is required. Its focus would be on examination of troubled banks.

3. The Federal Reserve Board, which has been responsible for the federal regulation of more than 1,000 state-chartered member banks and all of the approximately 5,000 U.S. bank holding companies, would maintain its regulatory power over the 50 key bank holding companies and retain veto power over the activities permitted to bank holding companies by the FBA.* It would also retain its regulatory power over state member banks (and under the proposal nonmember banks) until individual agreements could be reached with individual states by which the Fed would recognize the capacity of state superintendents to handle the regulation of their own state banks (and their holding companies as well).† The Fed would thus take over the regulatory power of the FDIC—at least until this authority is transferred to the states. The Comptroller of the Currency, however, has been granting charters to nonbank banks, so there is a question as to just how much additional power the Federal Reserve is gaining.

4. The state superintendents, where qualified, would obtain the power to regulate their banks without having to share this power with the Fed or the FBA.

5. Eligibility for regulation as a thrift institution would be based on the institution's functional activities rather than on its type of charter.

---

*To use its veto the Fed would have to determine by a two-thirds vote that "any such activity would undermine the stability of the entire U.S. banking system or have a seriously adverse effect on safe and sound financial practices." This is a specific recommendation set forth on p. 45 of the Bush Task Group draft recommendations.

†The FBA, the FDIC and the Fed set criteria for recognition of state superintendent authority over state-chartered banks. Once the criteria are established, the states can qualify, provided they meet the criteria.

A "portfolio test"* would be used to determine whether the institution maintains a minimum percentage of its overall assets in activities relating to residential housing finance. It could, if it chooses, continue to be regulated by the FHLBB and insured by the FSLIC. If it might not so qualify under this test, it would be considered to be a commercial bank and would be subject to a bank regulatory agency for control. This accent on functional regulation is a very positive determination. Thrifts have certain advantages over banks. They should justify these by a continued focus on housing finance, which public policy properly favors.

    6. The SEC and the Department of Justice would have an increased role. Under the current regulatory system, four agencies plus the SEC regulate the securities activities of banks and thrifts. Four agencies plus the Department of Justice also enforce the antitrust laws applicable to banks and thrifts. The Bush Task Group proposal would consolidate all securities regulation applicable to banks and thrifts in the SEC. Likewise, all antitrust responsibilities would be centralized in Justice. Surely, no one will quarrel with these changes.

    Where does this new program leave the two statutes that are of most concern to U.S. banks: the Glass-Steagall Act and the Bank Holding Company Act? Control over additional permitted activities under the Bank Holding Company Act — subject to exceptions for the largest bank holding companies and subject to the Fed veto power outlined — would, if the Bush report were adopted, be regulated by the new FBA in the case of national banks and by the state superintendents (who qualify) in the case of state bank holding companies. Complicated? The formula appears almost more complicated than before since it would involve three agencies rather than just the Federal Reserve Board.† In the case of Glass-Steagall, regulation will be less important than the action to be taken by Congress with respect to extending activities permissible for banks. This will be a problem for Congress to solve. As I have stated many times, if Congress does not act soon, it will not make any difference because the banks will free themselves of congressional inability to respond, through state action. One conclusion is certain: If the Treasury Department, acting through the FBA, were free to determine the activities in which a bank holding company might engage, the list would

---

*This means comparing assets engaged in housing with assets otherwise employed in bank activities.

    †See Figures 3 through 7 for diagrams outlining the Bush Task Group proposals as they affect the bank regulatory agencies. There may be new structural simplicity if the regulatory agencies agree to make it so.

be broad indeed—mutual funds, underwriting of government bonds, underwriting and sale of insurance, real estate brokerage, development, and investment would certainly be included in permissible activities. On the other hand, it is not likely that the Federal Reserve will willingly see its regulatory power abridged, to the extent it can avoid it. In fact it is being reduced. Nevertheless, it has quietly obtained, in the Bush Task Group proposals, control over a very important loophole indeed: the regulation of some 9,000 nonmember state-chartered banks that it will now regulate in place of the lenient FDIC, at least until such regulation has been turned over to the state superintendents who meet the qualifications established by the Fed, the FDIC, and the FBA.

Will the Bush Task Group recommendations be accepted by Congress? Past experience would indicate that this is not too likely. There have been numerous commissions established by prior administrations to consider the same problem: the Hunt Commission (1973), the FINE Study (1974/75), President Carter's Interstate Study (1979–81). (See Table 6-1, which lists all the bank regulatory restructuring proposals from 1919 to 1975.) All agreed "in principle" to loosen restrictions on bank activity and to make old laws more equitable.

Impact of the Bush Recommendations on Congress

The Reagan administration has truly done its best to urge congressional action on bank deregulation. In 1982 the Treasury had proposed a bill known as the Bank Holding Company Deregulation Act of 1982. It got nowhere in Congress but was successful in focusing attention on deregulation via the holding company. In 1983, FIDA was presented to the Congress. The Senate Committee on Banking, Housing and Urban Affairs in June, 1984 sent to the floor an amalgam of FIDA, the Garn bill, and the Proxmire bill which essentially was the Garn bill with modifications hammered out in Committee. The Committee had not had an opportunity to consider the Bush report and recommendations. But it appears likely, particularly in view of the attitude of the House that any really comprehensive overhaul of the regulatory system will have to be postponed until 1985 at the earliest, particularly since 1984 is an election year and Congress has shortened its session.

The structure of the regulatory system is really a secondary question. The most important question facing Congress relates to the powers that depository institutions and their holding companies should have under the economic conditions not only evident today but applicable

TABLE 6-1
Summary Of Restructuring Proposals: Centralize All or Some Federal Bank Supervision or Policy Making in One of the Following Agencies

	Federal Reserve System	Federal Deposit Insurance Corporation	Treasury	Bank Commission	New Agencies
1919–21 – Legislative proposals, 66th and 67th Congresses	X				
1937 – Brownlow Committee report			X		
1937 – Brookings Institution report		X			
1938 – Legislative proposal, 75th Congress			X		
1939 – Legislative proposals, 76th Congress		X			
1949 – Hoover Commission report					
1961 – Commission on Money and Credit report	X		X		
1962 – OCC Advisory Committee on Banking report			X		
1962 – FDIC Chairman Cocke's plan		X			

	OCC	FDIC	FRS
1963 — Legislative proposal, 88th Congress		X	
1965 — Legislative proposal, 89th Congress		X	
1965 — Legislative proposal, 89th Congress	X		
1965 — Independent Bankers Association of America plan			X
1969 — Legislative proposal, 91st Congress		X	
1971 — Hunt Commission report	X		
1974 — FRS Governor Sheehan's plan			X
1975 — FDIC Chairman Wille's plan	X		
1975 — Financial Institutions and Nation's Economy recommendation		X	

OCC = Office of the Comptroller of the Currency

FDIC = Federal Deposit Insurance Corporation

FRS = Federal Reserve System

Source: U.S. Government Accounting Office, The Debate on the Structure of Federal Regulation of Banks, issue paper, Washington, D.C., April 14, 1977.

in tomorrow's world of instant electronic communication. Whatever comprehensive action Congress might take in 1984 or 1985 might well prove unsatisfactory in the different money and credit environment that we can expect in 1986 or 1987. Change in banking methods is occurring very rapidly and the regulatory system will in due course have to be adjusted to market-place conditions.

Banking today is already a function of electronic communication. Under modern technology, is the Federal Reserve's function in clearing checks and money transfers between banks out of date and no longer relevant? Banks can debit and credit each other and their individual accounts instantly by means of electronic transfers. If banks can deal with each other and individuals can handle their deposits and payments in the same manner, where is the need for the imposing bank building where heretofore people transacted their business with their bank? This means that any business that deals with customers and customers' payments can act as a bank.

It is no surprise that the recent chairman of Citicorp, Walter Wriston, an innovative banker if there ever was one, could say that Citicorp feared the competition of only two concerns: IBM and AT&T. Recently, AT&T mailed out some 60 million credit cards, 20 million of which were mailed to long-distance users abroad. Those cards could be used to make cash transfers as well as charge calls. After IBM, the greatest users of computer equipment in the world are probably Sears Roebuck and American Express. Both are very much aware of the meaning of the coming electronic age.

How will the regulatory authorities be able to establish geographical limitations or product control for very long when this capacity to transfer credits and debits by electronics is already here? I would submit that we will go — and rather quickly — from county banking to state banking to regional banking and then promptly to international banking without much thought as to whether we have accepted interstate banking as a step along the way.

This is why the juridictional battles carried on by the Federal Reserve during the Bush Task Group hearings gave out such a scent of anachronistic concern with the past. As will be indicated in the next four chapters, the Federal Reserve Board should already have been concentrating on international lending rather than on domestic regulation. Our bank regulators have been living for too long in a world that is rapidly vanishing. Perhaps Congress is correct in allowing delays in deregulation since current recommendations may turn out to be irrelevant. Savings should earn a return no matter how deposits are labeled; transfers should be made instantaneously and across any boundary;

banks should give instant credit to their customers. Imagine delaying credits for a week in this age of the supercomputer!

What are the chances for a truly meaningful overhaul of the bank regulatory system in 1984? There has been enormous pressure on Congress to do so. The Comptroller of the Currency has warned that he cannot defer much longer action on the requests of national banks to establish or buy depository institutions in other states. More important, the leaders of the Congressional committees supervising the bank regulatory system know perfectly well that if the Congress takes no action, market forces will bring about such changes either through use of existing loopholes in the federal system or through state legislation, that Congress may never be able to restructure the system again to control banks as at present. If time permits, it seems very likely that legislation could be adopted to close the nonbank bank loophole, to permit regional banking, perhaps even to pass an amalgam of consumer protection legislation desired by the House along with much of the Garn bill. The Senate Banking Committee had already in June 1984 adopted and sent to the floor a revision of the Garn bill; the House Committee chaired by St. Germain has similarly, after many days of hearings, adopted a compromise version of the St. Germain package and sent it to the floor of the House. Both proposed bills would close the nonbank bank loophole with grandfather clauses which will undoubtedly be changed either before each chamber adopts a bill or in conference if bills are adopted by each chamber. If time does not permit passage of a bill by both houses of Congress and compromise of differences in conference, it is quite possible that an agreement will be reached for a moratorium to maintain the status quo until the next session of Congress. If a bill is passed by Congress and it does not extend the powers of the banks or their right at least to regional groupings, it is quite possible that President Reagan would veto whatever bill is presented to him for signature. One thing is clear: The difficulties of Continental Illinois Bank and Trust Company have made it much more difficult for Congress to agree on extending the powers of the banks. It should have, but hasn't, hastened the trend in Congress to allow the banks to extend their geographical reach for deposits.

An Alternative Recommendation

In such a coming banking age, what should be the role of the regulatory authorities? In Chapter 10 I will discuss the trend, as I see it towards the internationalization of monetary policy and the necessity of internationalizing bank regulation in an age of global electronic trans-

fers of money and credit. Here I wish to focus on domestic regulation of banks and thrifts. I will make a number of suggestions that will
anger some but hopefully convince others of their simplicity and good
sense. They are designed to cut drastically through our present overlapping system.

The needs of a central bank as it was conceived of in 1913 are today
irrelevant. As discussed in Chapter 2, one of the principal reasons for
the adoption of the Federal Reserve System was the necessity of transferring funds more quickly from one part of the country to another so
that banks would not get into difficulty from lack of credit because fund
transfers were too slow. All of this is unnecessary today. The Fed no
longer needs to exercise its former function as a clearinghouse. Does
it still serve a useful role as a lender of last resort? In Chapter 3 I pointed
out that the Fed discount window no longer holds a key function in U.S.
monetary policy. This leaves the Fed with control over monetary policy
through its control of bank reserves, which allows it, for better or for
worse, to increase the money supply rapidly or slowly. In order to do
this, does it need to regulate banks or holding companies? Certainly not,
except to control what U.S. banks do abroad, and this role the Fed — as
shown in Chapters 7 and 8 — has not to date done well. My strong recommendation would be to free the Federal Reserve from any role whatsoever in the regulation of either U.S. banks or their holding companies.
This does not mean that there should be no regulation but only that
the Federal Reserve should not do it. Since 90 percent of its time is spent
on regulation, the Fed could be turned into a much smaller organization — of thinkers and planners rather than comptrollers.

The Bush Task Group's suggestion of an FBA is a good one. It simply expands an existing agency, the office of the Comptroller of the
Currency. But the FBA should have much greater powers. It properly
belongs within the executive branch and within the Treasury Department. It should be *the* regulator of banks and bank holding companies
rather than having to share this power with two other federal agencies
and the state superintendents, as was proposed by the Bush Task Group.
Only the states, in the case of state-chartered banks, should have regulatory powers and only to this extent because the dual regulatory system
has in fact proved useful in the country's development. But no other
federal bank regulators should exist. Note that the Bush Task Group
did not concern itself with thrift institutions and their regulation because
there is no competitive pressure in the thrift area.

The principal problem with the federal insurance program for banks
and thrifts is quite simply that it is completely out of control today. Some

$1.8 trillion of customers' deposits are now federally insured. The financial services companies are constantly finding new ways of obtaining federal insurance for their customers in order to borrow funds more inexpensively and/or take greater risks with those funds at no risk to themselves. It is time for the government to blow the whistle on these tactics. I do not blame companies for trying to borrow at as low a cost as they can. I do blame Congress for allowing this to happen. The original purpose of insurance coverage was absolutely sound: Bank depositors (and by this, Congress meant small, unsophisticated depositors) were to have their deposits in banks, thrifts, or credit unions protected. But what has happened? Federal insurance is available to almost anyone. In addition, because of the FDIC's actions in merging rather than liquidating banks and mutual savings banks in difficulty, the FDIC has protected the large depositors as well as the small and thereby encouraged greater risk taking by the thrifts.

Federal insurance through the FDIC and the FSLIC for deposits of thrift institutions and credit unions plays a most important role because these institutions give small savers a return on their money while protecting their capital investments. These institutions then use their funds to encourage these same small depositors to buy homes or make small consumer loans as needed. This policy is sound.

The federal insurance program should not be used, however, by sophisticated investors who play the stock or commodities markets or who buy large CDs or who can take advantage of brokered deposits. No deposits in securities brokerage firms, commodities firms, or financial services firms should be insured. Congress needs to give immediate consideration to what has happened to its insurance program.

The FDIC should have no regulatory function other than the right to examine either state or national banks in difficulty. The FDIC should continue to be the insurer of bank deposits, but whoever heard of an insurance company giving cease and desist orders to its customers? In a system of separation of powers, I can see the FDIC performing a most useful function as a whistle-blower to the FBA and the state superintendents if they fail to do their jobs. The FDIC should have the power, as the Bush Task Group suggests, of setting insurance rates to fit the risk (as any insurer does) and to refuse or revoke insurance coverage in an extreme case. The mere threat of an insurance denial or revocation with full disclosure of the reasons for such an action should be amply sufficient to avoid the kinds of difficulties the FDIC faced with the Penn Square Bank or the Butcher family in Tennessee where its warnings and recommendations were repeatedly ignored.

Again, as the Bush Task Group report wisely suggests, the role of the SEC in bank regulation should be expanded. The principal nature of the SEC has been to require disclosure. There is no reason why disclosure cannot be as salutary to bankers as it has proved to be to businessmen. The adage that bankers cannot disclose what risks they are taking because their only asset is the public's confidence has no place in a country where bank deposits are insured. Nothing is more likely to cause bankers inclined to take undue risks to reconsider than the necessity of reporting the risks they have taken. In Chapter 8 I point out that Manufacturers Hanover loaned 169 percent of its capital to three Latin American countries. Can one imagine that the management of that bank would have done this if the loans had had to be disclosed?*

Finally, since the Federal Reserve is no longer to play the role of regulator, the Department of Justice should determine whether a given bank merger will raise antitrust questions. In my opinion, the Justice Department has not served the country well by deferring to the Fed on this question. The concentration of bank resources will raise much more important questions in the future as banking becomes a part of international communications networks with consequent new opportunities for monopolistic practices undreamed of at the present time.

It is also very useful to have both the SEC and the Department of Justice act as whistle-blowers to the bank regulators: the FBA and the state superintendents. Disclosure will invite regulatory review if public criticism ensues. Justice will not be reluctant to act because the regulatory authority has its own reasons for permitting a merger.

What about the regulation of thrift institutions and credit unions? There is no reason to change the FHLBB or its satellite, the FSLIC, except to provide over a reasonably short period of time that all three insurance agencies be consolidated into one. Deferral is recommended only because the problems of banks, thrifts, and credit unions may initially appear to insurance personnel to vary. What makes no sense at all even initially, however, is that the FDIC should insure some thrift institutions and the FSLIC others. There should obviously be immediate consolidation here. The role of the combined insurance agency will be that of an insurance agency maintaining its constant focus on troubled institutions, pressuring the regulatory agency—federal or state—to take action. If no action is forthcoming, the insurer raises premiums or

---

*See Chapters 8 and 9 for a more complete discussion of these matters. The new disclosure rules promulgated by the SEC in regard to foreign loans should result in greater care being exercised on the part of banks making foreign loans.

revokes coverage. This will make it more likely that regulations will be more effective.

If this plan were followed, there would no longer be any overlap of regulatory agencies or deferral by one so that action could be taken by another. The Fed's regulatory role would be clearly restricted to the activities of U.S. banks abroad where such control is a natural concomitant of monetary policy. The policy group at Treasury agree that this type of restructure would be preferable. Their concern is whether or not it is advisable.

If these steps were taken, U.S. authorities would really be preparing themselves for the kind of international banking and monetary system desirable for the future.

SUMMARY OF PART I – REGULATION OF U.S. BANKS AT HOME

This completes my analysis of domestic regulation of depository institutions in the United States. In Chapter 1 I laid out the broad regulatory framework and compared it with that in effect in other developed nations. Our system is very different: first, because regulatory power is shared between the federal government and the states; and second, because we have some seven federal regulatory agencies with different mandates from Congress and with a fair degree of overlapping authority. We clearly have no central bank in the sense that other developed countries do. We also have many more banking institutions than other countries as Table 6-2 indicates.

I believe, as Senator Proxmire and others do, that the multiplicity of banking institutions is a strength rather than a weakness. Regional banks have an important role to play in the U.S. economy.

In Chapter 2 I related just how our bank regulatory system has developed over the years. There are two important statutes to bear in mind here: the Glass-Steagall Act of 1933 and the Bank Holding Company Act of 1956. Both statutes were directed at specific problems but over the years they have become key elements in the regulatory process.

In Chapter 3 I analyzed the role of the Federal Reserve in its control over U.S. monetary policy. This is vitally important because the whole world depends upon a paper dollar monetary standard. Hence, the Federal Reserve's policies affect not only the economy of the United States but those of the rest of the world. In recent years the Fed's monetary policy has resulted in great volatility in interest rates and cyclical sav-

TABLE 6-2
Distribution of Banks by Number and Assets
(As of 12/31/82)

Type	Number	% of Banks	Assets (in billions)	% of Total Bank Assets
National Banks (OCC)	4,579	31.7%	$1,297	59.1%
State Member Banks (FRB)	1,039	7.2%	$421	19.2%
State Non-Member Banks (FDIC)	8,833	61.1%	$475	21.7%

Source: Bush Task Group Report (draft)—April, 1984, p. 9

ings from boom to recession and back to boom again. The Fed's policies have created inflation both at home and abroad, followed by recession in an attempt to halt the inflation through tighter control over the increase in the money supply.

In Chapter 4 I analyzed the effects of the Fed's most recent shifts in monetary policy and congressional efforts to save depository institutions from new competition instituted by commercial firms and financial services companies. As a result it is increasingly difficult to define either *money* or a *bank*. The paper dollar has ceased to be a store of value in a world in which everyone has become increasingly a debtor; in an electronic age, a bank has become whatever agency will give us a return on our savings as well as a process of making payment transfers.

In Chapter 5 I analyzed how the bank regulatory authorities had reacted to changes brought about by the Fed's shifts in monetary policy: the attempt by the depository institutions to extend the services rendered their depositors, both in terms of product and in terms of geographical outreach; conversely, the attempts by commercial firms, securities brokerage houses, and insurance companies to extend their own financial services in order to gain access to bank deposits while hopefully maintaining federal insurance coverage. The regulatory authorities have reacted differently to these new conditions, with the Federal Reserve attempting to preserve its jurisdiction, whereas both the Comptroller and the FDIC have tended to allow banks to expand their activities. The states, on the other hand, have encouraged out-of-state banks to come in, provided they will compete only outside the state. In the absence of congressional action, the result of these battles among the regulatory agencies and between the federal government and the states has been increasing chaos.

As Henry Wallich, one of the most thoughtful governors of the Federal Reserve, has so aptly put it:

> It has been said that America has some of the world's best banks and the world's worst banking system. Whatever can be claimed for the system, it is certainly unique. At one extreme there are thirteen money-center banks with total U.S. domestic deposits of $225 billion, about 15.6 percent of total domestic commercial bank deposits. At the other end, there are 1,934 insured commercial banks with assets of less than $10 million, the smallest one hundred of them having combined assets of $151.7 million.
>
> Duplication of authority, competition in regulatory laxity to attract constituents, conflicting treatment of similar institutions by different regulators, are among the deficiencies of the present system.[22]

In Chapter 6 I have analyzed the steps proposed by the Reagan administration and by certain members of both houses of Congress to restructure the regulatory system and to reallocate responsibilities among the federal regulatory agencies.

It is clear that action needs to be taken as rapidly as possible; that such action can only be taken by Congress; and that a consensus is slowly developing between the executive and legislative branches on the steps to be taken.

Throughout Part I I have briefly referred to the activities of U.S. banks outside the United States, activities that are also subject to supervision by the same three federal regulatory agencies: the Federal Reserve, the Comptroller of the Currency, and the FDIC. I turn now in the second part of the book to consideration of how well the regulatory authorities, and in particular the Federal Reserve, have discharged their responsibility for the actions of U.S. banks outside the United States.

NOTES

1. U.S. Congress, Senate, Committee on Banking, Housing and Urban Affairs, "*Disarray in the Marketplace*," speech presented by 98th Cong. 2nd sess. Donald T. Regan, Washington, D.C., March 28, 1984.

2. Ibid., p. 3.

3. *First Bancorporation* v. *Board of Governors*, 728 F. 2d434 (10th Cir. 1984), the so-called "Beehive" case.

4. U.S. Congress, House Committee on Banking, Finance, and Urban Affairs, "It's Time for a Rational Look at Deregulation," speech by Fernand St. Germain, Washington, D.C., 98th Cong., 2nd sess., February 29, 1984.

5. Ibid., p. 4.

6. Fernand St. Germain, Remarks to the Thrift Industry Banking Investment Conference, January 13, 1984, at Boca Raton, Florida.

7. See, for example, Del. Code Ann. Tit. 5 Sec. 761; N.Y. Banking Law, Sec. 96–98; and 100 Pa. Const. Stat. Ann. Tit. 7, Secs. 302–407.

8. Fla. Stat. Ann. 658.67(6).

9. Ind. Code Ann. 28.1.11.2; and Wisc. Stat. Ann. Sec. 221.04(9).

10. S.D. Codified Laws Ann. Sec. 51.18.30.

11. Cal. Fin. Code, Sec. 1338.

12. N.J. Stat. Ann. Sec. 17:9A.25.5(A)(2); N.Y. Banking Law 96(13); Ohio Rev. Code Ann. 1107.31; Ala. Code 5.5A-18(9); Ark. Stat. Ann. Sec. 67–501.1(M); Ind. Code Ann. 28-1-11-2; and S.D. Codified Laws Ann. 51–18–20.

13. The eight are Alabama, Alaska, California, Iowa, Mississippi, Missouri, Nebraska, and Rhode Island.

14. See U.S., Congress, Senate, Financial Services Industry—Oversight Hearings before the Committee on Banking, Housing, and Urban Affairs, 98th Cong. 1st sess., 1983 pp. 118–19.

15. See John A. Hawke, Jr., *Legal Times*, October 24, 1983, p. 16.

16. See the excellent discussion in Peter J. Wallison and Donald J. Toomey, "Continued Banking Deregulation Seems Inevitable." *Legal Times*, March 5, 1984, pp. 5–7.

17. *Securities Industry Association* v. *Comptroller of the Currency*, et al., 577 F. Supp. 252 (D.D.C. 1983), *appeal filed* No. 84-5026 (D.C. Civ. Jan. 13, 1984). The Federal District court held that the securities brokerage business is within the category of "general business" that national banks may conduct in their main office and is subject to the banking restrictions of the McFadden Act. Therefore, an office of a national bank that conducts brokerage activities is a branch subject to state law restrictions on the establishment of bank branch offices.

18. Letter dated June 1, 1983, from Secretary of the Treasury Donald J. Regan to Chairman Jake Garn of the Senate Committee on Banking, Housing and Urban Affairs, p. 2.

19. Public Law 96–221.

20. Undated memorandum of approximately January 1984 from Chairman Paul Volcker to the Bush Task Group; rebutted by William Isaac in "Who Should Supervise the Banks?" *Wall Street Journal*, January 16, 1984, p. 22.

21. Release entitled A *Blueprint for Return: Report of The Task Group on Regulatory Financial Services*, dated April 14, 1984.

22. Henry C. Wallich, "Banking Reform — The Case for Orderly Progress," *Banker* (London, England), May 1984, p. 1.

PART II

REGULATION OF U.S. BANKS ABROAD

Up to now the focus of this study has been on regulation of the domestic activities of U.S. banks and other depository institutions. The balance of the book will concentrate on the international scene — on the attempts of the regulatory agencies to supervise and control U.S. banking institutions in their foreign activities independent of whether they use a domestic affiliate to do so. Two preliminary differences here are important. First, we are no longer concerned with institutions other than banks and bank holding companies; so there are only three federal regulatory agencies involved: the Federal Reserve Board, the Comptroller of the Currency, and the FDIC.* Second, since 1978 state regulators have not played any role in supervising foreign lending by U.S. banks.

In Chapter 7 we will analyze the extent of regulation; the efforts of banks to circumvent domestic regulation through use of the Eurodollar market outside the United States; the activities of banks and bank holding company affiliates in foreign lending; and, finally, the position of the Federal Reserve Board in insisting upon continued control of the principal banks' activities abroad in order to carry on its functions with respect to U.S. monetary policy.

In Chapter 8 we will examine the dangers of default caused by excessive bank lending to the developing countries, particularly since 1979; the exposed position in which the U.S. money-center banks currently find themselves; and whether under current and foreseeable world economic conditions such loans are likely to be repaid.

In Chapter 9 we will explore the role that the international institutions, the Bank for International Settlements (BIS), the International Monetary Fund (IMF) and the International Bank for Reconstruction and Development (World Bank) may play in helping the central banks (including particularly the Federal Reserve), the commercial lending banks, and the borrowers find a long-term solution to bank lending policies that have turned out to represent very serious risks of default. In making this analysis, particular care will be given to explaining the changes in attitude on the part of the central banks and the ministers of finance to modifications that might be made in the responsibilities of the international financial institutions so that they might not only help to solve a serious current crisis but also be in a position to help avoid a repetition of similar crises in the future. Throughout this book, change has been highlighted. In international economic affairs, relationships between countries at a time

---

*If the Bush Task Group recommendations are eventually adopted by Congress, it would be expected that the FBA would handle examinations of U.S. banks abroad.

when the world has been in the process of unprecedented rapid develop-
ment have been undergoing rapid change. This requires flexibility, under-
standing, and a determination to accept the necessity of looking beyond
one's immediate national goals toward finding long-range answers to na-
tional problems that can only be solved through international cooperation.

In groping toward new answers, it should become apparent that inter-
national relationships in the area of finance are very similar to those in
trade, in services, and in politics. Indeed, the web is inextricable between
international trade and the repayment of loans made to developing coun-
tries and the Eastern bloc. As the value of some alternative solutions
becomes clear, it may also become obvious as to just how far we are being
forced to go to cure the financial errors of the past by developing increased
trade relationships in the future and new rules for investment from one
country to another.

Finally, in Chapter 10 we will be tying up the discussion by examin-
ing the advisability of convening a new international Bretton Woods con-
ference as rapidly as possible to remedy the one great error made in 1945
when the recommendation of John Maynard Keynes to create an interna-
tional bank to control monetary policy was unfortunately ignored. The
world has changed very much in economic terms since 1945: Countries
that were laid waste by six years of war have been built anew, colonial em-
pires have vanished, and new countries with peoples whose economic aspira-
tions do not differ from ours have appeared and begun a rapid industrializa-
tion process. As the power of the United States in global military or
economic terms has been reduced, there is a new opportunity to establish
a monetary system that will not rest on one currency as it does at present
on the paper dollar standard. The new monetary system would be estab-
lished on a new basis geared to growth without inflation and not subject
to the domestic politics of any single nation no matter how responsibly led.

7

REGULATION OF U.S. BANKS AND BANK HOLDING COMPANIES OUTSIDE THE UNITED STATES

THE STRUCTURE OF U.S. BANKS IN INTERNATIONAL FINANCE

U.S. banks engage in international activities principally through branches. As of December 31, 1982, there were over 800 foreign branches of U.S. banks with total assets of $350 billion, constituting over 70 percent of the international banking assets of U.S. banks and Edge Act corporations. There were also some 1000 foreign subsidiaries of U.S. banks, with those of the 200 largest U.S. banks accounting for 90 percent of their assets of $82 billion worldwide.

Member banks of the Federal Reserve System — whether national or state-chartered — may establish foreign branches with the approval of the Federal Reserve Board. After their establishment, branches of national banks are subject to examination by the Comptroller of the Currency, although the Fed may also require reports. State-chartered member bank branches are examined by the Fed. The establishment of foreign branches by state nonmember banks was brought under the authority of the FDIC by the Financial Institutions Regulatory and Interest Rate Control Act of 1978, thereby eliminating examination and control by state regulatory authorities.

In addition, in place of establishing a branch, a U.S. bank may invest directly in a foreign bank, subject to the same authorization procedure as in the case of branch banking.

A third method is the establishment of an Edge corporation by both member banks and bank holding companies. As was noted in Chapter 1, Edges have enhanced the competitive position of U.S. banks by permitting them to establish offices outside the state in which their headquarters are located and to engage in a wide range of international activities that would not be permitted domestically. The International Banking Act of 1978 removed the prohibition of foreign ownership and also eliminated a 10 percent reserve requirement. The act also required the Fed to review and modify its regulations on Edge Act corporations to enable them to be more competitive in rendering international financial services.

There are two types of Edge Act corporations: bank Edges and investment Edges. The bank Edges are located in virtually every significant U.S. financial center. They finance international trade transactions, foreign exchange, international deposits, and so on. The investment Edge is essentially a holding company for foreign investments. Because the Federal Reserve Act permits national banks to make foreign investments only in banks, foreign nonbank investments must be made either directly by a bank holding company or through an Edge subsidiary.

Subsidiaries outside the United States are generally established for one of three reasons:

- If the host country prohibits the establishment of branches of foreign banks; this is the case in Canada, Australia, and South Africa, for example;
- If foreign tax or banking laws favor subsidiaries rather than branches; or
- If the purchase of a local company enables the bank to gain rapid and less costly entry into a new market.

Investment Edges have proved to be an advantageous way to acquire foreign subsidiaries in interesting locations. At the end of 1979, foreign subsidiaries of Edges, mostly located in Western Europe, had assets in excess of $30 billion.

Under Federal Reserve Regulation K the extent of a bank's activities through ownership of a foreign company depends upon the extent of its control. If it owns over 50 percent of the voting stock, the sub may engage not only in banking but in certain other activities such as financing; leasing of both real and personal property; acting as a fiduciary; providing investment, financial, or economic advisory services; and engaging in general insurance brokerage.

The Fed's rules for operations abroad are therefore quite different from those permitted to domestic banks. The difference in approach goes back to the Federal Reserve Act of 1913 and the desire of Congress to compete abroad with foreign, particularly British, banks. Section 25 of that act enabled national banks to establish foreign branches, acquire ownership of foreign banks, and purchase stock in corporations organized to conduct "international or foreign banking" activities. Section 25(a) of the Federal Reserve Act, passed in 1919, established Edge Act corporations based in the United States but directed at international financial activities. As of December 31, 1982, there were 87 banking Edges with a total of 116 domestic branches and 17 foreign branches.

REGULATORY CONTROL OF U.S.
LENDING ABROAD

Strange as it may seem, the systematic monitoring of foreign lending only began in 1979 when the Fed, Comptroller of the Currency, and the FDIC formed the Interagency Country Exposure Review Committee (ICERC). Given what occurred between that date and 1983, in terms of excessive lending by U.S. banks to developing countries, it is appropriate to question the effectiveness of this committee.

The committee consists of nine members, two regional examiners, and one headquarters representative from each of the three agencies. It meets three times a year in Washington to "rate" country borrowers into six classifications: (1) strong—countries with no apparent economic, social, or political problems; (2) moderately strong—countries experiencing a limited number of identifiable problems not yet of major concern; (3) weak—countries experiencing problems deemed to be remediable; (4) substandard—countries where debt service has been interrupted or is threatened; (5) doubtful—countries where interest has been due and unpaid for at least one year and no definite prospects exist for obtaining foreign exchange; and (6) loss—countries guilty of protracted nonpayment, even though recovery may be forthcoming in the future.

The ratings are initially set by the Fed since it has better information than the other two agencies. The ICERC's rating list is highly confidential owing to its political sensitivity. The problems with the list and the ICERC generally are many. In September 1982 the GAO published a detailed analysis entitled *Bank Examination for Country Risk and International Lending*. In substance the analysis found that the commission's objectives needed to be better communicated, that its standards and administration could be improved, and that its impact was questionable.[1] For one thing, examiners were not required to follow up in subsequent examination reports on all outstanding prior recommendations or criticisms. It is certainly understandable that the three agencies would not impose country limits on banks. But it is difficult to understand why the commission has not insisted that the examiners review their country findings in detail with the banks, note their recommendations in their written reports, and take up the question again at a subsequent examination. It is even harder to understand why no written analyses of country conditions were made available to the banks examined. The GAO report found, for example, that special comments on country conditions were furnished the examined bank in only 1 of 13 examinations by the Fed.

It is certainly not possible for the lending banks to obtain the kind of country information available to the New York Fed, which is in constant touch with other central banks as well as with the IMF, the World Bank, and—almost on a daily basis—the BIS in Basel. Another very serious drawback is that the comments are prepared by country experts at the Fed in New York; they are reviewed with senior Fed officers; they are again reviewed at committee meetings; and only after general approval are they made available to the examined banks. This means that the information is necessarily out of date and watered down. The proof of the inadequacy of the commission's program is the surprise with which banks and their regulators greeted Mexico's admission in August 1982 that it could not meet its financial obligations. Since then the full story of excessive U.S. bank lending to developing countries has been gradually unfolding.

There would appear to be a real need to simplify systems and procedures here. Why is it necessary to have three separate agencies of the federal government examining foreign lending by U.S. banks? Should it not be possible to bypass the commission and have the New York Fed deal directly with the banks on country risk questions, advising the other agencies of its activities? We are dealing with a turf problem here, which, as will be discussed in a detailed analysis in Chapter 8, the United States can simply no longer afford. At the very least the Fed's country studies — promptly made available to the banks — should include projections on key economic variables for the future; analysis of the country's monetary and fiscal policies; discussion of performance under IMF agreements, if any; and an analysis of political and social developments including political stability, succession questions, external security threats, and relations with the United States and other countries. Should there be country limits imposed as other countries have done? In my opinion, not. If the banks are given adequate information, they should be expected to make the judgmental decision required. It would be well, however, to require detailed disclosure of foreign loans made by the banks in each country — not only to the government — but also to state enterprises and to the private sector as well, provided that the total of loans to any country amounts to more than a given percentage of the bank's capital or assets.

The SEC, whose function is to protect bank stockholders (a far different responsibility than the protection of depositors), has long taken the position that disclosure of foreign lending should be required of banks in their reports to the SEC.[2] Disclosure is always a better way to encourage responsible behavior than outright prohibition. Can we imagine, for example, that Manufacturers Hanover Bank would have loaned 284 percent of its equity to the four largest Latin American debtors — Mexico, Brazil, Venezuela, and Argentina — if this information had to be disclosed? Certainly the outside directors on the boards of banks would have demanded careful explanations before signing their names to reports which might have been required to disclose the extent of the 1979/82 U.S. bank lending to Latin American countries.

It is true that banks cannot lend more than 10 percent of their capital to any one "entity." But this is a meaningless regulation, as the Fed well knows, because most Latin American countries (and many European countries as well) have an infinite number of state-owned or -controlled corporations that represent, under the regulation, "separate borrowers." In 1971 in Italy, for example, when the government had difficulty in negotiating new loans, the loans were taken out by the oil company, the railroad, or other nationalized enterprises, and the funds were loaned, in turn, to the government. This regulation should certainly be reexamined because it serves no useful purpose and can only act to deceive the bank regulators into believing that there are limitations to foreign lending where none in fact exist.* What is true is that the nine principal money-center banks in the United States† have made loans in just two Latin American countries — Mexico and Brazil — in excess

---

*The SEC would require the banks to furnish three important pieces of information: the identification of countries that are not making timely payments of interest or principal in cases where loans exceed 1 percent of all loans outstanding, the amount of the exposure either in percentage or absolute terms, and the possible impact on the bank's financial condition or earnings.

Interestingly, the Comptroller has had a "means and purpose" test by which national banks must show that the individual borrower is required to pay from its own sources and that there are no guarantees from the national government. Otherwise, it is not a private loan.

†They are the Bank of America, Citicorp, Chase Manhattan, Manufacturers Hanover, Bankers Trust, Chemical Bank, First Chicago, Continental Illinois, and Morgan Guaranty.

of their combined capital. How can this be adequately explained by the Federal Reserve Board? And why have the regulatory authorities not required the banks to set aside more in loan-loss reserves against these outstanding loans?* Ostensibly the answer is that the Fed is now very concerned about the effect such action might have on the cost of bank CD's or on bringing about withdrawal of deposits.

The U.S. tax system adds one more unnecessary difficulty to the write-down of foreign bank loans by U.S. banks. Loan-loss reserves can only be established and deducted from taxable income up to a percentage fixed by law—at present 1 percent of "eligible" loans. Before 1969 the percentage had been 2¼ percent ever since the Great Depression. Today, most banks are close to their permissible maximum. This means that any write-down of additional loans will give the bank no deduction from taxable income in the absence of a demonstrable loss. Given the current situation with respect to the developing country loans of the major U.S. banks, the tax code is unrealistic. It is particularly so because it is so difficult to demonstrate to the tax authorities that a sovereign loan should in fact be written down or written off. The law should be changed. As it is, banks are being encouraged to avoid write-downs.

The accountants also have a problem with the bank lending practices to the developing countries. If a loan has been rescheduled, should not the auditors require that the status of the loan be changed? Take the case of a lawsuit brought against a bank or corporation. The accountant will inevitably require that the information be divulged in the company or bank's detailed annual report to the SEC on form 10-K. Yet loss from a rescheduled loan is often far more likely than payment in a pending legal action. The accountants have been caught in a quan-

---

*Under bank regulations in effect, banks do not have to increase their reserves against a loan if interest continues to be paid, regardless of rescheduling of principal payments. In Latin America since 1982 and earlier in Poland, interest was simply capitalized so that interest payments appeared to have been made while the principal owed merely increased.

On February 6, 1984, the Federal Reserve, the Comptroller of the Currency, and the FDIC did adopt, at the request of Congress, final regulations calling for the establishment of special reserves against problem loans made to foreign borrowers. The bank regulatory agencies will periodically identify the countries that have private or public borrowers that represent repayment risks and the amount of reserves banks will have to set aside against their foreign loans. The initial reserve requirement is 10 percent of impaired assets but may be eventually raised to 15 percent. The regulation also provides that loan restructuring fees must be deferred and recognized over the life of the loan as an interest adjustment.

dary here: the SEC wants disclosure; the Federal Reserve, however, understands that if the smaller banks in a syndicated loan subject to rescheduling demand to be repaid, the larger banks will have to pick up the additional burden. So, the Fed is not anxious to call attention to foreign lending difficulties. Chairman Paul Volcker made this very clear in a speech he gave in Boston in late 1982 indicating that the Fed would continue to regard bank lending to the countries of Latin American with patience and particular understanding.* Regardless of whether or not the Fed should not have strongly disapproved of excesses in lending, Volcker knows that it will be necessary not only to continue to reschedule many of these loans but also to make substantial new loans besides. If the Fed encourages the same banks that are already overexposed in Brazil, Mexico, and Argentina to make new commercial loans, how can it require that current loans be reported as in default and written down at a time when new loans are encouraged to be made to the same borrowers in difficulty?

This question will be discussed further when the role of the IMF is reviewed. However, note here that since August 1982 when the full extent of the Mexican debt problem became apparent to the banking authorities, Chairman Volcker has done everything in his power to make it possible for the borrowers to keep going, even when it required putting pressure on the commercial banks most heavily involved and the regional banks as well to maintain and even increase their loans in cooperation with loan packages designed by the IMF and the BIS.

What is much more difficult to understand is how — regardless of the failure of the central banks to urge caution — the money-center banks themselves could have continued to make loans to Latin American countries when it should have become apparent to all that there would be trouble ahead. In summer 1981, for example, the Mexican middle class began to exchange their overvalued pesos for U.S. dollars and transfer billions to banks in New York, Texas, Florida, and California. Yet as late as February 1982, those banks were loaning to Mexico over a six-week period an additional $8 billion. When we look back at this period of our history, it will be difficult to understand the behavior of these banks. There are perhaps several explanations that will help to clarify why the

---

*Paul Volcker, Speech to New England Council, Boston, November 16, 1982. Despite Volker's assurances, by 1984 the federal agencies had agreed on four classifications of foreign loans to determine which ones are likely to fall into default or require rescheduling. In May 1984, Venezuelan government and private sector loans were required to be classified as "substandard."

banks acted as irresponsibly as they appeared to have done in hindsight.

To understand what happened it is helpful to look at that peculiar development known as the *Eurodollar market*, which began in London around 1953 and grew to the point where in 1984 it is over $2 trillion gross and over $500 billion net. Some 75 percent of this amount is denominated in U.S. dollars; the rest is principally in deutsch marks, sterling, and yen. How could this market have grown as it did?[3] The answer is that it performed a very useful function over the years and proved very profitable to the participating banks. It was first useful in the early 1960s when President John F. Kennedy required U.S. firms seeking to expand overseas to borrow abroad for this purpose. Under President Lyndon Johnson, the funds grew through the financing abroad of the war in Vietnam. Then came the first quadrupling of the price of oil by OPEC in 1973/74, which instantly caused enormous numbers of dollars to be transferred to OPEC countries. These nations deposited the funds in dollars in London but permitted the banks to recycle them to the industrialized countries so that they might pay for their continued purchases of oil. When the second massive oil increase was instituted by OPEC in 1979/80, the developed countries had begun to make efforts to cut down on their oil purchases, but the rapidly developing countries—such as Brazil, Taiwan, and South Korea—needed much larger supplies of funds to nourish their expanding industrial base. The banks once again set out to recycle the new supply of oil dollars on deposit in the Eurocurrency banks; however, this time instead of financing U.S. multinationals or the developed countries, their borrowers became the developing countries. Since the supply of new dollars on deposit more than kept pace with reasonable demand, the banks began to pursue customers and paid little attention to whether the borrowings would be used to generate hard currency earnings or simply encourage domestic expansion. Since the money-makers among the banks were not the lenders in the London Interbank Offer Rate (LIBOR) market but the syndicate managers who organized the new loans, this, too, placed a premium on encouraging borrowers to borrow regardless of purpose. There was money to be made, and the banks vied against one another in fierce competition to put syndicates together.

The central banks paid little attention to what was happening. The Austrians, the Germans, and the British made loans to Poland; the Americans spearheaded loans to Latin America. By 1981 the Poles were in default. By August 1982 Latin American borrowers took a turn: Mexico, Brazil, Argentina, Chile, Venezuela, even Bolivia. Bank holding companies like Citicorp were making up to 70 percent of their total profits from foreign lending, and their executives were calling for more. Several reasons account for this phenomenon:

1. A primary reason why banks then made these questionable loans to developing countries was their desire to profit from the recycling process in 1980, as they had done after the first oil price increase.

2. Perhaps after the pressure of recycling, a second principal reason for the rash lending, at least insofar as American bankers were concerned, might be attributed to the change in bank psychology that has been alluded to throughout this book: the feeling on behalf of bank presidents that a bank should compete for profits much as a stockbroker or underwriter or merchant should, forgetting entirely that a bank is required by law to be concerned with the safety of its depositors unlike Sears or Merrill Lynch or even an insurance company, which has never been concerned primarily with the safety of the customer's investments or even the ultimate value of the individual's insurance policy. The new competition in the financial services area and the gradual acceptance by regulators that competition between banks and other financial services companies was something to be encouraged were epitomized by the attitude of the Secretary of the Treasury, Donald Regan, who had formerly been chief executive of Merrill Lynch.

At times it almost seemed as if the regulators had forgotten that the banks had a principal duty to return deposits to their owners on demand rather than to maximize earnings either for those depositors or for the bank's stockholders. The nature of banking became distorted. Not even the savings banks and savings and loans were exempt. The Garn–St. Germain Act of 1982 allowed these special institutions the same competitive role as the banks even though their purpose had always been to foster real estate development and municipal bond projects. The banks, despite Glass-Steagall, were in fact acting as underwriters in their foreign loans — except that it was they, and not their customers, who were directly at risk.

3. Another argument that such prestigious bankers as Walter Wriston of Citicorp or William Ogden of Chase made much of was that sovereign countries, unlike business corporations, could not go bankrupt. Solvency was therefore no more of a problem than it had been for the city of New York, although temporary illiquidity might in a given instance require the rescheduling of loans. Were they correct? We have still to find out whether the principal will be repaid in due course. All such loans are currently being rescheduled although on a short-term rollover basis. The same statements were made, as we have seen, by their

predecessor chief executives of the same banks in 1931. Countries did not go bankrupt then, but they renounced their foreign obligations and bondholders lost their money. Today's outlook is different. In the 1930s the U.S. government did not find it necessary to bail out the governments of poorer countries for fear that a revolution might bring to power a Communist government. If bondholders lost their money, they had taken the risk and paid the price. Now it is the banks' depositors who have taken the risk—without giving their consent, without knowing. They are, of course, protected by FDIC insurance, which is one more reason why the U.S. federal bank regulators should have been more concerned with foreign bank lending.

4. Another reason why the banks made constantly increasing loans to the developing countries was their conviction in 1980 that the inflationary cycle would continue and that in foreign trade, as in domestic investment, borrowers would profit from inflation by being able to repay ever larger loans through rising prices for their exports. Was the wealth of Brazil not inexhaustible if the country were developed? Were Mexico and Venezuela not large producers of oil? If oil continued to increase in price, so would other materials. But oil prices succumbed to the oil glut of 1982/83, and prices for raw materials collapsed, leaving the Latin American countries with smaller earnings from their export trade to meet ever higher interest payments. What no one had understood—including the bank regulators and especially the Federal Reserve Board—was that the tight-money policy instituted by the Federal Reserve Board in 1979 at the same time as the new oil price increase would cause much higher interest rates and a deflationary swing worldwide. As soon as it changed its monetary policy, the Fed should have warned the banks that their loans to raw materials producers such as those in Latin America would become very risky. The banks received no such warnings.

5. Some bankers may have thought that reducing the term of their loans to developing countries would reduce their exposure. As bankers they should have known that a loan to a sovereign borrower is simply rolled over when it cannot be repaid. In 1984, and for many years to come, these rollovers will become increasingly commonplace.

6. Perhaps the saddest reason for the increased lending to developing countries lay in the fact that it was the syndicate managers, not the interbank lenders, who made the big money in international lending. Money-center bankers with an international reputation, like David Rockefeller and Walter Wriston, became underwriters for the less sophisticated or smaller banks through the syndicate mechanism. The Arab depositors did not care. They knew that their deposits were protected

by the central banks and in particular the Federal Reserve as lender of last resort. They had only to avoid making direct loans to developing countries and to confine their money to the major lending banks, avoiding the smaller ones, which might not be worth saving in the event of defaults. Had the FDIC not saved all the depositors of Franklin National Bank and not just those who were covered by $100,000 of FDIC insurance?

What has been the reaction of Congress to the foreign lending practices of the major U.S. banks and to the inadequacy of federal bank supervision? Congress appears to be reluctant to take much action, perhaps because the problem is so serious and the situation in respect to many banks very fragile. In September 1982 there were congressional hearings at which a number of expert witnesses contended that the federal agencies had contributed to the crisis in international banking as a result of lax enforcement of banking regulations. One witness, Richard S. Dale of Brookings and the Rockefeller Foundation, called for an overhaul of international bank regulation through a "global approach to supervision which ensures that the operations of multinational banks are viewed in their entirety regardless of national secrecy laws." He said that regulators had "conspicuously failed" to deal with bank loans to countries like Mexico.[4] In a carefully worded article in the New York *Times* on February 27, 1983, Peter B. Kenen of Princeton pointed out:

> Blame must be borne most heavily, however, by the finance ministers and central bankers of the developed countries. They are the ones who left the banks with the task of recycling OPEC surpluses. They are the ones who produced the third great shock to the world economy — the recession and high interest rates that precipitated the debt problem.[5]

The Congress did consider legislation introduced by Senators John Heinz and William Proxmire, which would give the Fed new powers to raise loan-loss reserve requirements, to limit loans to countries deemed to be in trouble, and to spread rescheduling fees over the life of the loan. The additional funding for the IMF gave Congress the opportunity to add these provisions to the final legislation if adopted on the IMF funding.

One final area needs to be examined here. How did the U.S. bank regulatory system help to create the Eurodollar market? What steps, if any, have been taken to encourage the return of these funds to the United States? And what action might Congress take to make it advantageous for foreign funds to be invested in the United States at a time when domestic investment from domestic savings continues to lag?*

There is no question but that the regulations of the Federal Reserve Board greatly encouraged the development of the Eurocurrency market. As one author has stated:

> The remarkable development of offshore dollar banking is at bottom a history of regulatory myopia, together with a good bit of regulatory mismanagement. Also, unhappily, it is a story of regulatory futility — of the failure to grasp the implications of the changing world of high finance and to respond with forward looking and decisive policies. It is the history of trying to maintain the status quo in the face of market forces that could not be denied.[6]

These are harsh words. Yet they reflect one of the principal themes of this book: that both in domestic and international finance change has been constant in the last 30 years, and the regulatory authorities have neither foreseen nor adjusted to the consequences of the changes that have occurred, many of which have been a direct result of the actions of the regulators themselves.

Without Regulation Q (which sets maximum interest rates payable by U.S. banks on time and savings deposits) and Regulation D (which sets the minimum required reserves to be held by commercial bank members of the Federal Reserve System), the Eurodollar market might never have developed as it did. A study of bank deposits since the end of World War II shows how demand deposits went down steadily and time deposits grew as interest rates became increasingly volatile, for reasons discussed earlier.† The Eurodollar market proved to be a most attractive repository for U.S. bank funds because for a long period of time neither Regulation Q nor Regulation D were applicable. The London branches of U.S. banks could pay their depositors the going interest rate without regard to Regulation Q, and they were not — at least through the 1960s — subject to any reserve requirements under Regulation D. As early as 1918 the Fed had ruled that foreign branch deposits were not covered by reserve requirements. This lasted until October 1969 when the loophole was "partially" closed through a 10 percent reserve

---

*The Treasury has been urging Congress for some time to abandon the withholding tax on interest paid to foreigners on holdings of Treasury securities. Legislation was finally adopted in 1984.

†See Chapter 2. Also note the impact of Federal Reserve monetary policy discussed in Chapter 3.

requirement against increases in the total of net balances due from domestic offices of U.S. banks to their foreign branches. It freed up deposits raised abroad and parent borrowings, giving foreign branches a very significant cost advantage over domestic deposits; this freedom lasted until 1980 when the Fed announced changes in Regulation D to implement the provisions of the Monetary Control Act of 1980. However, not only has the freedom from Regulation Q remained; there is also no necessity to pay insurance premiums to the FDIC on foreign branch deposits.

Why did the Fed encourage the flight of bank capital away from the United States? Supposedly, to allow U.S. banks to compete on equal terms with foreign banks. But the effect has clearly been to discourage U.S. banks from financing U.S. businesses and to encourage loans to developing countries, which are then increasingly able to compete against U.S. goods in international markets. It was only on December 5, 1981, that the U.S. government took minimal action to bring Eurodollars home. On that date, international banking facilities (IBFs) began business in the United States, following a favorable Federal Reserve decision. The IBFs are allowed to conduct foreign banking business in the United States as though through a foreign branch, thus free of reserve requirements, interest-rate limitations, and insurance premiums. They are limited, however, to foreign clients and overseas subsidiaries of U.S. corporations. In the first 20 days of operation, no less than $47.2 billion of assets were transferred to the new IBFs. Hopefully, at least some $250 billion out of the $700 billion Eurodollar market will eventually find its way to the IBFs and be invested in the United States. This would mitigate a sad story of past regulatory mismanagement.

The Eurodollar market has led to some additional problems that have caused great difficulty not only for the Federal Reserve Board but for other central banks as well. I refer to the offshore havens, generally organized in tax-free countries or countries with strict secrecy laws such as Hong Kong, the Bahamas, Cayman Islands, Singapore, Panama, Luxembourg, Curacao, Monaco, the Jersey Islands, and other financial sanctuaries with no domestic banking business to speak of. Why have these proved so popular? What can or should be done to terminate the many abuses that these localities have permitted to the commercial banks operating abroad?

The banking world and most newspaper readers are now familiar with the Ambrosiano case if only because it involved the Vatican; the supposed assassination of a famous Italian banker, Roberto Calvi; and the legendary Michaele Sindona. To bankers, Ambrosiano was important because this small Luxembourg branch of the largest private bank in Italy was robbed of over $1.3 billion by means of transfers through Panamanian companies, some of which belonged to the Vatican. At any rate the money simply vanished. The Italian government refused to take responsibility, although central bank members of the BIS—including the central bank of Italy—had agreed in the Basel Convention of 1975 that the central bank of the headquarters country of a commercial bank should be legally liable for the actions of that bank's foreign branches. Here was an important case, with other banks (including U.S. banks) holding over $400 million of bad debts and the Italian government saying, "We are not responsible because the parent Italian bank belonged to the Vatican, and the Vatican under our law is a sovereign state." Finally in the spring of 1984 the Vatican agreed to pay out a substantial portion of the debt ($250 million). Accountants and high-level bank commissioners specially appointed have still been trying to ascertain what happened, but with the funds scattered, no one may now be held responsible for absconding with billions of dollars.[7]

Why have the central bank members of the BIS, who meet each month and talk to each other by phone almost every day, not been able to solve this mystery or at least come up with some agreed-upon rule that will make such looting of a branch bank impossible in the future? The answer is that there is at present no way to control what commercial banks may do internationally if they choose to establish branch banks in these havens that have no bank regulations other than tight bank secrecy laws. Is there an answer to this problem? Of course. It only necessitates that the central banks as a group, or the central bank of any individual country that wishes to exercise adequate control over its own commercial banks, refuse to allow branches to be established in these havens or require that any haven transactions be reported in detail and the books kept at headquarters regardless of the bank location's secrecy laws. Unfortunately, each developed country's banks have successfully persuaded their own banking authorities that for their own central bank to take such action would make it impossible for domestic banks to compete with the banks of other nations engaged in international financial transactions.

A more interesting example of what has been going on is the story of Citicorp and its Citibank banking subsidiary operating over 1,000 branches and subsidiaries all over the world in over 150 different countries and in many exotic tax and secrecy havens. How could the largest bank in the world be allowed to function in such a manner that it appeared to have circumvented tax statutes, reserve requirement regulations, and other laws without anyone being called to account? In an age of increasingly sophisticated electronic communications, are the central banks and the Federal Reserve Board in particular telling us that it is not possible to monitor what a commercial bank does abroad and that we must rely on the judgment and integrity of bank management to protect the bank's depositors? If this is the case, why does the Federal Reserve Board purport to supervise the activities of U.S. banks abroad?

Curiously enough, the Citibank story was not brought to light by any bank regulatory agency but by the SEC to whom an employee of the bank had revealed a part of the story. After a three-year investigation, the SEC decided on a split vote (3 to 2) not to prosecute despite the recommendation of its staff. The congressional subcommittee in the House, which has oversight responsibility over the SEC,[8] then decided to investigate why no action had been taken by that agency, which is responsible for protecting the interests of bank stockholders. Once again, no one appeared to be unduly concerned with the effect of these actions on the protection of depositors. This amounts to saying that if the bank is large enough, we need not worry about its solvency or the protection of its depositors. Like Brazil, it is too rich and too powerful to incur risks that might affect the depositors. This is an interesting theory.

Citibank was alleged to have breached the tax and exchange control regulations of various European countries, including France, West Germany, Switzerland, and Italy as well as certain Asian and Latin American nations in which it did business by "parking" certain foreign exchange transactions in tax and regulatory havens like Nassau in the Bahamas and indulging in fictional transactions between branches so as to turn short-term deposits requiring reserves into long-term deposits free of reserve requirements. There are indeed delicate ethical questions at play here very akin to the old conundrum that it is acceptable to act in such a way as to *avoid* taxation but that tax *evasion* is illegal.* Enormous profits were certainly involved. The SEC study found that in the 1974–78 period, Citibank earned $417 million from all foreign exchange transactions, of which at least $46 million involved parking. The system used in German transactions can serve as a brief example of how to avoid reserve requirements: A Citicorp German branch might deposit short-

*When the top management of Citicorp realized what had been going on, the practices were stopped and the bank's counsel was requested to make an exhaustive investigation of all acts complained of. The study clears the bank but itself raises many questions.

term money (for example, a three-month deposit) in a Citicorp offshore facility in Nassau, Luxembourg, Monaco, or the Bahamas and then immediately redeposit the money back in Germany—but as four-year money not subject to German reserve requirements. The bank's books would show the deposit at its true maturity, but the German regulators would have been neatly circumvented in the transaction.

Given the record of regulation by the Federal Reserve Board of the

TABLE 7-1
Member U.S. Banks Foreign Branches, June 30, 1982

	Number
Bank of America N T and S A (San Francisco and Los Angeles)	110
Bankers Trust Company (New York)	15
Chase Manhattan Bank NA (New York)	79
Chemical Bank (New York)	20
Citibank NA (New York)	219
Continental Illinois NB & TC (Chicago)	20
First Interstate Bank of California (Los Angeles)	8
First National Bank of Chicago (Chicago)	31
First National Bank of Boston (Boston)	51
Irving Trust Company (New York)	8
Manufacturers Hanover Trust Co. (New York)	24
Marine Midland Bank NA (Buffalo)	8
Mellon Bank NA (Pittsburgh)	5
Morgan Guaranty Trust Co. of New York (New York)	19
Rainier National Bank (Seattle)	6
Republic National Bank of New York (New York)	6
Security Pacific National Bank (Los Angeles)	8
Wells Fargo Bank NA (San Francisco)	6
Total	643

Note: These banks are the 18 largest.

Source: Compiled by the author.

activities of U.S. commercial banks outside the United States, it will perhaps appear surprising that the Fed has insisted with the Bush Task Group (on deregulation of banking) that it continue to regulate the largest U.S. banks. These include all the banks whose overseas activities the Fed has failed to supervise adequately. The reason given by the Fed in a detailed study furnished the Group was that it needed to continue to regulate the largest U.S. banks and bank holding companies in order to properly exercise its responsibility over monetary policy. As a result the Bush Task Group has recommended that the Federal Reserve Bank continue to regulate the 50 largest bank holding companies. This would effectively give the Fed regulatory responsibility over banks controlling well over 50 percent of all bank deposits in the United States.

The essential reason given by the Fed to the Bush Task Group for this continued regulatory role was that this was necessary because of the Fed's function to direct U.S. monetary policy. In fact, the principal bank holding companies, which control the largest money-center banks, are the entities which are responsible for excessive lending abroad. If the Bush recommendations are adopted, this will mean the Fed will exercise better supervision over U.S. banks abroad in the future. The extent of the power exercised by a small number of banking institutions active outside the United States, can be explained by the following:

As of June 30, 1982, 18 U.S. banks had 643 branches outside the United States (see Table 7-1). Of these, 2 banks — Citibank and Bank of America — had 329; 89 branches of U.S. banks were located in the Cayman Islands and 77 in the Bahamas as compared with only 14 in France and 27 in Germany. These figures provide some measure of the inadequacy of bank supervision of the activities of U.S. banks outside the United States.

NOTES

1. General Accounting Office, *Bank Examination for Country Risk and International Lending*, Washington, D.C., U.S. Government Printing Office, September 1982.

2. See Opening Statement by John D. Dingell, Chairman, Subcommittee on Oversight and Investigations of the Committee on Energy and Commerce, House of Representatives, 97th Congress, Washington, D.C., Sept. 17, 1982.

3. For a complete analysis of the Eurocurrency market, see Thibaut de Saint Phalle, *Trade, Inflation and the Dollar*, 2d Revised Edition, (New York: Praeger, 1984), chap. 5.

4. U.S., Congress, House, Committee on Energy and Commerce. Statement by Richard S. Dale, September 17, 1982, p. 16.

5. Peter B. Kenen, "The Costly Blunders of Central Bankers," New York *Times*, February 27, 1983, p. F3. Kenen is correct in finding central bankers and ministers of finance as a group having a heavy responsibility for the current debt situation. Under the current paper dollar monetary standard, however, it was the Fed that instituted, first, easy money and then the tight-money policy that lay at the root of the borrowers' problem along with the drop in the price of oil that occurred almost simultaneously. Borrowers were encouraged to borrow in the easy money period and then whipsawed when the Fed switched to its tight-money policy in 1979. Kenen's point is important, however, because the solutions to the problem, as discussed in Chapters 9 and 10, are going to require the utmost cooperation among central banks and the international financial agencies.

6. Franklin Edwards, "The New International Banking Facility: A Study in Regulatory Frustration," *Columbia Journal of World Business* (Winter 1981): p. 6.

7. Anyone interested in the full story of the financial dealings between Michaele Sindona, Roberto Calvi, the Mafia, the Instituto Per le Opere di Religione (IOR) in the Vatican, the Freemasons in Italy (the P-2), and the Christian Democratic party should read Luigi DiFonzo's *St. Peter's Banker* (New York: Watts, 1983). The Ambrosiano case is but a small part of this story.

8. U.S. Congress, House, Committee on Energy and Commerce, Subcommittee on Oversight and Investigation. Hearings on SEC insurance of investor information. Washington, D.C., September 1982. In 1983 the staff of the Senate Permanent Subcommittee on Investigations, in a 253-page study, called for increased scrutiny of offshore activities by the banking industry, law enforcement officials, U.S. bank regulators, and central banks.

8

INTERNATIONAL LENDING: PROBLEMS AND POSSIBLE SOLUTIONS

In this chapter we will examine the impact of commercial bank lending in the 1979–82 period and the means by which the enormous debt incurred may in time be repaid. What was the situation at the beginning of 1984? How did this enormous debt burden ever come about?

According to A. W. Clausen, president of the World Bank, by January 1, 1984, the total debt of the developing countries amounted to a staggering $800 billion. In 1983 alone, this debt increased by 33 percent, from $608 billion to $810 billion. The debt increase in Latin America has been particularly dramatic, owing to the lending activities there of the nine largest U.S. money-center banks. In 1982 the debt amounted to 280 percent of total exports from Latin America. Argentina, for example, had a debt-to-export ratio of 390 percent in that year; and Brazil, 345 percent. Interestingly enough, exports from Latin American countries were less than 50 percent of that of Asian countries and well below the exports of African and Middle East borrowers. It is as though in a brief period of a few years Latin American countries soaked up for their own internal development a substantial portion of the world's dollar liquidity. It was done essentially, as noted in Chapter 7, through the recycling of dollar surpluses from certain Middle East countries. These countries deposited, principally in U.S. banks, in London, their dollar funds accumulated from the massive increase in oil prices in 1979/80.

In 1983, commercial bank lending to these developing countries suddenly slowed dramatically as the banks began to understand the difficult position in which they found themselves as a result of lending too much too fast and out of proportion to the countries' capacity to repay. Perhaps even more important, direct investment in those countries went down in 1983 from $13 billion to $10 billion. Danger signals appeared in all directions.

THE CAUSES OF THE PROBLEM

How could such a situation have come about? Why was it allowed to happen? The causes can be briefly set forth:

1. The new OPEC oil price increase of 1979/80 was obviously an important factor. Even though the multiple was less than in the first oil shock of 1973/74, the effect was much worse because it started from a much higher base. In the earlier period the price per barrel went from $2.30 to $12; in the second, from approximately $13 to over $40 at its peak. When you consider the demands of developing countries that had been rapidly industrializing in the intervening years, it is easy to understand the effect of this massive new price increase.

2. The Federal Reserve's 1979 change in monetary policy to slow down the rapid rise in the money supply caused sharp increases in interest rates. The demand for dollars had escalated throughout the global economy as a result of the increase in oil prices. Yet at the same time, the U.S. Federal Reserve decided to move to a tight-money policy. Supply was reduced just as demand increased. The result was a classic increase in the value of dollars—hence, the price, that is, a rise in interest rates. This is not to say that the Fed was not right in correcting the excesses of the past. It was just that the timing and the lack of warning to the banks proved to be singularly unfortunate. At the time of the first oil shock in 1974 interest rates had been 4 percent. In 1980 they were approaching 20 percent.

3. The developing countries were already fully borrowed when OPEC increased the price of oil in 1979. In 1980, 60 percent of all new Eurodollar credits were going to the developing countries compared with 35 percent in 1974.

4. There was an enormous concentration of borrowing taking place: 20 developing countries were taking down 80 percent of the loans between 1974 and 1980; 5 countries alone—Brazil, Mexico, Argentina, South Korea, and the Philippines—borrowed half this amount.

5. Not to be outdone, the Eastern bloc countries increased their Eurodollar borrowings from $6 billion to $60 billion, with two thirds going to Poland, Hungary, and East Germany.

6. The major error of lenders and borrowers alike was not to foresee the deflationary impact of the new OPEC price increase, which was bound to reduce the volume of international trade (except for oil) and make it increasingly difficult for developing country borrowers to repay their loans.

7. The recession and oil glut of 1982 in turn diminished the flow of Middle East dollars into the Eurocurrency pool. OPEC itself became a borrower instead of a depositor of dollars. Loanable funds decreased.

8. In 1983 U.S. banks themselves became borrowers instead of lenders. As the economic recovery took further hold in the United States in 1984, U.S. banks continued to borrow heavily. This has caused the Federal Reserve to increase the money supply to the upper targets fixed by the Fed. It has obviously been trying to maintain the economic recovery while maintaining tight control over the money supply increase, hoping that interest rates would remain steady or increase only slightly.

9. Already as of mid-1982, nine developing countries needed over 90 percent of their foreign exchange earnings to meet their foreign debt; Argentina needed 179 percent of foreign exchange earnings. The developing countries were rapidly being forced to borrow additional amounts just to maintain industrial production for their export trade.

10. As borrowings by the developing countries have risen, the effects of changes in interest rates have become more significant. It is estimated that a 1 percent rise in interest rates may mean an additional $2 billion in what developing country borrowers have to pay in annual interest charges.

11. When OPEC increased the price of oil again in 1979, the developed countries made an enormous error in not creating their own buyers' cartel. In 1983 the U.S. government, faced with the opportunity at last to break the OPEC cartel, instead helped stabilize the price of oil at well over twice what it had been in 1978, thereby preserving the cartel. One wonders why, particularly since the Soviet Union is the world's largest exporter of oil and hence the biggest beneficiary of this price maintenance policy.

It is important to keep in mind three factors that affect the position of the lending banks:

1. No central bank really knows which banks are principally at risk in the excessive lending to the developing countries because banks are constantly lending to each other in the Eurodollar market. There is a very significant interdependence among the international financial institutions because of this fact. This means that if one large bank is unable to meet its commitments, many others will follow.

2. The central banks' definition of *performing assets* for banks is that interest must be paid but principal need not be. The effect of this is to encourage commercial banks to capitalize interest payments when

due, thereby constantly increasing the amount of principal owed. Developing country debts are not and will not be reduced. They will have a tendency to keep on rising, and indeed have been doing so steadily, if only because of this practice.

3. The banks have been operating with totally inadequate data in determining the extent to which to make loans to developing countries. How to remedy this serious flaw in the system will be the subject of subsequent analysis.

THE PARTICIPANTS

Since the U.S. commercial banks have loaned principally to Latin America, the focus will be on borrowers from this region. The principal borrowers are Argentina, Brazil, Mexico, Venezuela, and Chile.

Among the U.S. bank lenders principally at risk we have not only the nine major money-market banks but also a host of regional banks. It is important to remember that in Mexico alone over 1,400 U.S. banks were participants in loans when Mexico revealed its difficulties in August 1982. This makes any reschedulings very difficult, particularly since regional and smaller banks consider that they were enticed by the larger banks to participate in syndicates and, in an expanding U.S. economy, would prefer now to use their funds for domestic loans. In 1983 U.S. banks moved from being lenders to borrowers in the international money markets. In that year they borrowed $14.6 billion more than they loaned. The major bank lenders are faced not only with constant reschedulings of foreign loans but also with increased lending on an already very heavy base. As of mid-1982, Mexican credits alone represented almost 50 percent of the total capital of the nine largest U.S. banks; Brazil, 45 percent; and Argentina, 20 percent. Taken together, loans to these three countries represented 115 percent of the total capital of these banks. One is led to wonder once again why some of these banks did not increase their capital more aggressively during the stock market recovery of 1982/83 or why U.S. regulatory authorities did not make a greater effort to force them to do so.*

The international financial organizations also have an important role to play in the relations between developing country borrowers and the lending banks. Principal among these are the IMF, the World Bank,

---

*Undoubtedly, from management's point of view this may be due to the fact that bank shares have been selling at low prices in relation to their book value.

the BIS, and the InterAmerican Development Bank, which to date has played almost no role at all.

The U.S. regulatory agencies are, of course, very much involved (see Chapter 7). Since 1983 they have increased the capital ratios of banks and tightened the rules with respect to reserves against nonperforming loans. The SEC, as was noted, has also begun to take a closer look at the disclosure rules with respect to foreign loans. And since August 1982, when the Mexican loan difficulties were first divulged officially, Chairman Paul Volcker of the Federal Reserve has played a particularly important and effective role as an active participant in negotiations between the country borrowers and the commercial bank lenders, aided by the IMF and the BIS, and with the administration and Congress to make sure that a very difficult and delicate situation with respect to foreign loans by U.S. banks does not become more unmanageable.

Finally, the export promotion agencies in the developed countries need to be active participants also because the developing countries must continue to import equipment, machinery, and particularly spare parts if they are going to be able to continue to manufacture products for export. The maintenance of foreign trade by developing country borrowers is obviously essential if these loans are ever to be paid. The new Export-Import Bank program for Brazil of $1.25 billion was an important step taken by the U.S. government to meet these needs.

There has been a natural tendency on the part of individual governments (which are reluctant to impose austerity measures on their populations), on the part of certain banks (which would like to see the international agencies more adequately financed, so that they might be in a better position to make new loans to the developing countries), and on the part of the media to highlight the difficulties faced by the borrowers and by the banks in finding solutions to the debt problem. As in all such international economic relationships, politics and U.S. government policy also play an important role. Analysis indicates, however, that while the problem of loans to developing countries is a very difficult one, it is by no means unmanageable. Fortunately for the commercial banks, there are a minimum number of countries involved. Mexico, Brazil, Argentina, Venezuela, and Chile are the principal countries where U.S. bank lending has raised difficulties.

Mexico

In considering the importance of the Mexican debt of over $80 billion, it is essential to keep in mind the very great strengths of the Mexican economy. As one Mexican business leader put it to me:

We didn't throw away the money we borrowed. It went into plants and equipment and in educating a burgeoning middle class of trained technicians fully capable of managing a newly industrialized nation. We are not about to commit suicide by allowing a revolution just because we will have to tighten our belts for a period of time after two disastrous administrations. We now have a good President and we will help him succeed because we know what the alternatives are.

President Luis Echeverría Alvarez had thought of himself as a leader of the Third World and neglected the development of his country. President Jose Lopez Portillo had allowed corruption to flourish and lacked judgment. He kept the value of the peso artificially very high, so exports languished and as much as $30 billion fled the country. Then he revised his policy and reduced the value of the currency while increasing wages. The results were galloping inflation and no increase in exports. Then, after the money had fled, he foolishly nationalized the banks to seek a scapegoat for his unfortunate policies.

Under the new administration of President Miguel de la Madrid, much has been done to reverse the economic errors of the past. There is a determination on the part of government to make it work and a commitment to reduce corruption. The country has a strong middle class, enormous natural wealth in oil and silver, a revised investment policy to encourage foreign investment (as shown by the decision of the Ford Motor Company to establish a major plant in Mexico), and a flexible exchange rate policy that will gradually reestablish the value of the peso on a sound basis. It has an IMF package in place for $10 billion, and commercial bank loans have been increased and rescheduled.

In 1982 the lending banks treated Mexico with singular severity, demanding a rate of 2¼ percent over LIBOR plus a fee of 1¾ points for a $200 million premium paid when the first $1.7 billion was disbursed. With the help of Paul Volcker, who intervened on behalf of the Mexicans, the banks have since improved their terms for Mexico. The notion on the part of certain New York bankers that they are entitled to extraordinary fees and higher interest rates (supposedly justified by the higher risks) for rescheduling loans that should never have been made does not seem defensible, particularly where the borrower is making a real effort to cooperate and to initiate policies that will eventually enable the banks to be repaid in full. The U.S. bank regulatory authorities have now discouraged this practice of charging large rescheduling fees by requiring that they be amortized over the life of the loan and considered as additional payments of interest. Mexico's problem will be on its way to solution unless the price of oil should suddenly decline to less than $25 per barrel. Mexico's future is dependent upon its ability to sell its oil at close to current prices.

Brazil

At the end of 1980 Brazil owed approximately $90 billion to the international commercial banks, most of them American. At the end of 1984 it is expected that the Brazilian debt will have reached $100.8 billion through capitalization of interest, direct or indirect, and through additional loans. This increase assumes repayments of principal and interest of $18.7 billion during the year.

Compared with Mexico, the psychological situation in Brazil is the reverse and therefore more serious. Mexico found a highly competent government succeeding two disastrous administrations. Brazil has just come out of 18 years of military rule and has held its first democratic elections since 1962. Instead of a new cohesiveness born of desperate circumstances, there is a tendency to accentuate diversity of ideas and rebellion against the past—even though during the period of military rule the country went through a period of extraordinary economic development. One has only to visit Itaipu and understand that 87 percent of the machinery in place in that immense hydroelectric development in a jungle region was built in Brazil to realize what industrialization of the country has accomplished in less than 20 years. Brazil is an industrial giant today and passed Canada in GNP over two years ago.

It also has all the problems of rapid industrialization in addition to its debt, with 10 percent of its population in Greater São Paulo, a flight to the cities, and high unemployment with an unbalanced economy. Under these circumstances, how much austerity can the social fabric of Brazil withstand to meet payments due the international commercial banks? It will depend on a number of factors, including: (1) the price of oil (Brazil's new industrialization requires massive importation; a $5 per barrel reduction in price is equivalent to $1 billion of savings in a year); (2) the rate of inflation (Brazilian indexation ensures both constant inflation and painless adjustment, but this cannot continue); (3) the extent of maintenance of food subsidies; and (4) the growth of partial unemployment. Above all, it depends upon the temper of the people and their national willingness to adjust their standard of living downward, at least temporarily. The debt cannot be a permanent problem. In relative terms the debt per inhabitant is only $720, while it is $2,600 in Venezuela and $6,000 in the United States. As bankers are ceaselessly repeating, Brazil is a very rich country awaiting further development of its natural resources wealth.

Perhaps the greatest problem in Brazil is the proliferation of state-owned businesses, which have been allowed to function as independent states within a state, refusing even to submit their budgets for approval and importing what they want. Petrobas, Electrobas, and the like have to be brought under control, and there are over 500 of these state-owned companies.

Under certain assumptions, Brazil can meet its indebtedness problem. These are (1) that the trade surplus of $6.1 billion in 1983 will increase to $9 billion in 1984 and keep on rising, a target which is likely to be exceeded; (2) that the LIBOR rate averages 10.5 percent and that the banks do not try to treat Brazil as they did Mexico with rescheduling fees and increased interest rates; (3) that the $1.5 billion Paris Club rescheduling become effective; (4) that the commercial banks reschedule $4.5 billion in 1984 and make $5.2 billion in new loans; (5) that the export finance agencies in the OECD countries make special credits available ($1.25 billion from the Export-Import Bank of the United States is already in place); and (6) that oil imports can be reduced even further (in 1983 imports were down 11.6 percent) which also seems very likely.

The IMF put up $4.9 billion when the commercial banks agreed to put up an additional $4.4 billion on top of their existing loans. So far, however, only 50 percent of the 830 banks involved in Brazilian loans have agreed to lend more. Their prior loans have been used, and the IMF funds repaid a bridge loan from the BIS outstanding for 11 months. The demand for new advances is great; and by the time new loans are made, they have to be used to repay prior obligations. It is an endless attempt to catch up to past indebtedness. If agricultural development which does not require large amounts of foreign capital can be sharply expanded (which should be possible), then at least employment and the problem of food supplies for the poor and the hungry will be alleviated. For eventual debt repayment, the problem is certainly not impossible, if the government remains in strong hands for the next several years until confidence is restored.

Venezuela

For Venezuela the debt problem is very much more difficult, again for different reasons. Venezuela has been a rich country since the 1920s because of its oil, but it has never really used its wealth either to develop its other vast natural resources or to bring education to its people until very recently. When OPEC increased its price for oil, Venezuela borrowed more.* Why were these funds not used to develop new oil fields, the nickel deposits, or even the country's heavy oil deposits?

Venezuela is a country of the very rich and the very poor who move to Caracas to find work; the rest of the country remains relatively as undeveloped as ever. With a $34 billion debt — $2,600 per inhabitant — of which $10 billion is short-term debt due from the government, and no agreement with the IMF as of March 1984, Venezuela must count on its foreign exchange earnings from oil. Yet oil revenues have been declining with the decline in the price of oil. Just recently, however, the price for heavy crude like the Venezuelan has risen.

The new President Jaime Lusinchi, elected in 1984 is from the Christian Democratic Party, the same party as that of President Carlos Andres Perez, who preceded the prior government and was unfortunately not a capable administrator. The government's strongest backer has been the Labor Confederation, which is not likely to favor an austerity program. While exchange controls are in effect and the currency has been devalued again, there is no plan yet in effect for economic development or control. Venezuela is still the world's biggest importer of Scotch whiskey. It imports 70 percent of its food although it could readily develop its own agricultural potential. Gasoline is still 40 cents per gallon. The prospects for the future do not look bright unless policies change. The problem in Venezuela is that it became oil-rich in the 1920s and there has been for 60 years no need on the part of the government leaders or the wealthy class to make a special effort to foster development.

Argentina

Argentina is one of the wealthiest countries in the world, rich in natural resources. It has oil and gas, it exports grain and meat, and it has a highly educated middle class. In 1880 the population of Brazil and Argentina were essentially the same; in 1984 Argentina has some 28 million inhabitants, whereas Brazil has 130 million. The first has a static society, the second highly dynamic.

How can one explain why the country is so highly indebted, why it has had so much bad government for so long, and why its inflation

---

*When I lectured there in 1975 and 1976, I was continuously being asked by businessmen why a country that was so rich was constantly borrowing from the banks. The official explanation given me was that since rates were low this was a good time to borrow and keep the funds invested until needed for development projects.

rate is the highest in Latin America? Its foreign debt had reached $45 billion by 1984, of which almost $3 billion represented new indebtedness incurred by the military government in 1983 to purchase arms to replace those lost in the Falklands War with Great Britain. In early 1984 it elected a new civilian government without incidents, and President Raúl Alfonsin appears to have established control over the military. He has not, however, reached an agreement with the IMF, and in the meantime arrears of principal and interest on the foreign debt are mounting steadily. The President has declared that his policy is growth and expansion of the economy rather than the IMF normal program of import control, increased taxes, and elimination of subsidies to bring down inflation. In Brazil in 1979, when Delfim Netto first came to power as economic minister, his policy was based on growth as well, but he had to reverse course 180 degrees. The same will probably sooner or later have to happen in Argentina. Alfonsin believes the banks will accept continued deferral of interest payments rather than see his fragile government replaced by the Peronist labor confederation. The large U.S. banks are in a difficult position: 40 percent of Manufacturers Hanover's capital is represented by $1.2 billion of loans to Argentina; Citibank, Chase, and Morgan Guaranty each have approximately 19 percent of their capital in Argentinean loans.

As in Brazil, the principal problem in Argentina is the state ownership of businesses. State-owned companies account for 50 percent of the country's gross domestic product (GDP). They are badly managed and deficit ridden, yet there is no plan to return these companies to private ownership. A careful economic plan is urgently needed: the government deficit must be reduced, monetary policy needs to be eased, import controls on semimanufactured goods should be loosened, and letters of credit with U.S. banks must be renewed. In the meantime price controls are in effect, and Argentinean manufacturers, although anxious to cooperate with the new civilian government, are not making money. It is difficult for the first civilian government in many years to realize that what is needed in such a situation is less government rather than more. Inflation in March 1984 was still 11 percent, and yet the President refuses to cut government spending or reduce a swollen bureaucracy.

Some years ago Finance Minister Martinez de Hoz tried to make Argentina competitive again by keeping the peso strong and allowing imports to come in through tariff reductions. His policy, not unlike that of President Reagan's, resulted in a decline of exports as the currency strengthened. He also ratcheted up interest rates to cure hyperinflation, but he let government expenses soar and budget deficits increased sharply. Today's government blames him for the 24 percent decline in the industrial sector between 1977 and 1982, the 6.8 percent reduction in GDP, and the sharp decline in real images. Can we see an eventual parallel in current U.S. policies?

Chile

In Chile the military still rules. This country, which a few years ago had more stability than any other Latin American country, went through a disastrous Socialist revolution that was followed by a military takeover with General Augusto Pinochet still in power. This was the country where monetarist theories were going to bring back prosperity under strong government. It did not succeed because the economic policies used lacked flexibility, particularly with regard to exchange rates. Had the currency been allowed to devalue, exports would have increased because Chilean products would have become more price-competitive. Chile is a country poor in natural resources. Its principal export has been copper, and the world price of copper has severely declined in the last few years. Now with $20 billion of foreign debt, an unpopular government, and rising unemployment, the country appears to have lost its direction.

How could Latin America be in such difficulty when U.S. commercial banks have advanced more money in recent years to these countries than the U.S. government did after World War II to Europe? Why did the one succeed and the other fail? Did Europeans work harder? Were they better governed? Were they simply more determined after six years of war?

POSSIBLE SOLUTIONS

The Role of the IMF

After considerable difficulty the capital of the IMF was doubled to $90 billion in 1983, with an additional General Agreement to Borrow of $27 billion. The failure to move more quickly was due in large part to the fact that it took so long for the Reagan administration to understand the importance of the IMF's role in helping the developing countries take the unpleasant political steps that would make it possible for them to reschedule their debts. How can this increase in funds, amounting in reality to only some $55 billion,* enable this international agency to help reschedule over $800 billion of developing country debt? Nevertheless, if the Latin American debt is ever repaid, it will in large part be attributable to the role of the IMF. The reasons for this are many. The organization is apolitical, it treats the rich as well as the poor with equal severity, it does not play either politics or favorites, and it is currently headed by a man with remarkable judgment, energy, and single-mindedness of purpose, Managing Director Jacques de Larosière.

Jacques de Larosière

Jacques de Larosière is the managing director of the IMF. His experience has been that of a typical senior French civil servant. Born in 1930 of an aristocratic family, he does well all that is expected of his background: he is an accomplished horseman, fisherman, and skier; he has a beautiful apartment in Paris and country homes elsewhere in France; and he is an art connoisseur. His experience in international economic policy, like that of many Frenchmen destined for the higher reaches of the French civil service, was acquired in the Finance Ministry. In 1974 he became chief of staff to the finance minister, Valery Giscard d'Estaing, a man of similar background and upbringing who went from finance minister to the presidency of France. De Larosière went on to become director of the Treasury and from there—in 1978 at the age of 48—to managing director of the IMF. He is a man of strong intelligence, he is highly disciplined, and he evidences great integrity and a moral courage born of an acceptance that what is right must succeed. Like many men of similar qualities, he is hardworking—a difficult taskmaster who is admired but not liked by his subordinates. At the same time, he is a shrewd but uncompromising bargainer, a man well aware of what needs to be done in the position he now occupies. The job of the IMF is to exact financial rectitude. Its managing director fits the international agency he represents perfectly. He will require that its conditionality be met regardless of political pressures. He is not a compromiser over principles. The world is fortunate in having a man of his stature, expertise, and dedication as managing director of the IMF. I would predict that he will turn out to have been an unusually good choice for what is today a most difficult and exacting position.

---

*The increase in quotas involves many weak or restricted national currencies from IMF member nations that have no value for loan purposes because they cannot be exchanged for 'hard' currencies.

IMF Policies

The IMF was created at Bretton Woods in 1945 for the purpose of making loans to countries in temporary balance of payments difficulties. It was not expected to have to solve severe economic structural problems, such as those today facing so many developing countries that have attempted to industrialize too quickly and with an inadequate infrastructure. Its policies are erroneously summarized by just one word: *austerity. Restoration of economic balance* would be a better phrase. In order to accomplish this, as a condition of its lending, the IMF requires the borrowing country to agree to the following basic program:

1. To reduce or remove government subsidies in favor of certain parts of the population: food, fuel, transportation, housing, and so on;
2. To devalue the currency in order to discourage imports and to encourage exports so as to earn more foreign exchange;
3. To raise taxes so as to reduce budget deficits and lower the inflation rate;
4. To regulate imports so as to eliminate luxury or unnecessary items;
5. To adopt legislation that will facilitate exports through credits, tax rebates, and the like; and
6. To eliminate or reduce investments in state enterprises, that is, to encourage private sector investment and a return to entrepreneurship at the expense of investment in large, bureaucratic state enterprises with little motivation for profit or innovation.

Cooperation Between IMF and Commercial Bank Lending

Because the IMF has limited resources of its own, it must — by persuading countries to accept its program — encourage the commercial banks to reschedule outstanding borrowings and make additional loans. The IMF's success during its 40 years of existence is such that banks know how well its programs have succeeded in country after country. Fortunately, while in 1984 developing country indebtedness is huge, there are really only a handful of countries faced with a level of indebtedness so high as to require that drastic steps be taken to restore their economic well-being. The IMF is a very positive force in international affairs because its policies have been proven to work.

As noted earlier, Chairman Paul Volcker of the Federal Reserve has been working very constructively with the managing director of the IMF to encourage U.S. banks to cooperate with the IMF in its efforts to bring constructive solutions to the Latin American debt problem. This means the rescheduling of old indebtedness and the granting of new loans at less-than-prohibitive interest rates or rescheduling fees.

The World Bank has also developed two new programs: "structural adjustment" lending, which means foregoing project or infrastructure loans in favor of long-term balance of payments lending where it is clear that the developing country in question is faced with more than "temporary balance of payments" difficulties; and cofinancing along with new commercial bank loans for additional balance of payments support. Both of these programs represent important additional help to those countries in extreme balance of payments difficulties. Above all, the international financial organizations are seeking to restore the confidence of the commercial banks in continuing to lend, because without this there will be no way to acquire sufficient time to bring about any permanent solution. It is the commercial banking system in the developed countries, after all, that alone has the financial capacity to make it possible over time to bring about a renewed financial stability to those countries that now cannot repay because they were encouraged by these same banks to borrow too much. Bank presidents like to say that countries are illiquid but not insolvent. They must participate in the restoration of that liquidity.

Former Managing Director Johannes Witteneen of the IMF recently made the suggestion that the IMF might constructively develop an insurance or guaranty program for the commercial banks' new loans to developing countries in difficulty. Such a program merits careful consideration because it would enable the IMF to put additional pressure on the banks to continue to lend. It would reduce the banks' risk, so that their interest rates might come down. It would also stretch the limited financial resources of the IMF further.

Necessity to Increase Trade and Investment

If the financial well-being of the so-called intermediate developing countries — Mexico, Argentina, and Brazil among them — is to be restored, the export trade of these countries must increase as their imports are held in check. There is a very close link between the growth of trade and repayment of borrowings. For this to succeed, however, it will be necessary for developing countries to maintain their importation of equipment and parts needed to continue to manufacture products for export. The Export-Import Bank program of $1.25 billion to finance needed exports to Brazil for this purpose is a constructive move and hopefully will be followed by the export financing agencies of other

countries. Another important factor will be the price paid for basic re-
source commodities: copper, other minerals, food products such as cof-
fee, and so on. But even though the recovery in the industrialized countries appears to be taking hold, prices of raw materials are very weak.
There is little sign in mid-1984 that the world economy is not still in
a deflationary cycle. As producer prices firm up, this will help the developing countries.

The Japanese may in the future, and should, participate more in
investments in Latin America and other developing areas, because they
have long since realized that trade cannot be a one-way street. If one
wishes to sell manufactured goods to the developing countries, one must
buy from them even if it means slowly reducing a steel-making capacity
that is the envy of the world. Obviously, it is impossible, as politicians
in the United States sometimes appear to imply, to export everything
from food to high-technology products unless we are prepared to buy
from others. Our economy seems able to produce almost everything.
While we need to do more to encourage our own exports, we must be
willing to import from others where price and quality are competitive
and we have no comparative advantage. The United States, it is true,
has changed the pattern of its international trade so that 40 percent of
our trade is now with the developing countries. But Europe is far more
protectionist toward the developing countries in its trade policies.

As the value of the dollar will probably tend to depreciate slowly
in the 1985/86 period, the developing countries will have an advantage
in developing their trade with Japan and Germany in particular so as
to get a better conversion rate into dollars to reduce their debt. Also,
as recovery gains in the West, there will be less of an incentive toward
protectionism. There should also be a tendency for oil prices to trend
downward. This will help countries like Brazil. Other programs that will
help developing countries to stabilize their debt are: special tariff reduction programs in the industrialized countries, new aid programs such
as the Reagan administration's Caribbean Initiative, and private sector
initiative for investment in Central and South America. Investment
must, at least partially, replace short-term lending because in the final
analysis national development depends upon long-term investment.

OTHER SUGGESTED SOLUTIONS

Many suggestions have been made by academicians, bankers, and
others about what should be done to solve the developing country indebtedness problem. Peter B. Kenen of Princeton has proposed that the

governments of the developed countries, including the United States, establish a new international institution — and call it the International Debt Discount Corporation — to issue long-term bonds to banks in exchange for the debts of developing countries.[1] The banks would be required to sell their loans at a discount of say 10 percent. The corporation would then reschedule the debts on a one-time, long-term basis, using the discount to reduce interest rates or grant a period of grace. Banks would neither be allowed to choose which loans they would discount nor to decide when to discount.

Felix Rohatyn of Lazard Frères also sees the necessity of converting short-term commercial bank debt into long-term debt using a new government agency, either national or international. He would propose a swap by the banks of their short-term, high-interest rate, Third World loans for long-term, low-interest rate paper issued by the new agency. This would require the banks to take substantial losses on their loans, but shaky banks would be aided by Rohatyn's additional government agency, which would be similar to the Reconstruction Finance Corporation that aided shaky banks and businesses during the depression years.

Norman Bailey, in charge of these matters at the National Security Council during most of the Reagan administration, has proposed an ingenious plan whereby banks would continue to receive interest on their loans, but the principal would be amortized over a long period through some part of the debtor countries' export earnings.[2]

Congressman Charles E. Schumer of Brooklyn has proposed a plan for the Mexican debt. His proposal would require the Mexicans to deposit large quantities of their oil in the U.S. Strategic Petroleum Reserve as a pledge against payment of Mexico's indebtedness to U.S. banks.

Minos Zombanakis, former governor of the central bank of Greece, has suggested that all Third World countries faced with a rescheduling of their debts should make 13-year agreements with the IMF as part of their general agreements with the IMF, thereby extending their outstanding commercial bank loans for this length of time. In return the IMF would guarantee years 11 to 13 if the loans had not been repaid in 10 years.[3]

Not to be outdone, two sets of British bankers — one from Barclays and the other Mackworth-Young of the Morgan Grenfell group — have also proposed the creation of a new agency backed by the central banks instead of the IMF and a swap of central bank bonds for outstanding bank loans. Barclay's suggestion would involve selling loans to the central banks at a discount, with central banks acting as collecting agent.

Mackworth-Young's idea involves a swap of non-interest-bearing notes for the troubled loans.

William H. Bolin, vice-chairman of Bank of America, and Jorge Del Canto, former director of the Western Hemisphere Department of the IMF, have proposed still another suggestion: to create a new organization affiliated with the World Bank but still separated from it — an Export Development Fund — that would be backed by the export credit agencies of the industrialized countries and that would finance the export of machinery and equipment in order to make it possible for the more developed developing countries (who owe the bulk of the borrowings from the commercial banking sector) to increase their exports and in this way pay off in time their current bank indebtedness.[4] The new agency would raise funds through borrowing in the Eurodollar market. Thus, outstanding loans would be paid off through further growth of the developing countries by means of new borrowings: not a very different scheme from that of President Alfonsin's in Argentina.

These proposals indicate the seriousness with which careful observers in different countries view the developing country debt problem. It is surprising that the principal New York bankers involved in these loans to Latin America have not expressed the same sentiments. William S. Ogden, retired vice-chairman of Chase Manhattan Bank and for a time head of the Institute of International Finance,* has repeatedly stated that the proposed swap transactions represent "a radical solution to a problem that does not now exist."[5] He sees only a temporary liquidity problem in the developing countries created by a recession that has now been replaced by a strong economic recovery. The managing director of the IMF, Jacques de Larosière, perhaps because he *must* believe solutions to the problem do in fact exist, has also said there is no global debt crisis because only a limited number of countries are involved. This makes it possible to contain the problem if everyone will cooperate.

There are also a number of commentators who believe strongly that the banks should not be bailed out. An Ad Hoc Committee on International Debt, headed by two well-known monetarists, Karl Brunner of the University of Rochester and Allan H. Meltzer of Carnegie-Mellon University, issued a report in February 1983[6] setting forth three principles backed by many conservatives who oppose any form of government intervention: (1) problems in international credit markets should

---

*This organization was created by a group of international commercial banks to collect country data of value to foreign lenders.

not be allowed to cause deflation; (2) uncertainty about repaying loans should not serve as an excuse for a new inflation caused by an increase by the Federal Reserve in the money supply; and (3) there should be no bailouts either of debtor developing country nations or of the banks that made unsound loans to them. Another monetarist, Treasury Undersecretary Beryl Sprinkel, in an interview with *Euromoney* magazine said, with a certain lack of understanding of the problem, "We're not in the business of bailing out banks. We do not try to direct our banks as to how to conduct their affairs."[7] And George Champion, chairman of Chase Manhattan Bank from 1961 to 1969, has recommended that banks immediately discontinue further loans to developing or Eastern bloc countries, dedicate at least 50 percent of their next five years' earnings to writing down their foreign loans, restrict any dividend increases, and increase their reserves by 0.25 percent of their total loans annually until the reserves reach at least 3 percent, preferably 5 percent.[8] The principal intellectual on the Federal Reserve Board, Governor Henry C. Wallich, in a speech entitled "International Commercial Banking from a Central Bank Viewpoint," said flatly:

> I do not regard as appropriate the various schemes for debt relief, buy-out of bank-held debt at a discount by some public agency, and similar devices. Certainly, central banks could not take over any part of these assets from banks, which would mean substituting LDC credit for domestic resources as backing for their currencies.[9]

In Wallich's opinion, large international payments due from developing countries need not be unmanageable, provided that the world economy resumes its expansion, that debtor nations do not prevent payment from being made, and that protectionism is avoided. Given these three conditions, Wallich is correct.

Developments in Mexico and Brazil since August 1982 have proved that developing countries with capable governments can solve their own problems and that we do not need new national or international agencies to solve current debt difficulties. Close collaboration by those concerned and common sense on the part of both banks and governments should prevent a global crisis from occurring. The important consideration is, however, how we can avoid a repetition of the current global debt crisis. Can we effectively learn from what happened to international lending between 1979 and 1982?

THE POLITICAL PROBLEMS

The nature of the problem can best be understood by looking at Mexico, Brazil, and Argentina. With Mexico, as pointed out, the banks not only raised interest rates on the 1982 rescheduling but also charged very high fees. In 1983 Paul Volcker of the Federal Reserve intervened in that year's negotiations on behalf of Mexico. Improved terms were given Mexico as a result. Now Mexico believes itself entitled to renegotiate the original package. Banks such as Security Pacific have long said the banks should volunteer better terms, particularly where—as in the case of Mexico—the country is cooperating with the IMF and meeting interest payments due the banks. Citicorp and other New York banks have taken the attitude that higher risk demands higher interest rates. They are adamantly opposed to renegotiation.

It is highly likely that the banks will in time have to soften their rates and extend the terms of the loans as well as make new loans. Otherwise the borrowers will never be able to meet their payments of principal. If they do not, or if the central banks and the IMF do not solve the problem for them through some swap transaction scheme as has been proposed, it is very likely that one or more nations will rebel and refuse to pay anything. If one nation does that, others will immediately follow. The international financial system will face disaster, and some international action will have to be taken. The New York banks have taken an enormous risk here. It will be particularly delicate to solve because renegotiation is extremely difficult and, worse, time-consuming. It has done little good to engage short-term one-year reschedulings because the next year the same problem has to be faced and the country debtors are under more pressure with each ensuing year to tell the banks they cannot pay.

U.S. bankers are convinced that the Fed will be forced to save them. But looking over the Fed's shoulder is the Congress, which is disinclined, for different reasons, to bail out the banks: the Republicans, because it is not the role of government to bail out private firms; the Democrats, because the banks were greedy and should suffer the consequences.

What of Brazil? In 1984 Brazil will need new bank loans—perhaps as much as $20 billion—to repay old loans and maintain its economy. It is currently being required to pay 13 percent interest. Despite reduced imports and greater exports, it is likely that the country's situation will not improve unless the term of its $100 billion borrowings is greatly lengthened and interest rates sharply cut. Who will force the banks to change their position? If the banks gave special conditions to Brazil, would it not be an admission that the same should be done for other developing countries? We run a terrible risk that both banks and countries are being frozen into positions that will surely bring about an eventual confrontation. Perhaps the most serious situation, however, is in Argentina — not because of need — but because the new Alfonsin government has no IMF program in place and is determined to solve its debt problem through expansion, regardless of its effect on the reimbursement of bank indebtedness. The risks in the international lending situation are enormous. One has the feeling that it will require an emergency for the central banks and the IMF to come up with a program that in one way or another will force a rapid rescheduling of commercial bank loans on a long-term basis with very different interest rates.* Until the emergency occurs, there is likely to be much discussion but very little action.

U.S. GOVERNMENT'S ROLE IN
LATIN AMERICA'S DEBT

The Reagan administration's propensity for participation in other countries' economic problems — despite its constantly professed ideology that market forces should not be interfered with — took an interesting turn at the end of March 1984. U.S. banks were faced with write-downs of Argentinean loans because Argentina had declared it would not pay by March 31 interest due the banks as of January 1, 1984. The banks would also have had to reverse accruals of interest as income on these loans. But at the last minute — supposedly at the instigation of the finance minister of Mexico — a complicated deal was worked out to meet the $500 million of interest due on Argentina's public sector borrowings. (Argentina still owes $2 billion of interest to all creditors even after this temporary, limited accommodation.) Under the arrangement Argentina put up $100 million, 11 bank creditors put up $100 million at a very much reduced rate of ⅛ percent over LIBOR, and four highly indebted

---

*The Federal Reserve is faced with a terrible quandary here. As interest rates rose in 1984 because of the failure of the administration and Congress to reduce government deficits, the crowding out process, which Chairman Paul Volcker of the Fed so fears, began to take effect and the prime rate rose significantly. The Fed could refuse to loosen its monetary policy, but this would cause further problems for the developing countries; or it could increase the money supply, which would lower rates temporarily but bring back inflation. Neither choice is satisfactory.

Latin American countries together advance $300 million (Mexico and Venezuela $100 million each; Brazil and Colombia $50 million each), with the promise by the U.S. government to repay the countries' advances as soon as the IMF has issued a new letter of intent to lend to Argentina. Did Argentina commit itself to reach an understanding with the IMF within 30 days? This appears unlikely, given the Argentinean government's difficulties at home already outlined.

What does this mean for the future, now that the U.S. government has intervened? Was it to protect the profits of major U.S. banking institutions? Will this now set the stage for a cartel of Latin American countries, knowing that they can take a very tough negotiating stance because they are dealing with the U.S. government and no longer with the international banks? Already the President of Mexico has called for a united front of debtor countries on the grounds that the reschedulings have been for too short a period of time and at exorbitant interest rates. (Note here that a 1 percent reduction in interest rate means $500 million less to the banks in annual interest income from Latin America.) Will the rate charged on this loan to Argentina of ⅛ percent over LIBOR — instead of the usual 1¾ percent to 2½ percent over LIBOR — constitute the new lending rate for rescheduled loans? This move on the part of the U.S. Treasury to help Argentina, the richest country in Latin America, raises all sorts of difficult questions. The banks themselves are not in accord. European lenders are under far less pressure than the American banks, which are in more deeply and must publish quarterly reports (and income adjustments) on nonperforming loans. Will the regional banks, faced with making new loans at very low rates, not prefer to write down their loans and not participate in new advances?

Now that the U.S. government has become involved as an active participant, it is hard to see how it will avoid being left with the ultimate loss. We may say that we "did it for Argentina," but to the Latin Americans it will be seen as a bailout of the banks and a willingness to act as guarantor on new loans. In international lending — as in foreign policy, witness Lebanon — once the government becomes an active participant rather than a helpful mediator, it takes over the ultimate responsibility.

NOTES

1. Peter B. Kenen, "A Bailout for the Banks," New York *Times*, March 6, 1983, p. F3.

2. See Norman Bailey, "The International Financial Crisis: An Opportunity for Constructive Action," monograph edited by Thibaut de Saint Phalle, Georgetown University Center for International and Strategic Studies, Significant Issues Series, 1983, pp. 27–36.

3. See Minos Zombanakis, "The International Debt Threat: A Way to Avoid a Crash." *Economist*, April 30, 1983, p. 7.

4. William H. Bolin and Jorge Del Canto, "LDC Debt: Beyond Crisis Management," *Foreign Affairs*, Vol. 61, No. 5, p. 1099 (Dec. 1983).

5. H. Erich Heinemann, "Third-World Debt Problem," New York *Times*, March 10, 1983, p. D5.

6. Carnegie, Rochester Conference on Public Policy, The Theory, Policy Institute, Elsevier Science Professor, Amsterdam, Netherlands 1983.

7. Peter Field, David Shirreff and William Ollard. "The IMF and Central Banks Flex Their Muscles," *Euromoney*, January, 1983, p. 41.

8. George Champion, "Foreign Debts: A Proposal for U.S. Banks," *Wall Street Journal*, January 11, 1983, editorial page.

9. Henry C. Wallich, "International Commercial Banking From a Central Bank Viewpoint." Remarks to the Allied Social Science Associates, December 29, 1983, at San Francisco, California.

9

HOW CAN
WE PROGRESS?

NEED FOR AN INTERNATIONAL
REGULATORY SYSTEM

In the last two chapters we have discussed how the U.S. bank
regulatory agencies have supervised lending by U.S. banks abroad; the
result of such lending since the last OPEC price increase, particularly
in Latin America; and what steps might be taken to assist these countries to meet their loan obligations in order to avoid default.

Default by one major borrower may well precipitate a chain reaction, with other countries following suit. From the standpoint of the
banks, one major default may cause other bank failures. In view of the
prevalence of bank-to-bank lending in the London Eurocurrency market,
it is impossible to judge accurately the effect of one bank's inability to
repay other banks. Because of this fact, it is essential that central banks
be prepared to cooperate fully to avoid a chain reaction effect from a
potential default on the entire international financial system. In the past,
banks have worked effectively together whenever a crisis has occurred —
in the Herstatt failure of 1974,* in controlling foreign exchange speculation, in swap transactions. The Basel Concordat of 1975 was held out
to be an agreement among the central banks to act as lender of last resort
to prevent defaults by branches of their national banks. Nevertheless, the
limits of the Basel Concordat have been shown by the failure of the central bank of Italy to act as lender of last resort for a branch bank of an
Italian bank, Banco Ambrosiano, located in Luxembourg. It is clear from
this unfortunate episode that the Basel Concordat contains gaps that

---

*The Herstatt bank was a small German bank that failed, leaving unpaid short-
term loans from other banks.

257

the central bankers should rapidly try to fill.* The world financial system simply cannot take the risk of not having a complete system in place to guarantee that there is a central bank ready to act as lender of last resort in every conceivable case that might occur. Herstatt was, after all, a very small German bank. The next default may occur because a large bank cannot repay its interbank loans.

What does this really indicate? And in which direction might the necessary cooperation of central banks be heading? These are the topics of this chapter. As the Japanese language says, the same character symbol that spells out disaster also stands for opportunity. The failure of the Federal Reserve Board and other central banks to control adequately foreign lending by the banks under their supervision makes it imperative that these central banks now collaborate closely so as to be prepared to contain the damage swiftly in the event that a worst-case scenario occurs. There is indeed a great opportunity here—and one that must not be missed. If handled correctly, there is a possibility that out of the failures of the past will come a chance to create a much better bank supervisory system that will be international rather than national in its scope. Such a system should be put in place as soon as possible.

In a world economy becoming increasingly interdependent, why should bank regulation continue to be parochial? It is certainly no answer for European central bankers to say that Latin America is a U.S. problem to be solved by the Federal Reserve's acting as lender of last resort or for Americans to say that the failure of Poland and other Eastern bloc countries to meet their obligations requires the Austrian or West German banking authorities to make others whole. Are we at the threshold, as a result of inadequate regulatory controls in the past, of taking the first hesitant steps toward the creation of a new international bank regulatory system? Will we then be ready to make another important move: toward the creation of a new monetary system that will no longer be controlled by one country as the present monetary system is dominated by the United States? This is an exciting prospect, no matter how distant it may appear at the present time. There are organizations in place to make all this possible. Furthermore, there are men of extraor-

---

*There has been a great deal of misunderstanding concerning the Basel Concordat of 1975. It was simply intended to indicate who should have primary responsibility for supervising the liquidity and solvency of banks. As John Heinmann, former Comptroller of the Currency, has said, "Few people understand that the Concordat deals only with supervision; lender of last resort has not been formalized at all."[1] It is this important step that remains to be taken.

dinary stature among central bankers and leaders of international financial organizations quite capable of supplying the necessary vision without regard to the kind of ideological limitations that prevented Secretary of the Treasury Regan for so long from appreciating the problem caused by excess lending by U.S. banks to Latin America.* Much has indeed been learned since August 1982. The momentum of international cooperation among ministers of finance and central bankers of the developed nations must not be allowed to falter or to fall into sterile recriminations. We are now at an important crossroads in the guidance of the international financial system. Objectivity must come from the central bankers rather than from national government officials concerned with trade or finance because they can necessarily afford to be less political in their judgments. Men like Paul Volcker, Jacques de Larosière, Fritz Leutwiler,[3] President of the World Bank A. W. Clausen, Andre de Lattre,[4] Otmar Emminger,[5] Karl Otto Pohl,[6] Johannes Whitteneen,[7] and Henry Wallich[8] are men with enormous experience and a global breadth of understanding. They are certainly capable of designing a suitable safety net to ensure that the international financial system is protected.

Before discussing what prospects may lie ahead for greater international collaboration among central bankers and the international organizations, it may be useful to analyze very briefly some developments that have been taking place at the BIS, the IMF, and the World Bank, slowly setting the stage for the gradual establishment of an international central banking system and, as a corollary, a new monetary system under its control.

THE BANK FOR INTERNATIONAL SETTLEMENTS

The BIS, as was noted earlier, is the successor organization to the group of central banks that originally came together after World War I to handle the reparations payments of the Central Powers that had lost the war. It is today a central bankers' club located in Basel that meets

---

*For an excellent explanation of U.S. interest in expanding the role of the IMF to ensure world economic stability, read the statement submitted by Donald T. Regan, Secretary of the Treasury, to the Senate Committee on Banking, Housing, and Urban Affairs on February 13, 1983.[2] This not only indicates how well Secretary Regan now understands U.S. interest in expanding the role of the IMF, but it also presents a very clear historical analysis of how the lending banks and the borrowing countries put themselves in a situation progressively more dangerous.

each month to discuss problems of common interest.* It has a small staff of highly qualified technicians who gather financial information from the central banks. The BIS publishes an annual report that gives useful information on the state of the world economy, warns of financial excesses, and makes recommendations for better financial management of the global economy. Its books are kept in Swiss gold francs valued as of 1930 because they have always been presented that way. It reinvests its funds in loans to central banks and has become very rich in the process. The funds at its disposal total $40 billion — more than the IMF until its recent capital increase. After the Mexican threat of default in August 1982 the BIS made available to the Mexican government what was expected to be a short-term bridge loan of $1.8 billion, pending Mexico's negotiation of longer-term financing from the IMF. Earlier it had granted Hungary a $500 million temporary advance. It has also advanced $1.5 billion to Brazil in short-term loans. The BIS does not, however, consider that it is its function either to bail out commercial bankers or to make even temporary loans to assist developing countries to meet their interest payments.

In making loans the BIS has normally followed certain simple rules: the loans must be short term (its central bank constituency insists on matching its short-term central bank deposits with the term of its loans); the loans must be backed by solid collateral; and automatic repayment terms must be in place. The BIS is hindered in considering the expansion of its role as an international lender of last resort because as a central bankers' club it must assume that individual central banks are properly exercising their function of policing their own nation's commercial banks. This proposition has now been proved wrong, as bank lending to the developing countries has demonstrated.

Is the BIS relevant in today's world? Why is a $40 billion institution of central bankers not doing more to address problems common to all? It does not seem to me to be an irrelevant question. In international banking, as well as economics, the most dangerous factor is inaccurate information. Despite its highly qualified staff, the BIS depends for its information on data furnished by the central banks, which, to state the situation honestly, is today of little use in determining the extent to which banks are overextended in their international lending. If the BIS is to be the key international bankers' institution it ought to be, then

---

*The bank's headquarters in Basel are located in a magnificent new building equipped with the latest electronic gadgetry for its meeting rooms and even with a wine cellar capable of holding 20,000 bottles.

it should decide that it must do more than just exchange whatever information member central banks choose to make available. It must have much more extensive and timely data, and it must have some method by which such data can be translated into forthright action.* The world does not need a $40 billion bankers' club. It needs bank control based upon highly accurate data and some sensible rules agreed upon by all to control the use by commercial banks of banking centers in odd parts of the world where bank secrecy and tax gimmicks invite control avoidance by the central banking system.

If the central banks are unwilling to exercise controls through such rules as they may agree upon together, would it not be preferable to disband the organization and turn over its holdings and its responsibilities to another organization such as the IMF? A pity this, because the world needs the kind of organization the BIS could be. Might it be reorganized? Here are some suggestions:

1. The central banks should require each individual member to furnish accurate and timely reports, according to a precise timetable, describing foreign loans extended by its commercial banks. Since practically all foreign loans are extended by banks in the so-called Group of Ten† countries and Switzerland — which are member countries of the BIS — this should not pose a problem. There should, however, be an agreement that each reporting bank must disclose loans made by its branches or subsidiaries regardless of secrecy provisions.

2. Any bank that refuses to divulge information about the activity of its branches should be forced to close that branch. If penalties are not exacted on a uniform basis for use of nonbanking bank centers such as the Bahamas, the Jersey Islands, the Cayman Islands, or similar locales, each nation's banks will claim it cannot compete. It should be made impossible for this argument to be used. Banks should have the right to compete fairly with one another, but the kind of practices outlined in the Citicorp case must not be allowed to continue. The best way to control this kind of activity is through rules adopted by central banks among

---

*Recognize, however, that statistical information useful to international bankers is very hard to get because of political considerations. Developing countries are borrowers and often request their bankers to treat information given at the time of a loan as confidential.

†Includes the United States, W. Germany, France, Japan, the United Kingdom, Belgium, Italy, Netherlands, Sweden, Canada, and, since 1984, Switzerland as an eleventh member.

themselves. So the BIS is logically the institution of choice to determine which rules commercial banks will be required to follow regarding international lending.

3. As a nonpolitical institution with central bank members and a highly competent staff, the BIS should hold itself out as willing to advise developing countries on the steps necessary to create a central banking entity capable of supervising its own commercial banks and of furnishing accurate data to its finance or treasury ministry on foreign borrowings or government guarantees of such borrowings. It should also be ready to offer advice regarding monetary or credit policies. Such information need not necessarily be made public, but it should assist individual central banks such as the Federal Reserve in seeing where debt problems might likely occur so that each can take action with its own commercial banks to avoid overlending to developing countries.

It seems clear that without some kind of common regulatory standards agreed upon by the world's principal central banks there can be no avoidance of the kind of problems discussed in Chapter 8. Host countries to branches of developed country banks are not going to regulate those branches because they will assume that the parent's regulatory agency will carry out the responsibility. But this cannot be expected to occur unless national regulatory systems are harmonized through some kind of binding international agreement to make sure all central banks apply the same rules to their individual national commercial banks. It would be simplest to do this through the BIS because this organization brings together the Group of 10 countries.

ROLE FOR CENTRAL BANKERS

If the BIS is going to default on this important function, the Group of ten or of five* should take action. Governor Henry Wallich of the Federal Reserve has addressed this need for greater coordination of national loans:

> There is a need to individually adopt our national laws and practices into an international framework so that they will accommodate and support each other instead of creating gaps or even conflicts that could pose a threat to the worldwide system.[9]

---

*Including the United States, W. Germany, France, United Kingdom and Japan.

The reader will remember the role played by Felix Warburg, the German banker, in the creation of the Federal Reserve System by the Federal Reserve Act of 1913. It would be interesting if a governor of the Federal Reserve Board, himself a banker and the son and grandson of a German banker, would play a key role in bringing about a true harmonization of banking regulation among the lending countries, which might avoid in the future the very serious problems we face today as a result of commercial bank overlending to the developing nations. In the United States there have been many men who have used the banking system to make personal fortunes. There are, however, few men who have understood the function of banking in its true sense of providing the means by which a country can develop its potential. Many were foreign born or sons of immigrants: Warburg, Eccles, Giannini, and Wallich should be numbered among these thinkers within the banking community.

Henry C. Wallich

Henry Wallich is the intellectual and the "European" among the governors of the Federal Reserve Board. Born in Berlin, Germany in 1914, he was educated in Germany, England, and the United States where he earned both an M.A. and a Ph.D. at Harvard. He did not come to the United States until 1935, became a citizen in 1944. For a time, after being in the export business and a commercial banker, he headed the foreign research division of the Federal Reserve Bank of New York. He was then for 23 years a professor of economics at Yale until he was appointed a governor of the Federal Reserve in 1974. He has written several books on foreign economic questions, many articles, and lectures constantly in the United States and abroad. He is also known as a connoisseur of German wines. Better than anyone on the Board, he understands the complexities of international finance, the needs of developing countries for capital in the development process, and how the banking system operates and is supervised in other developed countries. Son and grandson of well known German bankers, will he be able to bring to any reorganization of the U.S. regulatory system the same kind of input that we observed was provided by that other great German, Paul Warburg, in the design of the Federal Reserve System when it was adopted in 1913? He fully understands why the large U.S. money-center banks are in such trouble: Unlike their European, Canadian and Japanese counterparts, they do not have (and cannot have because of the limitations on interstate banking) the extensive branch system which allows deposit funds to flow to the central banking office in support of large loans in a highly-developed lending system. This makes it necessary for them to buy their funds. And this in turn makes them particularly vulnerable. Wallich has been warning of this for many years without success. He also understands that changes in the system are inevitably headed toward expansion of the powers of banks. Should banks be allowed to engage in other activities? Retail brokerage certainly, but insurance and real estate development probably not; nor is there any need for U.S. banks to be allowed to underwrite corporate securities again because in the United States — unlike other developed countries — we have a highly developed and efficient underwriting system handled by investment banks both nationally and regionally. I asked him why the Fed had allowed U.S. banks to engage in syndicated loans abroad to the extent they have. His answer was that if you did not allow American banks to do this, they would become noncompetitive with foreign banks which were freely allowed to engage in underwriting activities.

Wallich does not like regional banking as it is developing because the process is defensive in nature: Keep out the New York giants. He does not believe in geographical limitations. We discussed the reluctance of Congressional leaders like Senator Proxmire to allow the largest banks to acquire smaller banks. The solution to this problem, as Wallich sees it, is to limit the size of banks that can be acquired, perhaps by utilization of a bank's capital for this purpose. But here again he notes that American banks may be less competitive if the government requires that they increase their capital: foreign banks, for example, are only required to maintain a very low capital ratio.

Henry Wallich does not believe in consumer credit control, apart from the need to control overall credit expansion. Unfortunately, as I have noted in Chapter 3, this monetary control tool has been infrequently used in the United States. The 1984 sharp rise in installment debt has been unfortunately not sufficiently noted or any action taken by the Fed to control it. Monetary policy, as Henry Wallich knows, must be used to control excesses as well as encourage growth.

As government leaders in the United States come to realize in time the necessity to internationalize both monetary policy and bank supervision, it is hoped that Henry Wallich, like his predecessor Paul Warburg, will have a key conceptual role to play.

If one accepts the need for the harmonization I have discussed, how can it be accomplished this side of a light's striking the BIS tower in Basel while the bankers are gathered there? Three alternative ways might be suggested: participating countries could refuse to host banks head-quartered in nonparticipating countries; if branches abroad were subject to the same regulation as the parent regardless of country rules, this would obviously discourage branches in exotic nonbank centers; and a more drastic solution would simply be to reverse the Basel Concordat of 1975 as to nonparticipating countries and declare that the parent will not be responsible for any branch located in such jurisdictions. One has only to think of these alternatives to realize that if the central bankers really wish to prevent what has been happening in the supervision of lending abroad, the means to accomplish the desired end are very much at hand.

The only questions seem to be, Why has the required action not long since been taken? Given the caliber of the men involved, why has a leader not come forth to take the action everyone is waiting for? Why will it take a new disaster to cause central bankers to collaborate effectively together? After all, they do not even have the excuse of political accommodation. Any one of the alternatives mentioned would effectively put an end to the proliferation of commercial bank branches in locations chosen to avoid regulation and/or taxation. What a record of international permissiveness has been established for all to see! As a former chairman of the Federal Reserve has pointed out, we have here created a "competition in regulatory laxity."[10] It is high time this ended. This $40 billion institution earning $129 million a year has to think in broader terms and either take responsibility for a much closer collaboration among its constituent central banks or declare its own incapacity by going out of business. Its current role must be seen as thoroughly unsatisfactory in view of the problems facing the international banking system.

THE INTERNATIONAL
MONETARY FUND

The IMF was organized for a very special purpose. Its role, however, has all of a sudden been necessarily expanded to meet not the isolated case of a sovereign nation no longer able to meet its foreign exchange obligations but a large number of developing countries that have borrowed too much over too short a period of time to industrialize more quickly than their ability to generate foreign exchange to meet the terms of their indebtedness would permit. While the capital of the IMF has now risen by 47 percent through an increase in member country quotas from $67 billion to $99 billion, only about $60 billion is in funds that can be usefully loaned. The U.S. share of this increase is $5.8 billion, representing 18 percent of the total. In addition, the U.S. share of the increase in the General Agreement to Borrow is another $2.6 billion. Parenthetically, it should be noted that Saudi Arabia independently agreed to provide an additional $4 billion to the IMF in 1983, making up a $12 billion contribution over three years. So the IMF must work closely with the international commercial banks to maintain the requisite lending facilities to the developing countries in difficulty. This requires a maximum of cooperation from the individual central banks that supervise the lending banks as well as support from the Ministries of Finance in the developed countries. These must supply not only emergency financial assistance — as the U.S. government did in the case of Mexico in 1982 — but also political support, encouraging the efforts of the developing countries toward increasing their exports while reducing their imports.

One of the more immediate problems the IMF could help resolve in connection with its efforts to encourage the world's commercial banks to renew existing loans and advance new sums to the developing countries is the inadequacy of country economic data available to the banks. The World Bank has taken the position that financial data furnished by its country borrowers is confidential; and the IMF's information is too often out of date. In too many instances the IMF has not insisted on checking the data it receives. Such information should be more timely and accurate. A few years ago IMF teams trying to collect accurate data on Zaire's financial situation found themselves obliged to go to London to quiz the banks there on their loans to Zaire. The country's records were totally inadequate since any minister could enter into binding financial agreements and these were not necessarily reported to the central bank. The IMF staff needs to understand that inaccurate and no longer timely information is worse than no information at all. International financial statistics published by the IMF are, unfortunately, accepted by economists and bankers. Their system of reporting needs to be thoroughly overhauled. If data is not up to date, this fact should be apparent. If data has not been cross-checked, it should not be published or it should be published with appropriate caveats. Surely the IMF has staff enough to supply better information.

Without accurate data it is not possible to analyze country risk with any degree of certainty. Borrowing limits should, of course, include money loaned to a country's private banks, since these banks typically turn around and loan to their governments if they want to avoid nationalization (witness Mexico in 1982). Borrowing limits should also apply to private corporate loans, which are increasingly being guaranteed by their governments. All of these data are essential.

The U.S. Congress, in approving the increase in funding for the IMF, urged the organization to give "more complete and timely information" and asked the U.S. executive director to monitor the efforts of the IMF to improve its data. The January 1984 issue of *International Financial Statistics* attempted at last to do this.[11] It added six new tables providing credit flows between individual countries. These include cross-border interbank accounts, international commercial bank credits to nonbanks, and international deposits of nonbanks. Each table identifies banking activity by residence of borrower and lender. Astounding as it may seem, BIS statistics are only given by region and not by individual country. Surely, in an electronics age, the IMF can take immediate action with respect to furnishing timely and accurate data. Even a few years ago, for example, Argentinean data were five years in arrears. Of what possible value is such information? Will Jacques de Larosière, already in office five years, be able to bring about some changes within the organization?

The IMF needs to be forced to take a much broader view of what constitutes government loans. It should not have been necessary for the banks to create a new private organization, The Institute of International Finance located in Washington, D.C., to supply pertinent data on which the banks could rely in making foreign loans. That Institute of International Finance, organized in 1982, would be redundant if the BIS and the IMF were functioning effectively as monitors of financial information.

What is important to understand is that the new international financial crisis described in Chapter 8 must necessarily create a new and much more important role for the IMF. Even as careful an observer as Richard Cooper of Harvard University, former undersecretary of state for economic affairs in the Carter administration, has often expressed the view that the new responsibilities forced upon the IMF may result in that institution's becoming a true international central bank. At long last there is beginning to be close collaboration among the IMF, the central banks, and the financial agencies of the governments of the developed countries, which are now so concerned that the developing countries will not be able to meet their financial commitments.

What an opportunity indeed for de Larosière who had first to learn a hard lesson from the experience of the IMF in Turkey, Romania, and Hungary. In 1979 the IMF had had to lend Turkey $5.1 billion, with the additional help of an OECD Aid to Turkey consortium, after the commercial banks had withdrawn their loans. In Romania in 1981, the

IMF recovery program was skewed because the banks would not maintain their credits. In Hungary in the first quarter of 1982 the banks pulled out their short-term lines of credit, leaving no time for the IMF to work out a refinancing plan. No wonder that after the Mexican debacle of August 1982 de Larosière was determined not to allow the banks to bail out, leaving the IMF to save the situation. As a result it is the IMF that now determines what action the commercial banks are to take in rescheduling old indebtedness or making new loans. The banks have no recourse but to follow the IMF lead. The real test of 1984 has been in Argentina where in March 1984 the government asked the banks to lend more money when their interest payments remained unpaid and no IMF program was in place. Who will control this situation? An inexperienced new Argentinean government with little base of support, the IMF, the banks, or their central bank supervisors? Only time will tell whether common sense will spur that government to reestablish an agreement with the IMF and thereby maintain its bank credits.

As noted earlier, Chairman Paul Volcker of the Federal Reserve has been most helpful to de Larosière in his new assertive role at the IMF. On November 16, 1982, Volcker told the New England Council in Boston:

> An orderly adjustment program will frequently require at least transitional financing beyond amounts appropriate to, or feasible, for the IMF and official lenders. . . . Lending banks should be able to provide the necessary margin of finance. From the standpoint of the banks themselves, such restructuring and the provisions of some additional credit, alongside and *dependent upon agreed IMF programs,* will in some instances be the most effective and prudent means available to enhance the creditworthiness of borrowing countries and thus protect their own interests. In such cases, where new loans facilitate the adjustment process and enable a country to strengthen its economy and service its international debt in an orderly manner, *new credits should not be subject to supervising criticism.* [Emphasis added][12]

In this important pronouncement the chairman of the Federal Reserve had in effect called upon the managing director of the IMF to take the lead in managing international bank lending, promising his assistance insofar as U.S. banks were concerned. In Great Britain, the Bank of England ordered British banks to increase their loans by 7 percent of their existing exposure. Serge Robert, executive vice-president of Credit

Agricole in Paris, the world's largest bank, said: "The IMF is directing commercial bank credits more and more."

One discordant voice to the IMF funding has been Senator Jesse Helms of North Carolina who wrote a thoughtful article suggesting that the IMF might use its 103 million ounces of gold to aid developing countries in financial difficulty. He suggested borrowing by developing countries using advances of IMF gold to collateralize the loans upon acceptance of IMF conditionality. He also proposed:

> Another use of IMF gold would be as reserves for a new gold standard. But a gold standard — built on a gold-convertible U.S. dollar — would mean lower interest rates. That would lower debt servicing costs and ease debt refinancing.[13]

It is curious that in a period when the gold exchange standard has been abandoned by all developed nations and no central banker would propose going back to the gold standard, none of the central banks or national governments — including the United States — nor the IMF as well, are willing to dispose of one ounce of their gold reserves. Is there not a clear message here?

THE WORLD BANK

So much for the new role of the IMF. Is there also a new role for the World Bank in helping to solve the current financial crisis? In the last chapter, reference was made to two new programs developed by the World Bank. Should the World Bank now offer a rediscount facility for countries such as Argentina, Brazil, and Mexico? The World Bank's annual lending program has increased from $2 billion in 1973 to $11.3 billion in fiscal 1983, excluding appropriations made by its affiliates, the International Finance Corporation and its soft-loan window, the International Development Association. The bank's revenue from loans and investments has also grown sharply, to a total of $3.4 billion per year in 1982. Its subscribed capital went from $30.4 billion in 1973 to $49 billion in 1982, and its callable capital to $77 billion. Its borrowings have gone from $3.1 billion in 1973 to $8.5 billion in 1982. Since it borrows in the financial markets, why should the bank not offer a rediscount facility to private commercial banks at a rate that would not only reduce their exposure but lower the borrowers' cost? It could, furthermore, do this without violating its customary 1 : 1 gearing ratio and without in any way impairing its financial strength. As A. W. Clausen, its president, has stated, the Bank's financial strength is not an end in itself but rather a means to permit the bank to mobilize its growing volume of resources at the lowest possible long-term cost.

A. W. Clausen

Unlike his predecessor Robert McNamara, who had been president of the Ford Motor Company and U.S. Secretary of Defense in the Kennedy and Johnson Administrations, Tom Clausen is a banker's banker. He was appointed president of the World Bank after a long career at Bank of America in San Francisco where he became president and chief executive officer. Clausen is a consensus man rather than an innovator and a leader as was McNamara. In the United States there have been many competent commercial bankers; but very few men who have seen the opportunity to innovate along the trend-line of change to accommodate new business or political factors. By nature a commercial banker is not apt to be an entrepreneur. That is not normally his function. Yet there is a need at the World Bank in the current crisis for just that kind of understanding and drive that will make for leadership to solve creatively the problems of excessive bank loans to the developing countries without creating more than a temporary pause in the development process. Walter Wriston, recently retired chairman of Citicorp was that kind of leader, very creative, with a capacity to inspire his subordinates. Hopefully, Tom Clausen will be able to inspire the men around him at the World Bank to become part of a new creative effort at the Bank so much needed at the present time.

The World Bank has never tapped the commercial bank market. Its borrowings have been in the bond market. Its rediscount facility would be a first step toward participating, with the commercial banks, in loans to the developing countries, with the World Bank taking the later maturities and the commercial banks the earlier ones. Such a World Bank program would accomplish three important ends. First, it would reduce the cost of commercial bank credits to developing countries. Second, it would encourage the regional banks to continue to make new loans to developing countries since no country would default on a World Bank loan; otherwise, it would never be able to borrow again. This form of participatory financing is very similar to that which the Export-Import Bank of the United States has used so successfully in financing long-term U.S. foreign trade projects. And third, it would encourage developing countries to increase their foreign trade by providing for additional imports of equipment needed to service their foreign trade. This is in everyone's interest. We must not forget that developing countries account for roughly a quarter of the merchandise exports of the industrialized countries as a group but for 45 percent of Japanese and close to 40 percent of U.S. exports.

AN INTERNATIONAL CENTRAL BANKING SYSTEM?

What other suggestions can be advanced? The area of deposit insurance is certainly one to be explored. Each industrialized country appears to have a different approach to depositors' insurance.[14] This is one of the factors that makes it difficult for central banks to harmonize their regulatory procedures. The internationalization of deposit insurance rests on an unconditional willingness on the part of central banks to provide back-up loans to national deposit insurance funds such as the FDIC. What we need now is an International Deposit Insurance Corporation, as proposed by Canada's Herbert Grubel.[15] The advantage of such a scheme would be that it would provide not only for international examination of individual national banks, and additional premiums for insurance if warranted by risks taken. Such a scheme would certainly enhance confidence in international lending, now at a low ebb. It could not, of course, take effect unless and until governments were ready to regard regulation of international banking as an *international* rather than as a *national* problem.

One of the truly great leaders of the past ten years has certainly been Chancellor Helmut Schmidt of West Germany. After his defeat, he gave a lengthy interview that apeared in the *Economist* of February 26, 1983.[16] Among other matters, he discussed with apologies the monetary system of floating exchange rates that he, George Schultz, and Valery Giscard d'Estaing established in 1973. He went on to commend the commercial banks for their role in the growth of world trade since World War II. He commented on the recent excesses in lending to the developing countries by the banks and stressed the necessity of maintaining the growth of international trade — which benefits all countries, rich and poor alike. As he put it: "Credit creates trade, trade secures credit." He went on to say:

A particular danger is the growing tendency toward bilateralisation of trade policy, for instance by making the trade balance between two countries the criterion of whether free trade between the two countries is useful or damaging. If this bad habit spreads, we shall soon be back in the 1930s.[17]

Schmidt pleaded for a new collaboration among central banks to redesign a monetary system that will bring more stability and allow for increased trade. He asserted, after referring to Poland, Mexico, and the Ambrosiano Bank:

It would be wrong to conclude from these examples that the international banking and finance system is unable to cope with the difficult problems which the current world economic situation has imposed on it. But everybody — central banks, governments, international organizations and private creditor banks — will have to pull in the same direction.[18]

The question remains unanswered as yet. Will we find the necessary leadership at this point in our international financial difficulties to bring about the kind of collaboration indicated in this chapter to be so essential to renewed international economic stability?

NOTES

1. Dun's Business Month, February 2, 1983 at p. 48.
2. See U.S., Congress, Senate, Committee on Banking, Housing, and Urban Affairs, "IMF Resources, World Financial Stability and U.S. Interests." Statement by Donald T. Regan, February 13, 1983, Washington, D.C.
3. He has been chairman of the Swiss National Bank and president of the BIS, Basel, but resigned in 1984.
4. He is president of the Institute of International Finance, Washington.
5. He is the former president of the Deutsche Bundesbank.
6. He is the current president of the Deutsche Bundesbank.
7. He is the former managing director of the IMF and chairman of the Group of Thirty, a prestigious group of international bankers and academics.
8. Governor of the Federal Reserve appointed in 1974.
9. Remarks at the International Conference of Banking Supervisors, Washington, D.C., September 24, 1981.
10. See Richard Dale, "Safeguarding the International Banking System," Banker No. 132 (August, 1982) p. 49. Dale, then at the Brookings Institute, is a British banker who devoted several years to analyzing the questions discussed

in this chapter. His focus is on bank safety, a very important theme of this book.

11. International Monetary Fund, *International Financial Statistics*, January 9, 1984, Washington, D.C.

12. Peter Field, David Sherriff and William Ollard, "The IMF and Central Banks Flex Their Muscles." *Euromoney*, January, 1983, p. 40.

13. Senator Jesse Helms, "In a Pinch, The IMF Could Go For the Gold" *Wall Street Journal*, May 6, 1983, p. 28.

14. For a detailed discussion of the variety of depositors' insurance schemes in effect in the OECD countries, see Richard Dale "Safeguarding the International Banking System," *Banker* 132, (August 1982): p. 79.

15. Herbert G. Grubel, "A Proposal for the Establishment of an International Deposit Insurance Corporation," *Princeton Essays in International Finance*, no. 1331, July 1979.

16. Manfred Lahnstein, "Helmut Schmidt's Prescription." The *Economist*, February 26, 1983, pp. 19–30.

17. Ibid., p. 27.

18. Ibid., p. 24.

10

TREND TOWARD
AN INTERNATIONAL
MONETARY POLICY

A MUTUALLY DEPENDENT
GLOBAL ECONOMY

Both our government and our regulatory authorities need to con-
ceive of monetary policy in international rather than national terms. The
world is completely tied economically to the dollar, and so it is affected
by its exchange value and the rates of interest that dollar loans command.

The global economy is so interlocked today that the world's central
banks do not even know which banks are principally at risk in their foreign loans to the developing countries and the Eastern bloc. If one country defaults on its debt, it is highly likely that others will follow. The international financial system — owing to the failure of the central banks
in the developed countries to exercise their function of supervision adequately — is now hostage to its borrowers. If as a result of country debt
defaults one or more of the larger banks active in the Eurocurrency
market cannot meet its repayment obligations on interbank loans, the
banks of other countries will in turn have to default on their loans. The
central bank charged with supervision of the first defaulting bank should
act as the lender of last resort and pay off its obligations. But what of
the next bank in what has become an endless interlocking chain? Will
the central banks acting together and with the help of the international
financial institutions be able to act fast enough to avert a calamity? Will
national political self-interest permit them to move in concert? Ideology
can be a fearful problem here. The financial leaders watched in awe and
amazement when the U.S. Secretary of the Treasury at the IMF meeting
in Toronto in 1982 opined that foreign bank lending was quite sound
and that the IMF required no additional funding since the marketplace
could handle any problems that might come up. In fairness to Secretary

Regan, he reversed himself with great courage a few months later. But can we afford to put off consideration of worst-case scenarios, even if they might well be postponed by a year or two, if prompt action is so necessary in the event of any major financial default?

FAILURE OF THE
GOLD EXCHANGE STANDARD

What is the condition of the world economy today in financial terms? In 1973 the gold exchange standard, with the dollar as the key currency linked to gold, was abandoned. Floating exchange rates were substituted, that is, exchange rates that varied in their value relative to the dollar. This is tantamount to saying that in eliminating gold we substituted a paper dollar monetary standard. As a result the entire world is liquid or illiquid, able to make purchases or not, capable of investing or forced to defer capital goods expenditures simply because the U.S. Federal Reserve Board has decided to add to bank reserves in the United States or, conversely, to lessen the increase in the money supply, as it did from 1979 to 1982. In 1984 or 1985 will the Federal Reserve Board, in order to prevent the return of U.S. inflation, decide to tighten the money supply once again? If it does not, interest rates in the United States will rise because of the earlier sharp increase in the money supply in 1982/83. This has created a period of high consumer spending and capital investment. If the Fed does not continue to increase the money supply at the same pace or higher, the demand for money will cause interest rates to rise. If it does, interest rates will rise even more as the inflationary cycle returns once more. This is hardly a pleasant choice for the Board. How can this scenario be avoided?

The actions of the Federal Reserve Board over the past 20 years cannot be studied in terms of U.S. policy alone. I showed how increases in the money supply in 1967, to meet the costs of the war in Vietnam, and in 1970, to prevent bankruptcies of U.S. business firms, led to the events of August 1971 when President Nixon unilaterally declared that the United States would no longer meet its foreign obligations through transfers of gold bullion as required by the Bretton Woods agreements. The then-chairmen of the Federal Reserve, William McChesney Martin in 1967 and Arthur Burns in 1971, were both men of integrity and high repute. Yet they made decisions to increase the money supply in each case to comply with presidential requests made to satisfy temporary political needs—and the whole world was affected through the resulting spread of inflation. Today the financial relations of the entire world rest on a paper dollar monetary standard. Decisions made by the Federal Reserve Board to increase or tighten the money supply have therefore even greater consequence for other countries.

The fact is that if the money supply is increased in the United States, other countries are led to do the same in order to maintain approximately the same exchange rate relationship with the dollar. Take just one example, the case of West Germany. If the deutsch mark rises in value against the dollar, there is pressure on the Bundesbank to increase the money supply so as to decrease the value of the German currency. If it did not, German exports would be less competitive against U.S. goods. The result of these monetary relationships has been that West Germany, France, Japan, the United Kingdom, Italy, Canada, and other nations have all been adding to their money supply and increasing their government deficits in tandem with the United States.

Put in blunt terms, the effect of these monetary policies is that all the major democratic countries of the Western world (even Switzerland, because its economy is tied to that of West Germany) have increased their money supply over the last ten years, reduced the value of their currency through inflation, and increased their budgetary deficits.

A WORLD TOTALLY INDEBTED

There have been many instances in world history when a single country has been unable to meet its foreign obligations. This is, however, the first time in history when all the principal nations have been required to print new money because they would otherwise not be able to pay their debts. What are the central bank reserves of the Western democracies? Essentially, to the extent of approximately 70 percent, they are in dollar or dollar-denominated assets — that is, in the currency of a nation that owes over $1.5 trillion, with a government deficit that will increase by another 50 percent or so in the next few years. What is the position of these central banks and their assets if the United States should find itself in time unable to repay this huge debt? Under these circumstances is it possible to maintain the world's financial stability without devising a new monetary standard that cannot be subject to the excesses of any one country as at present?

In Chapter 9 I pointed out how the problems of the commercial banks arising from their excess lending to the developing countries have brought about much closer cooperation among the major countries' central banks and with the international financial organizations. At long last there is in this new collaboration the opportunity to create a monetary system free of national political imperatives. Lord Keynes, at Bretton Woods in 1945, pleaded with the Americans not to return to a gold exchange standard but to make of the IMF a true international central bank. The United States refused, preferring to preserve the dollar as the key reserve currency. In the years since Bretton Woods, the IMF has constantly proved the value of its original limited concept: to aid countries in temporary balance of payments difficulties. The conditions established for its loans have repeatedly enabled countries to restore their financial health by meeting these conditions, no matter how painful. Only the United States has been able to avoid the consequences of its abuses of sound monetary policy because since 1945 its currency has been the standard to which other countries have had to adjust. Unless we, too, are going to play according to the same rules as others, we will face increasingly unpalatable choices that will affect not only us but our children's children, as well. No thinking American would want to do anything to pass on such a burden to succeeding generations. What can we do to avoid this?

POSSIBLE SOLUTIONS

There are a limited number of alternatives:

1. We can return to a gold standard after working out the mechanics of such a move with the so-called Group of Five, or the Group of Ten, countries.* It would probably be preferable to arrive at an understanding with the smallest group because in monetary policy only bigger countries have a large enough money supply to exercise much independence. Such a system should provide for gradual increases in the money supply under some formula to raise the price of gold slowly so that as the world economy grows, the supply of world liquidity can also increase. As indicated in Chapter 3, any such system must also take into account the velocity of money.

2. We can change the statutes of the IMF to provide, as Keynes had suggested, that it function as a world central bank. As indicated in

---

*The Group of Five includes the United States, Japan, West Germany, the United Kingdom and France. The Group of Ten includes in addition to the first five, Netherlands, Belgium, Italy, Canada and Sweden. Switzerland became a member in 1983.

the preceding chapter, the world has come a long way toward accepting an important new role for the IMF. If it succeeds, (with the help of the principal central bankers) in restoring liquidity to the principal developing country and Eastern bloc borrowers, then governments should accept that the IMF play a continued important role in supervising international lending. If governments agree to this, there will then be an internal understanding that the IMF, rather than the individual central banks, will be regulating international lending limits. This would be a very important step forward.

3. In default of taking either of the first two alternatives, the United States may have to take the action already supported by the public in many states that there must be a constitutional provision requiring a balanced federal budget. By March 1984 such a constitutional amendment was only two states short of necessitating a constitutional convention for the purpose of voting on such an amendment. The balanced budget requirement has worked well in the states. There is no reason why it should not work on a national level. Wartime expenditures can (as was observed in the case of the Korean War), be met without monetizing the debt. In addition, the federal government has assets to pledge for a long-term, one-time loan from the public to reduce the federal debt substantially, to be secured not only in gold but also with federal lands. This would enable the government to convert its overwhelming short-term borrowings at high interest rates into very long term (10 to 20 years) debt at a low interest rate because the debt would be secured.

IN SUMMARY

In this book I have tried to show that over the years the Federal Reserve Board has taken upon itself powers that were never anticipated by the act of 1913. Congressional mandates are rarely precise. In the case of the Federal Reserve Act, it was made purposely imprecise because it was not the desire of many in the Congress to have a strong central bank. Furthermore, laws are interpreted by judges who try to find clarity in terms of the conditions at the time they are called upon for legislative interpretation. When laws are vague, men shape the wording and fill the unspoken gaps to give themselves the power they seek. This is the history of the Federal Reserve Board as analyzed in Chapter 2.

In Chapter 3 the monetary policy of the Federal Reserve was traced over the years and under different chairmen attempting in different ways to maintain growth in the economy while meeting political imperatives.

Not an easy task. Some chairmen succumbed to political pressure, particularly in election years. It was not my intent to focus criticism on the Board but to explain the difficulties it faces in developing a sound monetary policy. It has not become any easier over the years.

In Chapter 4 I looked at the changes brought about by recent developments in the financial marketplace — partly, unfortunately, because of the monetary policies of the Federal Reserve Board — and by congressional action designed to make the depository institutions more competitive in an inflationary and changing environment. The concepts of both money and credit have changed. This requires a new definition of the function and nature of banking. So, what is a bank, and what is money today? It is a fair question and one that has required of the regulatory agencies and of the Congress an understanding of the new methods of rendering financial services in the super computer age.

In Chapter 5 I examined the role of the regulators in adjusting to change while continuing to apply what they saw as their mandate from Congress under the Glass-Steagall Act, the McFadden Act, the Bank Holding Company Act, the Garn–St. Germain Act, and other legislation seeking to balance the protection of depositors with the advisability of allowing depository institutions to compete in a rapidly changing environment. The efforts of the regulators have certainly been made more difficult by court interpretations, that, while allowing for "the greatest possible deference" to findings of the regulators, make their own findings as to congressional intent. There are highly competent bank regulators. The difficulty of their function, trapped between Congress and the courts, needs to be better appreciated.

In Chapter 6 I tried to look into the future, to analyze the need for regulatory change, to examine the efforts of the Reagan administration and Congress to succeed in simplifying the regulatory maze, and to discuss what might be the result, given the continued efforts on the part of financial services institutions and commercial firms not subject to bank regulation to capture savings from the depository institutions and give the public better returns on their savings without losing the protection of government deposit insurance programs. Electronics will surely bring about rapid changes in national, and eventually international, banking practices.

The meaning of this electronic revolution in banking may perhaps be best illustrated by Sears' decision to get into electronic banking. In early June, 1984, it began test-marketing in Southern California a telephone-bill-paying service that enables consumers to pay a variety of invoices using funds drawn on any bank. The function of Sears in the process is to act as agent, electronically channeling the payments from the subscriber's bank account.

In Chapter 7 I turned my attention from domestic regulation and described how the federal bank regulatory agencies control foreign lending by U.S. banks. Here, too, recent developments in international banking have made the job of the regulatory agencies much more difficult than in the past. The regulators—especially the Federal Reserve Board, which is more concerned with domestic rather than foreign activities of U.S. banks—have allowed the major U.S. banks to overextend themselves abroad in recent years. Overextension has been permitted to occur under great pressure from the domestic banks. Understandably, they want to be allowed to compete freely with foreign banks not subject to the same regulatory strictures. Nevertheless, the results of inadequate federal regulatory supervision over foreign lending by U.S. banks will haunt us for many years.

In Chapter 8 I examined the results of this failure to control bank lending by U.S. banks abroad and how the developing countries now find it impossible to meet the repayment terms of their borrowings. The risks taken by the banks, the manner in which they have been handling borrowers' difficulties, and the possible role of the central banks as well as the international financial institutions were all analyzed. The threats to the international financial system are serious. Solutions may be available, provided the banks are willing to lend more and to respond with understanding to the borrowers' needs for longer repayment terms and fair rescheduling conditions. Here, the chairman of the Federal Reserve, Paul Volcker, who has not always been as concerned as he should have been on the extent of foreign lending by U.S. banks, is given a great deal of credit for his understanding and flexibility in encouraging the banks to "stay the course." The actions of other regulatory agencies are compared. There are serious differences of opinion among regulators. Chairman Volcker encourages banks to make new loans to Latin American developing countries, whereas the SEC, concerned with information made available to stockholders, has recommended that much more disclosure be made with respect to foreign loans. Both positions have merit. Should there be a priority in protecting the international banking system over the "right to know" of stockholders who might otherwise purchase bank stock without knowledge of the extent of troubled loans?

Finally, in Chapter 9 I discussed the effect of exaggerated lending by banks to developing and Eastern bloc countries on the future role of the IMF, the BIS, and central banks in controlling foreign lending.

The new role of the IMF in particular is carefully analyzed to determine whether or not its additional responsibilities are likely to jolt developed country governments into realizing that to protect the international banking system there simply must be some new rules on foreign bank lending agreed upon by the central banks and perhaps enforced by the IMF. What are the chances that this will result in acceptance by governments that the IMF must establish the rules with respect to foreign lending since it must finance the restoration of liquidity for the borrowers if the banks lend more than they reasonably should? Is this an opportunity to establish at last a true international banking system? From there to turning the IMF into a true international bank is but one more step. We hope, in due course, to find there a path to a world monetary system free of political pressures from any country, no matter how powerful. The collaboration of central bankers made necessary by the folly of recent commercial bank lending to developing countries may in this manner bring about a much more effective international regulatory system that will ensure the liquidity of individual national banks.

As society has progressed from village communities to states to countries and now to regional and international cooperation, it is essential that rules regarding the exchange of goods, banking, finance, insurance, and other forms of trade in goods and services be regulated by international agreement. The production of goods will continue to become more internationally sourced. Services will need to do the same. Given the importance of trade to the world community, it is vital that the monetary system itself be internationalized. To do this the old exchange rate system, whether fixed or floating, must be modified.

The world has become too small a place for artificial barriers to exist, making trade more difficult. The free exchange of goods so necessary for growth and development everywhere can only be made possible if banking transactions can be facilitated. This means the establishment of a monetary system that will control the money supply under international guidance. The revised system, in turn, must — with a minimum of interference — be designed to encourage economic growth while at the same time avoiding renewed inflation. It is possible to accomplish this. If we should fail to do so, the world faces the threat of continued international financial instability. If we succeed, the United States, other developed countries, and those in the painful process of development will all be the beneficiaries. In the final analysis, each country's economic growth depends on the economic development of its neighbors. We are truly part of one economic world today.

In this effort U.S. commercial banks must play an important role regardless of the bank regulatory system in place. So long as our currency remains, as it will, the world's key currency, I believe the banks will find a way to do this. Developments in electronic transfers and in satellite communications should make it possible. As Walter Wriston has so aptly put it:

> The old discipline of the *gold standard* has been replaced, in fact, by the discipline of the *communications revolution* . . . Modern technology has welded us into an integrated economic and financial marketplace which governments — and all of us — must learn to live with. The clock cannot be turned back . . . As the perception grows that we live in a world of limited resources and of unlimited demand, the world problem continues to be how to make maximum use of these resources. Helping to solve that problem has always been a banker's basic business — and with the tools now available, we have an opportunity for doing that job with a proficiency never seen before in history.[1] (Emphasis added.)

NOTE

1. Walter B. Wriston, Speech at International Monetary Conference, London, England, June 11, 1979, pp. 4, 6, 7.

BIBLIOGRAPHY

CHAPTER 1

Books

Bank Facts, 1983. Toronto: Canadian Bankers Association, 1983.

Campbell, Colin D., and Rosemary Campbell. *An Introduction to Money and Banking*, 4th ed. Hinsdale, Illinois: The Dryden Press, 1981.

Credit Union Report, 1982. Madison, Wisconsin: Credit Union National Association Inc., 1983.

Golembe, Carter H. *Federal Regulation of Banking.* Washington: Golembe Associates, 1981.

Hutchinson, Harry D. *Money, Banking and the U.S. Economy.* Englewood Cliffs, N.J.: Prentice-Hall Inc., 1980.

Luckett, Dudley G. *Money and Banking.* 3rd ed. New York: McGraw-Hill, 1984.

Marshall, Robert H., and Rodney B. Swanson. *The Monetary Process: Essentials of Money and Banking.* Boston: Houghton Mifflin Co., 1980.

Reed, Edward W. *Commercial Banking.* 3rd ed. Englewood Cliffs, N.J.: Prentice-Hall, 1984.

Spong, Kenneth. *Banking Regulation: Its Purposes, Implementation, and Effects.* Kansas City, Mo.: Federal Reserve Bank of Kansas City, 1983.

Journals

"Allowed to Play New Instruments, S&Ls Finally Making Sweet Music." *National Journal* (August 13, 1983):1690.

"American Banker Ranks the 300 Largest Commercial Banks." *American Banker* (August 19, 1983):57.

"American Banker Ranks the Top U.S. Thrift Institutions." *American Banker* (August 12, 1983):29.

"American Banker Ranks the World's 100 Largest Savings Banks." *American Banker* (August 5, 1983):11.

"Credit Unions in Transition." *United States Banker.* (May 1984):55.

"Financial Developments of Bank Holding Companies in 1982." *Federal Reserve Bulletin* (July 1983):508.

"Franchising and the Law—What There Is of It." *American Banker* (August 12, 1983):9.

"Legal Reserve Requirements: A Case Study in Bank Regulation." *Journal of Bank Research* (Spring 1983):59.

"Look for Growth of 10–12%: That's the 1983 Prediction for Growth in CU Savings and Loans." *Credit Union* (July 1983):42.

"Structural Reorganization of the OCC." *Bank Compliance* (September 1983):35.

"The Conflicting Roles of the Fed as a Regulator and a Competitor." *Journal of Bank Research* (Spring 1983):75.

"The Demand for and Supply of Deposits by Credit Unions." *Journal of Banking and Finance* (June 1983):285.

"What is a Commercial Loan?" *Federal Reserve Bank of Boston Economic Review* (July/August 1983):36.

Newspaper Articles

Weiner, Steve, and Robert Johnson. "Falling Short: Export Trading Firms in U.S. Are Failing to Fulfill Promise." The *Wall Street Journal*, May 24, 1984, p. 1.

Public Documents

Board of Governors of the Federal Reserve System. *The Federal Reserve System: Purposes and Functions*. Washington, D.C., 1974.

Conference of State Bank Supervisors. The Dynamic American Banking System—An Analysis of Proposals for Change of Geographic Structural Constraints. Washington, D.C.:1981.

Conference of State Bank Supervisors. *Why State Banking? A Question of Importance to All Bankers*. Washington, D.C.:1981.

Federal Deposit Insurance Corporation. *Banks & Branches Data Book, June 30, 1982*. Washington, D.C.: U.S. Government Printing Office, 1983.

Federal Deposit Insurance Corporation. *FDIC: Symbol of Confidence*. Washington, D.C.: U. S. Government Printing Office, 1982.

Federal Deposit Insurance Corporation. *1982 Statistics on Banking*. Washington, D.C.: U.S. Government Printing Office, 1983.

Federal Reserve. *The Monetary Control Act of 1980*. Washington, D.C.: December 1980.

Federal Reserve Bank of Richmond. *The Federal Reserve at Work*. 1979.

National Credit Union Administration. *Credit Union Share Insurance*. Washington, D.C.: 1983.

U.S. Congress, House. Committee of Banking, Finance and Urban Affairs. *Formation and Powers of National Banking Associations—A Legal Primer*. 98th

Cong., 1st sess., May 1983. Washington, D.C.: U.S. Government Printing Office.

U.S. Congress, House, Committee on Banking and Currency. Subcommittee of Domestic Finance. *The Federal Reserve System After 50 Years.* 88th Cong., 1964., Washington, D.C.

U.S. Congress, House. Committee on Banking, Finance and Urban Affairs. Oversight hearing on section 14(b)(1) of the Federal Reserve Act as amended by section 105(b)(2) of the Monetary Control Act of 1980. Hearings 98-1, Washington, D.C.: U.S. Government Printing Office, 1983.

U.S. Congress. House. Subcommittee on General Oversight and Renegotiation of the House Committee on Banking, Finance and Urban Affairs. Statement by Charles E. Lord. Washington, D.C. June 4, 1981. Also in *Quarterly Journal of the Office of the Comptroller of the Currency,* November 1981.

U.S. Congress. Senate. Committee on Banking, Housing and Urban Affairs. Statement by John G. Geinman. Washington, D.C. April 28, 1981. Also in *Quarterly Journal of the Office of the Comptroller of the Currency,* November 1981.

U.S. Federal Home Loan Bank Board. *Agenda for Reform: A Report on Deposit Insurance to the Congress from the Federal Home Loan Bank Board.* Washington, D.C.:1983.

CHAPTER 2

Books

Aldrich, Nelson, W. *The Aldrich Plan for Banking Legislation.* Boston: The Eliot National Bank, 1911.

Boltes, Albert S. *The Financial History of the U.S. from 1789-1860.* Vol. 3. New York: August M. Kelley, 1969.

Burns, Arthur F. *The Condition of the American Economy.* Washington, D.C.: American Enterprise Institute, 1979.

_____. *Reflections of an Economic Policy Maker: Speeches and Congressional Statements: 1969-1978.* Washington, D.C.: American Enterprise Institute, 1978.

Chandler, Lester V. *Benjamin Strong, Central Banker.* Washington, D.C.: The Brookings Institute, 1953.

Crawford, Arthur Whipple. *Monetary Management Under the New Deal.* New York: Da Capo Press, 1972.

Eccles, Marriner S. *Economic Balance and a Balanced Budget.* New York: Da Capo Press, 1973.

Glass, Carter. *Adventures in Constructive Finance.* New York: Doubleday, Page & Co., 1927.

Golembe Associates. *Commercial Banking and the Glass-Steagall Act.* Washington, D.C.: American Bankers Association, 1982.

Homer, Sidney. *The History of Interest Rates.* New Brunswick, N.J.: Rutgers University Press, 1963.

Hoyt, Edwin P., Jr. *The House of Morgan.* New York: Dodd, Mead and Co., 1966.

Hyman, Sydney. *Marriner S. Eccles.* California: Stanford University Graduate School of Business, 1976.

Johnson, Arthur M. *Winthrop W. Aldrich: Lawyer, Banker, Diplomat.* Boston: Harvard University, Division of Research, Graduate School of Business Administration, 1968.

Lekachman, Robert. *Inflation: The Permanent Problem of Boom and Bust.* New York: Random House, 1973.

Link, Arthur S. *Woodrow Wilson and the Progressive Era.* New York: Harper & Row, 1963.

Myers, Margaret G. *A Financial History of the U.S.* New York: Columbia University Press, 1970.

Nader, Marcus, and Dr. Jules J. Bogen. *The Bank Holding Companies.* Association of Bank Holding Companies, 1976.

Owen, Robert L. *The Federal Reserve Act.* New York: The Century Co., 1919.

Patman, Wright. *The Federal Reserve System.* Washington, D.C.: U.S. Government Printing Office, 1976.

Pelora, Ferdinand. *Wall Street Under Oath.* New York: Simon & Schuster, 1937.

Shoup, Lawrence H. *The Carter Presidency and Beyond: Power and Politics in the 1980s.* California: Ramparts Press, 1980.

Sobel, Robert. *Panic on Wall Street: A History of America's Financial Disasters.* New York: Macmillan Co., 1968.

Stephenson, Nathaniel Wright. *Nelson W. Aldrich: A Leader in American Politics.* New York: Kennikel Press, 1930.

Strong, Benjamin. *Interpretations of the Federal Reserve Policy.* New York: Harper & Brothers Publishers, 1930.

Studenski, Paul, and Herman E. Kruos. *Financial History of the U.S.* New York: McGraw-Hill Book Co., Inc., 1963.

Vennard, Wickliffe B. *The Federal Reserve Hoax: The Age of Deception.* 1962.

Warburg, Paul M. *The Federal Reserve System.* Volumes I and II. New York: Macmillan, 1930.

Wicker, Elmus R. *Federal Reserve Monetary Policy, 1917–1933.* New York: Random House, 1966.

Willing, Pearl. *The Federal Reserve System: A Study of its Impact on the Economy and Related Factors, 1950–70.* Ontario, Canada: Graduate Division of Philathea College, 1971.

Willis, Henry Parker. *The Federal Reserve System: Legislation, Organization and Operation.* New York: Ronald Press, 1923.

———. *The Federal Reserve: A Study of the Banking System of the U.S.* New York: Doubleday, Page & Co., 1915.

Journals

"A reinterpretation of the Banking Crisis of 1930." *Journal of Economic History* (March 1984):119.
"Banking Structure and the National Capital Market, 1869–1914". *Journal of Economic History* (June, 1984):463.
"The 'Business of Banking' in Historical Perspective." *George Washington Law Review* (August 1983):676.
"The Depository Institutions Deregulations and Monetary Control Act of 1980." *Federal Reserve Bulletin* (June 1980).
"Money Statistics of New England, 1785–1837." *Journal of Economic History* (June 1984):441.

Newspaper Articles

Dunn, Robert M., Jr. "Why Is the Fed Suddenly So Important?" The *Washington Post*, June 22, 1983. p. A23.
Keynes, John Maynard. "Lord Keynes: Delighted With F.D.R. Economics." The *New York Times*, 1934. Reprint. April 10, 1983, p. F2.
Schlesinger, Arthur Jr. "The 'Hundred Days' of F.D.R." The *New York Times*, April 10, 1983, p. F1.

Public Documents

Aldrich, Nelson W. *Suggested Plan for Monetary Legislation*. Submitted to the National Monetary Commission in 1911. Washington, D.C.: U.S. Government Printing Office, 1911.
Board of Governors. *The Bank Holding Company Movement to 1978: A Compendium*. Washington, D.C.: U.S. Government Printing Office, 1978.
Board of Governors of the Federal Reserve System. *Historical Chart Book*. Washington, D.C.: U.S. Government Printing Office, 1982.
Brunner, Karl. *"The Voices of 'Failure' and the Failure of Monetary Policymaking."* Washington, D.C.: Shadow Open Market Committee, September 12–13, 1982.
Curry, Timothy J., and John T. Rose. *Multibank Holding Companies: Recent Evidence on Competition and Performance in Banking Markets*. Washington, D.C.: Board of Governors of the Federal Reserve System, December 1981.
Houpt, James V. *Performance and Characteristics of Edge Corporations*. Washington, D.C.: Board of Governors of the Federal Reserve System, January 1981.
Shadow Open Market Committee. *Policy Statement*. Washington, D.C.: March 15, 1982.
U.S. Congress. House. Committee on Energy and Commerce. Statement by Richard Dale. Washington, D.C. September 17, 1982.

Unpublished Material

Eccles, Marriner S. "The Postwar Price Problem: Inflation or Deflation." Address at meeting of National Conference Board, New York, November 16, 1977.

CHAPTER 3

Books

Ali, M. Rahmet. *Federal Reserve Policy (Monetary Policy of the U.S.) During Booms and Recessions.* New Delhi: Jamia Millia Islamic, 1968.

Bach, G. L. *Federal Reserve Policy-making.* New York: Alfred A. Knopf, 1950.

Bell, James W., and Walter E. Spahr, eds. *A Proper Monetary and Banking System for the United States.* New York: The Ronald Press Co., 1960.

Black, Stanley W. III, Glenn Canner, and Robert G. King. *The Banking System: A Preface to Public Interest Analysis.* Washington, D.C.: The Public Interest Economics Center, 1975.

Clifford, Jerome A. *The Independence of the Federal Reserve.* Philadelphia: University of Pennsylvania Press, 1965.

Currie, Lauchlin, B. *The Supply and Control of Money in the United States.* Massachusetts: Harvard University Press, 1935.

Harris, S. E. *Twenty Years of Federal Reserve Policy,* Massachusetts: Harvard University Press, 1933.

Willis, Henry P., and George W. Edwards. *Banking and Business.* New York: Harper and Brothers Publishers, 1922.

The Political Economy of Monetary Policy: National and International Aspects. Boston: Federal Reserve Bank of Boston, 1983.

Journals

Friedman, Benjamin. "Time to Re-Examine the Monetary Targets Framework." *New England Economic Review* (March/April 1982).

_____. "A Monetary and Fiscal Framework for Stability." *American Economic Review* (June 1948):245–264.

_____. "Monetary Policy: Theory and Practice." *Journal of Money, Credit and Banking.* 14 (February 1982):98–118.

Haywood, Charles F. "Political Control of the Money Supply is not Acceptable." *ABA Banking Journal* (July 1982):69–74.

_____. "An Examination of the Evolving Concept of an Independent Fed." *ABA Banking Journal* (June 1982):219–229.

Lawrence, Robert J. "Effects of Deregulation and Expanded Banking Activities on Bank Supervision." *Issues in Bank Regulation* (Autumn 1982):15–22.

Poole, William. "Federal Reserve Operating Procedures: A Survey and Evaluation of the Historical Record Since October 1979." *Journal of Money, Credit and Banking.* 14 (November 1982):575–596.

Storey, Donald R., and J. Anthony Boeckh, eds., *The Bank Credit Analyst: Investment and Business Forecast.* 10 (April 1984).

Tobin, James. "Monetary Policy: Rules, Targets, and Shocks." *Journal of Money, Credit and Banking.* 15 (November 1983):506–518.

Wallich, Henry C., and Peter M. Keir. "The Role of Operating Guides in U.S. Monetary Policy: A Historical Review." *The Federal Reserve Bulletin* (September 1979):679–691.

World Financial Markets: U.S. Monetary Policy Shift Reasons and Implication." *Morgan Guaranty Trust Company* (November 1982):1–5.

"Recent Techniques of Monetary Policy." *Federal Reserve Bank of Kansas City Economic Review* (May 1984):21.

"The Instruments of Monetary Policy." *Federal Reserve Bank of Kansas City Economic Review* (May 1984):3.

"Unresolved Issues in Monetary Policy." *Federal Reserve Bank of New York Quarterly Review* (Spring 1984):1.

Magazines

Cooper, James, and Gelvin Stevenson. "What the Fed Says is not What it Does." *Business Week,* June 7, 1982, 29.

Ehrbar, A. F. "How to Bring Rates Down." *Fortune,* June 24, 1982, 66–72.

Higgins, Byron, and Jon Faust. "NOW's and Super NOW's: Implications for Defining and Measuring Money." *Economic Review,* January 1983, 3–9.

Janssen, Richard F. "'Crating' Capital by Changing the Rules." *Business Week,* February 1, 1982, 20.

Lascelles, David. "Supermarkets on Wall Street." London *The Banker,* September 1982.

"The Fed Faces Its Critics . . . Live." *Fortune,* June 1, 1981, 89–91.

"The Fed's Plan for Economic Recovery." *Business Week,* December 13, 1982, 90–97.

"Where is US Monetary Policy Heading?" London: *The Banker,* July 1983, 53.

Newspaper Articles

Blustein, Paul. "Volcker's Dilemma: Fed Is Being Pushed To Both Curb and Spur Rise in Money Supply." *The Wall Street Journal,* June 7, 1984.

Clark, Lindley H. Jr. "Slump Drives Wedge Between Supply-Siders, Monetarists." *The Wall Street Journal,* Jan.4, 1983, p. 29.

Feldstein, Martin. "Why Short-Term Interest Rates Are High." *The Wall Street Journal,* June 8, 1982, p. 34.

Foldessy, Edward P. "New Bank Accounts May Force Fed to End Experiment in Monetarism." The *Wall Street Journal*, Dec. 1982.

Friedman, Benjamin M. "The Federal Reserve's New Monetary Policy: Applause for a Credit Guideline." The *New York Times*, Feb, 27, 1983, p. F2.

_____. "A Memorandum to the Fed." *Wall Street Journal*, January 30, 1981.

Friedman, Thomas L. "Fed's Policy of Tight Money." The *New York Times*, Sept. 12, 1981, p. Business 1.

Fuerbringer, Jonathan. "Fed's Interest Rate Dilemma." *New York Times*, June 15, 1982, p. D1.

Hall, Robert E. "A Bid for Tracking Nominal G.N.P." The *New York Times*, Feb, 27, 1983, p. F2.

Heinemann, H. Erich. "The Fed's Strategy." The *New York Times*, December 17, 1982, p. 1.

_____. "Monetary Control: A Partisan Debate." The *New York Times*, July 25, 1983, p. D1.

Kristol, Irving. "The Focus Is on the Fed." The *Wall Street Journal*, Feb, 12, 1982, p. 28.

Malabre, Alfred L. Jr. "Velocity Throws the Money Men a Curve." The *Wall Street Journal*, May 24, 1983, p. 36.

_____. "Supply of Money Supplies is Abundant; Problem: Which 'M' Counts?" The *Wall Street Journal*, January 22, 1981, p. 50.

Meltzer, Allan H. "Avoiding the Monetary Shoals." *Wall Street Journal*, May 9, 1979, p. 24.

_____. "A Monetarist Looks at the Federal Reserve." The *New York Times*, October 14, 1979, p. F16.

Nakagawa, Yukitsugu. "A Japanese View of U.S. Monetary Policy." *New York Times*, March 28, 1983, p. 23.

Newton, Maxwell. "Fed Still Suspect as 'Cabal' Undermines Reagan Policy." *New York Post*, September 22, 1981.

Quint, Michael. "Taming the Renegade Money Supply" *New York Times*, December 20, 1981, p. F8.

Tobin, James. "Stop Volcker From Killing the Economy." The *Washington Post*, August 15, 1982, p. B1.

Unpublished Material

Brunner, Karl, and Allan H. Meltzer. "Strategies and Tactics for Monetary Control" Prepared for the Carnegie-Rochester Conference on Public Policy, University of Rochester, April 1982.

Meltzer, Allan N. "Consequences of the Federal Reserve's Reattachment to Free Reserves." Presented at the Western Economic Association meeting, July 1981.

Volcker, Paul A. "The New Federal Reserve Technical Procedures for Controlling Money." Attachment to Chairman Volcker's testimony before the Joint Economic Committee, Washington, D.C., Feb. 1, 1980, p. 82.

Wallich, Henry C. "Changes in Monetary Policy and the Fight Against Inflation." Remarks read at a conference sponsored by the Cato Institute, January 21, 1983, Washington, D.C.

_____. "A Perspective on Federal Reserve Policy." Remarks read at meeting of the Steuben-Schurz Society and the U.S. Chamber of Commerce, July 6, 1982, at Frankfurt, Germany.

CHAPTER 4

Books

Duesenberry, James S. *Money and Credit: Impact and Control.* New Jersey: Prentice-Hall Inc., 1972.

Journals

"ATMs 1983: A Critical Assessment." *Bank Administration* (May 1984):24.

"Banking: Fed Lets Michigan BHC Establish Ohio Credit-Card Bank." *Regulatory and Legal Developments.* No. 226 (November 22, 1983):A-3.

"Count Debit Cards in Your Electronic Banking Game Plans." *American Banker* (May 22, 1984):7.

"Developments in Consumer Electronic Fund Transfers." *Federal Reserve Bulletin* (June 1983):395.

"U.S. Banker Round Table: ATM Networks and the Future of EFT." *United States Banker* (July 1983):24.

"Financial Services Companies Hope Consumers Will Buy One-Stop Shopping." *National Journal* (March 17, 1984):504.

"Financial Supermarkets in the United States." *Finance & Development* (March, 1984):18.

"Interest Rates and Bank Profitability: Additional Evidence." *Journal of Money, Credit and Banking* (August 1983):355.

"Money Market Deposit Accounts and Money Market Mutual Funds: True Competitors?" *Journal of Retail Banking* (Fall 1983):34.

"On the Economics of Private Money." *Journal of Monetary Economics* (July 1983):127.

"Regulatory Innovation: The New Bank Accounts." *Federal Reserve Bank of Chicago Economic Perspectives* (March/April, 1984):12.

"Ten Approaches to the Definition of Money." *Federal Reserve Bank of Dallas Economic Review* (March 1984):1.

"The Development of Terminal-based EFT Delivery Systems in the Eighties." *Federal Home Loan Bank Board Journal* (April, 1984):20.

"The Forces of Change in Retail Banking." *World of Banking* (July-August 1983):4.

Magazines

Dale, Richard. "Safeguarding the International Banking System." *The Banker*, Vol. 132, No. 678, August 1982, 49.

Hindle, Tom. "International Banking Survey: 'The Other Crisis.'" *The Economist*, March 26 1983, 3–90.

"How Building Societies See Their Role in the Financial Services Revolution." London: *Banker*, March 1984, 33.

"Putting World Trade Back on a Growth Course." London: *Banker*, March 1984, 23.

Newspaper Articles

Bennett, Robert A. "Deregulation Alters Banking." The *New York Times*, December 5, 1983, p. D1.

Carrington, Tim. "Just When Is a Bank Not a Bank? When It Is an Abomination." The *Wall Street Journal*, January 30, 1984, p. 1.

_____. "Cash Management Accounts Proliferating As Banks, Brokers Vie for People's Money." The *Wall Street Journal*, November 15, 1982, p. 31.

Hertzberg, Daniel. "Fed Lets U.S. Trust Take Florida Deposits, Opening Door Wider to Interstate Banking." The *Wall Street Journal*, March 30, 1974.

_____. "Banks Linking Cash Machines Across the U.S." The *Wall Street Journal*, November 16, 1983, p. 33.

Rowe, James L., Jr. "The Process Is Far From Neat: How Interest Rates are Determined." The *Washington Post*, May 20, 1984, p. 1.

Public Documents

Hess, Alan C. *Effects of Regulation on deposits and interest rates at savings associations*. Kansas City, Mo.: Research Division, Federal Reserve Bank of Kansas City, 1983.

General Accounting Office. *"Bank Examination for Country Risk and International Lending."* Washington, D.C.: U.S. Government Printing Office, Sept. 2, 1982.

CHAPTER 5

Books

Cart, Alan. *The Insider's Guide to the Financial Services Revolution*. New York: McGraw-Hill Book Company, 1983.

Glass-Steagall: The Collapsing Walls between Banks and Securities, May 16 & 17, 1983, Washington, D.C. New York: Executive Enterprises, Inc., 1983.

Major Events in the Financial Industry: January 1, 1982–August 15, 1983. Washington: Golembe Associates, Inc., 1983.

Rosenblum, Harvey. *Financial Services in Transition: The Effects of Nonbank Competitors.* Chicago: Federal Reserve Bank of Chicago, 1984.

Second Annual Financial Services Institute, New York: Practicing Law Institute, 1984.

Seligman, Barnard. *Money Market Funds.* New York: Praeger, 1983.

Sinkey, Joseph F. *Commercial Bank Financial Management.* New York: Macmillan, 1983.

Taxation of Financial Institutions: Commercial Banks, Thrift Institutions. 3 vols. New York: Matthew Bender, 1983.

The New Synergy Between Thrifts and Commercial Banks. New York: Law & Business, Inc., 1983.

Journals

Conover, C. T. "Quest for Powers in Financial Services." *Bankers Monthly* (February 15, 1984):18.

Hawke, John D., Jr. "Fed Smiles on Holding Company Expansion in 1983." *Legal Times* (January 16, 1984):11, 13–19.

Key, Sydney J., and James M. Brundy. "Implementation of the International Banking Act." *Federal Reserve Bulletin* (October 1979):785–796.

McAffee, James. "Order Approving Application by BankAmerica Corp., San Francisco, California, to Acquire the Charles Schwab Corp., a Retail Discount Brokerage Firm." *Federal Reserve Bulletin* (February 1983):105–117.

Nader, Ralph. "Regulators Who Kowtow to Bankers." *Business and Society Review* No. 36 (Winter 1980–81):37–42.

Roderer, David W. "Nonexistent Banking Law Warrants Closer Scrutiny." *Legal Times* (January 9, 1984):12, 14.

"A Banker's Adventures in Brokerland: Looking through Glass-Steagall at Discount Brokerage Services." *Michigan Law Review* (May 1983):1498.

"Bank Acquisition of Non-bank Firms." *Journal of Banking and Finance* (June 1983):213.

"Banker's Bank: An Institution Whose Time Has Come?" *Independent Banker* (June 1984):10.

"Banking Regulatory System Badly in Need of Reform." *Legal Times* (June 27, 1983):27.

"Banking: Court Decides ATM Is Branch, Puts Chill on Electronic Funds Transfer." *Regulatory and Legal Developments,* No. 75 (April 18, 1984):A10–11.

"Banking: Fed, Asserting Jurisdiction, Denies Mellon Bid to Acquire Heritage." *Regulatory and Legal Developments,* No. 81 (April 26, 1984):A8–10.

"Banking: OCC Imposes Non-Bank Bank Moratorium, Also Approves Four of 31 Dimension Non-Banks." *Regulatory and Legal Developments,* No. 91 (May 5, 1984):A16–19.

"Banks and the Insurance Industry." *United States Banker* (March 1984):61.

"Banks Controlled by Those Outside the Commercial Banking Industry." *American Banker* (August 19, 1983):18.

"Banks Control Money, But Who Controls Banks?" article from Banking & Finance: The Hidden Cost by Corporate Data Exchange in *Business and Society Review* No. 36 (Winter 1980–81):30–33.

"Congress is Hesitant About Moving to End Financial Industry Turmoil." *National Journal* (July 2, 1983):1372.

"Contagion Effects of Bank Failures: Evidence from Capital Markets." *Journal of Business* (July 1983):489.

"EFT Comes to the Corporate Suite." *Institutional Investor* (June 1983):151.

"Executive View of Deregulation: The Depository Institutions Deregulation and Monetary Control of 1980." *Journal of Retail Banking* (Spring 1983):52.

"Federal Reserve Board Proposed Revision of Reg Y." *Legal Times* (July 25, 1983):41.

"Implications of Deregulation for Product Lines and Geographical Markets of Financial Institutions." *Journal of Bank Research* (Spring 1983):8.

"Lending Limits Under Garn/St. Germain." *Southern Banker* (July 1983):28.

"Major Shift Seen in S & L Industry." *Mortgage Banking* (May 1984):47.

"Money Market Mutual Funds: An Experiment in ad hoc Deregulation: A Note." *Journal of Finance* (June 1983):1011.

"Mr. Volcker's Reappointment—What Significance for Banking Regulation." *Golembe Reports*, Vol 1983-5 (July 25, 1983):21.

"New Competition and its Implications for Banking." *Bank Administration* (July 1983):34.

"Profitability of Insured Commercial Banks in 1982." *Federal Reserve Bulletin* (July 1983):489.

"Retailers, Networks Compromise as EFT Programs Take Hold." *Bank Systems & Equipment* (March 1984):69.

"Separation Between Banking and Commerce Under the Bank Holding Company Act—A Statutory Objective Under Attack." *Catholic University Law Review* (Fall 1983):163.

"Special Report: The New Players." *United States Banker* (June 1984):25.

"The Carry-Forward Provision and Management of Bank Reserves." *Journal of Finance* (June 1983):845.

"The Emerging Financial Services Industry: Challenge and Innovation." *Federal Reserve Bank of Atlanta Economic Review* (April 1984):25.

"The Glass-Steagall Act and The Acquisition of Member Banks by Unregulated Bank Holding Companies." *Banking Law Journal* (July 1983):484.

"The Public Policy Issues of Payment System Regulation." *Issues in Bank Regulation* (Winter 1984):20.

"The Separation of Banking and the Securities Business: A View of the United Kingdom, West Germany and Japan." *World of Banking* (May–June 1984):12.

Law Cases

A.G. Becker Incorporated *v*. Board of Governors of the Federal Reserve System, *et al*., 693 Fed. 2d 136, U.S. Circuit Court, Washington, D.C. (1982).
Board of Governors of Federal Reserve System *v*. Investment Company Institute, U.S. Supreme Court, 450 U.S. 46 (1981).
New York Stock Exchange, Inc. and Investment Company Institute *v*. Smith, 404 F. Supp. 109, VSDC, D.C. (1975).
Securities Industry Association *v*. Comptroller of the Currency, *et al*., 577 Fed. Supp. 252, D.C.D.C (1983).

Magazines

Hector, Gary. "The Banks Invade Wall Street." *Fortune*, February 7, 1983, 44.
Lascelles, David. "Supermarkets on Wall Street." London: *Banker*, September 1982, 33.
"General Electric Credit: From financing Home Appliances to an Aggressive Source of Funds for Industry." *Business Week*, August 30, 1982, 54.
"Penn Square Revisited." Boston: *Bankers Magazine*, January–February 1984, 75.
"Target Marketing of Financial Services." London: *Banker*, April 1984, 51.
"The Golden Plan of American Express." *Business Week*, April 30, 1984, 118.

Newspaper Articles

Beazley, J. Ernest. "Five Banks Related to Butcher Brothers Expected to be Closed, Sold by Regulators." The *Wall Street Journal*, May 27, 1983, p. 3.
Hertzberg, Daniel, and J. Ernest Beazley. "Mellon National Takes Banks. Big Interstate Step by Seeking Approval for Banks in 15 Cities." The *Wall Street Journal*, April 16, 1984, p. 2.
Heylar, John. "Banks Cut Costs, Change Strategies As Deregulation Alters the Industry." The *Wall Street Journal*, May 29, 1983, p. 37.
Rowe, James L., Jr. "Citicorp's Big Lead in Race Toward Nationwide Banking." The *Washington Post*, January 29, 1984, p. G1.

Public Documents

Anderson, Clay J. *A Half-Century of Federal Reserve Policy-Making, 1914–1964*. Federal Reserve Bank of Philadelphia, 1965.
Federal Home Loan Bank Board. Combined financial statements 1982, FSLIC-insured savings and loan associations. Washington, 1983.
U.S. Comptroller of the Currency. *Decision on the Application by Security Pacific National Bank to Establish an Operating Subsidiary to be Known as Security Pacific Discount Brokerage Services Inc*. Washington, D.C.: U.S. Government Printing Office, August 26, 1982.

U.S. Congress. House. Committee on Government Operations. *Federal supervision and failure of United American Bank (Knoxville, Tenn.)* Hearings 98-1. Washington, D.C.: U.S. Government Printing Office, 1983.

U.S. Congress. House. Committee on Energy and Commerce. *Financial deregulation in New York State.* Hearing 98-1. Washington: U.S. Government Printing Office, 1984.

U.S. Congress. Senate. Committee on Banking, Housing, and Urban Affairs. *Competitive equity in the financial services industry.* Hearings 98-1 and 2. Washington: U.S. Government Printing Office, 1984.

Unpublished Material

Hawke, John D., Jr. "Securities Activities of Banks." Delivered to the Ray Garrett Jr. Corporate and Securities Law Institute, Northwestern University School of Law, May 27, 1982.

CHAPTER 6

Books

Bradfield, Michael, Thomas A. Brooks, and John D. Hawke Jr., eds. *Fifth Annual Workshop: Banking Expansion in the '80's.* New York: Law & Business, Inc., 1984.

Heimann, John G. "Forces for change in banking." In *Annual Review of Banking Law.* Boston: Warren, Gorham & Lamont, 1982.

Rhoades, Stephen A. *The Implications for Bank Merger Policy of Financial Deregulation, Interstate Banking, and Financial Supermarkets.* Washington: Board of Governors of the Federal Reserve System, 1984.

Journals

Barrett, Ford. "Judicial Review of Agency Cease and Desist Orders: The Gains and Losses for Financial Institutions." *Quarterly Journal* (OCC) (June 1983):1.

Conover, C. T. "Deregulation Poses Both a Danger and an Opportunity for Banks Because the Old Built-in Franchise Days Are Going." *American Banker* (June 27, 1983):18.

_____. "Breaking Brokered Deposits." *Southern Banker* (May 1984):64.

_____. "The Urgent Need for New Powers." *Bankers Monthly* (May 15, 1984):20.

Wallison, Peter J. "Consumer Bank Concept Deserves Continued Scrutiny." *Legal Times* (December 12, 1983):48–50.

Wallison, Peter J., and Donald J. Tourney. "Continued Banking Deregulation

Seems Inevitable." *Legal Times* (March 5, 1984).

Webster, Susan M. "Regulatory Plan On Broker Deposits Likely to Draw Fire." *Legal Times* (January 16, 1984):1, 4.

"A Special Issue on Bank Product Deregulation." *Federal Reserve Bank of Atlanta Economic Review* (May 1984).

"Are Brokers Being Made Scapegoats?" *United States Banker* (March 1984):36.

"Banking: Existing Antitrust Laws are Inadequate to Prevent Concentration in Banking, House Panel Told." *Regulatory and Legal Developments*, No. 92 (May 11, 1984):A3-5.

"Brokered Deposits: Issues and Alternatives." *Federal Reserve Bank of Atlanta Economic Review* (March 1984):14.

"Competitive Banking Business — Poised for Deregulation." *Banking World* (July 1983):30.

"Continental Illinois and the Case for Deposit Insurance Reform." *Golembe Reports*, Vol. 1984-5.

"Financial Disclosure and Bank Failure." *Federal Reserve Bank of Atlanta Economic Review* (March 1984):5.

"Industrials as Consumer Banks?" *Credit* (May–June 1984):17.

"Interstate Banking — One Step Closer: The Citicorp-Fidelity Savings Merger." *Journal of Retail Banking* (Fall 1983):8.

"Interstate Banking: The Drive to Consolidate." *New England Economic Review* (May–June 1984):11.

"Interstate Banking — A Time for Statesmanship." *Golembe Reports*, Vol. 1984-4, (May 18, 1984).

"Interstate Banking in Delaware." *United States Banker* (August 1983):14.

"Interstate Banking: Issues and Evidence." *Federal Reserve Bank of Atlanta Economic Review* (April 1984):36.

"Nonvoting Stock Investments — The advent of Interstate Banking." *Business Lawyer* (August 1983):1449.

"Regulatory Reform? Treatment of Symptoms Isn't Enough." *American Banker* (August 24, 1983):4.

"What is the Role of Government in a Major Restructuring of Financial Institutions in the 1980's?" *Journal of Bank Research* (Spring 1983):25.

"The 'New Englande Experiment' in Interstate Banking." *New England Economic Review*. (March–April 1984):5.

"The Depository Institutions Deregulation Committee: Did it Achieve the Goal?" *Banking Law Journal* (February–March 1984):100.

"The Garn Bill — Transcript of a Dialogue That Never Took Place; And of One That Did." *Golembe Reports*, Vol. 1984-3, (March 28, 1984).

"The Midwest Prepares for Interstate Banking." *Federal Reserve Bank of Chicago Economic Perspectives* (March–April 1984):3.

"The Case for Deposit Brokerage." *United States Banker* (May 1984):46.

"The Future of Deposit Insurance: An Analysis of the Insuring Agencies' Proposals." *Federal Reserve Bank of Atlanta Economic Review* (March 1984):26.

Magazines

"The New Shape of Banking." *Business Week*, June 18, 1984, 104.

Newspaper Articles

Hill, G. Christian. "Battered Rescuers: Agencies That Insure Bank, Thrift Deposits Face Major Problems." The *Wall Street Journal*, May 23, 1984, p. 1.

Public Documents

Avery, Robert B. *Discrimination in Consumer Credit Markets*. Washington, D.C.: Federal Reserve System, 1982

Board of Governors of the Federal Reserve System. *Federal Reserve Position of Restructuring of Financial Regulation Responsibilities*. Washington: U.S. Government Printing Office, 1983.

Depository Institutions Deregulation Committee. Proposed Bill to take away restrictions on Interest Payments by Depository Institutions. Washington, D.C. August 4, 1983.

Regan, Donald T. Secretary of the Treasury. "Statement on the Administration's Proposal for Financial Institutions Holding Company Deregulation." *Treasury News*. July 8, 1983.

"Delaware moves toward interstate banking: a look at the FDCS," *Federal Reserve Bank of Philadelphia Business Review*. (July/August 1983):17.

"Special Issue: Interstate Banking." *Federal Reserve Bank of Atlanta Economic Review* (May 1983): 4.

U.S. Congress. House. Committee on Banking, Finance and Urban Affairs. Subcommittee on Financial Institutions. "Administration Views on the Demand Deposit Equity Act of 1983." Statement by Hon. Thomas J. Healey, Sept. 28, 1983.

U.S. Congress. House. Committee on Education and Labor. "Oversight on Truth-in-lending Provisions of Student Financial Assistance Technical Amendments Act of 1982." Hearings 98–1. Washington, D.C.: U.S. Government Printing Office, 1983.

U.S. Congress. House. Committee on Government Operations. Subcommittee on Commerce, Consumer and Monetary Affairs. "Statement of the Honorable Peter J. Wallison, General Counsel of the Treasury, on the Proposed Rule of the Federal Deposit Insurance Corporation and the Federal Home Loan Bank Board to Restrict 'Brokered Deposits.'" *Treasury News*, March 14, 1984.

U.S. Congress. House. Committee on Government Operations. *Federal Reserve competition with the private sector in check clearing and other services*. Report 98–2. Washington: U.S. Government Printing Office, 1984.

U.S. Congress. House. Committee on Small Business. *Oversight of Regulatory Flexibility Act.* Hearings 97-1. Washington, D.C.: U.S. Government Printing Office, 1982.

U.S. Congress. House. "It's time for a Rational Look at Deregulation." Floor statement by Chairman Fernand J. St. Germain. Feb. 29, 1984.

U.S. Congress. Senate. Committee on Banking, Housing and Urban Affairs. *"The Credit Deregulation and Availability Act of 1983."* Hearings 98-1. Washington, D.C.: U.S. Government Printing Office, 1983.

U.S. Congress. Senate. Committee on Banking, Housing and Urban Affairs. "Testimony of the Honorable Donald T. Regan, Secretary of the Treasury, on the Need for Holding Company Deregulation." *Treasury News,* March 28, 1984.

U.S. Congress. Senate. Committee on Banking, Housing and Urban Affairs. "Testimony of the Honorable Donald T. Regan, Secretary of the Treasury, on the Administration's Proposal for Bank Holding Company Deregulation." *Treasury News,* July 18, 1983.

U.S. Congress. Senate. "Banking Geographic Deregulation Act of 1983." S. 2107. 98th Cong. 1st Sess., November 17, 1983.

U.S. Congress. Senate. "Depository Institutions Holding Company Act Amendment of 1983." S. 2134. 98th Cong. 1st Sess., November 18, 1983.

U.S. Congress. Senate. "To Limit the Acquisiton of Depository Institutions by Nonbanks." S. 2071. 98th Cong. 1st Sess., November 9, 1983.

U.S. Department of Justice. *Notice of the Proposed Limitations on Insurance on Brokered Deposits.* Washington, D.C. March 8, 1984.

U.S. Department of the Treasury. *Third Annual Report of the Chairman of the Depository Institutions Deregulation Committee on the Activities During the Year and on the Viability of Depository Institutions.* Washington, D.C. March 31, 1983.

U.S. Office of the Vice President. Task Group on Regulation of Financial Services. "Statement on Endorsing a Proposal to Reorganize Federal Agencies Which Regulate Commercial Banks." Washington, D.C. January 31, 1984.

Unpublished Material

Miller, Leslie A. "Commercial Bank Lending Under Deregulation." Thesis, Rutgers University, Stonier Graduate School of Banking, 1984.

Regan, Donald T. Letter to Hon. Thomas P. O'Neill Jr., concerning draft legislation entitled "Financial Institutions Deregulation Act of 1983." Washington, D.C. July 8, 1983.

———. "Deposit Interest Rate Deregulation and the Small Saver." Remarks before the DIDC. Washington, D.C. Dec. 15, 1983.

Volker, Paul A. Letter to Jake Garn supporting Administration's program concerning non-banking powers for bank and thrift holding companies. Washington, D.C. July 5, 1983.

CHAPTER 7

Books

DiFonzo, Luigi. *St. Peter's Banker: Michele Sindona.* New York: Franklin Watts, 1983.

Fraser, Robert D. *International Banking and Finance. Volume I: A Comprehensive Overview.* 6th ed Washington: R&H Publishers, 1984.

von Furstenberg, George M., ed. *International Money and Credit: The Policy Roles.* Washington: International Monetary Fund, 1983.

Western Hemisphere Commission on Public Policy Implications of Foreign Debt Guidelines for U.S. Policy. New York: America's Society, 1984.

Journals

Crane, Dwight B., and Samuel L. Hayes III. "The New Competition in World Banking." *Harvard Business Review* (July/August 1982):88–93.

Dale, Richard S. "Safeguarding the International Banking System." *The Banker,* Vol. 132, No. 678 (August 1982).

Edwards, Franklin R. "The New 'International Banking Facility': A Study in Regulator Frustration." *Columbia Journal of World Business* (Winter 1981): 6–20.

"Banking: Fed, Comptroller Propose Rules on Special Reserves Against International Loans." *Regulatory and Legal Developments.* No. 247 (December 12, 1983):A16–18.

"Export Trading Companies Emerge in Many Forms." *Business America* (March 19, 1984):3.

Magazines

Belcsak, Hans, and Brian Zimmer. "What if . . . ? Credit Crisis Could Destroy Eurodollar Market. A Worst-case Scenario." *Europe,* January–February 1983, 32–33.

Dizard, John W. "The End of Let's Pretend." *Fortune,* November 29, 1982.

Lascelles, David. "U.S. Bank Regulation After the Debt 'Crisis'." *The Banker,* January 1983, 21–23.

Wallich, Henry C. "A U.S. Regulator's View of the Debt Rescheduling Problem." *World of Banking,* May/June 1982.

"The Crash of 198?" The Economist, October 16, 1982.

"Worry at the World Banks." *Business Week,* September 6, 1982.

Newspaper Articles

Bennet, Robert A. "Less Risk More Worry for the Banks." The *New York Times*, October 10, 1982.

———. "Economic Scene: Free-Market Bank Controls." The *New York Times*, May 30, 1984, p. D2.

Carley, William M. "Close Encounters: Was Law Firm's Study of Citibank's Dealings Abroad a Whitewash?" The *Wall Street Journal*, September 14, 1982, p. 1.

Rowen, Hobart. "Nine Major Banks Highly Exposed on Third World Loans." *Washington Post*, October 24, 1982, p. F1.

———. "U.S. Backs Expanding IMF, Bank Lending." *Washington Post*, September 9, 1982, p. D1.

"Failing the Test: How Giant Frauds Elude Federal Bank Examiners." *Barrons's*, August 8, 1983, p. 13.

Public Documents

U.S. Congress. House. Committee on Energy and Commerce. Statement by Richard S. Dale, Rockefeller Foundation International Relations Fellow. Washington, D.C., September 17, 1982.

U.S. Congress. Senate. Committee on Banking, Housing and Urban Affairs. Statement by Paul A. Volcker on international lending by U.S. banks. April 21, 1983.

U.S. General Accounting Office. *Banking Examination For Country Risk and International Lending*. GAO/10-82.52 Washington, D.C., September 2, 1982.

CHAPTER 8

Books

Global Risk Assessments, Inc. *Global Risk Assessments: Issues, Concepts, and Applications in Business Environment Risk Assessment, Country, Investment & Trade Risk Analysis, Political Risk Assessment & Management*, Book I. Riverside, Calif.: Global Risk Assessments, Inc., 1983.

International Monetary Fund. *World Economic Outlook, a Survey*. 1984.

Organization for Economic Cooperation and Development. *External Debt of Developing Countries: 1983 Survey*. Paris: 1984.

———. *Geographical Distribution of Financial Flows to Developing Countries: Disbursements, Commitments, External Debt, Economic Indicators, 1979–1982*. Paris: 1984.

Nevitt, Peter K. *Project Financing.* 4th ed. London: Euromoney Publications, 1983.

Journals

"A Proposal for the LDC Debt Problem." *Columbia Journal of World Business* (Winter 1982):36.
"Assessing Country Creditworthiness." *Journal of Commercial Bank Lending* (July 1983):9.
"Bank Lending to Developing Countries: Problems and Prospects." *Federal Reserve Bank of New York Quarterly Review.* Vol. 7, No. 3 (Autumn 1982): 18–29.
"Can Continental Bounce Back?" *Institutional Investor* (August 1983):209.
"Debt Rescheduling: What Does It Mean?" *Finance & Development* (September 1983):26.
"Declaration of the Commercial Banks of Latin America on the External Indebtedness of the Continent." *World of Banking* (January–February 1984):6.
"International Report: Latin American Debt." *Bankers Magazine* (Boston) (May/June 1983):15.
"International Conference on Multinational Banking in the World Economy." *Journal of Banking and Finance* (December 1983).
"Is Time Running Out for Brazil?" *Institutional Investor* (International Edition) (April 1984):73.
"LDC Debt: Beyond Crisis Management." *Foreign Affairs* (Summer 1983):1099.
"Latin America: Looking for Financial Medicine." *Institutional Investor* (International edition) (July 1983):217.
"Lending Policies of Financial Intermediaries Facing Credit and Funding Risk." *Journal of Finance* (June 1983):873.
"Lending to Latin America: One Regional Banker's Perspective." *Journal of Commercial Bank Lending* (April 1984):34.
"Mexico: One Country's Attempt at Dealing With the International Liquidity Crisis." *World of Banking* (March–April 1984):9.
"On Third World Debt." *Harvard International Law Journal* (Winter 1984):83.
"Securities: Direct Access to Eurobond Market Complicated by Plans to Reduce Withholding Tax." *Taxation and Accounting* No. 237 (December 8, 1983): G3-5.
"Troubled Foreign Loans in Perspective." *Bankers Monthly* (February 15, 1984): 10.
"The Economies of Offshore Financial Centers." *Columbia Journal of World Business* (Winter 1982):31.
"The Great Debate over LDC Loan Swapping." *Institutional Investor* (May 1984):263.
"The Surprising Strength of the Interbank Market." *Institutional Investor* (International edition) (July 1983):111.

Magazines

Cooke, W. Peter. "International Supervision in Today's Banking Environment." *The World of Banking*, September/October 1982, 7.
Key, Sydney J., and Serge Bellanger. "International Banking Facilities: The Shape of Things to Come." *The World of Banking*, March/April 1982, 17.
Palmer, Jay. "The Debt-Bomb Threat." *Time*, January 10, 1983, 42.
Wallich, Henry C. "A U.S. Regulator's View of the Debt Rescheduling Problem." *The World of Banking*, May/June 1982, 39.
Zombanakis, Minos. "The International Debt Threat: A Way to Avoid a Crash." *The Economist*, April 30, 1983, 11.
"A New Approach to International Indebtedness." London: *Banker*, June 1983, 25.
"Adventures in the Loan Trade." *Harper's*, September 1983, 22.
"Chase: From Lending to Financial Engineering." *Euromoney*, August 1983, 36.
"Global Debt: Assessment and Long-term Strategy." *World Financial Markets* (Morgan Guaranty Trust Company of New York), June 1983, 1-23.
"How the EEC Pulled in the Banks." London: *Banker*, August 1983, 20.
"International Banking Survey." *Economist*, March 24-30, 1984, 5.
"International Debt Crisis: The Next Phase." London: *Banker*, July 1983, 25.
"International Debt Crisis: The Practical Lessons of Restructuring." London: *Banker*, July 1983, 33.
"Is Mexico Making a Comeback?" *Euromoney*, July 1983, 44.
"Spain and the Euromarkets." *Euromoney*, July 1983, 18.
"The Battle of Wills Over Argentina's Debt." *Business Week*, February 6, 1984, 63.

Newspaper Articles

Hertzberg, Daniel. "Banking Behemoth: Citicorp Leads Field In Its Size and Power — And In Its Arrogance." The *Wall Street Journal*, May 11, 1984, p. 1.
Kenen, Peter B. "Third-World Debt: Sharing the Burden — A Bailout Plan for the Banks." The *New York Times*, March 6, 1983, p. F.3.
Lever, Harold. "The Road to Solvency." The *Wall Street Journal*, June 7, 1984.
Lewis, Paul. "U.S. Banks Net Borrowers Abroad." The *New York Times*, January 26, 1984, p. D1.
Lowenstein, Roger. "Mismanagement Caused Venezuela's Credit Crunch." The *Wall Street Journal*, May 18, 1984, p. 30.
Witcher, S. Karene. "U.S. Banks Told to Label as Substandard Venezuela Loans, in Move Seen as Political." The *Wall Street Journal*, May 11, 1984.
Wriston, Walter B. "Banking Against Disaster." The *New York Times*, September 14, 1982, p. 27.

Public Documents

U.S. Congress. House. Committee on the Budget. *Export financing issues and foreign assistance.* Hearings 98–1. Washington, D.C.: U.S. Government Printing Office, 1983.

U.S. Congress. Senate. Committee on Banking, Housing and Urban Affairs. *Export-Import Bank proposal of credit to Brazil and Mexico.* Hearings 98–1, Washington: U.S. Government Printing Office, 1983.

U.S. Congress. Senate. Committee on Banking, Housing and Urban Affairs. *Proposed solutions to international debt problems,* Hearings 98–1. Washington, D.C.: U.S. Government Printing Office, 1983.

Unpublished Material

de Saint Phalle, Thibaut. "The International Financial Crisis: An Opportunity for Constructive Action." In *Significant Issue Series,* pub. Center for Strategic and International Studies, Georgetown University, Washington, D.C., 1983.

Wallich, Henry C. "International Commercial Banking From a Central Bank Viewpoint." Remarks to the annual meeting of the Allied Social Science Associates, 29 December 1983, San Francisco, California.

CHAPTER 9

Books

Griffith-Jones, Stephany. *International Lenders of Last Resort: Are Changes Required?* London: Midland Bank International, 1984.

Helleiner, Gerald K. *The IMF and Africa in the 1980's.* Princeton, N.J.: International Finance Section, Department of Economics, Princeton University, 1983.

Institute for International Economics. *IMF Conditionality.* Washington: 1983.

Wallich, Henry C. *Insurance of Bank Lending to Developing Countries.* New York: Group of Thirty, 1984.

Williamson, John. *A New SDR Allocation?* Washington: Institute for International Economics, Cambridge, Mass. Distributed by MIT Press, 1984.

The International Monetary Fund and the Private Markets. New York: Group of Thirty, 1983.

Yearbook of International Organizations, 1983/84, Vol. 1, organization descriptions and index. 20th ed. Munchen, New York: K. Saur, 1983.

Journals

Edwards, Franklin R. "The New International Banking Facility—A Study in Regulatory Frustration." *Columbia Journal of World Business* (Winter 1981).

Heimann, John G. "The Effects of Political, Economic and Institutional Development on International Banks." *Journal of Banking and Finance* (December 1983):615.

North, Christopher M. "Risk Minimization for International Lending in Regional Banks." *Columbia Journal of World Business* (Winter 1981).

Wallich, Henry C. "A U.S. Regulator's View of the Debt Rescheduling Problem." *World of Banking* (May/June 1982).

"International Banking on Hold?" *Journal of Commercial Bank Lending* (June 1984):26.

"The Evolution of International Banking Competition and its Implications for Regulation." *Journal of Bank Research* (Spring 1983):39.

"The New International Banking." *Banca Nazionale Del Lavore Quarterly Review* (September 1983):263.

"The Role of International Development Institutions in International Project Financing: IBRD, IFC and Co-financing Techniques." *International Lawyer* (Fall 1983):615.

"The World Bank's New Cofinancing Initiatives: Legal Mechanisms for Promoting Commercial Lending to Developing Countries." *Law and Policy in International Business*, Vol. 15, No. 3 (1983):911.

Magazines

Dean, James W., and Tan H. Giddy. "Six Ways to World Banking Safely." *Euromoney*, May 1981, 129–135.

Field, Peter, David Shirreff, and William Ollard. "The IMF and Central Banks Flex Their Muscles." *Euromoney*, January 1983, 35–42.

Hakim, Jonathan. "International Banking Survey: 'A New Awakening.'" *The Economist*, March 24, 1984, 5–78.

"IMF Policies in Developing countries: The Case for Change." London: *Banker*, April 1984, 31.

"The 100 Largest Commercial Banking Companies Outside the U.S." *Fortune*, August 22, 1983, 184.

"Where Should the Fund Go From Here?" London: *Banker*, June 1983, 41.

Newspaper Articles

Farnsworth, Clyde A. "A Dramatic Change at the I.M.F." The *New York Times*, January 9, 1983, p. F1.

Helms, Jesse. "In a Pinch, the IMF Could Go for the Gold." The *Wall Street Journal*, May 6, 1983, p. 28.

Pine, Art. "Central Banks' Bank Resists Change." The *Wall Street Journal*, December 15, 1982, p. 35.

Public Documents

Board of Governors of the Federal Reserve System. *Report to Congress on bank supervision in the Group of Ten Nations and Switzerland*. Washington: 1984.

Unpublished Material

Emminger, Otmar. "Can We Achieve a More Stable International Monetary System?" Remarks to the Lehrman Institute, May 5, 1982, New York.

CHAPTER 10

Books

Byrd, William A. *China's Financial System: The Changing Role of Banks*. Boulder, Colorado: Westview Press, 1983.
Cline, William R. *International Debt: Systemic Risk and Policy Response*. Washington, D.C.: Institute for International Economics, 1984.
Hanley, Thomas H. *Electronic Banking: Yesterday, Today and Tomorrow*. New York: Salomon Brothers, 1984.
Skully, Michael T. *Financial Institutions and Markets in the Far East: A Study of China, Hong Kong, Japan, South Korea and Taiwan*. New York: St. Martin's Press, 1982.

Journals

Cline, William R. "Managing the International Debt Crisis." *Transatlantic Perspectives*, 10 (December 1983):6–9. From a monograph "International Debt and the Stability of the World Economy." Published by Institute for International Economics, September 1983.
"Current and Future Status of Retail Banking in Latin America." *World of Banking* (July–August 1983):16.
"Floating Exchange Rates." *Journal of Monetary Economics* (May 1983):321.
"Short-term Mutual Investment Funds—A New Innovation of the French Money Market." *World Banking* (July–August 1983):24.
"Trade and Debt: The Vital Linkage." *Foreign Affairs* (Summer 1984):1037.
"The Development of Technology in Japanese Consumer Banking." *World of Banking* (July–August 1983):10.

"The Mending Wall: The Rise of the Universal Financial Market." *World of Banking* (March–April 1984):16.

Newspaper Articles

McMurray, Scott, and Maile Hulihan. "London Exchange Accepts Firm Set by Prudential Unit." The *Wall Street Journal*, December 21, 1983, p. 50.
Rowe, James L., Jr. "Corporate Profits' Surge Expected to Continue." The *Washington Post*, January 8, 1984.

Unpublished Material

Martin, William McChesney. "Toward A World Central Bank?" Speech delivered to the Per Jacobsson Foundation, 14 September 1970, Basel, Switzerland.

INDEX

ABOUT THE AUTHOR

Thibaut de Saint Phalle is an international and financial lawyer, teacher, banker, and author. He is counsel to the national law firm of Vorys, Sater, Seymour and Pease of Columbus, Ohio, and Washington, D.C., where he heads the International Finance Department. In addition, he is an Adjunct Senior Fellow of the Georgetown University Center. From 1981 to 1983, he was the first holder of the William M. Scholl Chair in International Business at the Georgetown University Center for Strategic and International Studies and director of its International Business and Economic Program. From 1977 to 1981, he was a Director of the Export-Import Bank of the United States. Prior to that he was financial vice-president of a multinational company and responsible for its foreign operations; partner of an international law firm in New York; partner in an investment banking firm, in charge of its international banking operations; and Professor of International Law and Finance at the International Management Institute of the University of Geneva, Switzerland.

De Saint Phalle has written numerous articles on banking, law, finance, and trade and has coauthored two books on international economics: *The Dollar Crisis* (1963) and *Multinational Corporations* (1976). On international trade he has written *Trade, Inflation and the Dollar* (1981; rev. ed., 1984).